INTRODUCTORY FINANCIAL ACCOUNTING
Third Edition

PRENTICE HALL SERIES IN ACCOUNTING
Charles T. Horngren, Consulting Editor

INTRODUCTORY FINANCIAL ACCOUNTING

Third Edition

Gerhard G. Mueller
UNIVERSITY OF WASHINGTON

and

Lauren Kelly
UNIVERSITY OF WASHINGTON

PRENTICE HALL, Englewood Cliffs, New Jersey 07632

Library of Congress Cataloging-in-Publication Data

Mueller, Gerhard G.
    Introductory financial accounting.—3rd ed./Gerhard G. Mueller
and Lauren Kelly.
       p.   cm.—(Prentice Hall series in accounting)
    Rev. ed. of: A new introduction to financial accounting/Robert
G. May, Gerhard G. Mueller, Thomas H. Williams.
    Includes index.
    ISBN 0-13-485616-3
    1. Accounting. I. Kelly, Lauren. II. May, Robert G.
New introduction to financial accounting. III. Title. IV. Series.
HF5635.M92 1991
657'.48—dc20   90-42939
                                         CIP

Acquisitions editor: *Joseph Heider*
Production editor: *Anne Pietropinto*
Interior design by: *Penelope Linskey*
Cover design by: *Bruce Kenselaar*
Cover photo by: *Loyd C. Heath*, *Professor of Accounting*
Manufacturing buyers: *Trudy Pisciotti and Bob Anderson*

© 1991 by Prentice-Hall, Inc.
A Division of Simon & Schuster
Englewood Cliffs, NJ 07632

This is a revised edition of *A New Introduction
to Financial Accounting* by Robert G. May,
Gerhard G. Mueller, and Thomas H. Williams.

Printed in the United States of America
10 9 8 7 6 5 4 3 2

ISBN 0-13-485616-3

Prentice-Hall International (UK) Limited, *London*
Prentice-Hall of Australia Pty. Limited, *Sydney*
Prentice-Hall Canada Inc., *Toronto*
Prentice-Hall Hispanoamericana, S.A., *Mexico*
Prentice-Hall of India Private Limited, *New Delhi*
Prentice-Hall of Japan, Inc., *Tokyo*
Simon & Schuster Asia Pte. Ltd., *Singapore*
Editora Prentice-Hall do Brasil, Ltda., *Rio de Janeiro*

To: Kent, Lisa, and Jeff

Janel

Contents

PART TWO

PART FOUR

Preface

The 1990's have brought renewed challenges to the structure and effectiveness of accounting education. In 1971, the Price Waterhouse Foundation-sponsored Study Group on Introductory Accounting issued its report. The first and second editions of this book, *A New Introduction to Financial Accounting*, were written by Professor Robert G. May (University of Texas), Gerhard G. Mueller (University of Washington), and Thomas H. Williams (University of Wisconsin) in response to the concepts and recommendations of the Study Group. This third edition follows closely on that tradition and addresses directly recent challenges to the traditional technical approach typically characterizing the first course in accounting.

In 1985, the AAA Bedford Committee concluded, "Accounting education as it is currently approached requires major reorientation between now and the year 2,000."[1] In 1989, the chief executives of the (then) eight largest public accounting firms issued a report stating, "Individuals seeking to be successful in the diverse world of public accounting must be able to use creative problem-solving skills in a consultative process. They must be able to solve diverse and unstructured problems in unfamiliar settings."[2] The growing admonitions to reexamine accounting education led to the establishment of the Accounting Education Change Commission in 1989. Its purpose is to foster substantive change in the education of future accounting professionals. This book responds to the need for a new approach to accounting education at the introductory level.

The first course in accounting is traditionally taught from the procedural perspective of double entry bookkeeping. Under this approach, students learn techniques to account for numbers representing economic events and transactions. Even though students may become good technicians, they frequently fail

[1] AAA Bedford Committee, Future Accounting Education: Preparing for the Expanding Profession, Special Report of the American Accounting Association Committee on the Future Structure, Content, and Scope of Accounting Education, 1985.
[2] Perspectives on Education: Capabilities for Success in the Accounting Profession.

to understand why the double entry paradigm is used and what the resulting financial statements mean. This book uses a decision-making approach as the foundation for explaining the need for and role of accounting information in a modern economy. The use of financial accounting information in making investment decisions is the focus from which the concepts and processes involved in preparing financial statements are explained.

The book is comprised of four parts. Part One contains Chapters One and Two. The first chapter introduces the role of accounting information in making decisions about business enterprises. Chapter Two describes the use of the present value model for making investment decisions.

Part Two contains five chapters devoted to the basic accounting framework. Chapter Three concerns the accrual basis, income determination, and preparation of the income statement. In Chapter Four, preparation of the balance sheet is addressed by developing an understanding of its major components: assets, liabilities, and owners' equity. The statement of cash flows is covered in Chapter Five, using the framework of cash flows from operating, investing, and financing activities. Chapter Six addresses limitations of the historical cost assumption in financial accounting and considers general price-level adjustments and current costs as alternative measurement bases. In Chapter Seven, accounting information systems and the debt/credit mechanism are described.

Part Three contains four chapters elaborating upon the theoretical and technical issues that arise in applying the financial accounting framework. Chapter Eight addresses revenue recognition topics such as long-term contracts and credit sales. Complex measurement issues relating to inventory and long-lived assets are the topic of Chapter Nine. Chapter Ten concerns the accounting for liabilities such as leases, income taxes, and pensions. Accounting for ownership issues relating to corporate shareholders and intercorporate investments is described in Chapter Eleven.

Part Four addresses professional issues related to the provision and use of accounting information. In Chapter Twelve, the financial accounting policy-making process is described, with particular attention to the role of accounting information in the functioning of market economics. Chapter Thirteen covers the traditional use of accounting information in financial statement analysis. The auditing profession and its importance to the credibility of the financial reporting system are addressed in Chapter Fourteen.

These four parts have been constructed such that each is freestanding and can be used in combination with any other part. Instructors of a one-quarter first introduction to accounting may choose to omit Part Three, with no loss of continuity. Schools where the introductory course is taught in one semester or two quarters would have sufficient time to cover some of the more detailed topics addressed in Part Three. The institutional topics in Part Four can be deleted entirely. Alternatively, these chapters can be used as the initial chapters covered by instructors who prefer to establish more depth regarding the social and professional roles of financial accounting before addressing the workings of the accounting system.

Users of the second edition of this book will observe that the length has been shortened from 18 to 14 chapters. Great attention has been given to making the text more readable. Significantly shorter chapters and a simplified writing style make for more efficient and effective learning. Throughout, the goal was to create a concise exposition without overwhelming technical details. A logical sequence of material has been followed, reducing the amount of mechanical or rote learning required. All technical aspects covered have been completely updated to current standards.

The intrinsic idea of this edition is consistent with the concept originated by the Price Waterhouse Study Group. We owe a special debt of gratitude to Professors May and Williams for their role in translating the Study Group report into a viable textbook—and later refining the sequence of subject matter and exposition of the text from the first to the second editions.

Our colleagues, Professors Judith Requist and William Wells at the University of Washington, gave us many specific suggestions on the manuscript that we were able to use. Colleagues at other universities reviewed the manuscript for this book and provided much appreciated, helpful comment. The group of reviewers includes Dean Robert Carver, Jr. (Southern Illinois University at Edwardsville) and Professors Jay D. Cook, Jr. (Washington and Lee University), William T. Geary (College of William and Mary), James K. Loebbecke (University of Utah), Maryanne Mowen (Oklahoma State University), Mohamed Onsi (Syracuse University), Alan K. Ortegren (Southern Illinois University at Edwardsville), Shahrokh Saudagaran (Santa Clara University), Edmund Scribner (New Mexico State University), and P. van Essen (Higher School of Economics, The Hague, Netherlands). Quite a number of informal comments were received from Ph.D. students using this text in sophomore classes—this source of help is thankfully acknowledged.

Mss. Irene Childs, Kelly Foy, Debbie Malestky, and Diane Robinette at the University of Washington provided invaluable assistance in producing useable copies of this manuscript through the many stages during which it was being tested in actual classroom settings. Messrs. Andrew Boyd and Ali Salama provided significant help with the problem and solution material.

As is customary for projects of this type, the co-authors accept full responsibility for all errors of commission and omission. We invite feedback from colleagues who have an opportunity to use this book.

Gerhard G. Mueller
Lauren Kelly

The Role of Accounting

CHAPTER ONE

This book is an introduction to the role of financial accounting in society. To place the topic in its proper context, Chapter One begins with a general discussion of the uses of accounting information. The focus then narrows to financial accounting, or the use of information about business enterprises by parties external to these enterprises. Sections of Chapter One describe how people make decisions, the characteristics of business enterprises, and decision making in relation to the business entity.

WHAT IS ACCOUNTING?

Accounting is frequently described as the language of business. It is used to communicate financial and other information to people, organizations, and governments who need to make decisions.

Accounting. The function of accounting is to provide quantitative information, primarily financial in nature, about economic entities that is intended to be useful in making economic decisions—in making reasoned choices among alternative courses of action.[1]

In this definition, information is knowledge helpful in reaching a conclusion. Accounting information is used in many sectors of society. To illustrate, the uses

[1] American Institute of Certified Public Accountants, *Statement of the Accounting Principles Board No. 4*, "Basic Concepts and Accounting Principles Underlying Financial Statements of Business Enterprises" (New York: AICPA, 1970), paragraph 40.

of accounting information about individuals, business enterprises, nonbusiness organizations, social programs, and units of government are discussed below.

Information About Individuals

Accounting information about individuals is used in the following cases. Individual credit is typically extended only after the prospective borrower has furnished an accounting of his or her private financial affairs. For example, banks evaluating applications for home mortgages or other forms of consumer credit need this type of information. Scholarship committees of colleges and universities use accounting data when they evaluate the financial needs of student applicants. Candidates for political office make public their income and property owned. Income tax collectors need accounting information since a large share of tax revenues collected by state and federal governments comes from individuals.

Information About Business Enterprises

Owners of businesses, creditors, suppliers, management, taxing authorities, employees, and customers need accounting information about business enterprises. For example, owners may examine accounting information to determine if they should expect to receive dividend payments from a firm. Users with indirect concerns about business enterprises include financial analysts and advisors, stock exchanges, lawyers, regulatory and registration authorities, financial press and reporting agencies, trade associations, labor unions, and the public at large. These parties continually evaluate business firms and make decisions about them or on their behalf; for example, in helping the business raise funds.

Information About Nonbusiness Organizations

Nonbusiness organizations such as churches, hospitals, the United Way, the Boy Scouts of America, the Red Cross, political parties, and trade or professional associations also must provide financial information. The general public needs enough information about the financial status of these organizations to determine whether to make private contributions to them and, if so, in what amount.

Information About Social Programs

Similarly, administrators of social programs must adequately report on the success of their programs. For example, day care centers which receive business, community, and governmental support need to account for how their funding is used. All such programs must provide an assessment of resources spent and program benefits achieved.

Information About Units of Government

The leaders of governmental units use a wide variety of accounting information. Tax policy at all levels of government cannot be formulated without accounting information about present and potential tax bases within the particular jurisdiction. National income data are needed to measure the productivity of the total economy and the distribution of economic resources. This type of information supports the formulation of national economic, monetary supply, foreign trade, and investment policies.

Although accounting information is used extensively throughout society, it is only one part of all the information needed by decision makers. Few decisions are or should be made on the basis of accounting information alone. At the same time, most decisions with financial or economic implications can be improved with the use of accounting information.

FOCUS ON FINANCIAL ACCOUNTING

Accounting has been described as providing information about various types of entities to facilitate economic decision making. This broad scope cannot be adequately covered in a single textbook. Thus the focus of this book is narrowed to one category of information users: those parties external to the accounting entity.

External Users of Information. External users of information concerning an accounting entity are those interested parties whose decisions relate to the entity, but who are not employed by the entity to direct its activities or utilize its resources.

External users of information include investors, customers, suppliers, and taxing authorities; that is, interested parties who are not employees of the enterprise. The entity these individuals are evaluating is the subject of the accounting information.

Accounting Entity. An accounting entity is any individual or organization that (1) uses economic resources to achieve a purpose; (2) has an identity of its own; and (3) is of interest to one or more individuals for decision-making purposes.

All the parties in the previous section can be considered accounting entities. The key characteristic of such organizations is that they are of decision interest in and of themselves, and that their activities can be distinguished from the activities of other entities. This includes a vast number of decision-relevant parties. In this text we narrow the focus to the business enterprise as the accounting entity of interest. Business entities dominate our economy, as they control the bulk of productive resources. They are also the most frequent focus of decisions by external parties. By narrowing the focus to external users of information about the business entity, we are limiting ourselves to the subject matter of financial accounting.

Financial Accounting. Financial accounting provides a continual history quantified in money terms of economic resources and obligations of a business enterprise and of economic activities that change those resources and obligations.[2]

DECISION MAKING

Information is primarily used to facilitate decisions regarding the allocation of scarce resources. Society is faced with virtually unlimited wants and needs. However, our resources, the means to satisfy those wants and needs, are in limited

[2] AICPA, *Statement of the Accounting Principles Board No. 4*, "Basic Concepts and Accounting Principles Underlying Financial Statements of Business Enterprises" (New York: 1970), paragraph 41.

supply. We can classify the resources available to satisfy wants and needs as (1) land, or natural resources; (2) labor, or the capacity of the individual for mental or physical output; (3) capital, or any implement, technology, or learned technique that increases the output of our resources; and (4) entrepreneurial ability, or the creative and leadership capacity to organize other individuals and resources to produce products and services.

Members of society must continually make decisions to resolve the conflict between unlimited wants and needs, and limited means to satisfy those wants and needs.

Decision Making.   Decision making is the process of choosing from among alternative courses of action using criteria adopted by the decision maker.

We can depict the decision-making process in stages similar to those illustrated in Exhibit 1–1. Each of these stages will be discussed separately and illustrated by an individual making a career decision. The role of accounting is to provide information for use in this decision-making process.

Identifying the Problem

The decision-making process begins when an individual feels the need to take a course of action. The problem must then be identified. In defining the problem, the decision maker states the criteria that will determine the choice of one action over another for satisfying a need. These criteria can be formulated as objectives.

Statement of Objectives.   A statement of objectives is an expression of the decision maker's preferences in terms of the consequences of potential courses of action.

For example, an individual may decide he or she would like to become a professional. This is a statement of objectives. Two courses of action might achieve this goal: attending law school to become a lawyer or attending business school to get an MBA. However, the individual has limited financial resources available for tuition. Thus a constraint on the action taken is the cost of attending school. In this manner, the set of constraints and the statement of objectives provide a framework for the evaluation of alternatives leading to a choice, as well as prescribing what information will be useful to the decision maker.

Evaluation of Alternatives

As in the example of the aspiring professional, the decision maker may face two or more alternatives, each of which possesses different desirable attributes. In such cases, it is useful to define a common denominator to evaluate the alternatives.

EXHIBIT 1–1

Stages in the Decision-making Process

Need Felt	Problem Identified	Information Sought about Alternatives	Alternatives Evaluated	Conclusion or Action Selected	Action Taken if Appropriate	Outcome Reviewed; New Needs Emerge

Different decision outcome attributes can then be translated into this common denominator for greater ease of comparison. The decision is thus simplified to a selection of the alternative that scores highest on the common denominator. Thus if the individual who wants to become a professional decides maximization of earnings is a criterion for choosing a career, the starting salaries of lawyers and MBAs would be a common basis upon which to evaluate the alternatives.

The Role of Information

After defining the problem, the decision maker should have some idea regarding what aspects of the alternative courses of action might affect the constraints and attainment of objectives. Usually the outcomes from the alternative courses of action cannot be predicted exactly. This gives rise to uncertainty in the decision setting.

> **Uncertainty.** Uncertainty is the condition of not knowing at the time of decision precisely what the outcomes of relevant future events will be; that is, not knowing precisely the consequences of alternatives courses of action.

For example, our ambitious professional is uncertain as to what future employment opportunities and salaries will be upon graduation. Uncertainty can never be eliminated altogether, but it can be lessened by information. A more formal definition of information can now be given.

> **Information.** Information is data that improves the decision maker's understanding and predictions of the outcomes of uncertain future events.

The decision maker is essentially interested in the results or consequences of the different decision alternatives. With greater information, the knowledge about the outcomes from a decision usually increases. However, this does not mean that more facts are always better, since the decision maker may be confused by additional data. Defining a problem indicates what features and characteristics about each alternative must be investigated to make the best choice. Thus a particular problem definition prescribes what information is relevant.

> **Decision Relevance.** Information is relevant with respect to a specific decision situation if it will improve predictions regarding future events related to the decision.

For example, the individual choosing between law school and business school would obtain information about the cost of tuition, potential number of jobs, average starting salaries, and the like.

Decision making is not simply a matter of choosing the most desirable alternative. Rather it is the process of finding the best combination of the expected outcome and the amount of resources needed to follow a specific course of action. Information improves the expected outcome of a decision. But information is costly. Fortunately there are individuals (such as accountants) who can produce the information needed by decision makers at a cost lower than producing it on their own. These persons are called information specialists.

> **Information Specialist.** An information specialist is an individual who devotes resources to producing decision-relevant information for use by others.

The need for an information specialist arises when large numbers of individuals make decisions involving similar courses of action. For example, business newspapers such as *The Wall Street Journal* contain articles about specific corporations that are of interest to many investors. Information produced by a specialist has value to many decision makers, provided it is decision relevant. Since the specialist can provide information at a lower cost than would be incurred by others individually gathering the same facts, decision makers often pay for such services. Thus decision makers oftentimes use more information at a lower cost and make decisions with greater expected benefits. The role of the information specialist to enable the functioning of an economy is served by accountants.

THE BUSINESS ENTERPRISE

This book focuses on the role of accounting in supplying information to decision makers concerned about the business enterprise. To understand the characteristics of these decision makers, their common decision problems and the information they need, the role of the business enterprise in the free enterprise, or market, system is reviewed next.

The Enterprise Function

Entrepreneurs are individuals who provide products and services in response to demand by potential customers. They organize factors of production such as natural resources and labor to produce specific goods and services. They also take the risk that the price they receive for the goods or services may not exceed the cost of production. Presumably, entrepreneurs are motivated by the expectation that sales prices will exceed costs by a sufficient amount to justify the effort expended and the risks taken. In performing their dual role of organizing and risk taking, entrepreneurs usually structure themselves as a business enterprise.

> **Business Enterprise.** A business enterprise is an organization comprised of one or more individuals, capital goods, and other resources, whose purpose is to produce specific products or services for sale.

Thus the business enterprise is a means of coordinating the activities of individuals engaged in production processes, often of a fairly large scale involving a high degree of division of labor and specialization. Additionally, the business enterprise is a means of dividing or sharing among many individuals the enterprise function itself by obtaining funds to finance the business. When an entrepreneur sees an opportunity for profit in the production of a product or service, the necessary factors of production must be secured first. Then these factors must be organized and used to produce and sell the product or service to others. Significant resources are needed to accomplish these steps. Before the sale of products or services starts to bring in cash, the enterpriser may have to pay for buildings, equipment, and other capital goods, as well as for materials and wages. Even after starting a business, there is a time lag before the sale of products and services brings in cash. This requires the ongoing commitment of money capital.

> **Money Capital.** Money capital is the cash or cash equivalent of other resources committed to a business enterprise to enable it to procure and meet its obligations to pay for capital goods, labor, material, and other factors of production.

A central part of the enterprise function involves the provision of money capital and the acceptance of the attendant risk that the sales proceeds may not cover the costs of production. Individual enterprisers may not possess adequate funds and thus may borrow money in exchange for fixed interest payments, or arrange for other persons to share the enterprise function with them as owners. However it is financed, the business organization provides a means of breaking down a large opportunity for profit into a number of smaller individual opportunities.

Kinds of Business Enterprises

There are three traditional kinds of business enterprises: proprietorships, partnerships, and corporations. All are recognized by accountants as economic units or entities with an existence separate from that of their owners. They differ from each other in legal status, ownership and management relationships, extent of ownership risk or liability, duration of life and dissolution, and transferability of ownership interest. Exhibit 1–2 summarizes these differences.

Proprietorship. A proprietorship is a personal business, formed unilaterally by a single individual. It exists as an organization devoted to production activities, and it separates those activities and the resources devoted to them from the entrepreneur's private life. Legally, however, a proprietorship does not constitute a separate entity. It is identical with the owner and therefore cannot be involved in any legal relationship or action except in the name of the owner. If, in the

EXHIBIT 1–2

Comparative Features of Types of Business Enterprises

Type of Business Enterprise	Proprietorship	Partnership	Corporation
Legal Status of Business Entity	Not a separate legal entity	Not a separate legal entity	Separate legal entity
Owner-Management Relationship	Separation only by owner choice	Separation only by partnership agreement	Separation; owners influence management indirectly
Risk of Ownership	Owner's personal fortune at stake	At least one partner's personal fortune at stake	Limited to loss of interest in benefits of ownership
Duration of Life	Expires by choice or death of owner	Expires by withdrawal or death of a partner	Indefinite life span; possibly unlimited
Transferability of Ownership Interest	If sold by the proprietor, the business is reconstituted under new ownership	Partnership share cannot be sold without agreement of other partners; new partnership is formed	Usually transferable

conduct of the business, the business causes harm to a person or property, the proprietor may be held responsible (or legally liable) not only to the extent of the resources committed to the business, but also for everything else personally owned. A proprietorship may be dissolved by the proprietor at will, and it automatically dissolves upon the proprietor's death. Proprietorships are often small service-oriented businesses, or retail establishments such as gas stations, bakeries, bicycle repair shops, and the like.

Partnership. Partnerships resemble proprietorships except there is more than one owner. A partnership is an association of individuals and does not possess a legal identity separate from its owners. It enters into legal relationships or actions in the names of the partners, most often jointly. Usually, each partner can legally bind the partnership by his or her own actions. While some partners may be able to legally limit their liability for damages to others caused by the partnership as a whole, one or more partners are always liable to the full extent of their personal fortunes. Unless otherwise agreed, each partner is entitled to participate in conducting the business and to use its resources.

A business partnership is formed when two or more individuals agree to combine their efforts or other resources in an activity aimed at generating and sharing profits. Unless a partnership agreement specifically provides otherwise, partnerships dissolve upon the death, withdrawal, or bankruptcy of any one partner. Usually a partner cannot transfer his or her interest in a partnership without consent of the other partners. Partnerships are generally larger in scope than sole proprietorships and are illustrated by accounting and law firms.

Corporation. In contrast to proprietorships and partnerships, corporations are legal entities separate from their owners. This means that legal actions can be conducted by or against the corporation in its own name. The owners, called stockholders or shareholders, do not have a direct voice in the conduct of the business, cannot directly use or own its resources, and cannot legally bind it by their actions. The stockholders have the right to vote for the directors who manage the corporation and to share in the profits generated by its activities.

In exchange for limited power over the resources of the business or its management, owners of corporations have flexibility and legal protection not possessed by proprietors or partners. First, owners can sell their shares of stock to others without the consent of other shareholders. Thus the corporation can have an indefinite life, with ownership being transferred from person to person. Second, shareholders cannot be held liable for the actions of the corporation for an amount which exceeds their ownership proportion of the resources and profits of the corporation. Large business activities needing huge amounts of money capital are organized as corporations: airlines, computer manufacturers, and steel firms are examples.

Transferability of ownership and limited liability are characteristics which provide an ideal way for dividing the enterprise functions between management (those who recognize production opportunities and direct activities) and owners (those who take the risk associated with supplying money or physical capital). Persons who contribute money capital but not management talent to a business may wish to limit the risk they accept in the business's activities. They would be much less willing to back enterprising and creative managers if they could be held liable for all corporate actions and responsible for these actions to the full extent of their personal wealth. Furthermore, owners who disagree with the actions taken by management can terminate their ownership relationship by selling their interest, rather than calling for dissolution of the whole business. The appealing features of corporate ownership result in large amounts of money capital that can be raised to complement management skill. Thus corporations have become the dominant form of business for organizing large-scale production in modern market economies.

DECISIONS RELATED TO THE BUSINESS ENTERPRISE

Earlier in this chapter we described different categories of users of information about business enterprises. We noted that information specialists like accountants emerge to provide information for users who have common decision problems and need financial information. This section identifies some common types of decisions made with regard to the business enterprise.

Internal and External Decision Makers

Decision makers concerned with the business enterprise can be described as internal or external, according to how their individual decisions relate to the enterprise. External users of information were defined at the beginning of this chapter.

Internal Users of Information. Internal users of information are those individuals who are employed to direct the activities of the enterprise (managers) or to utilize its resources to achieve the goals of the enterprise (other employees).

Internal users are concerned with choosing among decision alternatives or opportunities available to the business enterprise itself. Common types of decisions made by managers and other employees include whether to make or buy component parts, pricing of new and existing products, volume of operations to break even, whether to lease or purchase equipment, and budgeting for internal departments. External users view the business enterprise as one decision alternative or opportunity available to them. With this distinction in decision interest between the two groups, it is easy to see why accounting has responded separately to the needs of each—managerial accounting for the internal group and financial accounting for the external group. Although many of the accounting concepts, tools, and approaches applied to the problems of the two groups are the same, the differences in their decision interests mean they require different information. Thus for purposes of study, as well as accounting practice, we deal with these two branches of accounting separately. Again, this book focuses on accounting for the business enterprise from the perspective of the external decision makers.

Types of External Decisions

There are two classes of external decisions: an individual's investment decisions and the distribution of enterprise benefits.

Investment Decisions. An individual's investment decision involves an exchange of present resources for rights to resources in the future. The investors in a business include its present and prospective creditors and owners. Investors may acquire the rights of creditors or owners by either (1) paying cash (or other goods and services) directly to the business; or (2) buying the transferable rights of present creditors or owners.

A creditor receives a contractual obligation from the business (1) to pay a specified amount of money, called the principal amount, after a specified time interval; and (2) to periodically pay a specified amount, or rate of interest, on the principal amount. A mortgage note from a business firm to a bank to repay $10,000 on December 31, 1997 and 10 percent interest each year before then is a credit obligation.

An owner receives ownership interest in all rights and properties owned by the business enterprise in proportion to his or her ownership percentage. Also received is the right to share proportionally in (1) the distributed profits of the business (e.g., dividends from corporations); and (2) the proceeds remaining after sale of the business's resources and discharge of obligations, in case of dissolution. A shareholder might pay $100 per share to acquire 1,000 shares of a corporation's stock. This would give the owner the right to receive any dividends which are declared (e.g., a $1 per share or a total of $1,000), as well as a proportionate share of the firm's resources if the entity ceases to exist.

Present creditors and owners may decide to sell their rights in the business for cash or other consideration, provided the rights are transferable. In the case of nontransferable ownership interests in partnerships, this can be accomplished by dissolution of the partnership and settlement with the withdrawing partner. Both the acquisition and the sale of creditor and ownership rights in a business are decision alternatives to the investor, since both involve an exchange of present resources (the capital contribution or price paid or received) for rights to future benefits (interest and principal payments for creditors; ownership interests, dividends, or withdrawals for owners). Together, present and prospective investors constitute an important class of external users of information about businesses.

Distributions of Enterprise Benefits. At the time of deciding about an investment in a business, present and prospective owners are concerned with the future benefits to be received from ownership. For example, shareholders are interested in the dividends they will receive from their investment. As time passes, owners will be concerned with receiving some of those expected benefits as cash payments from the business. Owners are the residual beneficiaries of the business. They are thus interested in information about the activities of the enterprise, as well as its ability to distribute money or other resources to them.

Residual Beneficiaries. Residual beneficiaries are parties whose rights and claims remain after all existing statutory and contractual rights and claims (e.g., bills, wages, taxes) have been satisfied.

Thus the owners must wait until all obligations to employees, creditors, the government and other parties have been paid before they receive final distribution of corporate resources.

SUMMARY

This chapter began with a definition of accounting and a description of its more common uses in society. Then the focus narrowed to financial accounting for business enterprises and its specific relevance to external decision makers. Exhibit

1–1 presented the various stages in the decision-making process. The basic elements include identifying the problem, evaluating alternatives, and using information to reduce uncertainty. This latter stage often involves the use of specific information such as accounting.

Next considered was the role of the business enterprise in a market economy. Exhibit 1–2 portrayed the principal characteristics common to the three traditional kinds of business enterprises: proprietorships, partnerships, and corporations. Money capital is needed to operate any business enterprise, but especially the large-scale functions of the modern, complex corporation. Finally, the topic of making decisions related to the business enterprise was discussed. Both internal and external decisions are made regarding the enterprise. Focusing on external decision makers, their decision interests were divided between investment decisions involving creditors and owners, and the distribution of enterprise resources.

Questions for Review and Discussion

1–1. Define
  a. Accounting
  b. Accounting entity
  c. External users of information
  d. Financial accounting
  e. Statement of objectives
  f. Constraints
  g. Uncertainty
  h. Information
  i. Decision relevance
  j. Information specialist
  k. Business enterprise
  l. Money capital
  m. Internal users of information
  n. Residual beneficiary

1–2. Who might use accounting information about individual persons and for what purpose?

1–3. List ten different parties who benefit from having accounting information about business and public organizations. Also give some benefits from the information.

1–4. What motivates the production of goods and services in a market economy?

1–5. What is the role of the entrepreneur in a market economy? Why would an entrepreneur undertake this role? What methods or devices do entrepreneurs employ to raise sufficient money capital for their business endeavors?

1–6. What is an information specialist? Why do information specialists exist; that is, what function do they serve? List five types of information specialists and give reasons for the existence of each.

1–7. What is the role of a business enterprise in a market economy?

1–8. Describe the three traditional forms of business enterprise. Why is the corporation the dominant form of business enterprise (in terms of resources controlled) in a modern market economy?

1–9. Distinguish between internal and external decision makers. How do their individual decisions relate to the business enterprise? What are the two major classes of decisions about the enterprise made by external parties?

1–10. In general, what are the advantages of using quantitative information? What are the disadvantages?

1–11. Various governmental agencies have an interest in business enterprises (as external users of information). Describe some of these interests and the kinds of information that might be relevant to them.

1–12. Decision making is defined as the process of choosing among alternative courses of action according to some criteria adopted by the decision maker.

    a. Given that a decision maker is faced with a problem, can the decision maker elect not to make a decision regarding the problem?

    b. Must the decision maker always obtain information prior to making a decision?

    c. Should the decision maker always obtain information prior to making a decision?

1–13. Decision makers need good information to make economic decisions. Do you agree or disagree? Defend your position.

1–14. More information is always better than less. Do you agree or disagree? Defend your position.

Problems

1–1. When Does Accounting Begin? John Berg has always wanted a duplex. In 1991 an uncle bequeathed to him $24,000. Even before he received these funds, Mr. Berg signed an agreement with a seller to use $500 from his savings for the purchase of a lot suitable for construction of a duplex. An architect friend prepared, cost-free, six preliminary sketches of a building that might be erected on the property. Mr. Berg then began tentative negotiations with a construction company. He estimated that he would be able to finance a building project at a total cost of $250,000.

After the construction company assured Mr. Berg that his building project was feasible, he hired the architect to prepare blueprints. At the same time, Mr. Berg contacted two commercial banks, three savings and loan associations, and several insurance companies to obtain financing for the project. He also signed a conditional purchase contract for the building site for $22,000.

After the blueprints were finished and three competitive construction contract bids were obtained, it became clear that Mr. Berg's credit was insufficient for financing the duplex project. Two weeks later he received his uncle's legacy and compensated the architect for her services. He then bought himself a new automobile and made a down payment of $15,000 on a small house which he intended to offer for rent.

At what point should the accounting process have started for Mr. Berg's real estate investment project? Defend your opinion in a short essay.

1–2. Accounting Measurement Problem. Green Lake is a large lake in Queen City. Its beautiful beaches and parklike setting make the surrounding residential area very attractive. After much negotiation, the Urban Development Company obtained a building permit from the City Planning Commission to erect a six-unit apartment building directly adjacent to and partly protruding out over Green Lake.

Construction began immediately. At this time, several neighborhood residential associations and environmental groups filed a lawsuit to have the building permit declared void because the planned structure would obstruct views of existing property owners and generally deface the immediate environs of the lake.

After the Urban Development Company had invested about $300,000 in the Green Lake apartment project, a court ordered demolition of the construction project as well as restoration of the site to its original condition. Demolition and restoration would cost approximately $100,000.

How might accountants measure the economic worth of this project on the day before the legal decision? What difficulties do you foresee in making such measurements? Who sustained the loss in the situation described?

1–3. Accounting Information Effects. The ownership interests in large corporations are bought and sold as stock on the New York Stock Exchange. Stock prices generally fluctuate daily. Would you expect accounting information made available to stockholders to influence stock prices? If so, what do you think is the nature of this influence? What other types of information do you think might affect stock prices?

1–4. Accounting Entity. Sears, Roebuck and Company is headquartered in Chicago. It operates many retail stores, a large mail-order business, scores of warehouses, and certain production facilities. Also, many manufacturers produce merchandise under a Sears label through various license agreements.

In several metropolitan areas, Sears has as many as a dozen retail stores. Its sales territories are divided into regions, and the company operates companies in Canada, Mexico, and South America.

List three parties who would benefit from accounting for each of the following: (1) each individual store; (2) all stores in a metropolitan area; (3) all stores in a region; (4) all stores in the United States; (5) the mail-order segment of the business in the United States; (6) production and licensing activities in the United States separated from all other operations; (7) all business in the United States combined; and (8) total combined worldwide business. What is the most appropriate unit of accounting for Sears, Roebuck and Company?

1–5. Duality in Bookkeeping. Keeping track of items owned and owed is the first step in the bookkeeping process, a major tool of accounting. List ten items that you feel might constitute the property (or resources) of a small manufacturing company. Also list ten claims (or obligations) that various parties might have against the company. (Hint: *Machines and cash-in-bank are examples of property; accounts payable and stock sold to the owners are claims.*)

1–6. Accounting Periods. The Northern Smelting Corporation operates a large phosphorus smelter in Poca, Idaho. During 1991 several scrubbing towers and other pollution control equipment were installed to reduce the phosphorus content of emissions from the smelter's smokestacks. The equipment cost $5.4 million; the installation and test costs amounted to $0.6 million. Engineers estimated that the new equipment would have to be replaced 12 years later.

The management of Northern Smelting prepared an annual accounting information report for its shareholders. Should the entire $6 million expenditure be allocated somehow over the next 12 years? If so, how? State five reasons why annual business reports seem desirable, and also five reasons why they might be undesirable.

1–7. Purchase of Information. *The Wall Street Journal* is a major weekday business newspaper in the United States. Aside from its usefulness for managerial and economic policy-making purposes, it is advertised as a source of direct benefits for personal money management and financial planning.

Propose a numerically expressed scheme by which a family could evaluate whether it should subscribe to (i.e., purchase the information contained in) *The Wall Street Journal*. Would this evaluation scheme to appropriate for other individuals (e.g., an individual looking for a new car)?

Present Value Approach to Investment Decisions

CHAPTER TWO

Chapter One discussed personal investment decisions made by external parties having an economic interest in the business enterprise. Starting in Chapter Three, we will study different types of information about business enterprises that accountants can provide to external parties for making investment decisions. In this chapter we discuss the nature of personal financial investment decisions and how individuals make them. The chapter is divided into two sections. The first describes these investment decisions and some of their general characteristics. The second develops the present value model for choosing between alternative investments. This model serves as a basis for discussion of the types of information about a business enterprise that are relevant to investors.

THE INVESTMENT DECISION PROBLEM

The Objective of Investment Decisions

Economic decisions, including investment decisions, are made to increase an individual's well-being; that is, to enhance the satisfaction of wants and needs. Such decisions usually deal with the material or physical means to attain this satisfaction—our wealth.

Wealth. Wealth is the command over present and future goods and services owned or controlled by an economic unit as of a point in time.

Thus, an individual's wealth is composed of both the material possessions currently owned and all future possessions to be acquired. This economic concept is clearly difficult to measure, a problem inherent in the practice of accounting.

Investment decisions involve the exchange of present goods and services for rights to goods and services in the future. Thus investment decisions can be thought of as exchanges of wealth in one form (usually rights to present goods and services) for wealth in another form (rights to future goods and services). Buying and selling creditor and ownership rights in a business involves an exchange of present wealth (the price paid or capital contribution made) for rights to future benefits (interest and principal payments for creditors; dividends, withdrawals, and proceeds from sale for owners). For example, an individual may decide to loan a business entity $5,000 (his or her present wealth) for the right to receive $5,000 in four years and 10 percent interest each year before then (his or her future wealth). These decisions are made with the objective of maximizing wealth. The implication of this objective is that the investment decision maker must be able to assess or measure the wealth sacrificed (in the example, $5,000 now) and the wealth expected in return ($5,000 after four years and $500 interest in years one through four).

The Decision Setting

In order to be explicit about how individuals choose between alternative investments, we assume that investments are composed exclusively of cash flows. The importance of cash in our discussion of investment decisions is not that it represents the only relevant aspect of investment decisions, but that it is a relevant and quantifiable feature of practically all such alternatives. Additionally we assume that all cash flows can be specified with certainty in terms of their amount as well as time of occurrence. In this simplifying framework, investment decisions involve cash flow alternatives that differ only with respect to the magnitude and/or timing of their cash flows.

Example 2–1 | An individual has two possible investment alternatives, investment A and investment B, each requiring an initial outlay of $100 but promising different cash inflows (returns) at the end of the next five years. Exhibit 2–1 shows these cash flows.

Which alternative should the individual choose? At first glance it may appear that investment B is better, since it promises $160 over five years in return for a $100 investment, whereas investment A promises only $155 in total. Such a

EXHIBIT 2–1

	Initial Outlay	Returns At the End of Year:					Total Returns
		1	2	3	4	5	
Investment A	− $100	$40	$35	$30	$25	$25	$155
Investment B	− 100	25	30	30	35	40	160

conclusion implies that the $10 and $15 greater inflows in years four and five promised by investment *B* are worth more in combination than the $15 and $5 greater inflows in years one and two promised by investment *A*. Although one person may prefer the higher, excess inflows received later from investment *B*, a second individual may prefer the lower, excess inflows received earlier from investment *A*. The present value model of investment decision making developed in the next section is a way to determining which of the two different sets of cash flows will benefit an investor more.

THE PRESENT VALUE DECISION MODEL

The present value model for decision making involves the concepts of time preference for money, future value, and present value. These techniques are used to evaluate investment opportunities which differ in terms of the magnitude and/or timing of the cash flows.

Time Preference for Money

Most individuals value more highly the opportunity to have a given sum of money now rather than the same amount at some future date. This is true for two basic reasons. First, money is the means by which people acquire goods and services. And most people prefer present consumption to future consumption of the same goods and services. Second, there are usually opportunities to put present cash to work earning additional cash. For instance, an individual offered $100 today can usually take the $100 now, put it in a money market account, and withdraw that amount plus the interest in one year. This observation gives rise to the concept of time preference for money.

> **Time Preference for Money.** An individual's preference for a given amount of money now, rather than the same amount at some future time, is called time preference for money.

Time Preference Expressed as a Rate. A person's time preference for money can be characterized in terms of an interest rate. The individual asks, "If I am offered either possession of $10 today or the right to have some greater amount one year from today, at what greater amount would I be exactly indifferent between the two opportunities?" If the answer to this question is $11, it implies that $11 to be received one year from now is equivalent in value to having $10 in hand right now. This means that the strength of the individual's time preference for money can be designated by the 10-percent-per-year differential (time preference rate) that was added to get $11. Similarly, if it only takes $10.50 to be received one year from now to make the individual indifferent, the time preference rate for money is 5 percent. Note: A commonly used synonym for time preference rate is the term discount rate.

Using the Time Preference Rate. Knowledge of a specific time preference rate helps individuals to evaluate investment problems by translating different amounts offered at different times to an equivalent amount of value at the present. A common point of reference (the present) is thus established.

Example 2–2 | Consider an individual with a time preference rate of 10 percent. If someone offered this person a chance to have $1,155 one year from now in exchange for giving up $1,000 today, should the offer be accepted? The answer is yes. When a person's time preference rate is 10 percent, we know that he or she is indifferent between any amount today and 110 percent of that amount one year hence. An individual should thus favor the opportunity to receive more than 110 percent of the amount one year from now. If the amount offered one year from now is less than 110 percent of an immediate payment, the individual should favor the immediate payment.

Now we can ask the question. Between $1,000 today and what amount one year from today would the individual be indifferent? The answer is obtained by asking: What amount is exactly 110 percent of $1,000? Multiplying $1,000 by 1.10, we get $1,100. Since the alternative being offered, $1,155, exceeds $1,100, the individual should favor the opportunity to receive $1,155 one year hence.

An equivalent way to approach the situation is to ask the question: Between what amount today and $1,155 one year from now would the individual be indifferent? The answer is obtained by asking: Of what amount is $1,155 exactly 110 percent? Dividing $1,155 by 1.10 we get:

$$\frac{\$1,155}{1.10} = \$1,050$$

or more than the $1,000 that the individual is asked to give up today. This calculation means that if the individual had been asked to give up $1,050 to get $1,155 back after one year, he or she would not really care which offer was taken. This is the point of indifference for that individual. Since the actual offer calls for a sacrifice of only $1,000 to get $1,155 back after one year, the individual should take it. He or she only has to give up $1,000 to receive something that is equivalent to having $1,050 right now.

Determining the Time Preference Rate. Two considerations affect an individual's time preference for money: (1) the present level of consumption enjoyed; and (2) the attractiveness of opportunities available. First, consider the contrast between an individual existing at the subsistence level versus one who is very wealthy. The former person is not likely to be able to think of a rate high enough to justify forgoing present survival for opulence in the future, while the latter individual may be willing forgo additional present consumption at a fairly low rate. Second, an individual will consider other investment opportunities in determining the time preference rate. For example, if an alternative investment will yield a 15 percent return (such as cash in a money market account), this is the opportunity sacrificed by the selection of the alternative investment.

Opportunity Rate. An investor's opportunity rate is the rate that can be earned on the best-known investment alternative.

An investor will be indifferent to an investment alternative if it promises a return equal to the opportunity rate, and will favor any new alternatives promising returns higher than the opportunity rate. Of course, new alternatives with a rate of return higher than the previously used opportunity rate imply the investor should increase the opportunity rate being used to evaluate investments. New alternatives offering less than the opportunity rate of return will be rejected. Thus the investor's time preference rate is equivalent to his or her opportunity rate.

Future Value

Once an individual has established his or her time preference for money, the amounts that would be required for postponing possession of cash for any period can be determined. A two-year period, for instance, is nothing more than two successive one-year periods. If the individual has a time preference rate of 10 percent and has agreed to give up $1 for one year, he or she would have $1.10 at the end of the year in exchange for the original $1. If at the end of the first year the $1.10 was recommitted for an additional year, he or she would have $1.21 at the end of the second year ($1.10 × 1.10 or $1 × 1.10 × 1.10). Notice that for any time after the first year, a return must be received on the first-year return as well as a return on the original amount invested. When the returns are called interest rates, this concept is described as compound interest. The same reasoning can be extended to a third year. Having $1.21 at the end of the second year, an individual would feel indifferent between holding it or giving it up for one more year for a return of $1.21 × 110 percent, or approximately $1.33 ($1 × 1.10 × 1.10 × 1.10). In other words, he or she is indifferent between $1.00 now and $1.33 to be received at the end of three years. The formula for future values is used to represent symbolically the amount that an individual would demand after any number of years in return for $1 given up initially at any rate of interest.

Future Value of One Dollar. Let r represent the decimal equivalent of the individual's time preference rate for one period (0.10 per year in the previous discussion). And let n be the number of years before payoff. Then the future value (amount of cash) an individual would require in return for $1 given up for n years at r rate, represented as $FV_{(n,r)}$, is equal to

$$FV_{(n,r)} = \$1 \times (1.0 + r)^n$$

Example 2–3 | For the example just used, r is 0.10, so the term in parentheses would be 1.10. To represent the inflow from a sacrifice of $1 for three years, we raise 1.10 to the power of $n = 3$:

$$FV_{(3,0.10)} = \$1 \times (1.10)^3$$

$$= \$1 \times (1.10)(1.10)(1.10)$$

$$= \$1.33$$

Future Value of Any Amount. The procedure used for the sacrifice of $1 can also be used to determine the future value for any number of dollars initially sacrificed. Let S be the number of dollars to be sacrificed for n years. The future value is equal to

$$FV_{(n,r)} = S \times (1.0 + r)^n$$

Example 2–4 | The future value of $9 invested for three years at 10 percent is nine times the future value for $1, or

$$9 \times \$1(1.10)^3$$
$$\$9 \times 1.33 = \$11.97$$

It is now possible to compare cash inflows and outflows that occur over several time periods, given an individual's time preference rate per period.

Example 2–5 | Assume an individual with a time preference rate of 10 percent per year is offered an opportunity to pay out $55 now for a return of $68 after two years. Should the offer be taken? The answer is yes. Such an individual would be indifferent between having $55 now and having $55 \times (1.10)^2$, or 55×1.21, or $66.55 two years from now. Since $66.55 is less than the return of $68 being offered, the individual should be willing to give up $55 now to receive $68 two years from now.

Present Value

It is often more convenient and appropriate in investment decisions to work from future cash flows to their present values. As we will see, this is a reversal of the future value concept just discussed.

Present Value. The present value of a future cash flow is the amount of current cash that leaves a decision maker indifferent between it and a specified amount of cash to be received or paid at a future date.

Having concluded that an individual is indifferent between $1 now and $1 \times (1.0 + r)$ one year from now, we can ask the reverse question: How much would he or she give up now to get a payoff of $1 at the end of one year? Assuming a time preference rate of 10 percent, the value today of receiving $1 in one year can be thought of as similar to the relationship a $1 sacrifice today bears to an inflow of $1.10 after one year. Using the symbol $PV_{(1, 0.10)}$ to represent the present value of $1 to be received in one year at a 10 percent time preference rate:

$$PV_{(1, 0.10)} = \frac{\$1}{\$1.10} = \$.909$$

This means that with a time preference rate of 10 percent, the present value of $1 to be received one year from now is 90.9 cents. That is, one dollar is 110 percent of 90.9 cents.

Present Value of One Dollar. The symbolic form of the present value calculation is:

$$PV_{(n,r)} = \frac{1}{FV_{(n,r)}} = \frac{1}{(1.0 + r)^n}$$

Notice that the present value of $1 to be received at the end of n years at r rate is the reciprocal of the future value to be received from investing $1 for n years at r interest rate.

Present Value of Any Amount. The present value of any amount, *P*, can be found by multiplying the present value of $1 by *P*. Symbolically:

$$PV_{(n,r)} = P \times \frac{1}{(1.0 + r)^n}$$

For example, we can determine how much cash is equivalent in value to $100 to be received three years from now (*n* = 3) if the time preference rate (*r*) is 10 percent. The present value of each of those dollars is

$$\frac{1}{(1.0 + 0.10)^3} = 0.751$$

Therefore, the present value equivalent is 100 times that factor (100 × 0.751), or $75.10.

Relationship Between Present Value and Future Value. The compound interest effects are the same in present value as in future value calculations. As seen earlier, present value arithmetic is the reciprocal of future value arithmetic. Thus any point in time may be reached in a number of different ways. Exhibit 2–2 demonstrates this relationship graphically, where the present and future values of having $100 at the present, point (a), are shown. For example, when starting at point (a), the future value of point (c) is determined (assuming *r* = .10) as $100 × FV$_{(2,0.10)}$ = $121. However, when starting at point (d), valuing point (c) is a present value calculation. We know that point (d) is the future value $100 × FV$_{(3,0.10)}$ = $133. The present value one year earlier (point (c)) is then $133 × PV$_{(1,0.10)}$ = $121. This is equivalent to the future value two periods from the present.

Annuities. A series of periodic future cash flows identical as to their amount is called an annuity. The present value of such a series can be determined by summing the present values of the individual flows. However, because an annuity

EXHIBIT 2–2

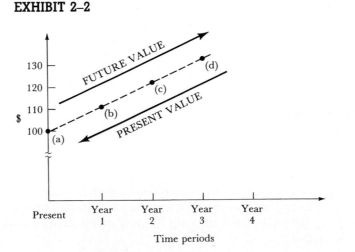

Time periods

consists of a stream of the same amount of cash flows, we can use a shortcut in determining its present value.

Example 2–6 | Suppose we wish to determine the present value of $1,000 to be received at the end of each year for three years, and that the appropriate time preference rate is 10 percent. The calculation is as follows:

Year	Cash Flow	$PV_{(n,0.10)}$	Present Values
1	$1,000	.909	$ 909
2	1,000	.826	826
3	1,000	.751	751
		2.486	$2,486

Since the annual cash flow amount is a constant ($1,000), we can algebraically sum the present value factors and then perform one multiplication. The result is the same:

$$\$1,000 \times (.909 + .826 + .751) = \$1,000 \times 2.486$$
$$= \$2,486$$

The same arithmetic convenience exists for the future value of an annuity. In that case we would sum the future value multiplication factors and apply that term to the constant cash flow of each period. Thus the future value of receiving $1,000 at the beginning of each year for three years is

$$\$1,000 \times (1.33 + 1.21 + 1.10) = \$1,000 \times 3.64$$
$$= \$3,640.$$

Present Value and Future Value Tables. Precalculated tables of present value and future value factors are available for use in place of the formulas used in the earlier examples. Appendix A in the back of the book contains these tables. Table A–1 has the present value factors for receiving $1. To use Table A–1, find the present value of $1 to be received at the end of n periods at r rate as the number at the intersection of the nth row of the column labeled r rate in the table. Table A–2 is organized in the same way for future values of $1, at the end of n periods and at r rates of interest. And Table A–3 contains the precalculated present value factors to be used with annuities.

The Net Present Value Decision Model

The present value of individual cash flows can be combined to get a single total present value for comparing alternative investment opportunities.

Example 2–7 | Return to the unresolved choice between investments *A* and *B* in Example 2–1. Using a time preference rate of 10 percent, present values can be determined for the cash flows of investments *A* and *B*, as shown in Exhibit 2–3.

EXHIBIT 2–3

	Initial Outlay	Returns At the End of Year:				
		1	*2*	*3*	*4*	*5*
Investment *A*:						
Cash flows	−$100	$40	$35	$30	$25	$25
Present value of $1 at 10%	1.00	0.909	0.826	0.751	0.683	0.621
Present value of cash flows (line 1 × line 2)	−$100	$36.36	$28.91	$22.53	$17.08	$15.53
Investment *B*:						
Cash flows	−$100	$25	$30	$30	$35	$40
Present value of $1 at 10%	1.00	0.909	0.826	0.751	0.683	0.621
Present value of cash flows (line 1 × line 2)	−$100	$22.73	$24.78	$22.53	$23.91	$24.84

Calculating Net Present Values. Looking at investment *A*, we observe that the receipt of $40 one year from now is equivalent to receiving $36.36 today. Likewise, the receipt of $35 two years from now is equivalent to $28.91 today. Similar observations can be made regarding the other three years' payoffs. Any opportunity combining $40 at the end of the first year and $35 at the end of the second would be worth $36.36 plus $28.91, or $65.27 in total today. Each of the two promised cash flows has been measured on the same numerical scale: its present dollar value. The total present value of a set of promised future cash flows is the sum of the present values of all the individual periodic cash flows. When an investment opportunity involves initial and future cash inflows and outflows, we can sum the present values of the inflows and the outflows separately and find the difference between the sums. This gives us a criterion, called the net present value, for comparing alternative investments.

Net Present Value. The sum of the present values of the future cash inflows minus the sum of the present values of the future cash outflows is the net present value of an investment opportunity.

Example 2–8 | Returning to investment *A*, the total present value of the inflows is

$$\$36.36 + \$28.91 + \$22.53 + \$17.08 + \$15.53 = \$120.41$$

The total present value of the outflows is $100, or the amount of the initial outlay. The net present value of investment *A* is therefore $120.41 − $100 = $20.41.

Interpreting Net Present Values. The interpretation of the net present value number is very useful for decision-making purposes. The present cash value of the outlay required to enter into investment *A* is $100. The present value of the benefits (cash inflows) from doing so is $120.41. Therefore the act of paying out

$100 to enter into investment *A* is equivalent to paying $100 and immediately receiving $120.41 in return. The difference is $20.41, or the net present value of investment *A*. The investor should find this an attractive alternative unless some other course of action, like investment *B*, promises an even greater net present value and the investor is constrained to making one $100 investment. To find out if *B* is more attractive we follow the same procedure as with the calculation of the net present value of investment *A*.

Example 2–9 | The total present value of the inflows from *B* equals

$$\$22.73 + \$24.78 + \$22.53 + \$23.91 + \$24.84 = \$118.79$$

The total present value of the outflows is the $100 initial outlay. The net present value of *B* is therefore $118.79 − $100.00 = $18.79. From the decision maker's perspective, undertaking investment *B* is equivalent to immediately receiving $18.79.

Assuming only one investment can be made, the decision maker should prefer investment *A* to investment *B*, since the net present value of investment *A* ($20.41) exceeds that of investment *B* ($18.79). In this manner, calculating and comparing net present values provides a criterion or a decision model for choosing between investment alternatives.

Summary of the Net Present Value Model. An individual who can specify a time preference rate for money can calculate a present value, or an amount of current cash that is equivalent to a certain amount of cash to be received or paid at the end of specified future periods. This allows calculation of net present values of investment alternatives as described in the following steps and illustrated in Exhibit 2–4. For each investment alternative

1. Specify the cash inflows and outflows for each period (i.e., the amount and time of occurrence).
2. Calculate the present value of each individual cash inflow and outflow.

EXHIBIT 2–4

1. Specify cash inflows and outflows in each period.

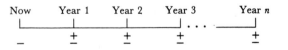

2. Translate individual cash flows into present value equivalents.

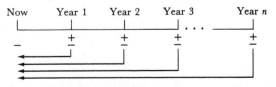

3. Sum positive and negative present values.

4. Difference is net present value (*NPV*).

5. Compare with *NPV*s of other alternatives.

3. Sum the present values of all the positive and all the negative cash flows.
4. Find the net present value by calculating the difference between the total present value of the positive cash flows and the total present value of the negative cash flows.

Some investment alternatives may be mutually exclusive, such that by investing in one alternative the investor uses all his or her investment funds or such that all other alternatives would be redundant investments (and thus not provide the expected returns). For example a small business owner may need only one delivery vehicle so that the investment decision concerns which type of vehicle to buy. To choose among such investments, the decision maker should select the alternative with the largest net present value. In other situations, the investor may have adequate investment funds and the alternatives being considered may be independent investments. For example, buying stock in IBM Corporation does not preclude receiving benefits from buying stock in Apple Corporation. In this situation, the decision maker should make all investments with a positive net present value until his or her investment funds expire.

Present Value, Wealth, and Income

At the beginning of this chapter, wealth was defined as the command over present and future goods and services owned or controlled by an economic unit as of a point in time. Investment decisions have been described as exchanges of present goods or services for rights to goods and services in the future. When such decisions lead to greater quantities of goods or services in the future (assessed at their present value), wealth is increased. The present value decision model was used to choose, from among all known and available investment alternatives, those alternatives whose net present value is positive (or that alternative whose net present value is the greatest when only one investment is to be made). This criterion uses present value as a means of measuring wealth.

Return to the decision problem concerning investments *A* and *B*. Prior to selecting an investment, the individual has wealth in the form of $100 in cash. After selecting investment *A* and paying the $100 initial outlay, investment *A* replaces the $100 cash. Because cash is the medium by which an individual most frequently acquires goods and services (the components of wealth), we make an inference about an individual's wealth from cash. That is, we say that an individual who has $100 cash feels as wealthy as the goods and services that can be commanded with $100 cash. In assessing the present value of investment *A*, we said that a person with a time preference of 10 percent per year would value investment *A* exactly as he or she would value $120.41 in cash today. In this sense, the wealth of an individual is measured or valued as current cash on hand plus the present value of the future cash inflows and outflows to be received from all noncash wealth items.

Valuation.　Valuation is the measurement (quantification) of wealth in money terms.

The net present value of an investment opportunity may be thought of as the improvement in wealth that will result from selecting an investment opportunity. Choosing investment alternatives on the basis of maximum or positive net present value improves the wealth position of an individual to the fullest;

EXHIBIT 2–5

	Returns At the End of Year:				
	1	*2*	*3*	*4*	*5*
Investment *A*:					
Cash flows	$40	$35	$30	$25	$25
Present value of $1 at 10%	1.00	.909	.826	.751	.683
Present value of cash flows (line 1 × line 2)	$40.00	$31.82	$24.78	$18.78	$17.08

(*Note: This analysis is prepared at the end of year one.*)

that is, it maximizes that person's wealth as measured in terms of present values at the time of decision.

As we will see in Chapter Three, measuring income is central to making investment decisions. For an individual investor, income is the increase in wealth that occurs during a period of time. Recalling that we have defined wealth in present value terms, income is the change in the present value of an investment that occurs over time. For example, an individual who invests $100 now and receives a 10 percent annual return on his or her investment has income (or an increase in wealth) of $10 at the end of the first year.

Example 2–10 | Continuing with the illustration in Example 2–8, assume an individual has selected Investment *A*. The present value of the future cash inflows was determined to be $120.41 at the time the investment is made. At the end of the first year, the investor may be interested in measuring his or her wealth at that time and income during the year. Wealth at the end of year one would be the present value of all current and future cash receipts. This calculation is shown in Exhibit 2–5. Notice that each cash flow promised by Investment *A* is worth more at the end of year one than at the beginning (see Exhibit 2–3). This is because each promised cash flow is one year closer to receipt. The sum of the end-of-year-one present values is $132.46. This is the investor's wealth at this point in time. The change in wealth during the first year of the investment ($132.46 − $120.41 = $12.05) is the income from Investment *A* during year one.

Caveats

In the following discussion we consider the important assumptions which underlie the net present value approach to making investment decisions.

Time Preference Rate. One important feature of the approach is the dependence of a decision on the time preference rate selected. The outcome of a decision can be highly sensitive to the magnitude of the rate selected.

Example 2–11 | Return to the choice between investments *A* and *B* first described in Example 2–1. Suppose the investor's time preference rate was 18 percent, rather than the 10 percent initially used to compare the alternatives. Exhibit 2–6 uses the present value factors from Table A-1 in the Appendix to calculate the net present value of investments *A* and *B* at the time of the initial investment.

EXHIBIT 2-6

	Initial Outlay	1	2	3	4	5	Net Present Value
				Returns At the End of Year:			
Investment A:							
Cash flows	−$100	$40	$35	$30	$25	$25	
Present value of $1 at 18%	1.00	0.847	0.718	0.609	0.516	0.437	
Present value of cash flows (line 1 × line 2)	−$100	$33.88	$25.13	$18.27	$12.90	$10.93	$1.11
Investment B:							
Cash flows	−$100	$25	$30	$30	$35	$40	
Present value of $1 at 18%	1.00	0.847	.718	.609	.516	.437	
Present value of cash flows (line 1 × line 2)	−$100	$21.18	$21.54	$18.27	$18.06	$17.48	−$3.47

Notice that using 18 percent, the net present value of both investments is lower than when 10 percent was used. It is always true that an individual who places a higher time preference rate on money will assign a lower present value to a given number of dollars promised in the future than will an individual with a lower time preference rate. The present value formula supports this reasoning:

$$PV_{(n,r)} = \frac{1}{(1.0 + r)^n}$$

Since r, the time preference rate, appears in the denominator of the formula, we know that the greater r is, the less will be the present value of each dollar promised in any future period. Thus an individual who has a high time preference rate expresses a stronger immediate demand for money, either because of the urgency with which he or she wants to consume or the attractiveness of alternate investment opportunities. Also notice that the net present value of investment B is now negative. This indicates that the wealth given up ($100) is greater than the net present value of the wealth received from the investment. Thus under no circumstances should the investor accept this investment.

Uncertainty. In Chapter One, uncertainty was defined as not knowing at the time of decision the exact outcome of alternative courses of action. Under uncertainty, the best the decision maker can do is to choose the alternative that is expected to provide the greatest satisfaction. Uncertainty is involved at each stage in the decision process described in this chapter. In specifying the time preference rate, the decision maker may be unsure of what alternative opportunities are available and their expected rates of return. Deciding on appropriate alternative investments can be difficult. And specifying the timing and amounts of the cash flows often involves much uncertainty. Note that in all our discussions to this point we assumed such cash flows were known with certitude. The role of financial accounting information is to assist the external decision maker in projecting expected cash inflows and outflows from alternative investments. For example, information about the business enterprise's profitability helps the firm's shareholders predict the dividends to be received from stock ownership. Succeeding chapters in this book study the accounting information provided to investors to enable them to predict cash inflows and outflows.

SUMMARY

This chapter concerns the investment decisions made by parties external to the business entity. The objective of such decisions is to maximize wealth, or the possession of present and future goods and services. The decision setting was described as choosing among alternatives that differ with respect to the magnitude and/or timing of cash flows. The present value model is an approach for comparing alternatives. This model utilizes the time preference for money to establish the present as the point of reference for evaluating different investments. After discussing the concept and mechanics of future and present value, the net present value was defined as the sum of the present values of the future cash inflows minus the sum of the present values of the present and future cash outflows. The investment alternative offering the greatest or a positive net present value maximizes the decision maker's wealth and should be the alternative chosen.

Questions for Review and Discussion

2–1. Define the following terms:
   a. Wealth
   b. Time preference for money
   c. Opportunity rate
   d. Present value
   e. Net present value
   f. Valuation

2–2. Discuss the concept of wealth and its relationship to the concept of well-being.

2–3. Describe the characteristics of creditor and ownership investments and how they relate to wealth.

2–4. What justification is there (if any) for the assumption that investment alternatives offer strictly cash inflows and outflows as opposed to flows of wealth in other forms?

2–5. In developing the net present value model, this chapter ignores constraints on decision makers (such as limited budgets). What justification is there for ignoring such constraints, which are often present in real-world investment decisions?

2–6. Most individuals seem to exhibit a time preference for money. Give the reasons that might explain such a preference.

2–7. An individual's time preference for money may be expressed as a rate. Explain.

2–8. Discuss factors which influence an individual's time preference for money.

2–9. What relationship (if any) exists between an individual's time preference rate and opportunity rate?

2–10. Explain the economic significance to an individual of the following:

    a. The present value of an amount of money to be received at a future date.
    b. The present value of an obligation to pay an amount in the future.
    c. The future value of an amount invested or consumed today.

2–11. Describe an annuity and how the future and present value of annuities are determined. How does this differ from the receipt of $1?

2–12. Explain the relationship between future value and present value.

2–13. The net present value of an investment opportunity is the cash equivalent of the gain (loss) experienced by the investor in undertaking the opportunity. True or false? Explain.

2–14. List the five steps required to apply the net present value model.

2–15. Explain why investment decisions based on the net present value of available alternatives may be different if different time preference rates are used.

2–16. Given a future cash flow and an individual's time preference rate, what is meant by the statement that the individual is indifferent between the present value of the future cash flow and the future cash flow itself?

2–17. What must be specified before one can determine the net present value of an investment opportunity?

2–18. Present value (and therefore net present value) is an example of a common point of reference. Do you agree or disagree? Explain your answer.

Problems

2–1. Future Values of Amounts Invested. Determine the following future values utilizing a time preference rate of 8 percent:
    1. The future value of $5,000 to be invested now for a period of five years.
    2. The future value at the end of three years of an investment of $4,000 now and $4,000 one year from now.
    3. The future value at the end of eight years of an investment of $6,000 at the end of each of the first four years and a withdrawal of $5,000 per year at the end of years five through seven.

2–2. Present Values of Future Cash Flows. Compute the present value of each of the following cash flows utilizing a time preference rate of 12 percent:
    1. $1,000 cash outflow immediately
    2. $2,000 cash inflow one year from now
    3. $2,000 cash inflow two years from now
    4. $1,000 cash outflow three years from now
    5. $3,000 cash inflow three years from now
    6. $2,000 cash inflow four years from now

2–3. Net Present Value. Calculate the net present value of the total cash flows in Problem 2–2 utilizing a time preference rate of 12 percent.

2–4. Net Present Value of an Opportunity. Determine the net present value of a business opportunity that costs $1,000 initially and generates cash inflows of $2,000, $2,000, $3,000, and $1,000 at the end of years one through four, respectively. An additional outlay of $1,000 for maintenance will be necessary at the end of year three. The opportunity can be sold for $1,000 at the end of year four. The appropriate discount rate is 12 percent.

2–5. Investment Opportunity Evaluation. You have an opportunity to make the following three investments:

1. You can buy a piece of property for $4,000 today. At the end of four years you can sell the property for $6,000.
2. You can buy a copying machine for $3,500 today which will generate a cash inflow of $1,500 for each of the next four years.
3. You can invest in a business that will require investments of $2,000 now and $2,000 at the end of the first year. You will receive $5,500 from the business at the end of the fourth year.

Calculate the net present value of each of the three investment opportunities using a time preference rate of 8 percent.

2–6. Future Value of a Replacement Fund Program. The William Corporation currently uses equipment that will become obsolete in five years. To provide the necessary funds for replacement of the equipment, the company plans to invest $40,000 in U.S. securities now; $50,000 at the end of each of the next two years; and $60,000 at the end of the following two years. If these securities pay an after-tax rate of return of 4 percent, compounded annually, what amount will be available at the end of the fifth year?

2–7. Future Adequacy of a Saving Fund Program. Mr. E. K. Roarke wishes to provide for the college education of his six children. He estimates that each child will require $3,000 for each of the four years of college, payable at the beginning of the school year. The triplets are fifteen years old and will start college in exactly three years. The twins are fourteen and will start college in four years. The youngest child is seven years old and will start college in eleven years. If Mr. Roarke deposits $100,000 in a savings account that pays an annual interest rate of 6 percent, will he have provided for the college educations? What is the exact amount Mr. Roarke should deposit now to provide for the college educations?

2–8. Sensitivity of a Decision to Time Preference Rate. The Hobard Cattle Company needs grazing land for its cattle operation. It can either purchase the land outright for $160,000 or lease it for $10,000 per year on a 15-year lease. The rental fee is payable at the beginning of each year. In either case, the company must pay all taxes and maintenance costs. The land will be needed for 15 years, at which time it would be salable for $200,000. If the company required a before-tax rate of return of 8 percent for this type of investment, which alternative should it choose? If it requires 6 percent?

2–9. Present Value of an Investment in Common Stock. Ms. Janice Downs wishes to invest $10,000 for a five-year period. She is considering the purchase of Buford Company common stock, which currently pays an annual cash dividend of $2 per share. Ms. Downs expects that this dividend will be paid each year for the next five years and that the stock at the end of the five-year period will be selling for $30 per share. If investments of comparable risk yield a before-tax rate of return of 10 percent, what is the maximum amount Ms. Downs should be willing to pay for a share of stock? If the stock is currently selling for $25 per share, should Ms. Downs be willing to purchase it?

2–10. Present Value of an Investment in a Promissory Note. A promissory note is offered for sale on which the yearly interest payments are $45. There are ten interest payments still due, with the first one due one year from now. The principal amount, $1,000, is to be repaid at the end of the tenth year. What is the maximum amount an investor would pay for this note if he or she wished to earn at least 8 percent on this type of investment? If he or she wished to earn 10 percent?

2–11. Alternative Time Preference Rates. Two investors, Helene and Leslie, are considering the same investment, a corporate bond that is selling for $963. The bond has a face, or principal, value of $1,000 and will mature in one year; that is, the principal of $1,000 will be paid in exactly one year. The bond pays 5 percent interest per year on the principal, including the year of maturity. Thus in one year the bond will pay $1,000 principal plus $50 interest for the year to anyone who presents the bond for redemption at that time. Of the two investors, Helene has selected a higher time preference rate, 10 percent; Leslie's rate is only 8 percent. Will either or both of the investors buy the bond? Which one(s) and why?

2–12. Present Value of a Taxicab Business. You have an opportunity to invest in a taxicab business. The business owns one cab and has made the following estimates of future cash flows. Assume that these cash flows take place at the end of the year and that you consider them to be realistic.

1. Passengers pay $.76 per mile for cab service.
2. Gas, oil, tires, and other operating expenses are $.20 per mile.
3. The driver is paid $.16 per mile plus tips.
4. The present owner expects that the cab will carry passengers a total of 50,000 miles per year for the life of the automobile, which is three years. After three years the car will be worthless.
5. You have decided to invest if you can earn a before-tax rate of 10 percent on your investment.

What is the maximum amount you would pay to acquire the business?

2–13. Evaluating an Offer for the Taxicab Business. Assume you have purchased the taxicab business described in Problem 2–12. At the end of the first year, after you have withdrawn all the cash receipts, you are approached by an investor who offers you $36,000 for the business. Should you sell?

2–14. Determination of the Implicit Time Preference Rate. Mr. Curtis Driver owns a ferry service which carries workers to and from an offshore drilling rig. The rig will be operational for three years. When it is shut down, Mr. Driver plans to sell his business and retire. The contract under which the business operates pays a flat sum of $100,000 every year at the end of the year. Expenses amount to $75,000 per year. Mr. Driver withdraws $25,000 every year and expects to be able to sell his equipment for $30,000 when he retires. At the end of the first year, Mr. Driver is approached by an investor who offers him $68,192 for the business. Should Mr. Driver sell? (Hint: At what time preference rate would he be indifferent?)

2–15. Net Present Value: Sensitivity to Time Preference Rate. The company you work for, Starr Cutter, is a medium-size tool and die company that is interested in expanding its line of services to its customers. The company has decided to provide a new service that requires the purchase of one new machine. Two brands of the needed machine are available, brand *A* and brand *B*. The machines differ only in the way they affect the other costs of providing the new service to customers; that is, they have different break-in periods, rates of physical deterioration, maintenance requirements, and so forth, but they will provide the same output capacity. As a result, the following patterns of cash flows have been estimated for the two machines:

	A	*B*
Initial price of machine	$20,000	$21,500
Annual net proceeds:		
At the end of year		
1	$10,000	$ 5,000
2	10,000	10,000
3	10,000	10,000
4	5,000	10,000
5	5,000	10,000

You are asked to choose the best machine for the company to buy. Your first impulse is to compute a net present value for each machine, but you have run into a problem. The treasurer of the company thinks the time value of money to the firm is 10 percent (compounded annually), but the president insists it is more like 15 percent.

While they are debating the question, you decide to compute net present values at both interest rates, hoping that maybe one machine will prove better regardless of which rate is used. Does the same machine prove to be best for both interest rates? If not, explain.

2–16. Investment Opportunity Evaluation.   You have an opportunity to invest in a venture of five years' duration. The venture consists of initially buying a building that a company has constructed for its own use and then renting it back to the seller. The venture requires that the investors put up a total of $100,000 initially to buy the building. Net cash flows (rent less taxes, insurance, etc.) projected for the venture equal $20,000 per year for each of the five years. At the end of five years the original seller has the right to buy back the building at $75,000. This option is expected to be exercised because the price is less than the expected market value after five years and the building is essential to the original seller's business. All amounts received are to be split and distributed each year according to each investor's contribution to the initial outlay. You are considering buying a one-fifth share in the venture. Assume that your opportunity rate for investments of equivalent risk is 12 percent.

Required:

1. What is the maximum amount you would be willing to pay for a one-fifth interest in the venture?
2. What is the net present value of the opportunity to buy at $20,000 and how does this net present value relate to your objective of wealth maximization?

2–17. Comprehensive Present Value Problem.   Tri-Cities Tours is a small business that is for sale. The business is well known in the Tri-Cities area and has enjoyed consistent success. The company operates out of a small rented office. It owns two touring buses, each in good working condition. You are interested in buying the business and have been given access to all of its financial records for purposes of determining what you think it is worth. Based on your investigation you have made the following estimates:

1. Each of the buses will be operated for a total of 1.5 million passenger miles per year.

    (a) The average cash fare per passenger mile will be $.05.
    (b) Fuel, lubricants, and routine service will be $.01 per passenger mile.
2. Other yearly costs of operating the business are expected to be

Rent	$12,000
Wages and salaries	60,000
Bus overhauls	18,000
Insurance	10,000

3. The buses will no longer be suitable for the touring and charter business after three more years of operations. However, each is expected to bring $10,000 upon sale at that time.

Assume, unless otherwise stated, that the appropriate time preference rate is 10 percent.

Required:

1. What is the maximum amount you would be willing to pay for the company?

2. Suppose the asking price of the owner is less than the amount you calculated. List the factors that might explain the difference.
3. Assume that you bought the business and your time preference rate changed from 10 percent to 12 percent immediately after purchase. What would happen to (*a*) the future value of the business; and (*b*) the present value of the business? Explain in words why the effects you have indicated would occur.

Basic Concepts and Income Determination

CHAPTER THREE

This chapter begins our study of accounting as it is conventionally practiced. First we consider what type of information is most useful to external decision makers in making investment decisions. We describe the cash basis of accounting, which measures the firm's cash receipts and disbursements for a time period to determine net operating cash flow. Because this measure depends upon erratic cash flows, it does not provide adequate information for predicting future performance.

We next describe the accrual basis of accounting, which represents a more useful measure of the firm's performance. Here, revenue constitutes a measure of accomplishment, irrespective of the cash inflow received from the firm's activities. Expense is used as a measure of the sacrifice made to generate the revenue, irrespective of the cash outflow made for the sacrifice. Matching the expense incurred with the revenue of the period yields net operating income. Gains and losses from extraordinary events are adjustments to net operating income, yielding net income. The income statement summarizes the forgoing figures.

INFORMATION FOR MAKING INVESTMENT DECISIONS

The previous chapter described the decision model commonly used to make investment decisions. A primary input to this model is the anticipated net cash flow from the investment. This net cash flow consists of the outflows, usually the initial investment, and the inflows or return to the investor. For a creditor, these returns are periodic interest payments and principal repayment. For the owner, these returns are periodic dividends and proceeds from selling the ownership interest. The future cash flows to the investor must be predicted before the present value decision model can be used.

A central question in accounting concerns the type of information of greatest use to investors for making these cash flow predictions. Unless the enterprise itself generates cash in the future, it will be unable to distribute cash to its investors. Thus the creditor relies on the business having sufficient cash in the future to pay the interest due and to repay the initial amount borrowed. And the owner relies on the firm's successfully earning profits and having cash available for dividends. When the owner decides to sell his or her ownership interest, other potential investors' expectations regarding the firm's profitability and future cash availability determine how much will be received from selling the stock. For these reasons, the future cash flows expected by the enterprise are important information to the investor. This information enables investors to predict the amounts and probabilities of the cash payments the firm will make to them as creditors or owners.

As will be seen in this chapter, the firm's cash flows consist of cash receipts from sales, for example; and cash disbursements for salaries, rent, equipment, and the like. A central question now concerns what type of information the investor needs to predict the firm's cash flows. Most relevant would be expected sales, along with the probability of making and collecting the sales. This forecast in turn depends upon future prices and quantities demanded of the goods or services provided by the firm. Also relevant would be the expected future cash outflows. These cash payments depend upon the resources (e.g., materials, labor, buildings, etc.) needed to satisfy the expected demand, along with prices and payment terms for these expenditures.

Such forecasts are difficult, if not impossible, for investors to generate. Being outside the enterprise, creditors and owners do not take part directly in the business's operations and thus are not privy to the plans and intentions of the firm's management. Nor do they have access to the information needed to develop the firm's cash forecast, such as future products, prices, and resource needs. One possible way to rectify this situation would be to have the firm's management issue public forecasts of future cash flows for everyone's use. Management will have made such projections to help them make internal plans. Yet management may be unwilling to make public these forecasts because competitors could use the information about their strategies and intentions and because the forecast might be inaccurate. Additionally, management might be tempted to bias the estimated cash flows they report in order to attract investors. For these reasons, U.S. businesses do not publish forecasts of future cash flows.

This leaves the investor still in need of reliable information to forecast the firm's cash flows and thereby estimate future cash flows from the investment. One possibility would be to use information about the enterprise's present and past cash flows as a basis for forecasting the future. Because it is based on actual events and activities, this type of information is not as susceptible to bias and error as are forecasts. In using past information to forecast the future, we assume continuity of the events and activities engaged in by the enterprise. Although many aspects of the enterprise's activities may change over time (e.g., product lines or production processes), other important aspects remain constant or change slowly. For most firms, the process of generating cash flows remains more or less continuous. Thus the immediate past provides a benchmark from which to consider the future. Providing investors with information about the firm's present cash inflows and outflows enables them to predict future cash flows.

The cash basis of accounting records the cash receipts and cash disbursements of an enterprise. Following the discussion of the cash basis, we will consider whether this measure constitutes the best information for developing future expectations about the firm.

CASH BASIS

One obvious way of assessing the firm's performance (the financial success or failure of its activities) is to determine cash inflows and outflows over a given time period. This measure would become the investor's basis for predicting the enterprise's future performance.

Cash Basis. The cash basis of accounting reports the entity's cash receipts and cash disbursements during a specific time period.

This measure includes all the sources and uses of cash, whether from outside investors or business operations. When the cash flows associated with providing goods and services are isolated from other cash flows, we have net operating cash flow.

Net Operating Cash Flow. Net operating cash flow is the excess of total cash received by the enterprise during a period of time over total cash disbursed during the same period of time, excluding dividends or withdrawals paid to owners, repayment of long-term debt, or cash receipts from owners or long-term creditors.[1]

Net operating cash flow has two major advantages that make it attractive for reporting to outside investors. First, cash receipts and disbursements include factual data, not estimates. In this regard they are objective numbers. Second, current-period net operating cash flow represents a measure similar to the future-period cash flow information of interest to investors.

But net operating cash flow has at least one distinct disadvantage. When measured over short periods of time it may seriously misrepresent the long-run cash-generating ability of the enterprise. For example, many firms make large cash expenditures in one period to acquire such resources as buildings and equipment that will be used to produce the products and services of future periods' operations. It might be appropriate to associate a portion of their cost with these future periods. The entity may acquire merchandise, supplies, and other resources on credit during one period and use them to produce products and services in a period different from when these items are paid for in cash. Similarly, cash received in any given period may represent payments for products and services sold by the firm in earlier periods on a credit basis.

Thus there is not necessarily an association between the measure of effort (total cash expenditures) and the measure of accomplishment (total cash receipts)

---

[1] For the purpose of this chapter we will include in net operating cash flow the cash flows from investments such as the purchase and sale of property, plant, and equipment. When we discuss the Statement of Cash Flows in Chapter Five we will use the separate category, "cash flows from investing activities," as required by the Financial Accounting Standards Board, *Statement of Financial Accounting Standards No. 95*. Notice we have removed from net operating cash flows the cash flows from financing activities related to borrowing money and the owners' investment.

represented by net operating cash flow. In a period when the enterprise is growing and actively producing products and services, its net operating cash flow may be small or negative simply because it makes an expenditure for a new piece of equipment to enable production in the future. Whereas the act of buying a piece of equipment may be good for future cash-generating ability, it will have a negative effect on the current period's net operating cash flow. Similarly, in a period when an enterprise's activities decline, its net operating cash flow may be large and positive due to cash collections from customers for products and services sold in previous periods. These situations limit the usefulness of net operating cash flow as a prediction of the firm's future cash flows. Example 3–1 illustrates these points.

Example 3–1 | An investor group agrees to establish a local chain of 20 ice cream parlors. They name their company Fancy Flavors, Inc., and raise $150,000 in cash from the owners. They also obtain a renewable five-year bank loan of $600,000, at an annual rate of interest at 12 percent. Thus $750,000 in cash is invested to start Fancy Flavors, Inc.: $150,000 by the owners and $600,000 by a major creditor. By August 1, 1991, 20 store locations are found, 20 store managers employed, and all employees hired. On August 1, three months' rent is paid in advance, totaling $60,000. Various store furnishings and equipment are purchased at total cost of $600,000. The equipment will meet Fancy Flavors' business needs until it wears out in five years and then must be scrapped. Also purchased are supplies (cones, napkins, spoons, scrapers, etc.) for $20,000 cash; and ice cream for $30,000, with payment due at the time of the next delivery.

Business operations began on August 1. Additional operating facts for August are as follows:

1. Cash ice cream sales total $400,000 during the month. In addition, the firm provided ice cream for several large banquets for which payments totaling $50,000 will not be received until September.
2. By August 31, the firm paid salaries and wages for August totaling $120,000. In addition, $30,000 of salaries and wages for work done during August remained unpaid as of August 31. They will be paid on the first payday in September.
3. In total, Fancy Flavors purchased $165,000 worth of ice cream (including the initial order) from several dairy products companies. During August they paid $130,000 of this in cash, with the remaining $35,000 due at the first ice cream delivery date in September.
4. Miscellaneous cash expenditures totaling $10,000 were made for heat, light, and so forth during August.
5. An additional $10,000 worth of supplies was ordered and received in August, but will not be paid for until September.
6. At the end of the month, an inventory count at the 20 store locations determined that $20,000 worth of ice cream and $15,000 worth of supplies remained on hand at that time.

How should Fancy Flavors, Inc. assess its performance, or financially measure the success of its operations, for the month of August?

Exhibit 3–1 shows the net operating cash flow for August. Fancy Flavors' total cash receipts are the $400,000 cash sales. Notice that the $750,000 obtained

EXHIBIT 3–1

Fancy Flavors, Inc.

Net Operating Cash Flow for August 1991		
Total cash receipts		$400,000
Cash disbursements for:		
Equipment	$600,000	
Three months' rent	60,000	
Supplies	20,000	
Salaries and wages	120,000	
Ice cream	130,000	
Miscellaneous	10,000	
Total cash disbursements		940,000
Net operating cash flow		−$540,000

from the owners and from the bank loan are not included in the operating cash receipts. To get the net operating cash flow for the month of August, we find the difference between the total cash receipts of $400,000 and the total of the cash disbursements. The net operating cash flow is − $540,000. In other words, Fancy Flavors, after its initial establishment, experienced a net operating cash outflow or drain of $540,000 in the month of August. Yet this does not accurately measure performance for August because there is an indiscriminate matching of dollars received and dollars paid. That is, net operating cash flow treats each dollar received and expended as applying equally to Fancy Flavors' operations during the month of August. Yet the positive side of performance, the total cash receipts of $400,000, does not include $50,000 to be received in September for ice cream items sold to banquet customers in August. Similarly, the negative side of performance includes the entire $600,000 paid for equipment that will last five years, and $60,000 in rent that covers not only August, but September and October as well. In addition, the cash disbursements omit all of the $35,000 to be paid in September for the last delivery of ice cream that may have been used in August, and the $30,000 to be paid in September for work performed by employees during August. Thus we need a better financial measure of perform-ance that will associate the positive and negative aspects of operations with the appropriate time period.

ACCRUAL BASIS

As seen in the previous example, cash receipts in a period may arise from the firm's productive activities of previous periods, and cash disbursements may relate to activities planned for future periods. The accrual basis of accounting was developed as a measurement procedure that more properly associates the firm's financial results with its productive activities in a specific time period.

Accrual Basis. Accrual accounting records the financial effects on an enterprise of transactions and other events and circumstances that have cash consequences for the enterprise in the periods in which the transactions occur rather than only in the periods in which cash is received or paid by the enterprise.[2]

The accrual basis recognizes the financial effects of transactions and events in the period in which they happen. Thus the prices received for products and services and prices paid for resources used to sell products and services are allocated to the time period in which they affect the firm's financial performance. In accounting, the accrual basis measures periodic financial performance to determine the enterprise's income. In this regard, income is the accounting measure of the entity's change in wealth as that concept was discussed in Chapter Two.

Measuring Periodic Accomplishments

The assessment of the enterprise's performance using the accrual basis to measure income begins by determining the revenue earned during the time period.

> **Revenue.** Revenues are actual or expected cash inflows during a period from delivering or producing goods, rendering services, or other activities that represent the entity's business purpose.[3]

Thus revenue represents the sum of the selling prices of all products sold and services provided to customers during the current period, whether the sales are cash or credit. (Credit sales are sales for which the customer promises to pay at a later time.) Note that revenue does not include cash receipts in the current period which represent payments for products and services the customers received in an earlier period. However, revenue does include the selling prices of products or services provided during the current period for which cash will be received from customers in a later period.

Example 3–2 | In Example 3–1, Fancy Flavors actually received only $400,000 cash from customers during the month of August. But there was $50,000 worth of ice cream sold to banquet customers who promised to pay in September. Both the $50,000 promised and the $400,000 actually paid by customers in August are included in August revenue of $450,000. Note that the $50,000 due in September will not be included in that month's revenue.

Measuring revenue is a more subjective process than determining cash receipts. Rather than observing cash flows, we must now determine the time period when the enterprise provides the goods and services. The process of deciding when to include revenue in the current period's performance is handled by the realization principle.

> **Realization.** Revenue has been realized when goods or services are exchanged for cash or claims to cash. This usually occurs when the prices to be received for products and services become reasonably certain and have been earned by the enterprise.

The term "earned" in the definition means that the enterprise does not face any substantial additional production barriers or steps, such as delivery. This implies that a legally enforceable sale of a product or completion of a service has already

---

[2] FASB, "Concepts Statement No. 6, *Elements of Financial Statements*, December 1985, ¶139.
[3] Ibid., ¶78–79.

taken place. In Example 3–1, Fancy Flavors has realized the revenue of $50,000 related to the sale of ice cream to banquet customers in August because the merchandise has been delivered to the customer. All that remains is for Fancy Flavors to collect the money owed. Fancy Flavors has completed its performance and thus earned the amount charged for the sale. The realization of revenue triggers its recognition; that is, this establishes a time period in which the revenue should be included in current performance.

> **Recognition.** Recognition is the process of recording or including the financial measurement of a transaction, event, or circumstance in the entity's measure of current period performance.

Thus Fancy Flavors would recognize $450,000 revenue during the month of August because that amount had been realized, or earned, during that time period. Of course, over the whole life of the enterprise, the sum of all periods' revenues will equal the sum of all periods' cash receipts from sales of products and services. The differences between the revenue and the cash receipts of individual periods is almost always a matter of timing.

Measuring Periodic Effort or Sacrifice

To determine the enterprise's income as a measure of performance, we need to deduct the efforts expended during the period to earn the revenue being recognized. When measured in dollars these efforts are called expenses.

> **Expense.** Expenses are the outflows or costs of resources during a period used to deliver or produce goods, render services, or carrying out other activities that represent the entity's business purpose.[4]

Expenses are actual or expected cash outflows that occurred or will occur in order to produce the current period's revenue. The firm must hire employees, purchase supplies and materials, rent a manufacturing facility or retail establishment, and incur other such costs in order to have a product or service to sell. The costs related to acquiring such resources become expenses in the period when the resources were used to generate sales. Using the accrual basis to measure the entity's income means we must identify the specific resources (labor, material, and the like) which were used to earn the current period's revenues. This process is accomplished by employing the matching concept.

> **Matching.** Matching is the process of including the expenses incurred to produce and sell a product or service in the same time period as the revenues they generated.

In this manner, the matching process associates the efforts expended with the revenues earned to measure performance during a time period. Subtracting the expenses incurred from the revenue earned in a specific time period yields the firm's income. As we will see in the Fancy Flavors example, determining the revenues realized precedes identifying the expenses to be recognized in any given time period. We will use this example next to illustrate income determination and the matching process.

---

[4] Ibid., ¶80.

Example 3–3

Returning to the facts in Example 3–1, we can contrast the expenses that would be recognized during the month of August with the cash disbursements. Exhibit 3–2 shows this comparison.

In August, Fancy Flavors purchased equipment for $600,000 with an expected service life of five years, or sixty months. Assuming equal applicability of that service life to all sixty months, the cost of the first month's use would be $1/60 \times \$600,000$, or $10,000.[5]

Three months' rent of $60,000 was paid in advance, leaving two month's prepaid occupancy. This means that one-third, or $20,000 worth of occupancy, was used up. In the case of supplies, $30,000 worth was received during August, with $15,000 worth still on hand at the end of the month. Presumably this ending stock of supplies will be used by Fancy Flavors to earn revenue in September. Subtracting the $15,000 ending inventory from the total $30,000 purchased during the month implies the supplies used during August cost $15,000.

Even though Fancy Flavors only paid salaries and wages of $120,000 during August, salaries and wages for time actually worked to earn August's revenue amounted to $150,000. The additional $30,000 will be paid on the first payday in September. On the accrual basis, the entire $150,000 represents the salaries and wages expense for the month.

Fancy Flavors received $165,000 worth of ice cream from the manufacturers during August. Of that amount, $35,000 had not been paid for in cash at August 31 and $20,000 remained unsold. Subtracting the ending inventory of $20,000 from the total purchases of $165,000 implies that the cost of ice cream sold during August was $145,000.

The $600,000 bank loan carries an interest cost of 12 percent per year, or 1 percent per month. Therefore, $6,000 of interest was earned by the bank during August, and Fancy Flavors should recognize this amount as an expense related to the month's operations. Note there was no cash outflow as of yet for this expense.

Fancy Flavors also must recognize an obligation to pay federal income taxes. Assuming taxable income of $94,000, federal income tax expense would be $24,000 (approximately 26 percent). Since the taxes will be paid next year, there is no cash outflow during August.

Finally, there is no difference between the August cash disbursement and the miscellaneous expense recognized for heat, light, power, etc. This implies that all such items or services were used to produce the revenue of the month in which they were paid.

Notice that for equipment, rent, and supplies, the cash disbursements exceed the expenses recognized. In each case Fancy Flavors paid for more of the resource in August than was used to generate that month's revenues. Yet for salaries and wages, ice cream, interest, and federal income taxes, the expenses recognized for August exceed the cash disbursement. This recognition acknowledged that the sacrifice of a resource took place to produce August's revenue even though the related cash outflow has not yet occurred.

---

[5] The process of spreading the cost of equipment and other long-term productive resources over their serviceable life is called "depreciation." We will cover this concept more thoroughly in Chapter Four.

EXHIBIT 3–2

Fancy Flavors, Inc.

Cash Disbursements versus Expenses for August 1991

	Cash Disbursed in August	Expense Recognized in August
Nature of the sacrifice:		
Equipment	$600,000	$ 10,000
Rent	60,000	20,000
Supplies	20,000	15,000
Salaries and wages	120,000	150,000
Ice cream	130,000	145,000
Interest on loan	0	6,000
Federal income taxes	0	24,000
Miscellaneous	10,000	10,000
Total	$940,000	$380,000

Product and Period Expenses

At this point it is useful to draw a distinction between product and period expenses based on the nature of these costs. The matching principle requires that every resource used in production in a given period (1) be specifically identified with a particular product or service; (2) have its cost added with the costs of all other resources used to produce that product or service; and (3) be recognized as an expense in the period in which that product or service is sold. When a sacrifice for a resource is made, the accountant considers the way in which the resource is used. If use of the resource can be associated with a specific product or service, its cost is recognized as an expense in the period when the specific products are sold or services completed, at which time the related revenue is recognized. Product expenses include resource costs (like the cost of ice cream for Fancy Flavors), that logically attach to products. Product expenses are recognized as expenses in the period in which the particular product is sold. But if a resource is consumed during the period and its consumption bears no discernible relation to a specific present or future product or service, its cost is recognized as a expense in the period in which it is consumed or sacrificed. Such costs, like the managers' salaries, are called period expenses because they relate more closely to a specific time period than to an identifiable product or service.

Income

The matching procedure allows us to associate the positive results of performance (revenue) with the negative aspects (expenses) to yield a summary measure of the entity's activities during the time period (income). The entity's income is its increase in wealth over that time period in the same sense that income was a return on investment in Chapter Two. Thus income measurement represents essential information to enable the investor to predict future returns from being a creditor or owner.

Example 3–4 Since we have already calculated Fancy Flavors' revenue ($450,000) and expenses ($380,000) for the month of August, we can now determine income as the difference: $70,000 ($450,000 − $380,000).

We show the details of this calculation in an income statement, illustrated in Exhibit 3–3. As we would expect, the $70,000 income as a measure of performance for the month of August contrasts sharply with the company's net operating cash flow of −$540,000 calculated earlier.

Because income is the arithmetic difference between revenues and expenses, its properties as a measure of performance are a function of the way expenses and revenues are determined. Exhibit 3–4 summarizes the properties of revenue, expense, and income.

Gains and Losses. The measurement of income to this point has been limited to the differences between revenues and expenses. We now wish to add explicit recognition of other transactions, events, and circumstances which affect income.

Gains and Losses. Gains and losses are inflows or outflows of resources from transactions and other events and circumstances which affect the entity during a period but are incidentally related to the entity's business purpose.

Gains arise from events that are not routinely associated with providing the primary product or service of the business to customers. For example, a gain may result from the sale of equipment which is held for use in producing the businesses product rather than for sale to customers. Note that the distinction between revenues and gains depends upon the nature of the enterprise. For example, income from investments in securities might be revenue for an insurance company but a gain to a manufacturing concern. Analogous to gains, losses arise from events not generally associated with the primary business. Examples include theft losses, interest expense on amounts borrowed, and the like.

EXHIBIT 3–3

Fancy Flavors, Inc.

Income Statement
For the Month of August 1991

Revenue from sales of ice cream		$450,000
Less expenses:		
Equipment	$ 10,000	
Rent	20,000	
Supplies used	15,000	
Salaries and wages	150,000	
Cost of ice cream sold	145,000	
Interest on loan	6,000	
Federal income taxes	24,000	
Miscellaneous: heat, light, etc.	10,000	
Total expenses		$380,000
Income		$ 70,000

EXHIBIT 3–4

Summary of Accrual Accounting Income Concepts

	Definition (What?)	*Timing* (When?)	*Measurement* (How much?)
Revenue	Goods and services sold to customers during the current period	Recognized when goods have been delivered or services have been rendered	Price paid or agreed to be paid by the customer
Expense	Resources used to provide a product or service	Recognized in the period in which the related revenue is recognized (i.e., expense is matched against revenue)	Cost of resources consumed to provide the products or services delivered during the period
Income	Difference between revenue and expense of the period	Determined as a result of recognizing the related revenue and expense of the period	Difference between the total prices of products sold and services rendered and the total costs of resources used to provide those products and services

Example 3–5 | Recognition Equipment, Inc., included the following gain in its 1985 income statement: "The Company has from time to time entered into cross-licensing agreements with other major manufacturers of information-processing equipment whereby the companies exchange certain patent rights. As additional consideration, the Company has received payments of $382,000 in fiscal 1985 and $1,554,000 in fiscal 1983 after deducting expenses, which have been recorded as nonoperating income."

A special category of gains and losses has been established for very unusual or atypical events and transactions. This category is labeled extraordinary gains and losses.

Extraordinary Gains and Losses. Extraordinary gains and losses are inflows or outflows of resources due to clearly abnormal events or transactions. Such events are not a normal part of the operations of the business in the long run and they occur very infrequently.

While gains and losses result from events peripheral to the major activities of the business, they are not highly infrequent or unusual. That is, they can be expected to occur occasionally. Extraordinary gains and losses are much more uncommon. They arise from natural disasters, arson, expropriation of assets by a foreign government, litigation and lawsuit costs and awards, gains and losses from redemption of debt, and other such uncontrollable events. We include these in a separate category on the income statement to alert the reader that such events are not expected to recur in the foreseeable future.

Example 3–6 | An example of an extraordinary gain is found in Machine Technology, Inc.'s 1984 financial statements: "In February 1984, the Company became entitled to $248,000 of life insurance proceeds as a result of the death of an officer. This amount has been reduced by an award of $150,000 to the officer's widow less the related tax benefit of $75,000."

Example 3–7 | The eruption of Mount St. Helens gave rise to an extraordinary loss for Weyerhaeuser Company in 1980: "In May 1980 Mount St. Helens erupted and approximately 68,000 acres of the Company's timberlands were affected by the explosion of the mountain, slides and flooding. An extraordinary charge of $66,700 less related tax effect of $35,000 or $36,200 ($.29 per common share) was made to cover losses of standing timber, logs, buildings and equipment incurred during the initial eruption and, in addition, incremental reforestation costs and added logging and transportation costs incident to the salvage of flood-carried, blown-down and scorched timber. Salvage and reforestation operations are expected to continue for several years."

Once we include gains and losses with the entity's revenues and expenses, we have the accounting measure of income from continuing operations for the period.

Income from Continuing Operations. Income or loss from continuing operations is the difference between revenues from operations and related expenses, plus or minus gains or losses, for a given period of time.

Since extraordinary gains and losses are not a part of normal operations, they are not included in income from continuing operations. Instead, they are added to or deducted from income from continuing operations to obtain the accounting measure of net income. This determination gives us an estimate of the change in the wealth of the entity due to its operating activities.

EXHIBIT 3–5 (see Example 3–8)

Fancy Flavors, Inc.

Income Statement
For the Month of August 1991

Revenue from sales of ice cream		$450,000
Less expenses:		
Equipment	$ 10,000	
Rent	20,000	
Supplies used	15,000	
Salaries and wages	150,000	
Cost of ice cream sold	145,000	
Interest on loan	6,000	
Federal income taxes	24,000	
Miscellaneous (heat, light, etc.)	10,000	
Total expenses		380,000
Income from continuing operations		$ 70,000
Less tornado loss		5,000
Net income		$ 65,000

Net Income.   Net income or loss is income or loss from continuing operations plus or minus extraordinary gains or losses.

Example 3–8 | Suppose Fancy Flavors, Inc., experienced a power outage on August 31 that was due to a tornado. This resulted in the failure of their refrigerators and the loss of $5,000 worth of ice cream. Fancy Flavors did not have insurance covering natural disasters. Thus the $5,000 would be considered an extraordinary loss and shown on their August income statement as in Exhibit 3–5.

SUMMARY

This chapter focused on the information used to make investment decisions. The cash basis of accounting, considered first, measures net operating cash flow as the difference between the cash inflows and outflows of conducting business activities. Because this measure fails to associate efforts and accomplishments within the same time period, it is not very useful for predicting the firm's future cash-generating ability. The accrual basis of accounting is considered a better predictor of future performance. This method records transactions and events in the time period in which they occur, irrespective of their related cash flows. Revenue is recorded in the period that goods or services are sold. Expenses incurred to generate the revenue are matched or associated with the period when the revenue is recognized. Gains and losses are additional items included in the measure of income from continuing operations. Extraordinary gains and losses, because of their very infrequent and unusual nature, are not considered as part of income from continuing operations but are added to or subtracted from it to yield net income.

Questions for Review and Discussion

3–1. Define
   a. Cash basis
   b. Accrual basis
   c. Income from continuing operations
   d. Revenue
   e. Realization
   f. Recognition
   g. Expense
   h. Matching
   i. Product expense
   j. Period expense
   k. Gains and losses
   l. Extraordinary gains and losses
   m. Net operating cash flow
   n. Net income

3–2. Specify the personal cash flows to an investor and creditor from making an investment.

3–3. Are the business's cash flows important to the investor? Why or why not?

3–4. Are forecasts of the firm's cash flows useful? Why or why not?

3–5. Providing net operating cash flows for use by investors in making investment decisions is considered to have both advantages and disadvantages. Discuss both.

3–6. Compare the cash basis and accrual basis.

3–7. How does one determine if revenue has been earned? How does this relate to the realization and recognition principles?

3–8. The text states that revenue realization must precede expense recognition. Explain.

3–9. Distinguish between product and period expenses.

3–10. The timing of recognition of revenue generally determines when many expenses will be recognized. Explain why this is so. What kinds of expenses will generally not be subject to this pattern of recognition?

3–11. Net operating income is based on historical events.

    a. What are the reasons for this historical orientation when investors are concerned mainly with future cash flows in valuing prospective investments?

    b. How or why can historical measures of performance be used as indicators of likely future performance?

3–12. Distinguish between gains (losses) and extraordinary gains (losses).

3–13. Distinguish between income from continuing operations and net income.

3–14. Why are extraordinary gains and losses excluded from income from continuing operations?

3–15. Suppose that each year for the last several years the Ace Company recognized a significant extraordinary loss in its income statement entitled "Loss on uncollectible customer accounts." What would you conclude about the losses?

3–16. Income from continuing operations is not considered to be a forecast per se, though it is presumably relevant to investors who wish to forecast future cash flows. Under what conditions will the current period's income from continuing operations be an actual forecast of the next period's (or other future periods') income from continuing operations? Does knowledge of these conditions have any implications for investors?

Problems

3–1. **Net Operating Cash Flow for Predictions of Future Cash Flow.** Two years ago, John Jacobsen and Steve Block started a small delicatessen specializing in sandwiches. Steve wants to remain in the business, and John has agreed to sell his share if they can agree on a mutually satisfactory purchase price. Steve has suggested using past operating cash flows of the business as an indicator of likely future cash flows. John, on the other hand, believes that the past operating cash flows are not representative due to heavy initial cash outflows for purchasing equipment and relatively light cash inflows while the business was building up a clientele. Actual net operating cash flows for the first two years of operation were − $1,000 the first year and $6,000 the second year. They each have projected future annual net operating cash flows as follows:

		John (projected)	Steve (projected)
Year	1	$10,000	$ 6,000
	2	12,000	8,000
	3	14,000	8,000
	4	14,000	8,000
	5	16,000	8,000
	6	18,000	8,000
	7	20,000	10,000
	8	20,000	10,000
	9	20,000	10,000
	10	20,000	10,000

Required:

1. Assuming the business will last for only the ten years projected, what is the present value of the business in each case if their time preference rate is 10 percent?

2. Suppose you are John. How might you go about convincing Steve that your projections are more realistic based at least in part on the actual events and transactions of the business during the first two years?

3–2. Feasibility of Future Cash Flow Projections.   The Northern Construction Corporation is engaged in the construction of government projects. Three years ago the management of the firm believed that the number of government projects it would undertake would increase. Based on this premise, it projected net operating cash flows that were significantly larger than in the past. In the belief that this information was important to both current and potential stockholders, it supplied the following estimates of future net operating cash flows:

1982	$ 60,000
1983	75,000
1984	90,000
1985	120,000
1986	125,000
1987–1991	130,000

Unfortunately, in the years immediately following these projections there was a significant cutback in actual government expenditures. As a result, the company's realized net operating cash flows stayed approximately constant at a level of $60,000 over the ten-year period. The company's management saw little prospect for net operating cash flows to increase in the foreseeable future.

Required:

1. Assume that there are a total of 1,000 shares of stock in the corporation. If the shareholders' time preference rate is 10 percent, what are the present values of the shares for the two sets of circumstances? (Assume that net operating cash flows are distributed in full to owners in the year received.)

2. Suppose you had purchased shares based on management's first cash-flow projections (and had paid approximately their then present value). How might you react to the revised estimates? Why?

3–3. Net Operating Cash Flow as a Performance Measurement.   The Green Thumb Nursery was started five years ago to raise and sell trees and shrubs. The varieties that it grows require from three to five years to reach a salable size. As a result, it has experienced rather heavy cash outflows in the first five years of operation. Net operating cash flows for these years were as follows:

Year 1	$(60,000)
Year 2	(40,000)
Year 3	(42,000)
Year 4	(34,000)
Year 5	(6,000)

Because of these heavy cash outflows, the firm is in need of additional money and is currently attempting to attract new investors. It realizes that investors make investment decisions on the basis of prospective future cash flows, but it is hesitant to make such estimates public because of the potential legal liability if they do not materialize.

Required:

1. One alternative it has considered is simply presenting the historical operating cash flows, but it feels that they do not adequately represent the past performance or future potential of the firm. Comment on this alternative. Why may it be inadequate information for prospective investors?

2. How might the nursery present largely factual information that would be more likely to give investors an indication of potential future operating cash flows?
3. What sort of criteria should be used for providing the information for potential investors?
4. If you were in a position to supply all the additional money The Green Thumb Nursery needs, what information would you request?

3–4. **Net Operating Cash Flow as a Performance Measurement.**   The Coastal Trading Company's principal activity is the sale of fishing equipment, supplies, food, and clothing to the Alaskan fishing industry. Its business is highly seasonal. Outfitting boats during the months of June and July accounts for approximately 40 percent of its annual sales. As a result it uses these two months as an indicator of its performance for the year. During June 1991 it had sales of $172,000, of which $16,000 was paid in cash and the balance was sold on account. Also during June it received payments on account from May sales totaling $18,000. Merchandise sold during June included goods purchased in May totaling $43,000; goods purchased on account during June totaling $48,000; and goods purchased and paid for in June totaling $23,000. In addition, it paid accounts payable for merchandise received in May totaling $23,000. June salaries and wages, advertising, and miscellaneous expenses were paid as incurred and totaled $14,000.

In July, as the fishing season progressed, the company's sales declined to $82,000, of which $61,000 was paid in cash and $21,000 was sold on account. It received payments on account during July of $156,000. Merchandise sold during July had a cost of $52,000 and was purchased in previous months. There was no new merchandise purchased during July. July cash payments included wages and salaries, advertising, and miscellaneous expenses totaling $11,000, and payments on account for June purchases totaling $40,000.

Required:

1. Construct separate operating cash flow statements for June and July based on the information given.
2. Which month's cash performance is better? Explain.
3. Which month's cash performance, if either, is the better indicator of future performance of the company? Explain.
4. What are the problems associated with use of either statement alone as an indicator of likely future performance?
5. In August sales declined further to $63,000, of which $46,000 was cash and $17,000 was sold on account. Payments received on account from May and June sales totaled $20,000. Based on this information, what is total revenue for the three months? What are total cash receipts for the same period? Discuss the reasons for their similarity despite the use of different principles in determining each.

3–5. **The Maine Fish Company—Cash-Flow Performance.**   The Maine Fish Company has recently set up a new operation which will own and operate a chain of fish, chip, and chowder restaurants. It has hired Jane Robinson to manage the operation. Realizing that net operating cash flow is important to investors, it has decided to base her salary in part on the cash flows she generates. Specifically, she will receive 3 percent of the net operating cash flow in the form of an annual bonus. But Jane does not know this.

During the first year of operations, Jane was able to open a total of four new restaurants and make final plans for an additional three. She feels that this was a rather outstanding performance and as a result is looking forward to a substantial bonus. The following events summarize her activities for the year.

1. Purchased land for the four restaurants for $80,000.
2. Signed contracts for purchase of three additional pieces of property costing a total of $65,000 but has not yet paid for them.
3. Constructed the four restaurant buildings. Total cost was $143,000, and she expected they would last about 20 years each.
4. Purchased equipment for $62,000 she expected would last 10 years.
5. Hired six full- and part-time employees for each restaurant.
6. Paid for initial advertising for the four restaurants of $7,200.
7. Paid wages totaling $37,000 for the year.
8. Paid for food supplies totaling $66,000.
9. Miscellaneous expenditures for the year totaled $4,300.
10. Received cash from sales totaling $134,000. (All sales are for cash.)

In checking over her records at year-end, Jane found that she had virtually no unpaid bills outstanding, but had $3,000 in wages which were earned but as yet unpaid. Similarly, she had $2,000 worth of food supplies remaining at year-end.

Required:

1. Prepare a cash flow statement for Jane's operations for the year.
2. What is the likely amount of Jane's bonus? Do you think it adequately rewards her for her performance?
3. Can you suggest an alternative measure of performance on which to base Jane's bonus? How much bonus would she receive for the first year under your plan?

3–6. Analysis of Effects of Transactions. Following are some randomly selected business events of the Kline Company.

1. The company pays off a long-term bank loan.
2. Wages for the period are paid by the company.
3. An individual contributes cash to the company to become an owner.
4. The company makes cash sales.
5. One of the owners uses up company supplies for personal purposes.
6. The company buys stock in Allied Corporation.
7. Credit sales for the period are recorded.
8. The company pays in advance for an insurance policy.
9. An item of inventory becomes worthless (normal spoilage).

Indicate the effects of each event (positive, negative, or no effect) on the following:

1. Net cash flow.
2. Income from continuing operations.

3–7. Revenue Recognition. The National Manufacturing Corporation is preparing its income statement for 1991. It is using the realization principle for recognition of revenue and has the following events:

1. Signed a contract to sell for $60,000 machinery that it manufactures. Of this $60,000, $32,000 worth has been manufactured and delivered during the year. The balance is to be manufactured and delivered next year.
2. Sold $43,000 worth of machinery, all of which has been delivered. However, it has not yet received payment for these goods.
3. Completed manufacture of $82,000 worth of machinery for which it has no buyer as yet.
4. Received a partial payment of $15,000 as an advance for machinery that is to be manufactured and delivered next year. The total selling price of the machinery is $37,000.
5. Manufactured and sold machinery to various other customers during the year

totaling $172,000. At year-end, it had received payments for this machinery totaling $155,000. The remainder is to be collected next year.

6. Received payments totaling $35,000 for machinery that had been delivered to various customers in 1990.

Required:

1. Under the realization principle, how much revenue is attributable to the year's performance for each of these events? Explain your answer in each case.
2. Why is the realization principle used to recognize revenue?

3–8. The Matching Principle. Jack's Gardening Service is a small sole proprietorship. Prior to now, Jack has been measuring the success of his enterprise on the basis of cash flow. He would like to start using income from continuing operations as his measure of performance. He wants to match efforts (expenses) with last month's accomplishments (revenues). The relevant facts are as follows:

1. At the start of his business, Jack purchased a truck for $4,200. He estimated at that time that it would last five years.
2. He purchased other equipment at a cost of $1,200. He estimates that this equipment will have to be replaced at the end of year four.
3. During the past month, he paid out $72 for gas used in his truck and mowers during the month.
4. He paid wages to employees of $800 during the month, $200 of which was for time worked in the previous month.
5. Jack purchased $450 worth of fertilizer on account. At the end of the month, he had $200 worth of fertilizer remaining. He started the month with $50 worth of fertilizer.
6. On January 1 of the current year, he had paid for insurance for the year totaling $600.
7. At the end of the month, he paid his bookkeeper for three months' services, including services rendered in the current month. This totaled $165.
8. At the end of the month, Jack withdrew $750 from the business to pay personal living expenses.

Required:

1. Using the matching principle, what are Jack's expenses for the month based on the listed events? Explain your reasoning in each case.
2. Which of the events might be classified as product cost? Which are period costs?

3–9. Revenue Recognition. Alice McKinley operates a women's wear shop which produces custom-made and ready-to-wear women's outfits. During a recent month, the following events took place. Indicate how much revenue should be recognized for the month in each instance.

1. Customers were permitted to put clothing on layaway for deposits totaling $200. At the end of the layaway period the customers need not buy the items, in which case they forfeit their deposits. Otherwise the deposits apply against the price.
2. A customer picked up a custom-made outfit she had ordered. The customer paid the balance owed of $80, the difference between the $100 price of the dress and the deposit paid at the end of last month.
3. Other customers ordered outfits with total selling prices of $3,000. These customers paid 20 percent of the total price.
4. Received $2,000 for cash sales, some of which were out of the layaway sales.
5. Received $3,500 in cash payments on credit sales. The beginning balances due from customers totaled $4,000 but by month-end they totaled $5,000.

3–10. Accounting Principles. The realization and matching principles are fundamental in determining net operating income. Identify the principle that is most relevant to each of the following events.

1. Supplies originally costing $1,500, which had been used to produce goods sold during the period, are recognized as an expense.
2. Prepaid rent was reduced by $500, representing the amount expired for the period.
3. A customer order was received for 100 of the power tools manufactured by the company. The total sales price of the tools is $3,000.
4. Depreciation of equipment is $600 for the period.
5. An oil painting costing $3,000 increases in value to $5,000. No revenue is recognized as a result of the increase.
6. The sum of $500 is paid in advance for services to be performed next year, but current period's revenue is unaffected.
7. Wages earned but not paid at the end of 1991 are recognized as expenses in 1991.
8. Interest earned, but not received, on a loan made to an associate is recorded as income of the period.

3–11. **Net Operating Cash Flow and Income from Continuing Operations Contrasted.** George Craft owns and operates a boardinghouse near a large university. He started the business two years ago when he leased a large old house for $14,400 per year payable one-half on January 1 and one-half on July 1 of each year. The house accommodates fifteen students for both room and board at a monthly rate of $400 each and provides meals only to another ten students for $240 per month each. Mr. Craft bought furniture at a cost of $14,400 two years ago, and he estimates that it will last six years. He also bought food preparation equipment at a cost of $12,000, and he estimated this equipment will have to be replaced in five years.

During May of this year, he made food purchases of $3,880 on account and paid for April's purchases totaling $4,240. He estimated he had $960 worth of food on hand at the end of April and $760 worth of food on hand at the end of May. He employs one person who handles both cleaning and meal preparation for a salary of $2,600 per month. Heat, light, and other miscellaneous expenses for May totaled $292.

Mr. Craft is currently reevaluating the profitability of his investment. He is unsure whether to measure it on the basis of net operating cash flows or income from continuing operations.

Required:

1. Prepare a statement of net operating cash flows for May for Mr. Craft's venture.
2. Prepare an income statement for May.
3. Which is the better performance measurement (i.e., the better indicator of the long-run cash-generating ability of the venture)? Explain.

3–12. **Income from Continuing Operations and Net Operating Cash Flow Contrasted.** Diver Supply Company was recently formed by Tina Wilson to manufacture a new kind of wet suit for skin divers. In its first month of operation, the following transactions occurred:

April 1   Tina invested $10,000 cash in the business.
April 1   Purchased wet-suit material on account for $1,700. The account must be paid by May 10.
April 1   Hired two part-time employees to assemble wet suits at a salary of $200 each per month.
April 2   Purchased equipment for manufacture of the wet suits. She paid $7,200 for the equipment.

April   5   Signed an agreement with a local sporting goods store to supply wet suits for April and May delivery (one-half delivered each month). The total selling price was $3,600; $1,000 of which was paid at the time of the order, the remainder to be paid at the end of May.

April 30   Paid employees for month of April. Counted inventory and found there was $700 worth of material still unused. Delivered half the wet-suit order as scheduled.

Required:

Assume that the equipment has a three-year life with no salvage value, that no additional materials were purchased in April, and that there were no finished wet suits in inventory at the end of April.

1. Prepare a statement of net operating cash flow for the month of April.
2. Prepare an income statement for the month of April.
3. Compare the two statements. Which do you think is a better performance measurement? Explain.

3–13. Income from Continuing Operations and Net Operating Cash Flow Contrasted.   The Glider Company was formed on January 1, 1991 to sell supply items to glider fans. During the first month the following transactions occurred:

January   1   Owner invested $15,000 in the business.
January   1   Hired a part-time salesperson for $500 per month.
January   2   Purchased $5,000 of supply items for cash.
January   5   Purchased a delivery truck for $3,500 cash. The estimated life of the truck is five years, after which it will be sold for $500.
January 10   Purchased $2,000 of supply items using credit. First payment is due in March.
January 31   Paid the part-time salesperson the January salary.
January 31   Paid $500 of miscellaneous business expenses.
January 31   Sales receipts for January indicated $3,000 of cash sales and $1,000 of credit sales.
January 31   An inventory of the supply items indicated that $5,000 worth of supplies have not been sold.

Required:

1. Prepare a statement of net operating cash flow for January 1991.
2. Prepare an income statement for January 1991.
3. List and explain each difference of items and/or amounts between the two statements.

3–14. The Matching Principle.   The Custom Sign Company is a sole proprietorship started by John Smith during March of this year. When the business was started, Mr. Smith opened a checking account in the name of the business. Until now, he has been evaluating his monthly performance by the increase (decrease) in the balance of the firm's checking account. However, he realizes that net operating cash flow is not the only measure of performance and that net operating cash flow does not take into account the usage of equipment and services that were paid for in prior months. He has therefore decided to use income from continuing operations as a measure of monthly performance.

   At the end of September, he became concerned with properly determining and measuring expenses. Some of the notes that Mr. Smith made to himself include the following information:

1. On March 1, he purchased a truck for $10,800. He estimated that the truck would last for five years.
2. Immediately after the purchase of the truck, he purchased a generator for $1,200

and installed it in the truck. He estimated the life of the generator to be four years.

3. Other equipment purchases on March 1 totaled $540. The estimated life at the time of purchase was three years.

4. On March 1, he paid for the city and state licenses required to operate a commercial business. The cost of the licenses totaled $400, and the licenses expire on October 31.

5. Mr. Smith acquired an insurance policy effective March 1. The policy is for a three-year period, with prepayments of annual premiums on March 1. The annual premium for the first year is $480.

6. Mr. Smith rented a small building on April 1. The rental is $1,000 per month, with prepayments of three months' rent due every three months. He prepaid three months' rent on April 1 and July 1.

7. During the current month Mr. Smith purchased $80 worth of gasoline using a credit card. He also paid $120 for gasoline purchased in prior months.

8. He purchased $750 worth of sign materials during the month. He estimated the cost of the materials on hand at the beginning and the end of the month to be $200 and $150, respectively.

9. Mr. Smith withdrew $450 at the end of August to pay for his estimated September personal expenses, and withdrew $500 at the end of September for his estimated October personal expenses.

Required:

1. Using the matching principle, what are the September expenses for the Custom Sign Company? Explain your reasoning for each item included or excluded.

2. Which of the September expenses might be classified as product costs? Which are period costs?

3–15. Cash Flows and Net Income. Mary Morton owns and operates a photography shop which she started last year when she leased a studio. The annual rental on the studio is $2,400, with advance quarterly payments due on the first of January, April, July, and October.

In the year that she began her business, Ms. Morton made improvements to the studio for $1,800. She estimated they would last for five years. The cost of furniture and fixtures was $4,800. She estimated their useful life would be eight years and that the salvage value would be negligible. The photography equipment cost $2,700. The estimated life of the equipment is ten years, but she plans on trading in all equipment for new equipment every three years. The trade-in value represents one-third of the original purchase price.

During April of this year, Ms. Morton purchased $600 worth of film and other photography supplies on account, and paid all the outstanding statements for the prior two months' purchases in the amount of $400. She estimated that she had $200 and $300 worth of photography supplies on hand at the beginning and the end of the month, respectively.

Ms. Morton bills customers after they have ordered photographs from the proofs. During the current month, she billed customers in the amount of $2,800. She collected $2,700 from customers during the month.

Ms. Morton employs an assistant whose salary is $700 per month, paid at the end of each month. Miscellaneous expenses (including utilities) totaled $100 for April and were paid for in April. Ms. Morton withdrew $500 for personal expenses at the end of the month.

In prior months Ms. Morton had not tried to measure the profitability of the business, since she had no cash problems. However, she now anticipates an approximate 10 percent increase in the price of film and other photography supplies, and she plans to raise the salary of her assistant to $750. Therefore she is wondering how much effect the expected cost increases will have on profitability and whether or not she should revise her price schedules. She also is unsure whether to measure performance on the basis of cash flows or operating income.

Required:

1. Prepare a performance statement for April based upon net operating cash flow as a measure of performance.
2. Prepare an income statement for April.
3. Which is the better profitability measure (i.e., the better indicator of long-run cash-generating ability)? Why?

3–16. The following footnotes were found in the 1988 annual reports of Burlington Northern Railroad Co. and Capital Cities ABC, Inc., respectively:

A. Burlington Northern Railroad Co.

In November 1988, BNI and Railroad reached an agreement to settle an antitrust action filed by Energy Transportation Systems, Inc. ("ETSI"). This litigation covered claims by the plaintiff that BNI and Railroad unlawfully blocked construction of a proposed coal slurry pipeline from the Powder River Basin to Texas and Arkansas. The terms of the settlement involved a $100 million cash payment on December 1, 1988 and deferred payments of $25 million plus interest on December 1, 1989, 1990, and 1991. The entire amount of the settlement, $175 million, has been charged against Railroad income for the year ended December 31, 1988 and is disclosed in the Consolidated Statement of Income, net of $67 million in income taxes ($30 million deferred), as an extraordinary loss.

B. Capital Cities ABC, Inc.

In transactions related to the acquisition of ABC, and to comply with certain regulations of the Federal Communications Commission, during January 1986 the Company sold certain broadcasting properties and all of its cable television systems. The cash proceeds of these sales were $703,378,000 and resulted in an extraordinary gain of $279,996,000 (net of income taxes of $156,800,000).

Required:

Discuss the accounting treatment used by Burlington Northern Railroad and Capital Cities ABC for each of the events described in their footnotes. In particular, consider whether categorization as an extraordinary gain or loss is appropriate.

3–17. Gains and Losses. You and a fellow student, Jane Tucker, pool your resources of $1,000 each in cash and enter the business of selling lecture notes on campus at the beginning of the autumn quarter, 1991. You intend to operate the business, Tucker and Jones Enterprises, at least until the end of spring 1992. Of the original investment, at least $500 is needed to meet costs of supplies, insurance, and wages each quarter while awaiting collection of revenues. The remaining $1,500 is used as a down payment to purchase a printing press at a total cost of $2,500 (the bank lends you $1,000, interest-free). You expect that the press can be sold for $1,900 at the end of spring 1992, or for $1,100 at the end of spring 1993. You therefore depreciate the equipment at a rate of $200 per quarter. You and Tucker collect the materials and print the lecture notes which you sell to three distributors. The distributors are given until the end of each quarter to pay Tucker and Jones Enterprises.

In the next two quarters the following events occurred:

	Autumn	*Winter*
Credit sales to distributors	$2,200	$1,800
Receipts from distributors	1,800	2,050
Wages paid	550	600
Advertising and insurance paid	50	100
Supplies purchased on credit	600	250
Repaid part of bank loan	500	500
Payments to accounts payable	500	350
Supplies on hand at end of autumn	250	–0–

Additional information:

1. At the end of autumn, one of the distributors owed $400. No action was taken as he promised to pay early in the winter quarter, which he did. During the autumn $500 of the bank loan was repaid.
2. At the end of winter another distributor owed $150. The amount was written off as a bad debt because a telegram was received from him saying that he had gone out of business. Just at the end of winter quarter classes, vandals broke in and destroyed the printing press. The insurance company paid insurance proceeds of $1,150.

Required:

1. Prepare income statements for autumn 1991 and for winter 1992.
2. How did you classify the losses on bad debts and the printing press? Justify your treatment.
3. Assuming that the loss of the printing press is an extraordinary loss, explain how the income from continuing operations and the net income amount for winter 1992 might be used to evaluate the business.

3–18. Calculating Gains and Losses. In each of the following three different situations determine (a) the amount of gain or loss; and (b) whether the gain or loss is extraordinary or not.

1. The Fashionable Corporation specializes in high-fashion apparel. During 1991 the fashion market experienced very rapid changes in styles and consumer preferences which resulted in the sale of discontinued styles and related accessories for $250,000 and $50,000, respectively. The total costs of these items were $300,000 and $80,000, respectively.
2. Winthrop Chemicals, Inc., manufactures chemicals for the drug industry. During 1991 it was decided that some of Winthrop's storage equipment had become obsolete. The original cost of the equipment was $1.5 million. The equipment had been depreciated a total of $800,000. The equipment was sold for $750,000.
3. A freak electrical storm occurred one night causing a warehouse to catch fire and burn to the ground. The building and contents were insured for a total of $2.53 million. The original cost of the building was $1.5 million and it had been depreciated $750,000. The contents cost $1.2 million. After a thorough investigation, the storm was determined to be a most improbable act of nature. Insurance will be received in the full amount stated on the policy.

3–19. Classifying Losses. On March 24, 1989 the Exxon Corporation oil tanker Valdez ran aground in Prince William Sound off the coast of Alaska. Approximately 280,000 barrels of crude oil were released, coating the beaches and wildlife with oil. During the remainder of 1989, Exxon incurred significant costs to clean up the oil spill; for example, scrubbing the beaches and rescuing the sea life. Exxon anticipated further cleanup efforts might be necessary in the spring of 1990. Additionally,

Exxon faced more than 170 lawsuits for damage related to the oil spill (e.g., the impact on wildlife, recreational users, and commercial fishing activities), as well as class actions and a lawsuit by the state of Alaska. In their 1989 earnings report, Exxon reduced income by $2,545 million (before income taxes) for a provision for the costs associated with the Valdez accident. Net income for 1989 after subtracting this provision was $3,510 million.

Required:

Do you think Exxon's Valdez provision should be shown as a loss deducted before determining income from continuing operations or as an extraordinary loss? Explain your answer.

Basic Concepts and Balance Sheet Measures

CHAPTER FOUR

The previous chapter covered the basic principles underlying the preparation of the income statement. The income statement tells us the results from managing and operating the business; that is, how profitable the entity was from selling goods and services during the period. The balance sheet is equally important. It tells us what resources management has available to operate the business during the year. Additionally, it tells us where management got the money used to purchase those resources. The balance sheet gives us a framework for recognizing the events that affect net income during the period, as well as events that do not affect income determination. The purpose of this chapter is to develop an understanding of the entity's financial position through the three major components of the balance sheet: assets, liabilities, and owners' equity. We will illustrate how the financial position changes during a period via external transactions and internal adjustments.

FINANCIAL POSITION

The primary elements of the balance sheet are categorized as assets, liabilities, and owners' equity. This section defines and gives examples of these categories. The difficulties in measuring the balance sheet elements in dollars are also addressed. Of central importance to the discussion is the role of assets, liabilities, and owners' equity in the balance sheet equation.

The Elements Defined

Assets. Assets are probable future economic benefits embodied in resources that are owned by an entity as a result of past transactions or events (e.g., outright purchase or receipt of a gift).[1]

The firm's assets include all the resources available for use by management. To be of benefit to the firm, these resources must be expected to help management operate the business and earn net income in the future. The phrase "probable future economic benefits" means the asset will contribute to the firm's profitability. Specific types of assets include cash on hand; accounts receivable from customers; copyrights and patents; and land, buildings and equipment. Equipment, for example, will be used by a business to manufacture a product which can be sold at a profit. Thus the equipment has future economic benefits; that is, it will help the firm earn net income.

Liabilities. Liabilities are future sacrifices of economic benefits which arise from present obligations of the entity to provide assets or services to other parties in the future as the result of past transactions or events.[2]

Liabilities provide one source of money that management can use to purchase assets. They represent the debts of the firm from past borrowing. Examples include accounts payable to suppliers for merchandise delivered; wages and salaries due to employees for work performed; mortgages on land or buildings; and notes payable to creditors such as banks. These examples illustrate past events wherein external parties conveyed resources to the firm (e.g., merchandise, employee services, cash) in return for the firm's promise to pay at some future date. Liabilities require the outflow of assets or services from the firm (e.g., cash, warranty work) when they become due. This payment of the obligations with assets or services represents the future sacrifice of economic benefits.

Owners' Equity. Owners' equity is interest in the assets of an entity that remains after deducting its liabilities. In this sense it is the residual, or the assets which remain after liabilities have been paid. In a business enterprise, the residual assets represents the ownership interest.[3]

At the inception of the business, owners' equity equals the assets contributed to the firm by the owners. This amount is called paid-in capital. It represents the money the entity obtained from the owners to be used to purchase assets. Because the owners are the residual beneficiaries, their original investment is increased by the firm's net income and decreased by net losses and withdrawals such as dividends. The net income (or loss) and withdrawals which accumulate since the inception of the entity are recorded in retained earnings. Thus owners' equity itself has two components.

Paid-in Capital. Paid-in capital equals the resources contributed by the owners to the entity in exchange for ownership interests. It is the portion of owner's equity represented by the assets contributed by investors to become owners of the entity.

[1] FASB, "Concepts Statement No. 6," *Elements of Financial Statements*, December 1985, ¶25.
[2] Ibid., ¶35.
[3] Ibid., ¶49–50.

For example, if the firm's owners originally contributed $500,000 for their ownership rights, this amount would be shown as paid-in capital. The paid-in capital account is only increased when investors contribute additional resources to the entity in exchange for new ownership shares in the business, and decreased when old ownership interests are sold by investors back to the firm.

Retained Earnings.   Retained earnings equals the cumulative excess of net income over net losses and dividend distributions to or withdrawals by owners since the inception of the business. It is the portion of owners' equity represented by the cumulative profitability of the entity which has not been given to owners as a return on their investment.

Dividends are distributions of assets made to the firm's owners. They represent a sharing of the profitability of the entity with its owners. Conceptually, dividends are similar to withdrawals of profits made by sole proprietors and partners. In each period, the retained earnings account is increased by net income and decreased by net losses and dividends or withdrawals paid to the owners. The balance in the retained earnings account at the end of any period is the amount by which cumulative net income exceeds cumulative net losses, dividends, and withdrawals. For example, if, since its inception, the firm earned net income of $150,000 and distributed to its owners dividends of $90,000, it would have a $60,000 balance in retained earnings. This balance in retained earnings does not exist in the form of any specific asset (e.g., cash). Nor does it represent a legal claim which the owners have against the entity. Rather, the term "retained earnings" means only what it implies: the amount of earnings kept (retained) in the business.

Measurement of the Balance Sheet Elements

In constructing a balance sheet, we need to determine how to measure the components; that is, how to quantify them in money terms. Conventionally, assets, liabilities and owners' equity are stated at their historical cost, or the amount originally paid when the assets were acquired or liabilities incurred. This concept is the cost principle.

Cost Principle.   The amount sacrificed to acquire use of a resource is measured as the price paid.

More formally defined, a cost is a sacrifice made by the entity to conduct its economic activities; that is, whatever is given up or foregone by the entity so that it can consume, use, save, exchange, produce, or in general conduct its operations. This cost becomes the basis of all accounting for the elements of the financial statements. Thus all assets are recorded at the amount that was paid for them, regardless of changes in their prices and market values in future periods.

Example 4–1 | Suppose a business has two customers. One buys a product and pays $1,000 in cash. The second buys the same product and promises to pay $1,000 in 30 days. The business would show two assets, cash for $1,000 and accounts receivable for $1,000. Suppose the same business received supplies worth $3,000 and promised to pay for them in 60 days. The business would show supplies measured at $3,000 and accounts payable at $3,000.

Note that the amount to be received from the customer is equal to the product given in exchange for the customer's promise to pay. And the amount to be paid by the firm for a liability is equal to the cash, goods, or services received in exchange for the liability. Thus assets acquired through purchase are measured in the financial statements at the amount of cash or other assets given up plus the liabilities incurred.

Example 4–2 | Assume a store acquired merchandise for sale to customers. It paid $500 at delivery and promised to pay $1,500 in two weeks. Their merchandise purchased would be shown as an asset for $2,000, equal to the $500 cash paid plus the $1,500 liability incurred.

Admittedly, this measurement approach for assets is not entirely consistent with the definition for assets given earlier. There it was stated that assets are future economic benefits, implying we should measure them at the price they will bring when sold or the market value of the products and services they will produce. Measurement on this basis would require forecasts of unknown cash flows from future events. For example, we would need to estimate future selling prices for the firm's products. Because these amounts are uncertain, we use instead the original cost as an objective basis for measurement.

Financial Position

Measurement of the three elements of the balance sheet gives the firm's financial position, or balance sheet, at any specific date.

Balance Sheet. A balance sheet depicts the financial position of the enterprise, or its financial status, consisting of the monetary amounts assigned to its assets, liabilities, and owners' equity, as of a point in time.

Because owners's equity is measured as a residual amount, the financial position or balance sheet is always in equality. This relationship is expressed as the accounting equation.

The Accounting Equation. Since the measurement of owners' equity derives from the amounts assigned to assets and liabilities, the following equality must always hold:

$$\text{ASSETS} = \text{LIABILITIES} + \text{OWNERS' EQUITY}$$

This equation reflects the fact that the firm's liabilities and owners' equity are the entity's sources of money to pay for the firm's assets. Thus the money obtained (liabilities and owners' equity) equals the cash on hand and spent for noncash assets. The remainder of this chapter illustrates how the balance sheet equation is used to record the financial events and transactions of the entity.

RECOGNIZING EVENTS

This section describes the recording of economic events or transactions and how they affect the financial status of the firm. The illustrations demonstrate how the accounting equation maintains its equality. We will distinguish between external transactions arising from outside events and internal adjustments necessitated by the accrual basis. The illustrations are based on the Fancy Flavors, Inc., problem introduced in Example 3–1.

External Transactions

Many events that affect the financial status of the enterprise are exchange transactions between the enterprise and other economic entities. These events are referred to as external transactions. Their effect on Fancy Flavors, Inc., is illustrated using specific events. To do so, we will expand the three major elements of the balance sheet to more specific components. For example, assets will be comprised of cash, equipment, and prepaid rent; liabilities will include accounts payable and accrued liabilities, and bank loan payable; and owners' equity will include paid-in capital and retained earnings.

Original Investment. The first event in Fancy Flavors' history was the investment of cash of $750,000. The owners invested $150,000 and a bank loan in the amount of $600,000 was secured. The effect of these events on Fancy Flavors' financial position can be represented as follows:

ASSETS = LIABILITIES + OWNERS' EQUITY
CASH = BANK LOAN PAYABLE + PAID-IN CAPITAL
$750,000 = $600,000 + $150,000

The investment has put $750,000 in cash under the control of the business. The owners' direct investment plus the bank loan represent the sources of the cash. Note that we can use either the three major elements of the balance sheet directly, or the specific accounts making up the elements, to record the transaction.

Acquiring an Asset. The next event was the purchase of equipment for $600,000 cash. This event reduces the cash account, but increases the equipment account by an equal amount. The effects of this transaction are shown in Exhibit 4–1. The event line indicates that the purchase results in a decrease in cash of $600,000 (denoted by the parentheses around the $600,000 in the Cash column) and an increase in another asset, equipment, by the same amount. Notice that the equipment is recorded at its cost, or the $600,000 cash sacrificed. When the elements of the event line are added to the prior total of their respective accounts, the result is a new financial position.

Note that the prior position satisfies the equality condition of the accounting equation—the total of the assets equals the total liabilities plus total owners' equity.

EXHIBIT 4–1

	Assets		=	Liabilities	+	Owners' Equity
	Cash	+ Equipment	= Bank Loan Payable	+ Paid-in Capital
Prior Position	$750,000 +	0 =	$600,000	+	$150,000
Event: Purchase of equipment	(600,000)	600,000			
New Position	$150,000 +	$600,000 =	$600,000	+	$150,000

The event line also satisfies the equality condition—it represents offsetting plus and minus changes to the asset side of the equation. Thus the new position line also satisfies the equality condition. The total assets (cash of $150,000 plus equipment of $600,000) equals the sum of the liabilities ($600,000) and owners' equity ($150,000).

Prepaying for a Service or Benefit. In the first month of operations, Fancy Flavors paid for three months' rent totaling $60,000. Prepaid rent is an asset because upon prepayment, the enterprise has a right to occupy buildings that can be used to produce goods and services and therefore contribute to future net income. In prepaying rent, the enterprise gives up one asset, cash, and receives another asset, the right to occupancy. As seen in Exhibit 4–2, the effect on the financial position is similar to the effect of the purchase of equipment.

Recognizing All of the Events of an Accounting Period—A Financial Position Worksheet. Rather than determining a new financial position after each event, we can consider the effects of all events of the first month's operations on one worksheet. A worksheet is a schedule with a column for each of the specific elements (accounts), which constitutes the entity's financial position. In Chapter Seven we will see that the worksheet is the basis of many computerized accounting systems. A new financial position is computed as of the end of the month, taking into account all the events of the month at once. Notice, however, that after recording each separate event, the equality of the financial position must be maintained, even if it is not separately calculated. Exhibit 4–3 represents the worksheet for the month of August. Each event line in the exhibit is numbered and discussed in the following section, with the exception of numbers 1 and 2, which were previously described. There are a few more headings in Exhibit 4–3 because as we consider more types of events, we need more accounts. Note that three zeros (000s) are omitted from all amounts appearing in Exhibit 4–3, such that each individual number is expressed in thousands of dollars.

Purchase of Supplies for Cash (Line 3). Fancy Flavors purchased supplies for $20,000 cash. Cash is decreased by $20,000 as indicated by the (20) in the Cash column of line 3. Supplies are recorded at their cost of $20,000 as indicated by the 20 in the Supplies column of line 3. Note the effect on total assets is zero; one type of asset has replaced another of equal amount. This event provides an inventory of supplies on hand which Fancy Flavors can use in operating its business as the need for supplies arises.

EXHIBIT 4–2

	Assets			=	Liabilities	+	Owners' Equity
	Cash	+ Equipment +	Prepaid Rent	=	Bank Loan Payable	+	Paid-in Capital
Prior Position	$750,000 +	0 +	0	=	$600,000	+	$150,000
Event 1: Purchase of equipment	(600,000)	600,000					
Event 2: Prepayment of rent	(60,000)		60,000				
New Position	$ 90,000 +	$600,000 +	$60,000	=	$600,000	+	$150,000

EXHIBIT 4–3

Fancy Flavors, Inc.

Financial Position Worksheet
(amounts in thousands)

Event	Cash	+ Accounts Receivable	+ Prepaid Rent	+ Ice Cream Inventory	+ Supplies	+ Equipment	+ Accumulated Depreciation	=	Accounts Payable and Accrued Liabilities	+ Bank Loan Payable	+ Paid-in Capital	+ Retained Earnings
Prior Position	$750									$600	$150	
1. Purchase of equipment	(600)					$600						
2. Prepayment of rent	(60)		$60									
3. Purchase of supplies	(20)				$20							
4. Purchase of ice cream				$30					$30			
5. Additional ice cream purchases				135					135			
6. Payments for ice cream purchased	(130)								(130)			
7. Additional supplies purchased					10				10			
8. Sales	400	$50										$450
9. Miscellaneous expanses paid	(10)											(10)
10. Payment of salaries and wages	(120)											(120)
11. Cost of ice cream sold				(145)								(145)
12. Cost of supplies used					(15)							(15)
13. Recognition of expired rent			(20)									(20)

EXHIBIT 4–3 (cont.)

Fancy Flavors, Inc.

Financial Position Worksheet
(amounts in thousands)

Event	Cash	Accounts Receivable	Prepaid Rent	Ice Cream Inventory	Supplies	Equipment	Accumulated Depreciation	=	Accounts Payable and Accrued Liabilities	Bank Loan Payable	Paid-in Capital	Retained Earnings
14. Recognition of equipment depreciation							$(10)	=				(10)
15. Recognition of salaries and wages								=	30			(30)
16. Recognition of interest on loan								=	6			(6)
17. Recognition of federal income tax obligation								=	24			(24)
18. Tornado loss				(5)				=				(5)
19. Dividends	(10)							=				(10)
New Position	$200 +	$50 +	$40 +	$15 +		$600 +	$(10)	=	$105 +	$600 +	$150 +	$55

Purchase of Merchandise on Account (Line 4). Fancy Flavors purchased $30,000 worth of ice cream, postponing payment until delivery of the second order of ice cream. A liability was incurred by exchanging a promise to pay its supplier, an accounts payable, for an asset, ice cream. This asset is an inventory of ice cream which ensures Fancy Flavors will have ice cream available to meet customer demands. Merchandise of this nature is often categorized as inventory. To record this transaction, line 4 contains a 30 in the Ice Cream column and a 30 in the Accounts Payable and Accrued Liabilities column, recognizing an increase in both assets and liabilities.

Additional Merchandise Purchases (Line 5). The original statement of the facts in Example 3–1 indicated that the total ice cream purchases for August amounted to $165,000, including the first purchase of $30,000 recognized on line 4. This means that an additional $135,000 was purchased. Thus line 5 shows a further increase in the stock of ice cream of 135 and an additional increase in the obligation to pay the ice cream supplier.

Payments for Merchandise Purchases (Line 6). Example 3–1 indicated that of all the ice cream deliveries received in August, only the last, in the amount of $35,000, had not been paid for by the end of the month. Hence $130,000 of the total $165,000 ice cream deliveries was paid for during the month. Line 6 represents the effect by reducing cash by 130 and reducing accounts payable and accrued liabilities by 130. Notice that no change is recognized in the inventory of ice cream since the supplier is being paid for ice cream that previously has been delivered and recorded.

Additional Supplies Purchased (Line 7). Before the end of the month an additional $10,000 supplies was purchased on account, with a promise to pay the supplier later. Hence line 7 shows an increase in the Supplies column of 10 and a matching increase in the liability, accounts payable.

Income Measurement within the Financial Position Framework

We now consider the relationship between the revenue of an enterprise and the changes in financial position that result from revenue recognition. When an enterprise provides products and services to customers in a period, the entity receives new assets in the form of cash or promises to pay from customers. Since no new obligation (liability) arises, the increase in assets is matched by an equal increase in owners' equity. Owners' equity is defined in such a way that this is always true (Owners' Equity = Assets − Liabilities.) But it is also theoretically correct. Revenue is the measure of accomplishment of the enterprise, and accomplishments should improve the owners' interest in the enterprise. Thus revenue is recognized as an increase in owners' equity in the same period that we recognize increases in cash and promises to pay from sales to customers. Recall that within owners' equity we distinguish between paid-in capital (the amount the owners invested) and retained earnings (the cumulative income of the firm after payment of dividends). Accordingly, revenue is recorded in retained earnings.

Revenue Recognition (Line 8). Fancy Flavors' sales of ice cream cones for cash during its first month of operations were $400,000. Sales of banquet desserts on credit totaled $50,000, none of which has been collected as of the end of the month. Thus there has been an increase in cash of $400,000 and an increase in accounts receivable of $50,000. Line 8 indicates an increase in cash of 400, an increase in accounts receivable of 50, and a total increase in the retained earnings component of owners' equity of 450.

The matching principle requires that we record the resource sacrifices made to earn revenue in the same time period in which the revenue is recognized. To recognize expenses we must record decreases in the assets used to produce the products and provide them to customers. These assets were sacrificed to produce products, not to decrease the liabilities of the enterprise. Thus there is no decrease in liabilities, but rather a decrease in the retained earnings component of owners' equity. Just as retained earnings is increased to record the firm's accomplishments through revenues, it must be decreased by the expenditures made to earn those accomplishments. This is because expenses represent the effort or sacrifice made by the entity which decreases the owners' interest in the enterprise.

Miscellaneous Expense (*Line 9*). Miscellaneous expenditures (heat, light, power, etc.) totaling $10,000 were paid in cash during August by Fancy Flavors. Since this example does not associate such expenditures with sales of future periods, we consider the whole $10,000 an expense of the current period. On line 9 we recognize a decrease in cash and in retained earnings of 10.

Salaries and Wages (*Line 10*). The $120,000 wages and salaries actually paid to employees during August constitute resource sacrifices made during the month to provide ice cream products to customers. These salaries and wages must be matched against August revenue as expense. On line 10 we recognize a decrease in cash for wages paid of 120 and a decrease to retained earnings for the same amounts.

Internal Adjustments

The events recorded to this point arise from Fancy Flavors' transactions with persons and entities existing separate from the enterprise. Internal adjustments (typically made at the end of an accounting period) are changes in the enterprise's financial position that are evidenced by observation of events within the entity. Many of these internal observations have to do with a physical sacrifice of resources for the revenue recognized. Revenue is usually recognized in connection with an external transaction of the current period; that is, a sale of product to a customer. But an expense is not always evidenced by an external transaction of the current period, such as the wages, salaries, and miscellaneous expenses in our example. In many cases, expense recognition is a matter of determining how much of asset's original cost should be recognized as an expense in a period subsequent to when the asset was acquired in an external transaction. This process is illustrated using Fancy Flavors.

Merchandise Sold (*Line 11*). Of the total purchases during August, ice cream with a cost of $20,000 was still in the freezers at the end of the month (before the tornado). Since $165,000 was purchased in total, this means that $145,000 was conveyed to customers in return for their cash and promises to pay. The internal observation that $20,000 of ice cream remains on hand tells us that a total sacrifice of ice cream originally costing $145,000 was made to generate the month's sales revenue of $450,000. On line 11 the 145 is recognized as a reduction in the stock of ice cream with a corresponding reduction in retained earnings representing the expense of ice cream sold.

Supplies Used (Line 12). Similar reasoning applies to the recognition of the cost of supplies used. A total of $30,000 of supplies was purchased during August. The internal observation is that supplies costing $15,000 was used up during August. Their cost should be matched against August revenues as an expense. On line 12 there is a decrease in supplies of 15 and a corresponding decrease in retained earnings of 15.

Expired Rent (Line 13). On line 2 we recognized the payment of three months' rent in advance. As of the end of the month, one-third of the total occupancy rights have been used. On line 13 we recognize a one-third reduction in the asset equal to 20, along with a concurrent 20 reduction in retained earnings for rent expense.

Depreciation of Equipment (Line 14). The cost of the equipment purchased at the beginning of August was recorded as an asset which is expected to serve the business for five years, or sixty months. Some of the original cost of such long-lived assets must be recognized as an expense in each period of the asset's useful life—ideally, in proportion to the decline in its service potential that is actually consumed in each period. However, it is usually difficult to accurately measure the amount of the service potential which expires. The usual practice is to estimate how long the asset will last and then choose a systematic pattern of apportioning its original cost to each of the periods in its expected life. The simplest of these patterns is called the straight-line method of depreciation, in which an equal share of the original cost is associated with each period of the life of the asset.

Using the straight-line method, we apportion $10,000 of the cost of the equipment to the first month of operations. (Based on an estimated life of five years, or sixty months, and a cost of $600,000, the per-month allocation is $600,000 ÷ 60 = $10,000.) Line 14 shows a reduction of retained earnings of 10 in the month of August and a corresponding entry in the Accumulated Depreciation column. Accumulated depreciation is a separate account (called a contra-asset account) that offsets the equipment account. It is created to recognize the reduction in the future economic benefits of the asset and it always has a negative balance that acts to reduce the equipment account's balance. To record the depreciation expense, we increase the magnitude of the negative accumulated depreciation account by $10,000, which is tantamount to decreasing the equipment account itself. In this manner the recorded amount in the equipment account remains at its original cost. The accumulated depreciation account is used to reduce the asset's original cost to an amount representing the cost apportioned to the remainder of the asset's useful life.

Recognition of Salaries and Wages (Line 15). In addition to the $120,000 in cash paid to employees for salaries and wages, another $30,000 was earned by employees but not yet paid by August 31. These additional employee services must be recognized as an expense in August since they enabled Fancy Flavors to earn that month's revenue. Because the salaries and wages are unpaid, they represent a liability by Fancy Flavors to its employees. Accordingly, line 15 records a 30 increase to accounts payables and liabilities and a 30 decrease to retained earnings.

Recognition of Interest Expense (Line 16). The recognition of one month's interest expense on the bank loan is an additional adjustment related to August's operations. While the loan benefits (i.e., the availability of the cash) were utilized during August, interest on the loan of $6,000 is not actually due until a later point in time. Thus line 16 shows 6 as an increase in accounts payable and accrued liabilities, as well as a decrease in retained earnings.

Recognition of Federal Income Tax Expense (Line 17). A future tax obligation relating to operations during the month of August is recognized on line 17. Since this represents an expense of the current period which has not been paid for in cash, it is shown as an increase of $24,000 in accounts payable and accrued liabilities and a decrease of $24,000 in retained earnings.

Tornado Loss (Line 18). As a result of a failure of its freezers from a power outage caused by a tornado, Fancy Flavors lost $5,000 of its ice cream inventory. This is an extraordinary loss which was not covered by insurance. It is reflected on line 18 by a 5 reduction in the inventory of ice cream and a corresponding decrease to retained earnings. Since extraordinary gains and losses are included in the firm's net income, they are correspondingly reflected in retained earnings.

Dividends (Line 19). Because operations were profitable during the month of August, Fancy Flavors decided to pay its owners $10,000 of dividends. Line 19 shows this as a decrease in cash of 10 and a reduction of retained earnings by 10. This treatment is consistent with recognizing that dividends are a distribution of cumulative earnings, and thus come from the firm's retained earnings account. And since dividends represent a withdrawal of resources by the owners, they decrease the total owners' equity.

Balance Sheet

Exhibit 4–3 shows how the various elements of financial position are affected by each external transaction and internal adjustment. The new balance for each account is found by adding to the original balance all increases and subtracting all decreases indicated in the column of that account.

Example 4–3 | To illustrate, consider the cash account. Upon establishment of the business, the enterprise had a stock of $750,000 cash. During the month it experienced an inflow of cash from sales of $400,000. In addition, there were outflows of cash during the month represented by the numbers in parentheses in the Cash column. When subtracted, the balance of cash at the end of the month is $200,000, as shown at the bottom of the Cash column.

Applying the same procedure to other columns gives the end-of-month balances in all the other accounts.

The $15,000 inventory of ice cream, like the remaining stocks of all other assets, represents the original cost of resources that have not yet been consumed in the production of revenues. They will be recognized as expense and matched against revenue of future periods when the products they help to create are sold to customers. The ending financial position of one period is the beginning financial

EXHIBIT 4–4

Fancy Flavors, Inc.

Statement of Financial Position
As of August 31, 1991

Assets:		
Cash		$200,000
Accounts receivable		50,000
Prepaid rent		40,000
Ice cream		15,000
Supplies		15,000
Equipment	$600,000	
Less accumulated depreciation	(10,000)	590,000
Total assets		$910,000
Liabilities and Owners' Equity:		
Accounts payable and accrued liabilities		$105,000
Bank loan payable		600,000
Owners' equity		
Paid-in capital	$150,000	
Retained earnings	55,000	205,000
Total liabilities and owners' equity		$910,000

position of the next period. It carries forward information about resources available for future performance. Since financial position is a way of characterizing the resources and obligations that are in the possession of the enterprise at a point in time, it conveys information to external investors about the ongoing ability of the enterprise to generate cash.

The balance sheet (or statement of financial position) is an organized array of the names of the components of the financial position and the amounts by which they have been measured. The balance sheet is captioned to identify the enterprise, the nature of the statement, and the point in time for which the financial position is being determined. Exhibit 4–4 illustrates the balance sheet of Fancy Flavors as of the end of August. Notice that the two sides of the financial position equation are presented separately—all assets first, followed by all liabilities and owners' equity. Notice too that their totals are equal (they balance each other). To construct a balance sheet at the end of any period, it is necessary to transfer the new balance of each account in the worksheet in Exhibit 4–3 to its place on the face of the balance sheet in Exhibit 4–4.

Income Statement

The income statement also can be prepared from the financial position worksheet in Exhibit 4–3. The income statement for Fancy Flavors' August operations has already been illustrated in Exhibit 3–5 and is reproduced in Exhibit 4–5. The income statement is a presentation of recognized revenue and expenses for a period, along with the residual, net income (loss). The income statement is captioned to identify the enterprise, the nature of the statement, and the period in the life of the enterprise covered by the statement. Given a financial position worksheet, complete with respect to all events and adjustments affecting financial position for a period of time, we construct an income statement by listing the changes in retained earnings that are due to recognized revenues and expenses during the period. Referring back to Exhibit 4–3, it is seen that each of the numbers appearing in the Retained Earnings column (with the exception of dividends) appears on the income statement opposite a description of the event that it represents. The total expenses are then subtracted from total revenue to determine net income.

In combination, the recognized accomplishments (revenues) and related expenses increase owners' equity by the amount of net income. In other words, net income is the recognized net increase in the ownership interests of the enterprise that results from its productive activities and any extraordinary gains or losses. Thus net income is that portion of the total increase or decrease in owners' equity that is due to the recognized productive performance of the enterprise during the period. Note that the increase in owners' equity during the period due to net income is matched by an increase in the excess of assets over liabilities. The income statement is a descriptive statement of how and to what extent the recognized accomplishments (revenues) and efforts (expenses) of the enterprise altered the ownership interest in the business during a period of time. Along with additional owners' investments or withdrawals of assets during the period, the income statement explains the change between two levels of owners' equity—that at the beginning of the period and that at the end of the period.

In the Fancy Flavors example, the $65,000 net income and $10,000 withdrawal for dividends completely explains how the ownership interest in the enterprise went from an initial level of $150,000 to $205,000 at the end of August. Thus the income statement bears a well-defined relationship to the beginning and ending balance sheets of the period that it covers. Note that while net income for a period may be large, the firm may not be able to distribute cash dividends

EXHIBIT 4–5

Fancy Flavors, Inc.

Income Statement For the Month of August 1991		
Revenue from sales of ice cream		$450,000
Less expenses:		
Equipment depreciation	$ 10,000	
Rent	20,000	
Supplies used	15,000	
Salaries and wages	150,000	
Cost of ice cream sold	145,000	
Interest on loan	6,000	
Federal income taxes	24,000	
Miscellaneous (heat, light, etc.)	10,000	
Total expenses		380,000
Income from continuing operations		$ 70,000
Less tornado loss		5,000
Net income		$ 65,000

to owners equal to net income. Net income measures the increase in assets of all kinds in excess of liabilities. Net income may be substantial, but the net assets of the firm may not be in readily distributable form (i.e., cash). Instead, the assets may be in the form of large amounts of receivables from customers, inventory buildup, substantial investments in buildings and equipment, and the like.

SUMMARY

This chapter covered the fundamental concepts underlying the balance sheet. The basic elements comprising the balance sheet were defined: assets, liabilities, and owners' equity (paid-in capital and retained earnings). These components are measured at their original cost: the amount sacrificed to acquire the asset and the amount received from incurring a liability and selling stock. When arranged in a balance sheet, these elements demonstrate the accounting equation in which assets equal liabilities plus owners' equity.

With the use of an example, the effects of external transactions on a firm's financial position were demonstrated. These transactions arise from events with parties outside the firm. Each transaction has a balancing effect on the financial position so that the accounting equation remains intact. Typical external transactions include investments by owners and creditors; purchase of equipment, supplies, merchandise, and other assets; payment of liabilities; sales to customers; collections from customers; and payment for expenses related to the sales.

Internal adjustments were described as transactions recorded as a result of observing events within the firm. The examples illustrated involved recording the portion of assets acquired in previous periods which were used in the current period. This included the merchandise that was sold, supplies used, rent expired, and depreciation on equipment employed during the period. Internal adjustments also involve recording expenses not yet paid, such as salaries and wages, interest expense on amounts owned, and unpaid federal income taxes.

Both the external transactions and internal adjustments were recorded in corresponding categories of assets, liabilities, and owners' equity on the financial position worksheet. Itemizing the revenues and expense in the retained earnings account gave us the income statement. Totaling the columns for each account gave us the ending amount and the balance sheet.

Questions for Review and Discussion

4–1. Define

   a. Assets
   b. Liabilities
   c. Owners' equity
   d. Paid-in capital
   e. Retained earnings
   f. Cost principle
   g. Balance sheet
   h. The accounting equation

4–2. Owners' equity is not measured directly. True or false? Explain your answer.

4–3. Because of the way that owners' equity is measured, the sum of the amounts assigned to the assets of the enterprise is equal to the sum of the amounts assigned to the liabilities plus owners' equity. Show that this is true.

4–4. Explain why owners' equity is divided into paid-in capital and retained earnings.

4–5. Explain the distinction between an external event and an internal adjustment. What is the significance of the distinction in the accounting cycle?

4–6. Strictly speaking, the usefulness of the financial position framework is that is provides a worksheet for processing transactions and calculating income. True or false? Explain your answer.

4–7. Explain why revenue is recognized as an increase in owners' equity.

4–8. Explain why expense is recognized as decreases in owners' equity.

4–9. Income from continuing operations explains the difference between the beginning and ending owners' equity of the business for a given period. True or false? Defend your position.

4–10. Suppose a company distributed cash dividends to owners equal to only one-half of its net income for a period. What are the implications of such a dividend policy for investors interested in the business? How would you describe the effect of such a policy on the business to someone who knows nothing about accounting (i.e., nothing about net income)?

4–11. The owner-manager of Small Business Limited is very pleased with the recent growth of his business and its prospects for future growth. Net income, he notes, is up 20 percent over last year. He therefore decides to withdraw 20 percent more than he did last year but is informed by his accountant that insufficient cash is available. "What is income for," he rages, "if not to tell you how much you can spend?" As his accountant, what would your answer be?

4–12. In the ordinary course of events, the revenue for a period is recognized in connection with external events, whereas expenses are often recognized only as the result of internal adjustments. Do you agree or disagree? Explain your position.

4–13. When an asset is acquired it is measured at its original cost—the amount of cash or other assets and liabilities given in exchange for it. Does this amount represent the worth of the asset to the firm? Defend your answer.

4–14. Suppose that at the end of the business year a business immediately sold all of its assets to various buyers and paid off all of its liabilities. Would the resulting cash available for the owners be equal to the year-end owners' equity figure? Explain your position.

4–15. One of the things that distinguishes accrual accounting from strictly cash basis accounting is the recognition of internal adjustments. Do you agree or disagree? Explain your position.

Problems

4–1. **Inventory Stocks and Flows.** Arnhem Distributors began 1991 with 5,000 units in inventory costing $2,500. It purchased 12,000 more units at $.75 per unit. By the end of the year, 3,000 of the units purchased during the year were left.

Required:
1. What was the cost of the units sold?
2. What would have been the cost of the units sold if the company had begun the year with 5,000 units costing $.80 per unit? (The rest of the facts remain the same.)

4–2. **Account Analysis.** The following events are observed during 1991:
1. Total purchases of supplies at a cost of $450.
2. Supplies costing $80 (purchased in 1990) are returned.
3. Accounts payable of $300 is paid (the $300 accounts payable arose from purchases of supplies on credit during 1990).

4. Supplies expense for 1991 is $270.

5. At the end of 1991, $400 of supplies are on hand.

Required:

Determine the cost of supplies on hand at the beginning of 1991.

4–3. Determining Net Income. On July 31, 1991 Janice, who owns Pike Street Antiques, drew up a statement of financial position for her business.

Assets:			*Liabilities and Owners' Equity:*	
Cash		$ 4,000	Accounts payable	$ 3,500
Merchandise		8,000	Wages payable	200
Accounts receivable		1,500	Loan from finance	
Prepaid rent		300	company	2,500
Fixtures and fittings	$3,000		Total liabilities	$ 6,200
Less accumulated			Owners' equity	9,600
depreciation	(1,000)	2,000	Total liabilities and	
Total assets		$15,800	owners' equity	$15,800

Given:

1. Sales for August were $6,500.

2. During August, a total of $700 was paid out for wages. Janice's shop assistants had not been paid for the last two days of August, which meant that $70 was owing to them.

3. The statement of financial position at the end of August showed that total accumulated depreciation of fixtures and fittings was $1,075.

4. By the end of August, only one week's rent ($150) was still prepaid. Janice had paid an additional $450 to her landlord during the month.

5. An additional $2,000 worth of merchandise was purchased during the period. $6,500 was still on hand at the end of the period.

6. Interest on the loan amounted to $40 for August. Janice paid the $40 on August 31.

Required:

Produce an income statement for Janice's business for the month of August 1991.

4–4. Transaction Analysis. The 6–10 retail store reports the following financial position statements for last year:

	(Amounts in Thousands)	
	January 1	December 31
Cash	$ 10	$ 12
Accounts receivable	20	25
Merchandise	30	32
Plant and equipment	60	66
Accumulated depreciation	(10)	(14)
Total assets	$110	$121
Accounts payable to suppliers	$ 15	$ 22
Owners' equity	95	99
Total liabilities and owners' equity	$110	$121

Transactions during the year were

1. Cash collections from customers, $145,000.

2. Cash payments to suppliers, $95,000.

3. Purchases of equipment (in cash), $6,000.
4. Cash dividends to owners, $5,000.

Required:
Compute the following:

1. Sales revenue for the year.
2. Purchases of merchandise during the year.
3. Cost of merchandise sold during the year (using purchases calculated above).
4. Depreciation expense for the year.
5. Income from continuing operations for the year.

4–5. Accounting Arithmetic. On December 31, 1991, the Machinery account represents two machines. One was purchased on January 1, 1988 for $20,000 and the other was purchased for $10,000. The depreciation expense on these machines (both have the same estimated life) in 1991 was $3,000, computed on the straight-line basis. Total accumulated depreciation for both machines at December 31, 1991, was $15,000.

Required:
On what date was the $10,000 machine purchased?

4–6. Product versus Period Expenses. Langley Developers began operations on January 1, 1991, with $600,000 in cash, contributed by a number of wealthy financiers. Two projects were commenced immediately—the Lakeside scheme and the Peninsula project. During the first three months of 1991, the following events occurred:

January	Land at Lakeside was purchased for $100,000. Land on the Peninsula was purchased for $200,000.
February	Land surveys necessary for eventual subdivision and sale of the properties were conducted at a cost of $10,000 ($4,000 for Lakeside; $6,000 for Peninsula).

March	Contractors cleared the land at both projects at a cost of $55,000:
	    $30,000 for Lakeside and
	    $25,000 for Peninsula.
	Roads and drainage were established at Lakeside at a cost of $15,000.
	On March 30 the Lakeside project was sold for $230,000.

During the three months a total of $18,000 was paid in wages and salaries for head office staff. Other general and administration expenses amounted to $30,000. All transactions in the period were cash transactions. During the period April 1 to June 30, general and administration expenses were $29,000; head office salaries and wages were $16,000. Roads and drainage were established at the Peninsula project at a cost of $48,000. A new project (the Condo plan) was commenced during June, with the purchase of a tract of land at a cost of $70,000. A land survey was conducted at a cost of $10,000. On June 28 the Peninsula project was sold for $350,000.

Required:

1. Produce an income statement for Langley Developers for the three months ending March 31, 1991. List the total assets of the corporation as of March 31.
2. Perform the same functions for the period April 1 to June 30.

4–7. Applying the Accounting Cycle.

July 1	Smith and Kline deposited $1,000 each in a bank account under the name of the Campus Record Center. They paid $1,200 for three months' rental of a shop, and after arranging a $500 loan from the bank, spent $700 on equipment such as record racks and a cash register. The partners expect this equipment to last five years and have proceeds of $100 on disposal.
July 2	Hired Sally Sullivan as salesperson at $400 a month.
July 3	Purchased records on credit at a cost of $1,500.
	Purchased general supplies for cash at a cost of $100. Were billed by the university newspaper $60 for advertisements.
July 4–12	Cash sales of records $950; paid advertising bill.
July 11	Paid $20 for insurance to the end of the month. Purchased 200 records at a cost of $2 per record (credit transaction).
July 12	Paid $500 to record suppliers.
July 12–31	Paid Sally her monthly wage.
	Recorded sales (cash) $1,000.
	Repaid the bank, including interest, with a payment of $510.
	Paid $60 for insurance to October 31.
	Paid $50 to a local artist for a personal appearance at the store.
	Paid $250 to record suppliers.
	Counted record stock and found stock costing $1,300 still on hand.
	Counted general supplies and found supplies costing $80 still on hand.

Required:
Produce a worksheet and an income statement for the Record Center for the month of July 1991. Draw up a statement of financial position as of July 31, 1991.

4–8. Applying the Accounting Cycle. The Cruiseline professional football team started operations in September 1990. The following activities took place during the first three months (first quarter) of the next year:

1. Collected $50,000 from season ticket holders.
2. Occupied office space with annual rental fees of $10,000, which was paid in advance on January 1, 1991 when the lease started.
3. On January 1 Cruiseline borrowed $20,000 from a local bank and agreed to pay 8 percent interest.
4. Paid salaries of $40,000 on March 31 for the first quarter. Players have earned an additional $10,000, but that will be paid on April 15.
5. Owners withdrew $5,000 for personal uses.
6. On March 31 the team bought a practice field for $20,000 cash.
7. On January 1 the team bought $6,000 worth of office supplies on credit.
8. A count of supplies at March 31 revealed that $2,000 worth of supplies were still on hand.

Required:
Prepare a worksheet to record the foregoing events. Make sure all internal adjustments are recorded at March 31. Since January 1 balances are not given, do not attempt to calculate balances at March 31.

4–9. Applying the Accounting Cycle. Five years ago, several individuals got together and started a business called Copy Fast Corporation. The business consists of several part-time employees and some high-speed dry-copying equipment. Small (several-page) copying jobs are done for cash for people who walk in off the street. Large jobs are done for regular customers on a competitive-bid basis. The balance sheet of the business as of the end of its third year is as follows:

Copy Fast Corporation

Statement of Financial Position
As of the End of Year Three

Assets:			Liabilities and Owners' Equity:		
Cash		$ 4,000	Accounts payable		$ 2,500
Accounts receivable		3,000			
Supplies and paper		6,000	Owners' equity		
Equipment	$15,000		Paid-in capital	$10,000	
Less accumulated			Retained earnings	8,000	18,000
depreciation	(7,500)	7,500	Total liabilities and		
Total assets		$20,500	owners' equity		$20,500

During year four the following events are recognized:

1. Cash sales of $9,000 and credit sales of $20,000 were made.
2. Paper and supplies worth $10,000 were purchased on account.
3. Rent of $2,400 for the year was paid in cash.
4. The equipment is estimated to last five years and bring $2,500 upon resale at the end of that time.
5. Wages of $9,000 in total were paid, all in cash.
6. At year-end $7,000 worth of supplies and paper were still on hand, and $2,000 of the total accounts receivable from customers had not been paid.
7. The business paid all but $4,000 of its total accounts payable by year-end.
8. The owners withdraw cash equal to net income at year-end.

Required:
Record the effects on financial position of these events in worksheet form. Prepare an ending balance sheet and an income statement for year four as well.

4–10. Applying the Accounting Cycle.

January 1–5	Kathy Wright places $18,000 in a bank account entitled Seaside Enterprises.
	Three months' rent (amounting to $1,200) was paid by Kathy for a wharfside building to be used for a restaurant. Kathy bought cooking equipment at a cost of $5,000. She paid $3,000 and was granted thirty days' credit for the balance. The equipment will have a life of four years and is expected to bring a price of $1,000 on its disposal.
	Kathy purchased supplies costing $2,000 on credit. She hired cooks, waitresses, and a resident band. The total payroll of $2,000 will be paid every two weeks. Kathy purchased furniture costing $6,000 for cash. The furniture will last ten years and have $1,200 salvage value.
January 6	The Seaside Restaurant opened.
January 6–31	Wages were paid totaling $4,000 ($700 was owed by Kathy at the end of the month). An additional $2,000 was paid for guest performers, and $6,000 worth of supplies of food and drink were purchased on credit. Suppliers were paid $7,000 (including the $2,000 owed for cooking equipment). Kathy withdrew $500

in cash for her own personal use. Supplies costing $2,200 were still on hand at the end of the period. Revenue from meals for the month amounted to $15,500 (all paid in cash).

Required:

Produce a worksheet and an income statement for January, and a statement of financial position as of January 31, 1991.

4–11. Identifying Changes in Owners' Equity and Income Measures. For each of the following events, indicate its individual effect on (*a*) owners' equity; (*b*) net income for the period; and (*c*) income from continuing operations for the period.

1. The company pays off a bank loan.
2. Wages for the period are paid by the company.
3. One of the owners contributes cash to the company.
4. The company makes cash sales.
5. One of the owners uses company supplies for personal purposes.
6. The company buys a small percentage of the outstanding stock of X Corporation.
7. The company receives cash dividends on shares owned of X Corporation.
8. Depreciation of equipment is recorded.
9. Rent expense for the period is recorded.
10. Owner contributes a motor vehicle to the corporation in exchange for additional shares.
11. Advertising expense for the period is recorded—it is not yet paid.
12. The company pays cash dividends.
13. Three years' insurance is paid in advance.
14. Sales on credit are made.
15. Supplies are used by the company.
16. A motor vehicle owned by the company is sold for more than its unexpired cost.
17. A ship owned by the company is confiscated in a foreign port during a revolution.

4–12. Identifying Changes in Owners' Equity and Income Measures. Owners' equity is affected by each of the following transactions. Construct a table showing the ultimate effect of each transaction on retained earnings, paid-in capital, net income, and income from continuing operations.

(Note: (*1*) *Many of the items will have an effect upon more than one of the measures;* (*2*) *the kind of business under consideration may be different from item to item, as indicated; and* (*3*) *it is assumed that the balances in paid-in capital and retained earnings are sufficient to absorb any appropriate decreases.*)

Example:	Paid-in Capital	Retained Earnings	Net Income	Income from Continuing Operations
Wages expense of $300	None	(300)	(300)	(300)

1. Sales revenue of $600.
2. Gain of $100 from sales of machinery (not purchased for resale).
3. Owners were paid dividends of $1,000.
4. Sales returns by customers of $80.
5. Additional new owners contributed $5,000 to business.
6. Uninsured loss from destruction of merchandise by arson ($200).

7. Depreciation expense of $1,000.
8. Newspaper company is forced to pay $5,000 damages in libel suit (not covered by insurance).
9. Partner signs over the title of his or her car (market value $3,000) to the business in exchange for a larger share in ownership.
10. Investors' club earns $500 in cash dividends.
11. Land speculation company earns $400 profit on sale of land.
12. Manufacturing company earns $1,000 profit on the condemnation of land for a freeway.
13. Partner is paid a $600 salary as the actual manager of the business.
14. A machine that had not been fully depreciated was unexpectedly determined to be completely worn out. It originally cost $5,000; depreciation to date is $4,000.

4–13. Levels and Changes in Owner's Equity. Bob Menzies is the sole owner of a plumbing business, Menzies Plumbing Company. On December 31, 1990, the company's statement of financial position showed total assets of $15,000 and total liabilities $2,000. On December 31, 1991 owner's equity was $18,000.

Required:

1. What was the owner's equity on December 31, 1990?
2. If total assets were $23,000 on December 31, 1991, what were total liabilities at that date?
3. If there were no withdrawals from the business or contributions to the business by Bob, what was the net income for 1991?
4. If Bob had contributed $2,000 in cash to the business in 1991, what would net income for 1991 have been?
5. Ignoring number 4, what would the net income for 1991 have been if Bob had withdrawn cash of $4,000 during 1991?
6. What would net income have been if, during 1991, Bob had contributed the $2,000 and withdrawn the $4,000?
7. Given the information in number 6, what revenue must the company have earned during 1991 if total expenses were $3,000?

4–14. Relationship Between Accounting Equation and Income Statement. Partial statements of financial position for the Eckto Company show

	December 31, 1990	*December 31, 1991*
Total assets	$10,000,000	$12,000,000
Total liabilities	1,500,000	1,000,000

During the 1991 calendar year, the total revenue generated by normal business operations was $14 million. The sum of $900,000 was received from the sale of additional shares of stock, and dividends of $200,000 were paid.

Required:
Using the information supplied, prepare a summary conventional income statement for the Eckto Company for the year ended December 31, 1991.

4–15. Financial Statement Relationships. The statement of financial position for the Larson Electronics Corporation, which was based on the conventional accounting model, reflected the following information:

	December 31, 1990	December 31, 1991
Total assets	$5,200,000	$5,800,000
Total liabilities	1,200,000	1,000,000

During 1991 the total revenue generated by normal business operations was $10 million. In addition, the company sold to the City (after condemnation) a parcel of land it had owned for several years at a gain of $200,000. The corporation declared and paid cash dividends to its shareholders amounting to $500,000 in 1991.

1. What was the value of owners' equity on December 31, 1991?
2. What was Larson's net income for 1991?
3. What was Larson's income from continuing operations for 1991?
4. What was the amount of the expenses associated with normal business operations recognized by Larson Electronics Corporation during 1991?

4–16. Financial Statement Relationships. The statement of financial position for the GX Corporation, which was based on conventional accounting, reflected the following information:

	December 31, 1990	December 31, 1991
Total assets	$2,600,000	$2,900,000
Total liabilities	600,000	500,000

During 1991 the total revenue generated by normal business operations was $5 million. In addition, a parcel of land the corporation had owned for several years was condemned by a local government for use as a park. The proceeds of the condemnation sale were sufficient to result in an after-tax gain of $100,000. The corporation declared and paid cash dividends to its shareholders amounting to $250,000 in 1991. No additional shares of stock were sold during 1991.

Required:

1. What was the amount of GX Corporation's owners' equity on December 31, 1991?
2. What was GX's net income for 1991?
3. What was GX's income from continuing operations for 1991?
4. What was the amount of the expenses associated with normal business operations recognized by GX Corporation during 1991?

4–17. Financial Statement Relationships. Certain data from the 1991 comparative statement of financial position for the YDC Corporation follow. The corporation uses the conventional accounting model.

	December 31, 1990	December 31, 1991
Total assets	$8,300,000	$9,200,000
Total liabilities	2,500,000	4,100,000

During 1991 the total revenue generated by ordinary business operations was $15 million. In addition, the company sold a truck it had owned for a few years at a gain of $6,000 net of tax. A most unusual flood during 1991 resulted in enormous damage to a warehouse. A total loss of $2.5 million net of tax and insurance proceeds was incurred as a result. There was no new owners' capital contributed during 1991 and no cash dividends were paid that year because of the flood loss.

Required:

1. Amount of YDC's owners' equity on December 31, 1991
2. Net income of YDC Corporation for 1991
3. Income from continuing operations of YDC Corporation for 1991
4. Normal business expenses of YDC Corporation as recognized during 1991

4–18. Accounting Equation Analysis. The following information is taken from the financial records of the Talisman Corporation:

Totals as of:	*December 31, 1989*	*December 31, 1990*	*December 31, 1991*
Assets	$23,000	$50,000	$?
Liabilities	4,000	18,000	20,000
Owners' equity	?	?	?
During year:	*1989*	*1990*	*1991*
Net income	$10,000	$?	$16,000
Withdrawals by owners	?	8,000	6,000
New investments by owners	12,000	5,000	10,000

The first year of operations for Talisman Corporation was 1989.

Required:

1. Withdrawals during 1989.
2. Net income for 1990.
3. Total assets at December 31, 1991.

4–19. Statement of Retained Earnings. Following is the statement of retained earnings from the 1991 annual report of Millipore Corporation. The letters *a*, *b*, and *c* have been substituted for certain intentionally omitted numbers.

Retained Earnings	*Year Ended December 31, 1991*	*Year Ended December 31, 1990*
Balance at beginning of year	$ (a)	$30,678,000
Net income	9,585,000	8,865,000
Deduct cash dividends declared:		
1991 $.15 per share	1,247,000	—
1990 $.11 per share	—	(c)
Balance at end of year	$46,967,000	$ (b)

Required:
For letters *a*, *b*, and *c*, give the dollar amount that appeared in the Millipore Corporation statement.

4–20. Statement of Retained Earnings. Following is the statement of retained earnings from the 1991 annual report of Super Retail Corporation. Figures are intentionally omitted at spaces marked *a*, *b*, *c*, and *d*.

Retained Earnings	Year Ended December 31, 1991	Year Ended December 31, 1990
Balance at beginning of year	$ (d)	$58,243,000
Net Income	(a)	(c)
Deduct cash dividends declared:		
1991 $.23 per share	(b)	—
1990 $.30 per share	—	2,700,000
Balance at end of year	$66,322,500	$63,043,250

Required:
Determine the dollar amounts represented by *a* through *d* which appeared in the statement.

(Note: *The number of shares of stock outstanding was constant during the year 1991.*)

4–21. Recognition of Effects of Events on Financial Position.

Required:
Indicate the row number, the account (column), and the amount of all numbers missing in Exhibit 4–6 on page 84.

4–22. Recognition of Effects of Events on Financial Position. On the Jones Printing Service worksheet are entered the effects on financial position of all the external events and internal adjustments related to the startup and first month of operations of a small company.

Jones Printing Service

Financial Position Worksheet

	Cash	Supplies	Prepaid Rent	Accounts Receivable	Equipment	Accumulated Depreciation	Notes Payable	Paid-in Capital	Retained Earnings
1.	$8,000							$8,000	
2.	(4,000)				$10,000		$ 6,000		
3.	5,000						5,000		
4.	(3,000)	$3,000							
5.	(3,600)		$3,600						
6.	3,500			$2,000					$5,500
7.						$(100)			(100)
8.			(300)						(300)
9.		(2,600)							(2,600)
10.	$5,900	$ 400	$3,300	$2,000	$10,000	$(100)	$11,000	$8,000	$2,500

Required:
Give a description of an event or adjustment likely to have produced each numbered entry in the worksheet.

EXHIBIT 4–6

Mastermind Enterprises Worksheet

Description	Cash	Accounts Receivable	Mer-chandise	Prepaid Rent	Equipment	Accumulated Depreciation	Accounts Payable	Wages Payable	Interest Payable	Mortgage Payable	Paid-in Capital	Retained Earnings
1. Prior position	$1,500	$1,000	$2,500	$200	$6,000	$(1,500)	$1,750	$ 0	$100	$3,000		$2,850
2. Cash sales	1,300											
3. Purchased mer-chandise on credit							500					
4. Credit sales												2,000
5. Paid rent in ad-vance				100								
6. Receipts from cus-tomers		(2,500)										
7. Payments to sup-pliers	(1,000)											
8. Purchased equip-ment with cash	(1,000)											
9. Credit sales of $1,500												
10. Paid wages	(700)											
11. Paid advertising	(300)											
12. Paid interest owing	(100)											
13. Purchased mer-chandise with cash	(200)											
14. Depreciation												
15. Merchandise used			(900)									(800)
16. Rent expense for period												(150)
17. Accrued wages								200				
18. Interest expense for period (not paid)												(80)
19. Contribution by owner	2,000											
20. New Position	$											

4–23. Relationship of Financial Position and Statements of Change. The following statements for John Gorton Enterprises are presented at the bottom of this page and on page 86.

Additional information:

1. There were no contributions or withdrawals by the owners during January 1991.
2. No credit sales during January 1991.
3. All merchandise was bought on credit. During January, merchandise costing $1,600 was purchased.

Required:

Prepare a statement of financial position as of January 31, 1991.

(Hint: *The income statement and statement of cash flows are both change statements. They provide information about the month's increases to and the decreases from items in the December 31 statement of financial position given first. For example*)

Cash balance, December 31, 1990	$ 5,000	(from prior statement of financial position)
Additions	6,000	(from statement of cash flows)
	$11,000	
Subtractions	1,750	(from statement of cash flows)
Cash balance as of January 31, 1991	$ 9,250	

John Gorton Enterprises

Statement of Financial Position
As of December 31, 1990

Assets:		
Cash		$5,000
Prepaid rent		100
Merchandise		400
Equipment	$2,400	
Less accumulated depreciation	(800)	1,600
Total assets		$7,100
Liabilities and Owners' Equity:		
Accounts payable		$1,000
Interest payable on bank loan		100
Bank loan		2,000
Owners' equity		
Paid-in capital	$2,000	
Retained earnings	2,000	4,000
Total liabilities and owners' equity		$7,100

John Gorton Enterprises

Income Statement
For Month Ended January 31, 1991

Revenue		$6,000
Less Expenses:		
Merchandise used	$1,500	
Rent	150	
Equipment depreciation	400	
Interest on bank loan	25	
Wages	600	
Total expenses		2,675
Income from continuing operations		$3,325

John Gorton Enterprises

Statement of Cash Flows
For Month Ended January 31, 1991

Inflows:	Cash sales		$6,000
Outflows:	Accounts payable	$1,000	
	Rent	100	
	Interest	50	
	Wages	600	
	Total outflows		1,750
	Net cash inflows		$4,250

4–24. Net Income and Owners' Equity. You are at the monthly meeting of the Campus Investors Club. The club's investment in McMahon Corporation is to be discussed. The club has a 10 percent interest in the corporation and receives 10 percent of any dividends that the corporation pays to its stockholders. You were responsible for bringing the 1991 financial reports of McMahon Corporation to the meeting but have discovered that you have neglected to do so. You discover that today's newspaper has a brief article on the McMahon Corporation, from which you can glean the following information:

	1990	1991
Sales	$ 60,000	$ 65,000
Total assets	120,000	125,000
Total liabilities	90,000	80,000

Sales are the only form of revenue for McMahon Corporation.

Required (each question is independent unless otherwise stated):

1. Assuming there were no dividends paid and no contributions made by stockholders to the corporation during 1991, calculate the corporation's 1991 net income figure.
2. Assuming that there were no dividends paid but that the corporation's stockholders contributed an additional $10,000 (in proportion to their previous holdings) in cash during 1991, what would be the corporation's net income for 1991?

3. Now assume the same facts as in number 2, except that you now recall the Campus Investors Club received a cash dividend of $2,000 from McMahon during 1991. What would be the 1991 net income for the corporation now?
4. Using the net income figure derived in number 3, what would be McMahon Corporation's total expenses for 1991?
5. You have a sneaking suspicion that the sales figure given for 1991 is wrong. You are also satisfied that the figure for net income that you derived in number 3 is correct. If the total expenses incurred by McMahon Corporation for 1991 were $60,000, what should the sales figure have been?

4–25. Recognition of Accountable Events. Indicate whether the following events result from internal adjustments (*A*) or external transactions (*T*).

1. Recorded purchase of $500 worth of supplies on credit.
2. From a count of supplies, calculated and recorded the cost of merchandise used as $400.
3. Recorded $700 depreciation of machinery.
4. Recorded the expiration of $200 of prepaid rent.
5. Recorded payment of advertising bill of $25.
6. Recorded withdrawal of $300 cash by a partner in the business.
7. Recorded $300 as wages owed by business at end of period.
8. Cash dividends earned by the business were recorded as revenue.

4–26. Cash and Withdrawals. Albany Rentals is a car rental firm which has been operating for several years. The owners have followed the practice of withdrawing cash equal to the net income of each period. The beginning of 1991 balances in the accounts of the business are as follows:

Assets:			Liabilities and Owners' Equity:	
Cash		$ 1,000	Accounts payable	$ 2,000
Accounts receivable		2,500		
Gas and oil supplies		500		
Motor vehicles	$16,000			
Accumulated			Owners' equity	15,000
depreciation	(3,000)	13,000	Total liabilities and	
Total assets		$17,000	owners' equity	$17,000

During 1991 the following events were recorded:

Cash rentals earned	$4,000
Credit rentals earned	4,000
Purchases of gas and oil supplies (credit)	1,500
Rent paid for 1991	2,000
Depreciation expense for 1991	2,500
Supplies on hand at end of year	250
Repairs expense (all paid)	700
Payments on accounts payable	2,750
Receipts from accounts receivable	1,000

All amounts are in thousands.

Required:

1. Record the information for 1991 on a financial position worksheet.
2. Produce an income statement for 1991.

3. Discuss whether the owners are able to follow their usual withdrawal policy. Explain your reasoning.

4–27. Uncertainty and Income Measurement. Max and several associates decide to go into business operating a charter bus service at tourist resorts. They commence the business on January 1, 1990 by placing $1 million in a bank account out of which the business purchases ten buses for $750,000. They decide that each year they will withdraw all the net income that the business earns. The buses are expected to have useful lives of five years, at the end of which Max and his associates expect to sell them for $15,000 each. Following are the other bus company transactions for 1990 and 1991:

	1990	1991
	(Amounts in Thousands)	
Cash fares	$1,200	$1,300
Charter fares (credit)	500	350
Insurance paid	150	70
Wages paid	750	700
Payments from customers	200	350
Gas and oil supplies purchased on credit	200	160
Payments to suppliers	50	310
Gas and oil on hand at year-end	40	0
Repairs and maintenance (all paid)	180	190
Insurance cost unexpired at year-end	50	0

All events for 1990 are recorded on the financial position worksheet on the next page. At the end of 1991 Max discovers to his horror that because a travel agency went bankrupt, the business will never collect $100,000 of the $300,000 that had been owing from 1990 and the debt must be considered a total loss. During 1991, one of the buses is totally destroyed in a civil disorder—a hazard not covered by the company's insurance.

Required:

1. Record all the facts as they took place in worksheet form for 1991. (Do not forget the depreciation of the bus.)
2. Draw up an income statement for each of the two years.
3. In drawing up the income statement, did you show the losses on the customer's bad debt and from the destruction of the bus as extraordinary losses? Why or why not?
4. Assuming that the loss of the bus is considered an extraordinary loss, explain the implications in the long run to the company if 1992 withdrawals equal (*a*) income from continuing operations; and (*b*) net income.

4–28. Conventional Accounting Transaction Interpretation. Following are a set of transactions and events for a hypothetical corporation for the year just ended. Interpret each according to the accrual accounting method and, in a table, (1) indicate the accounts or elements of the corporation's financial position that are affected by each item, giving the account name, amount, and direction of change (distinguish between paid-in capital and retained earnings); and (2) indicate the amount and direction of the effect of each item on income from continuing operations. (Item one is used as an example.) If you feel you have to make any significant assumptions in order to interpret an item, show them as a footnote to your answer table.

Max's Bus Company

Financial Position Worksheet 1990
(amounts in thousands)

Description	Cash	Accounts Receivable	Prepaid Insurance	Supplies	Buses	Accumulated Depreciation	Accounts Payable	Retained Earnings	Paid-in Capital
Balances, January 1, 1990	$1,000								$1,000
Bus purchase	(750)				750				
Cash fares	1,200							1,200 (R)	
Credit fares		500						500 (R)	
Insurance	(150)		50					(100) (E)	
Wages	(750)							(750) (E)	
Customer payments	200	(200)							
Supplies				200			200		
Payments to suppliers	(50)						(50)		
Supplies used				(160)				(160) (E)	
Repairs and maintenance	(180)							(180) (E)	
Depreciation expense						(120)		(120) (E)	
Withdrawal	(390)							(390) (W)	
Balances, December 31, 1990	$ 130	$300	$50	$ 40	$750	$(120)	$150	$0	$1,000

(R) Revenue

(E) Expense

(W) Withdrawal

1. The company had a total of beginning supplies inventory and purchases for the year with a cost of $20,000. The supplies remaining at year-end originally cost $1,000.
2. Rent for the year amounted to $2,400. However, it had been paid in a two-year rent payment prior to the beginning of the year.
3. Equipment originally costing $20,000 and depreciated to date in the amount of $12,500 was lost due to a freak accident at the beginning of the year. Insurance proceeds were $9,000.
4. Sales for cash amounted to $15,000. New credit sales equaled $75,000. Goods were delivered to customers who had advanced the full selling prices of $10,000 last year.
5. At the beginning of the period the accumulated depreciation on assets employed in the business was $225,000. At the end of the period it was $250,000.
6. New owners contributed $90,000 cash to the corporation.
7. Wage and salary payments made during the year equaled $55,000. However, wages of $5,000 were owed to employees at year-end for work already performed. No wages were owed at the beginning of the year.
8. Dividends of $20,000 were declared and paid to owners during the year.

Example:

	Income Measures Affected	
Accounts Affected	Income from Continuing Operations	Net Income
1. Supplies inventory Retained earnings	$(19,000)	$(19,000)

4–29. **Recognizing Effects of Events on Financial Position.** For each of the following events relating to the Antique Weavers Company, indicate the effect upon the individual accounts in the company's financial position. Treat each event independently, and do not do a worksheet. Indicate in each case whether the event is an external transaction (T) or an internal adjustment (A). Expenses and revenues are to be identified as such. For example:

Event:

> Incurred and paid advertising of $200
> (T) Assets (cash)—decrease of $200
> Owners' equity (returned earnings)—decrease of $200

Events:
1. Purchased wool from suppliers on credit for $1,000.
2. Purchased weaving machine for $5,000, paying $2,500 in cash with the bank paying the balance.
3. Placed advertisements in the local paper at a cost of $180. Payment has not yet been made.
4. Paid $1,800 rent for the next 18 months.
5. Paid $800 wages owed for work done in the preceding period.
6. Paid $500 to bank in repayment of a loan.
7. Made sales of $3,000 to a major retailer who paid cash of $1,500 and promised payment of the balance within 30 days.
8. One of the owners contributed a delivery van (market value $2,000) to the company.

9. Depreciation of equipment for the period—$150.
10. The retailer (in number 7) returned some goods, claiming he was overstocked. Antique Weavers gave him a credit note for $500 (i.e., reduction in the amount payable).
11. Discovered at the end of the period:

    a. Wool supplies used during period cost $300.
    b. Amount of prepaid rent that expired during the period was $500.
    c. Wages owing at end of the period were $250.
    d. Interest owing at the end of the period was $80.
12. Paid a $500 cash dividend to owners.

4–30. Recognition of Adjustments. The Custom Sign Company's financial position worksheets (Exhibits 4–7 and 4–8) contain the external cash transactions based on information available in problem 3–14. Also, the worksheets contain external cash transactions based on the following additional information:

1. Materials purchased through August 31, 1991 (paid for by check): $3,000.
2. Cash withdrawals for personal expenses through July 31, 1991: $1,000.
3. Total of gasoline credit card statements paid by check through August 31, 1991 (treated as an expense when paid): $300.
4. Cash received from customers through August 31, 1991: $6,200.
5. Cash received from customers during September: $1,800.
6. Original investment, $10,000 cash.

For purposes of convenience, prepaid licenses, prepaid rent, and prepaid insurance have been grouped into one account—prepaid expenses. The long-lived assets account includes the pickup, generator, and other equipment. The accumulated depreciation account may be used for depreciation on all long-lived assets.

Required:

1. Complete the financial position worksheet as of August 31, 1991 by

    a. Recognition of external transactions not involving cash up through August 31, 1991 (if any).
    b. Recognition of adjustments for the period March 1, 1991 through August 31, 1991.

2. Complete the financial position worksheet as of September 30, 1991 by:

    a. Recognition of external transactions not involving cash in September (if any).
    b. Recognition of September adjustments.

3. Prepare a statement of financial position as of September 30, 1991. What is the net income for September?

(Note: *You must refer to problem 3–14 in order to complete this problem.*)

4–31. Recognition of Internal Events. The financial position worksheets in Exhibits 4–9 and 4–10 contain the external cash transactions based on information available in problem 3–15. Also, the worksheets contain external cash transactions based on the following additional information.

1. The photography studio was opened on October 1, 1990. At that time the lease officially began, and Ms. Morton paid for the improvements, furniture and fixtures, and photography equipment.
2. Ms. Morton hired her assistant on November 1, 1990. Her salary is paid by check on the last working day of each month.

EXHIBIT 4-7

Custom Sign Company

Financial Position Worksheet

Description	Cash	Materials	Prepaid Expenses	Long-lived Assets	Accumulated Depreciation	Accounts Payable	Paid-in Capital	Retained Earnings
1. Original investment	$100,000						$100,000	
2. Purchase of truck	(10,800)			$10,800				
3. Purchase of generator	(1,200)			1,200				
4. Purchase of other equipment	(540)			540				
5. City and state licenses	(400)		$ 400					
6. Insurance premium	(480)		480					
7. Quarterly rental, April 1, 1991	(3,000)		3,000					
8. Quarterly rental, July 1, 1991	(3,000)		3,000					
9. Purchases of material	(3,000)	$3,000						
10. Withdrawals through July 31, 1991	(1,000)							(1,000) (W)
11. Payment of gasoline credit card statements	(300)							(300) (E)
12. Cash receipts from customers	6,200							6,200 (R)
13. Withdrawal at end of August	(450)							(450) (W)
Positions after cash events through August 31, 1991	$82,030	$3,000	$6,880	$12,540	$0	$0	$100,000	$4,450

(R) Revenue

(E) Expense

(W) Withdrawal

EXHIBIT 4-8
Custom Sign Company

Financial Position Worksheet

Description	Cash	Materials	Prepaid Expenses	Long-lived Assets	Accumulated Depreciation	Accounts Payable	Paid-in Capital	Retained Earnings
Beginning Position: September 1, 1991	?	?	?	?	?	?	?	?
1. Purchase of materials (paid by check)	$ (750)	$750						
2. Payment of gasoline credit card statement	(120)					$(120)		
3. Withdrawal at end of September	(500)							$(500) (W)
4. Cash receipts from customers	1,800							1,800 (R)

(R) *Revenue*

(W) *Withdrawal*

EXHIBIT 4–9

Mary Morton Photography Studio

Financial Position Worksheet

Description	Cash	Accounts Receivable	Film and Supplies	Prepaid Rent	Long-lived Assets	Accumulated Depreciation	Accounts Payable	Paid-in Capital	Retained Earnings
1. Original investment	$15,000							$15,000	
2. Improvements	(1,800)				$1,800				
3. Furniture and fixtures	(4,800)				4,800				
4. Photography equipment	(2,700)				2,700				
5. Quarterly rental on November 1, 1990	(600)			$ 600					
6. Quarterly rental on January 1, 1991	(600)			600					
7. Salary of assistant for November 1, 1990 through March 31, 1991	(3,500)								$(3,500) (E)
8. Payments on account for film and photography supplies	(2,000)						$(2,000)		
9. Receipts on account from customers	10,000	$(10,000)							
10. Miscellaneous expenses	(800)								(800) (E)
11. Cash withdrawals	(2,400)								(2,400) (W)
Position on March 31, 1991 *before* recognition of external events not involving cash and adjustments	$5,800	$(10,000)	$0	$1,200	$9,300	$0	$(2,000)	$15,000	$(6,700)

(E) Expense

(W) Withdrawal

EXHIBIT 4–10

Mary Morton Photography Studio

Financial Position Worksheet

Description	Cash	Accounts Receivable	Film and Supplies	Prepaid Rent	Long-lived Assets	Accumulated Depreciation	Accounts Payable	Paid-in Capital	Retained Earnings
Beginning Position, April 1, 1991	?	?	?	?	?	?	?		?
1. Quarterly rental on April 1, 1991	$ (600)			$600					
2. Payments on account for film	(400)						$(400)		
3. Salary of assistant	(700)								$(700) (E)
4. Miscellaneous expenses	(100)								(100) (E)
5. Cash withdrawal	(500)								(500) (W)
6. Receipts on account	2,700	$(2,700)							

(E) *Expense*

(W) *Withdrawal*

3. Payments on account for film and photography supplies totaled $2,000 for the period October 1, 1990, through March 31, 1991.
4. Receipts on account from customers totaled $10,000 for the period October 1, 1990 through March 31, 1991.
5. Payments for miscellaneous expenses totaled $800 for the period October 1, 1990 through March 31, 1991.
6. Cash withdrawals totaled $2,400 for the period.
7. Original investment, $15,000 cash.
8. Unpaid amounts due from customers were $700 and $800 at the beginning and the end of April, respectively.

For convenience, leasehold improvements, furniture and fixtures, and photography equipment have been lumped into one account—long-lived assets. The accumulated depreciation account may be used for depreciation on all long-lived assets.

Required:

1. Complete the financial position worksheet as of March 31, 1991 by:

   a. Recognition of external transactions not involving cash up through March 31, 1991.
   b. Recognition of adjustments for the period October 1, 1990 through March 31, 1991.
2. Complete the financial position worksheet as of April 30, 1991 by:

   a. Recognition of external transactions not involving cash in April.
   b. Recognition of April adjustments.

3. Prepare a statement of financial position as of April 30, 1991.

(Note: You must refer to problem 3–15 in order to complete this problem.)

Statement of Cash Flows

CHAPTER FIVE

The previous chapters concerned two of the three primary financial statements found in annual reports: the measurement of income for the income statement and the valuation of assets, liabilities, and owners' equity for the balance sheet. This chapter covers the third major financial statement, the statement of cash flows. This statement shows the flow of cash within the firm and associates these flows with their underlying causes in terms of the activities of the enterprise. The objective of this chapter is to demonstrate the need for cash flow information and to illustrate the preparation of a statement of cash flows. Cash flows arise from operating, investing, and financing activities. This distinction will be used to interpret the information about cash flows.

THE NEED FOR CASH FLOW INFORMATION

The primary purpose of the statement of cash flows is to provide information about the firm's cash receipts and disbursements during a period of time. In Chapter Three, predictions of future cash flows from investment decisions was described as a major need for information by creditors and owners. Investors need to predict future cash flows from interest, dividends, principal repayment, and return of capital. Future cash flows to the investor depend upon the firm having adequate cash to make payments. Information about current cash flows of the firm is useful for predicting future cash flows to the investor.

The importance of these disclosures was recognized by the FASB when it issued SFAS No. 95 requiring all firms to prepare a financial statement explaining cash receipts and disbursements.[1] This requirement elevates cash flow disclosures to an importance equal to that of the income statement and balance sheet. As stated by the FASB:

> The information provided in a statement of cash flows, if used with related disclosures and information in the other financial statements, should help investors, creditors, and others to (a) assess the enterprise's ability to generate positive future net cash flows; (b) assess the enterprise's ability to meet its obligations, its ability to pay dividends, and its need for external financing; (c) assess the reasons for differences between net income and associated cash receipts and payments; and (d) assess the effects on an enterprise's financial position of both its cash and noncash investing and financing transactions during the period.[2]

Chapter Three stated that the accrual basis is more useful than the cash basis for predicting the long-run cash-generating ability of the enterprise. The present discussion about the usefulness of cash flow information is not meant to diminish the usefulness of net income as a measure of performance. Net income measures the change in net assets that results from the firm's operations, giving equal weight to changes in assets and liabilities of all kinds. For example, sales revenue is interpreted as an accomplishment of the period, independent of whether the revenue has resulted in a cash receipt or a receivable from the customer. The income statement alone does not give information about changes in the specific types of assets, liabilities, and owners' equity—an important aspect of a company's history. Exclusive reliance on net income as a long-run indicator may cause the investor to overlook current shortfalls in the actual flow of cash through the business.

A prime example of the deficiencies in sole reliance on net income is the 1975 bankruptcy of W.T. Grant. Until 1974, W.T. Grant had consistently reported net income. Yet examination of the financial statements reveals that during the ten years prior to bankruptcy, W.T. Grant generated no cash from operations. In fact, the company continually obtained additional monies from outside investors to make up for the internal drain on cash reserves.[3] Yet it was not until 1974 that W.T. Grant reported its first net loss. Had investors been informed about W.T. Grant's cash flows, they would have been apprised of the company's financial difficulties much earlier than they were from the income statement.

Nor do the beginning and ending balance sheets adequately reveal the causes of the change in the firm's cash position. Such comparative statements depict only the cumulative effects of all the transactions that affected the composition of assets, liabilities, and owners' equity, not the dynamics of the changes that took place during a period. That is, only the net change in an account (e.g., cash) can be observed. No information is revealed regarding the specific transactions which caused the cash account to change. The statement of cash flows explains the specific changes that occurred in the balance sheet accounts and their related cash flow effects—the short-run financial impact of a firm's activities.

---

[1] Financial Accounting Standards Board, *Statement of Financial Accounting Standards No. 95*, "Statement of Cash Flows," November 1987. This chapter is based on the requirements set forth in SFAS No. 95.

[2] Ibid., paragraph 5.

[3] James A. Largay III and Clyde P. Stickney, "Cash Flows, Ratio Analysis and the W.T. Grant Company Bankruptcy," *Financial Analyst's Journal*, July–August 1980, pp. 51–54.

CASH FLOWS FROM OPERATING, INVESTING, AND FINANCING ACTIVITIES

Before describing the procedures underlying the preparation of the statement of cash flows, it is useful to consider the types of business activities that impact cash during the year. The firm's cash balance can be increased by (1) profitable operations; (2) a decrease in noncash assets (e.g., land sold for cash or a note receivable collected); and (3) an increase in liabilities or owners' equity (bonds payable issued or common stock sold). Likewise, the firm's cash balance can be decreased by (1) a loss from operations; (2) an increase in noncash assets (equipment purchased for cash); and (3) a decrease in liabilities or owners' equity (notes payable reduced or dividends paid). The objective of the statement of cash flow is to explain change in the cash account according to the managerial activities that cause them. These activities can be classified as operating, investing, and financing. As we will see, this classification becomes the basis of the format used to prepare the statement of cash flows.

Operating Activities. Operating activities are those transactions and events directly related to the regular production and delivery of goods and services to customers. Cash flows from operations are the cash effects of the transactions that impact net income. Included are the cash receipts from the sale of goods or services and cash payments for expenses such as merchandise inventory, wages, supplies, interest, taxes, and the like. A company such as W.T. Grant may have cash used by operations, even though net income is positive, if accounts receivable are slow to be collected and inventories are building up instead of being sold. Cash flow from operations was illustrated in Chapter Three when we discussed the cash basis of measuring performance.

Investment Activities. Investing activities consist of those transactions and events that relate to the acquisition and disposition of assets such as buildings, equipment, land, and other resources which provide the capacity over time to carry out the operations of the business. Cash inflows related to investment activities arise from collections on loans made to others (e.g., notes receivable) and proceeds from selling property, plant, and equipment. Thus the sale of land would be a cash inflow from investing activities equal to the amount paid by the buyer. Cash outflows arise from direct loans made to other entities, purchase of another firm's common stock, or acquisition of property, plant, and equipment. For example, lending monies to an outside party would be an increase in notes receivable and a cash outflow from investing activities.

Financing Activities. Financing activities relate to acquiring funds from and making payments to creditors and owners. Cash receipts from financing activities arise from bonds, mortgages, notes, and other short- or long-term borrowing as well as the sale of common stock. Borrowing funds from a bank increases notes payable and is considered a cash inflow from financing activities. Cash outflows relate to repayments of amounts borrowed as well as reacquisition of the firm's common stock and payments of dividends or withdrawals by the owners. Repayment of the note would be a cash outflow for financing in that period.

The effects of operations, investing activities, and financing activities arise from the management of a business over its natural operating cycle. Operating plans, in conjunction with financing and investment considerations, determine a desired level of investment in various assets. Cash to acquire the desired assets must be secured from new creditor or owner sources via financing activities. Such funds are then available for investing in the assets necessary to support operations. Actual operations, in turn, produce cash flows from sales (collections of accounts receivable) to replace resources used to provide products and services and to make payments to creditors and owners. In this manner, all changes in cash can be viewed as the result of either operating, investing, or financing activities. Furthermore, the financial implications of all operating, investing, and financing activities are reflected in changes in cash in one period or another. When the statement of cash flows is prepared, the cash effects of operating, financing, and investing activities are shown separately to facilitate an evaluation of the three types of management functions. This enables the investor to separately analyze the various sources and uses of cash and assess trends in the firm's activities. Had such disclosures been available for W.T. Grant, investors might have been alerted to the fact that cash balances were being replaced through financing activities rather than as a normal course of operations.

PREPARING THE STATEMENT OF CASH FLOWS

The firm's beginning-of-period and end-of-period balance sheets are used in conjunction with the income statement and other relevant information to prepare the statement of cash flows. (Note that the previous period's ending balance sheet is used for the beginning-of-period account balances, as they are one and the same.) Preparation of this statement involves three general steps: (1) analyzing changes in the balance sheet accounts in conjunction with other information to determine their effect on cash; (2) using this analysis to calculate cash flows from operating activities; and (3) preparing the statement of cash flows from these analyses. These steps are explained in this section and summarized in Exhibit 5–1. The process is illustrated by continuing the Fancy Flavors, Inc., example from Chapters Three and Four.

EXHIBIT 5–1

Preparation of the Statement of Cash Flows

1. **Analyze and Categorize Changes in Balance Sheet Accounts**
    a. Calculate the change in cash.
    b. Calculate the change in each noncash account.
    c. Obtain additional information to explain specific causes of the changes in noncash accounts.
    d. Categorize the change in each noncash account as from operating, investing, or financing activities.
2. **Calculate Cash Flow from Operating Activities**
    a. Cash receipts from customers
    b. Cash payments for merchandise
    c. Cash payments for operating expenses
3. **Prepare the Statement of Cash Flows**
    Arrange the information into a statement with three distinct categories: cash flows from operating, investing, and financing activities.

Example 5–1 | The example used to illustrate preparation of the statement of cash flows continues with Fancy Flavors, Inc., for their second month of operations, September 1991. The comparative balance sheets for August 31, 1991 and September 30, 1991 are found in Exhibit 5–2. (The only change from the August 31, 1991 balance sheet found in Exhibit 4–4 is that accounts payable and accrued liabilities are shown separately.) The income statement for September 1991 appears in Exhibit 5–3 (on page 102). Additional information for September includes the following:

1. Equipment with an original cost of $90,000 and accumulated depreciation of $1,500 was sold for $88,500 cash. Accordingly, no gain or loss has been recognized.
2. Equipment costing $150,000 was purchased during the month. A bank loan of $60,000 was used along with $90,000 in cash. The equipment is expected to have a useful life of five years.

Analyzing the Balance Sheet Accounts

Change in Cash. The first step is to determine the change in cash during the period. This is done by using comparative balance sheets (beginning-of-period and end-of-period) and calculating the increase or decrease in cash. This net change in the cash account is what we want to explain with the statement of cash flows. Notice for Fancy Flavors, cash increased during September by $64,500 (from $200,000 to $264,500). This net change is the focus of our analysis in preparing the statement of cash flows.

EXHIBIT 5–2

Fancy Flavors, Inc.

Comparative Statements of Financial Position

	August 31, 1991	September 30, 1991
Assets:		
Cash	$200,000	$ 264,500
Accounts receivable	50,000	65,000
Prepaid rent	40,000	20,000
Ice cream	15,000	30,000
Supplies	15,000	10,000
Equipment	600,000	660,000
Less accumulated depreciation	(10,000)	(19,500)
Total assets	$910,000	$1,030,000
Liabilities and Owners' Equity:		
Accounts payable	$ 80,000	$ 60,000
Accrued liabilities	25,000	30,000
Bank loan payable	600,000	660,000
Owners' equity		
Paid-in capital	150,000	150,000
Retained earnings	55,000	130,000
Total liabilities and owners' equity	$910,000	$1,030,000

EXHIBIT 5–3

Fancy Flavors, Inc.

Income Statement
For the Month of September 1991

Revenue from sales of ice cream		$600,000
Cost of ice cream sold		200,000
Operating expenses		
Rent	$ 20,000	
Supplies used	20,000	
Salaries and wages	180,000	
Equipment depreciation	11,000	
Interest on loan	6,600	
Miscellaneous (heat, light, etc.)	12,400	
Federal income taxes	30,000	280,000
Net income		$120,000

Change in Noncash Accounts. The second step is to analyze the change in each noncash account together with any additional information available to further explain the cause of each change. As discussed in the previous section, these changes can be categorized as arising from three distinct activities: (1) operations, as in activities relating to sales (accounts receivable) and expenses (prepaid expenses, inventories, depreciation, accounts payable, accrued liabilities); (2) investing, as in long-term assets such as land, equipment, buildings; and (3) financing, as in long-term liabilities (notes payable) and owners' equity (paid-in capital and retained earnings due to income and dividends). All these changes are interpreted as having an effect on cash during the period.

The account analysis and categorization for Fancy Flavors is shown in Exhibit 5–4. Note the individual account changes in Fancy Flavors have been detailed with the additional information we were given regarding the sale and purchase of equipment. This elaboration is important for determining if there are categories of increases or decreases in balance sheet accounts that may represent separate sources and uses of cash. Thus a net change in depreciable assets needs to be divided into the source of cash from dispositions, the use of cash for acquisitions, and the change due to depreciation. (Note that depreciation is categorized as relating to operations since it is associated with an expense found on the income statement.)

The first four accounts following cash in Fancy Flavors' balance sheet are assets which relate to sales (accounts receivable) and expenses (prepaid rent, ice cream, and supplies). Therefore, the changes in these accounts have been categorized as relating to operations in Exhibit 5–4. The equipment account increased by $60,000 during the month. However, we know the net increase is the result of two separate transactions: the sale and purchase of equipment. In September, Fancy Flavors sold equipment at its book value: $90,000 original cost minus $1,500 accumulated depreciation. Both these amounts are removed from the appropriate accounts and the net decrease in assets of $88,500 is interpreted as a source of cash during the month.

In general, special attention must be given to the sale of a fixed asset. To

EXHIBIT 5-4

Fancy Flavors, Inc.

Changes in Noncash Accounts
For the Month of September 1991

Account	Increase (Decrease)	Category
Accounts receivable	$ 15,000	Operations
Prepaid rent	(20,000)	Operations
Ice cream	15,000	Operations
Supplies	(5,000)	Operations
Equipment		
Disposition	(90,000)	Investment
Acquisition	150,000	Investment
Accumulated depreciation		
Disposition	(1,500)	Investment
Depreciation	11,000	Operations
Accounts payable	(20,000)	Operations
Accrued liabilities	5,000	Operations
Bank loan payable	60,000	Financing
Paid-in capital	0	
Retained earnings		
Net Income	120,000	Operations
Dividends	(45,000)	Financing

measure net income for the period, we calculate a gain or loss based on the difference between the proceeds from sale and the unexpired cost (book value) of the asset. In preparing the statement of cash flows, the effect on cash arises from the proceeds of the sale. Thus the statement of cash flows reflects a source of cash equal to the total proceeds received from the sale of an asset, and net income must be adjusted to exclude the effect of any gain or loss from the sale.

Because Fancy Flavors received the book value from the sale of its equipment, there was no gain or loss to be removed from net income. The net change in the equipment and accumulated depreciation accounts represents the entire proceeds from disposition of the asset.

In addition, Fancy Flavors acquired equipment during the month, partially by incurring a bank loan payable. This illustrates that a change in a noncash account can lack a direct effect on cash. Examples include acquiring property with a note payable or converting debt into common stock. Although these transactions do not directly involve cash receipts or disbursements they are included in the statement of cash flows as if they were a source or use of cash. The two noncash account changes are treated separately, thereby imputing to the transaction an effect on cash. This is done to provide information about all the investing and financing activities of the period, even if they did not directly involve cash, since they will likely affect the future cash flows of the firm.

For Fancy Flavors, only the $90,000 cash expenditure directly involved cash. However, the $60,000 increase in bank loan payable will be shown as a source of cash in cash flow from financing activities, and the entire cost of the equipment is classified as a use of cash in cash flow from investing activities.

Continuing with the account analysis in Exhibit 5–4, the $11,000 increase in the accumulated depreciation account is categorized as relating to operations because it is an income statement expense. (Note the amount of the current-period depreciation expense can be observed from the income statement in Exhibit 5–3.) Likewise, changes in the current liability accounts (accounts payable and accrued liabilities) are labeled as affecting cash from operations since they arise from expenses recognized on the income statement (cost of ice cream sold, salaries and wages, and the like).

Although the bank loan was incurred directly to purchase equipment (an investing transaction), it is considered a financing activity because it is an increase in a liability. If the incurrence of the loan resulted in a cash inflow, its classification as a financing transaction would be straightforward. We do not change the categorization because cash was not involved in the transaction.

No common stock has been sold or purchased, so there is no change in the paid-in capital account. Had there been such a transaction, it would be considered a financing activity.

The net change in a firm's retained earnings for the period must be divided into (1) the increase (decrease) due to net income (loss); and (2) the decrease from dividends. For Fancy Flavors, the net increase of $75,000 in retained earnings during September must be more fully examined. We know that retained earnings was increased by September's net income, $120,000. But the net change in retained earnings is only an increase of $75,000. This implies that dividends of $45,000 were paid during September, thereby reducing the retained earnings account.

Cash Flow from Operating Activities

The next step in preparing the statement of cash flows is to separately calculate cash from operations, using the analysis of the changes in the balance sheet accounts to adjust the income statement to the cash basis.[4] The objective is to calculate net operating cash flow as the difference between operating cash receipts (cash collections from customers) and cash disbursements (cash payments for purchases and operating expenses). The general approach is to adjust each income statement item to obtain the related cash flow.

Cash Receipts from Customers. Beginning with revenues, to determine cash flows from operations we need cash receipts from customers. The balance sheet account which causes revenues to be on the accrual basis is accounts receivable. Suppose we observe from the comparative balance sheets that the accounts receivable balance has decreased from the beginning of the period to the end of the period. We could conclude that not only were the current period's sales collected in cash, but also some from the previous period. Thus cash receipts from customers are equal to the revenue plus the net decrease in accounts receivable during the year. On the other hand, suppose the accounts receivable

---

[4] This section determines cash flow from operating activities using the direct approach whereby each income statement account is adjusted to the cash basis. The appendix to this chapter explains the indirect approach whereby the effects of accruals and deferrals are removed from net income. Both approaches yield the same cash flow measure. The difference lies in how the information is depicted.

balance had increased from the beginning of the period to the end of the period. We could then conclude that not all of the current period's sales were collected in cash. Some of the sales are represented by the net increase in accounts receivable. To determine cash receipts from customers, we would subtract from revenue the net increase in accounts receivable. Note that during any given year, the net change in accounts receivable can only be an increase, decrease, or no change.

$$\text{REVENUE} \quad \begin{array}{c} + \text{ DECREASE IN ACCOUNTS RECEIVABLE} \\ \text{OR} \\ - \text{ INCREASE IN ACCOUNTS RECEIVABLE} \end{array} = \begin{array}{c} \text{CASH RECEIPTS} \\ \text{FROM CUSTOMERS} \end{array}$$

At this point it may be helpful to consider what happens to accounts receivable during any given year. The beginning balance in accounts receivable is collected in its entirety during the year. This provides a cash inflow equal to the beginning amount. However, the ending balance is created entirely during the year, representing current sales that are not collected in cash. Thus an alternative, but equivalent, way of determining cash receipts from operations is from the following equation (where cash receipts is the unknown):

BEGINNING ACCOUNTS RECEIVABLE + SALES
  − CASH RECEIPTS FROM CUSTOMERS = ENDING ACCOUNTS RECEIVABLE.

Determining cash flows from operating activities is illustrated in Exhibit 5–5 using the Fancy Flavors example. The account analysis in Exhibit 5–4 indicated that Fancy Flavors' accounts receivable experienced a net increase of $15,000 during the month of September. The beginning balance of $50,000 was collected during September, providing a cash inflow. But, $65,000 of the current period's sales were not collected during the month. The net increase in accounts receivable of $15,000 represents the reduction to revenue to obtain cash receipts from customers during September of $585,000.[5]

Cash Payments for Merchandise. Next we need to adjust cost of sales to cash payments for merchandise. Here we recognize that the firm not only acquires the goods sold during the period, it also purchases merchandise for inventory. If the inventory balance increases from the beginning of the period to the end of the period, the firm purchased merchandise both for sale during the current period and to build up its stock of inventory. The net increase in inventory must be added to cost of sales to determine merchandise purchased during the period. On the other hand, the inventory balance could fall from the beginning of the period to the end of the period. This indicates that not all of the merchandise sold came from purchases made this period; some came from the stock of goods on hand at the beginning of the period. The net decrease in inventory is subtracted from cost of sales to get purchases during the period. An alternative, but equivalent, way of determining merchandise purchases (the unknown) is from the following equation:

BEGINNING INVENTORY + PURCHASES − COST OF SALES = ENDING INVENTORY

---

[5] Equivalently, beginning accounts receivable ($50,000) plus current period sales ($600,000) minus ending accounts receivable ($65,000) equals cash receipts from customers ($585,000).

EXHIBIT 5–5

Fancy Flavors, Inc.

Cash Flows from Operating Activities
For the Month of September 1991
(Direct Method)

Revenue:	$600,000	
Increase in accounts receivable	(15,000)	
Cash receipts from customers		$585,000
Cost of ice cream sold	$200,000	
Increase in ice cream inventory	15,000	
Decrease in accounts payable	20,000	
Cash payments for ice cream		(235,000)
Operating expenses:	$280,000	
Decrease in prepaid rent	(20,000)	
Decrease in supplies	(5,000)	
Increase in accrued liabilities	(5,000)	
Equipment depreciation	(11,000)	
Cash payments for operating expenses		(239,000)
Cash flow from operating activities		$111,000

Furthermore, not all the merchandise acquired during the current period is necessarily paid for in cash. The firm may use short-term credit in the form of accounts payable. If accounts payable increase from the beginning of the period to the end of the period, not all of the purchases represent a cash outflow; some are financed with accounts payable. The net increase in accounts payable is subtracted from cost of sales to obtain cash payments for purchases. Alternatively, the accounts payable balance could fall from the beginning of the period to the end of the period. This implies not only were the current period's purchases paid for in cash, but also some of the previous period. The net decrease in accounts payable would be added to the cost of sales to obtain cash payments for purchases. An alternative, but equivalent, way of determining cash payments for purchases (the unknown) is from the following equation:

BEGINNING ACCOUNTS PAYABLE + PURCHASES − CASH PAYMENTS
= ENDING ACCOUNTS PAYABLE.

The adjustments to determine cash payments for purchases are summarized below:

$$\text{COST OF SALES} \quad \begin{array}{l} + \text{ INCREASE IN INVENTORY} \\ \quad\quad\quad\quad \text{OR} \\ - \text{ DECREASE IN INVENTORY} \\ + \text{ DECREASE IN ACCOUNTS PAYABLE} \\ \quad\quad\quad\quad \text{OR} \\ - \text{ INCREASE IN ACCOUNTS PAYABLE} \end{array} = \begin{array}{l} \text{CASH PAYMENTS} \\ \text{FOR PURCHASES} \end{array}$$

Referring to Exhibit 5–5, we see two adjustments made to cost of sales to determine cash payments for ice cream. The inventory increased, showing not only the purchase of ice cream sold in the current period, but also the purchase of an additional amount to build up the stock on hand. The net decrease in accounts payable indicates that some of the previous period's purchases were paid for, as well as the purchases made in September. Thus cash payments for ice cream totaled $235,000.[6]

Cash Payments for Operating Expenses. Operating expenses also must be re-stated to the cash basis. Prepaid expenses may have been recorded that relate to cash expenditures to be used in operations in later periods. Examples include prepaid rent, insurance, and the like. An increase in prepaid expenses from the beginning of the period to the end of the period indicates that not only were the current period's expenses paid for in cash, but also the amount represented by the increase in prepayments. The net addition to prepaid expenses must be added to operating expenses to get current period expenditures. On the other hand, a decrease in prepaid expenses indicates that not all of the current period's operating expenses were paid for in cash. Some have come from the expenses prepaid in previous periods. The net decrease in prepaid expenses must be subtracted from operating expenses to get current period expenditures. Once again, an alternative approach to solve for current expenditures is as follows:

BEGINNING PREPAID EXPENSES + CURRENT EXPENDITURES
− OPERATING EXPENSES = ENDING PREPAID EXPENSES.

Furthermore, not all of the operating expenses recognized during the current period are necessarily paid for in cash. Some may be liabilities such as accrued wages or interest payable. If the accrued liabilities increase from the beginning of the period to the end of the period, not all of the operating expenses resulted in a cash outflow. Some are represented by the net increase in accrued liabilities. This net increase must be subtracted from operating expenses to obtain cash payments for operating expenses. On the other hand, accrued liabilities may decrease from the beginning of the period to the end of the period. In this case not only were the current period's expenses paid for in cash, but also some that were payable from a previous period. The net decrease in accrued liabilities must be added to operating expenses to get cash payments for operating expenses. Alternatively, we can solve for cash payments for operating expenses from the following equation:

BEGINNING ACCRUED LIABILITIES + CURRENT EXPENDITURES − CASH PAYMENTS
= ENDING ACCRUED LIBILITIES.

The adjustments leading to cash payments for operating expenses are summarized below:

---

[6] Equivalently, cost of sales ($200,000) plus ending inventory ($30,000) minus beginning inventory ($15,000) equals purchases ($215,000). Beginning accounts payable ($80,000) plus purchases ($215,000) minus ending accounts payable ($60,000) equals cash payments for purchases ($235,000).

income. Likewise, for a decrease in accounts payable, cost of sales is increased, while net income is reduced. Notice in Exhibit 5–8 Fancy Flavors' net income has been reduced for the $20,000 decrease in amounts payable. And an increase in accounts payable is a reduction to cost of sales, or an increase to net income.

Similar logic is used for the adjustments to net income necessary for operating expenses to get cash flows from operations. An increase in prepaid expenses is an addition to operating expenses to obtain the cash outflow, and thus a reduction to net income in the indirect method. A decrease in prepaid expenses is a reduction to operating expenses and therefore an increase to net income. Notice in Exhibit 5–8 the addition of $20,000 to Fancy Flavors' net income from the decrease in prepaid rent. If accrued liabilities decrease during the period, the cash outflow for operating expenses exceeds the income statement amount, and net income must be reduced in the indirect method. An increase in accrued liabilities is a decrease to operating expenses and thus an increase to net income. Therefore, we have added $5,000 for the increase in accrued liabilities in the Fancy Flavors example.

Finally, net income must be increased by the period's depreciation expense since no cash outflow related to this item was experienced in the current period. In Exhibit 5–8, we have added the $11,000 equipment depreciation to Fancy Flavors' net income.

Notice the $111,000 net cash flow from operating activities using the indirect approach for the Fancy Flavors' transactions in Exhibit 5–8 is the same amount determined using the direct method in Exhibit 5–5.

Questions for Review and Discussion

5–1. Define or describe
 a. Cash flows from operating activities
 b. Cash receipts from cutomers
 c. Cash payments for merchandise
 d. Cash payments for operating expenses
 e. Cash flows from investing activities
 f. Cash flows from financing activities

5–2. Explain how a company earning a substantial annual income can become financial embarrassed; that is, not be able to pay its obligations when due. Does this mean that net income is really not a useful measure of performance?

5–3. The Financial Accounting Standards Board requires companies to include a statement of cash flows in their annual report. Why do they consider this information useful to investors?

5–4. Identify and describe the major business activities that give rise to cash flows.

5–5. Describe the steps that you would follow in preparing a statement of cash flows.

5–6. Describe the procedures used in the direct method to determine cash flows from operating activities. What are the advantages of this method?

5–7. Explain why the net change in accounts receivable can be used to determine cash collections from customers.

5–8. (Appendix) Describe the procedure and rationale for calculating cash provided by operations, beginning with income from continuing operations.

5–9. (Appendix) What advantages, if any, are there to calculating cash provided by operations by starting with income from continuing operations rather than by reviewing the transactions of the enterprise for the period?

5–10. In recognizing sources and uses of cash other than from operations, cash flows are often imputed where no physical flow of cash actually took place. Explain why this is done.

5–11. Cash provided by operations would equal income from continuing operations were it not for certain items entering into the calculation of income from continuing operations. Name some typical items of this sort. Explain their treatment in deriving cash provided by operations from the income from continuing operations figure.

5–12. In general, would you expect cash provided by operations to be greater than, equal to, or less than income from continuing operations? Defend your position.

5–13. (Appendix) In deriving cash provided by operations from net income, changes in current assets and liabilities are added to, or subtracted from, income. Are such changes therefore sources or uses of cash? In what sense can such items be considered sources or uses of cash? Give examples and explain.

Problems

5–1. Preparing a Statement of Cash Flows. A worksheet describing the first year of operations of a new business is shown in Exhibit 5–9 on the next page.

Required:
1. Prepare a 1991 income statement.
2. Determine the cash flows from operations using the direct method.
3. (Appendix) Determine the cash flows from operations using the indirect method.
4. Categorize the remaining sources and uses of cash as investing and financing activities.
5. Prepare a statement of cash flows.

5–2. (Appendix) Calculating Cash Flows from Operations. The following information was taken from the financial statements of Calendar Company for 1988–1991.

	December 31, 1988	December 31, 1989	December 31, 1990	December 31, 1991
Cash	$ 5,000	$12,000	$14,000	$ 6,000
Accounts receivable	8,000	10,000	6,000	14,000
Inventory	12,000	9,000	12,000	16,000
Prepaid insurance	0	0	2,000	1,000
	$25,000	$31,000	$34,000	$37,000
Accounts payable	$ 5,000	$ 7,000	$12,000	$ 8,000
Accrued wages payable	0	0	3,000	2,000
	$ 5,000	$ 7,000	$15,000	$10,000
Net income	$10,000	$15,000	$18,000	$20,000
Depreciation expense*	$ 3,000	$ 4,000	$ 4,000	$ 5,000

* Assume that depreciation is the only cash expense.

Required:
For each of the years 1989, 1990, and 1991, and for the three-year period ended December 31, 1991, prepare a computation of the cash provided by operations using the indirect method.

5–3. Cash Flow from Operations. Using the worksheet shown in Exhibit 5–10 on the following page, satisfy the following requirements:
1. Determine the cash flow from operations using the direct method.
2. (Appendix) Determine the cash flow from operations using the indirect method.

EXHIBIT 5–9

Hobie's Bus Company

Financial Position Worksheet for 1991

Description	Cash	Accounts Receivable	Supplies Inventory	Bus	Accumulated Depreciation	Accounts Payable	Notes Payable	Paid-in Capital	Retained Earnings
Balances, December 31, 1990	$ 0	$ 0	$ 0	$ 0	$ 0	$ 0	$ 0	$ 0	$ 0
Initial investment by owners	6,000							6,000	
Purchased bus for $2,500 cash and $5,000 note	(2,500)			7,500			5,000		
Cash fares	12,000								12,000 (R)
Credit fares		5,000							5,000 (R)
Payment of one-year insurance premium	(1,000)								(1,000) (E)
Wages paid	(7,500)								(7,500) (E)
Customer payments	2,000	(2,000)							
Supplies purchased			2,000			2,000			
Payments to suppliers	(500)					(500)			
Payment of principal and interest on note	(1,300)						(1,000)		(300) (E)
Supplies used			(1,600)						(1,600) (E)
Repairs and maintenance paid	(1,800)								(1,800) (E)
Depreciation expense					(1,200)				(1,200) (E)
Withdrawal	(3,600)							(3,600)	
Balances, December 31, 1991	$ 1,800	$3,000	$ 400	$7,500	$(1,200)	$1,500	$4,000	$2,400	$3,600

(R) Revenue
(E) Expense

EXHIBIT 5–10

Buena Vista Enterprises

Financial Position Worksheet for 1991

Description	Cash	Accounts Receivable	Merchandise	Prepaid Rent	Equipment	Accumulated Depreciation Equipment	Accounts Payable	Wages Payable	Interest Payable	Mortgage Payable	Paid-in Capital	Retained Earnings
Beginning Position	$1,500	$1,000	$2,500	$200	$6,000	$(1,500)	$1,750	$ 0	$100	$3,000	$4,850	$ 0
Cash sales	1,300											1,300
Purchased merchandise on credit			500				500					
Credit sales		3,500										3,500
Paid rent in advance	(100)			100								
Receipts from customers	2,500	(2,500)										
Payments to suppliers	(1,000)						(1,000)					
Purchased equipment	(500)				1,000					500		
Mortgage payment	(1,000)									(1,000)		
Paid wages	(700)											(700)
Paid advertising	(300)											(300)
Paid interest owing	(100)								(100)			
Purchased merchandise with cash	(200)		200									
Depreciation of equipment						(800)						(800)
Merchandise used			(900)									(900)
Rent expense for period				(150)								(150)
Accrued wages								200				(200)
Interest expense for period (not paid)									80			(80)
Contribution by owner	2,000										2,000	
Ending Position	$3,400	$2,000	$2,300	$150	$7,000	$(2,300)	$1,250 ·	$200	$ 80	$2,500	$6,850	$1,670

Required:
1. Prepare an income statement for the period.
2. Determine the cash flows from operating activities.
3. Prepare a statement of cash flows.

5–7. (Appendix) Preparing a Statement of Cash Flows from Other Statements. Following is the financial position of the Herbert Medical Clinic at December 31, 1990 and 1991.

	December 31, 1990	December 31, 1991
Cash	$ 40,000	$ 45,000
Accounts receivable	80,000	70,000
Inventory	20,000	25,000
Equipment and furnishings	100,000	125,000
Accumulated depreciation:		
Equipment and furnishings	(40,000)	(55,000)
	$200,000	$210,000
Accounts payable	$ 15,000	$ 18,000
Accrued wages payable	5,000	2,000
8% notes payable, due June 30, 1991	50,000	0
Owners' equity:		
Paid-in capital	100,000	140,000
Retained earnings	30,000	50,000
	$200,000	$210,000

During 1991 the clinic reported a net income of $110,000.

Required:
From the information contained in these statements, and stating any assumptions that are logical and necessary, prepare a statement of cash flows for the year 1991.

5–8. (Appendix) Resource Flows from Operations. The financial position of Teton Village Restaurant, Inc., at December 31, 1990 and December 31, 1991, is as follows:

	December 31, 1990	December 31, 1991
Cash	$ 4,000	$ 2,000
Inventory	8,000	7,000
Land	20,000	20,000
Building and equipment	40,000	50,000
Accumulated depreciation:		
Building and equipment	(12,000)	(15,000)
	$60,000	$64,000
Accounts payable	$ 6,000	$ 2,000
Mortgage payable	25,000	30,000
Owners' equity:		
Paid-in capital	20,000	25,000
Retained earnings	9,000	7,000
	$60,000	$64,000

During 1991 Teton Village Restaurant, Inc., reported a net income of $12,000.

Required:

1. Determine the cash flows from operations for 1991.
2. In addition to the cash provided by operations, list other possible sources and uses of cash during 1991 and whether they are due to investing or financing activities. Indicate any assumptions you made.

5–9. Preparing Statements of Cash Flows from Other Financial Statements and Supplemental Information.   The financial statements for the Whitten Manufacturing Company have the amounts shown in thousands.

	December 31, 1991	*December 31, 1990*
Current assets:		
Cash	$ 15	$ 20
Accounts receivable	30	25
Inventory	60	50
Prepaid expenses	5	10
	$110	$105
Property, plant, and equipment (net)	330	295
	$440	$400
Current liabilities:		
Accounts payable	$ 20	$ 25
Accrued expenses	15	10
Estimated income taxes payable	30	25
	$ 65	$ 60
Owners' equity:		
Paid-in capital	$240	$220
Retained earnings	135	120
	$375	$340
	$440	$400

Income Statement for 1991

Net sales	$480
Cost of sales	330
Gross profit	$150
Operating expenses (including depreciation expense of 10)	75
Net income before taxes	$ 75
Provision for federal income taxes	35
Net income	$ 40

Required:

1. Compute the amount of dividends declared and paid during 1991, the value of equipment purchased during 1991, and the value at which capital stock was sold during 1991.
2. Prepare a statement of cash flows using the direct method to determine cash flows from operating activities.

5–10. (Appendix) Preparing a Statement of Cash Flows.   The financial position of the Bulloch Corporation at December 31, 1990 and December 31, 1991 follow.

	December 31, 1990	December 31, 1991
Cash	$ 25,000	$ 21,000
Accounts receivable	15,000	12,000
Inventory	40,000	50,000
Display equipment	25,000	40,000
Accumulated depreciation:		
Display equipment	(5,000)	(8,000)
Delivery truck		6,000
Accumulated depreciation:		
Delivery truck		(1,000)
	$100,000	$120,000
Accounts payable	$ 30,000	$ 25,000
10% notes payable, due September 30, 1994		10,000
Owners' equity:		
Paid-in capital	50,000	60,000
Retained earnings	20,000	25,000
	$100,000	$120,000

Required:

The corporation reported a net income of $25,000 for 1991. During the year 1991 no disposition of long-lived assets or retirements of capital stock place. From the information presented and stating any assumptions that are logical and necessary, prepare a statement showing cash flow from operating activities.

5–11. Comprehensive Statement of Cash Flows. The financial statements for the Cramer Corporation are as follows (amounts in thousands):

	December 31, 1991	December 31, 1990
Current assets:		
Cash	$ 3,000	$15,000
Accounts receivable	10,000	5,000
Inventory	10,000	5,000
Prepaid rent	4,000	2,000
	$ 27,000	$27,000
Notes receivable	8,000	0
Land	36,000	15,000
Plant and equipment	109,000	60,000
Accumulated depreciation	(18,000)	(10,000)
Total Assets	$162,000	$92,000
Current liabilities:		
Accounts payable	$ 32,000	$ 3,000
Accrued wages payable	10,000	12,000
	$ 42,000	$15,000
Bonds payable	40,000	0
Owners' equity		
Paid-in capital	70,000	70,000
Retained earnings	10,000	7,000
	$ 80,000	$77,000
Total liabilities and owners' equity	$162,000	$92,000

Income Statement for 1991

Sales	$100,000
Cost of sales	73,000
Gross profit	$ 27,000
Operating expenses	23,000
	$ 4,000
Gain from sale of land	5,000
Net income before taxes	$ 9,000
Provision for federal income taxes	5,000
Net income	$ 4,000

Other information includes the following:

1. A note receivable was received from selling land with an original cost of $5,000.
2. Depreciation expense is included in operating expenses.

Required:
Prepare a statement of cash flows using the direct method to determine cash flows from operating activities.

5–12. **Interpreting the Statement of Cash Flows.** Exhibit 5–12 shows the statement of changes in financial position (statement of cash flows) from the 1985 annual report of Boise Cascade Corporation and Subsidiaries.

Required:

1. Why are depreciation and cost of company timber harvested added to net income to get cash provided by operations? Is depreciation a source of cash?
2. Gain on sales of operating assets is shown as a reduction to net income to yield cash provided by operations. Explain this treatment.
3. Why are receivables added to net income to get cash provided by operations? What does this adjustment imply?
4. Why are inventories added to net income to get cash provided by operations? What does this adjustment imply?
5. What might be contained in other current assets? Why is the change in this account deducted from net income to get cash provided by operations?
6. Why are accounts payable and accrued liabilities subtracted from net income to get cash provided by operations? What happened to short-term liabilities related to operations during the year?
7. Cash provided by operations is more than twice the net income figure for the year. What explains the vast difference? Is this a good situation?
8. Notes payable is shown as a negative figure in cash provided by financing. What does this indicate?
9. Suppose Boise Cascade had issued some notes payable during 1985. How would this be shown? Should the proceeds be netted against payments made on notes payable to show one amount for the net change in notes payable?
10. Under cash provided by investment, $196,346 is shown as the proceeds from the sale of operating assets. Can the book value (original cost minus accumulated depreciation) of the assets sold be determined from the statement of changes in financial position?
11. Suppose Boise Cascade had received a long-term note from the buyer of the operating assets, rather than cash. Would this affect the treatment of this transaction?

EXHIBIT 5–12

Statements of Changes in Financial Position
Boise Cascade Corporation and Subsidiaries

	Year Ended December 31, 1985 (expressed in thousands)
Cash Provided by Operations	
Net income	$ 104,290
Items in income not (providing) using cash	
Depreciation and cost of company timber harvested	176,320
Deferred income tax provision (benefit)	29,254
Amortization and other	9,718
Gain on sales of operating assets (Note 1)	(31,485)
Receivables	11,284
Inventories	37,807
Other current assets	(2,165)
Accounts payable and accrued liabilities	(110,444)
Current and deferred income taxes	(5,437)
Cash provided by operations	$ 219,142
Cash Provided by (Used for) Financing	
Notes payable	(33,000)
Additions to (payments of) long-term debt, net	(21,094)
Cash provided by (used for) financing	$ (54,094)
Cash Provided by (Used for) Investment	
Sales of operating assets	196,346
Expenditures for property and equipment	(330,192)
Expenditures for timber and timberlands	(6,558)
Purchases of common stock	(13,807)
All other, net	14,959
Cash used for investment	$(139,252)
Cash Dividends Paid	
Common stock	(51,912)
Preferred stock	(10,218)
	$ (62,130)
Increase (Decrease) in Cash and Short-term Investments	(36,334)
Balance at Beginning of the Year	73,865
Balance at End of the Year	$ 37,531

12. The amount received from the sales of operating assets is shown separate from the expenditures for property and equipment. Explain this format.
13. Purchases of common stock is shown as a cash outflow in determining cash provided by investment. What does this imply? Why isn't it shown under cash provided by financing? Where would the proceeds from sale of common stock be shown?
14. Cash dividends paid are shown in a separate section. Where else might this cash outflow be shown?

15. Boise Cascade is explaining the change in cash and short-term investments, rather than just cash. What is included in short-term investments? Why are they considering this equivalent to cash?

16. Boise Cascade's cash balance decreased by $36,334 during 1985. Can you use the statement of changes in financial position to explain this change?

Accounting for the Effects of Changing Prices

CHAPTER SIX

In the earlier chapters we studied different ways of generating economic information useful for business and investment decisions. In turn, we learned about the cash basis of accounting and the accrual basis of accounting. We established that the accrual basis is conventionally used throughout financial accounting in the United States. Prior to that, we introduced the concept of net present value as an economic decision-making criterion.

This chapter introduces two additional types of accounting measurement: price level adjustments and current cost measurements. Both methods directly recognize effects of changing prices, which may be caused by technology changes (e.g., improved assembly line automation or more efficient microchips for pocket computers); specific supply and demand changes (e.g., high demand for housing on the West Coast or oversupply of tobacco products); or general price trends (e.g., increasing energy prices or cheaper air fares). Since changing prices affect economic decision making, it is important to be able to determine their effects.

Example 6–1 | Assume your grandmother gives you $10,000 to help defray the expenses of your university education. Suppose that you do not need the cash until a year from now, and invest it in an insured bank certificate of deposit (CD) which pays 9 percent interest. Thus, a year later, you have $10,900 in the bank.

Now assume that the inflation rate during this same period was 10 percent. Are you economically better off after you earned the bank interest? Obviously not! In terms of purchasing power at the end of the year, it would take $11,000 to be as well off as you were at the beginning of the year. So despite the receipt of the $900 bank interest, you suffered an economic loss. Moreover, the loss is even greater because the $900 interest income is taxable.

Price level adjustments require the use of price indexes to measure the impact of inflation on the business entity. This approach restates all accounting numbers to the same price index level, which is typically the one current at the end of the period covered by the financial statements. This approach also is used to assess monetary gains and losses from being a debtor or a creditor during times of inflation.

Current cost measurements involve the determination of replacement costs of physical assets like inventories, machinery and equipment, buildings, and land at the current balance sheet date. Current cost accounting is used to assess holding gains and losses from owning physical assets during periods of price changes. Both of these alternative measurements typically result in net income amounts and balance sheet numbers different from corresponding figures produced by conventional accrual basis accounting.

Why bother with the effects of changing prices for accounting purposes? The answer is that price changes, when present, distort conventional accounting numbers. Prices of goods and services are the basis of accounting measurements, just like yards measure progress in a football game, tons the cargo loaded on a truck, and degrees Fahrenheit the severity of a fever in the human body. The yard measure in football is absolutely constant—from game to game, between all teams playing, and year after year. Similarly constant are weight measures like tons or heat measure like degrees Fahrenheit.

How fair would a football game be if different teams used yards of different lengths? The home team might like to measure their yards at 32 inches each and require yards of 40 inches in length for the visiting team. This is the type of thing that happens in accounting when changing prices are not recognized. Some transactions are measured and reported in "old" dollars; for example, when a building was purchased 20 years ago. Other transactions are recognized in terms of "today's" dollars, as when a new roof is installed on the building. If purchasing power of the dollar (illustrated in Example 6–1) changed during the intervening 20 years, we really use yardsticks of different lengths to measure the original building purchase and later the cost of replacing its roof. The measuring unit is still the dollar, but its economic value (purchasing power) has changed. If we pretend that no change has occurred and add "old" and "current" dollar amounts indiscriminately, we surely distort the results of our accounting procedures.

CHANGING PRICES AND PRICE INDEXES

Prices of all goods and services in the economy do not rise and fall together. Some rise or fall faster than others. Therefore it is always important to distinguish between changes for prices of specific goods and services, and those for categories of prices in general. Health care costs are rising in most countries while computer hardware costs are falling. These are examples of specific price changes occurring at disparate rates.

General price changes are related to groups of goods or services and are often measured by price indexes. For example, the U.S. Department of Labor

EXHIBIT 6–1

Selected Price Changes

	Average Prices		
	Year 1	*Year 2*	*Year 3*
Small personal computer	$ 600	$ 500	$ 450
Monthly apartment rental	300	400	450
Physical examination	250	300	325
Case of auto oil	50	75	100
Woman's dress suit	300	375	425
	$1,500	$1,650	$1,750

publishes quarterly the gross national product (GNP) deflator, and monthly the consumer price index for all urban consumers (CPI-U). The GNP deflator is a percentage that can be applied to the entire economic output of the country to neutralize the effects of price changes. Deflated GNP dollars are sometimes referred to as real GNP.

Consumers are also interested in how changing prices affect them. By assuming what it takes for an average family to purchase shelter, food, and other essentials, prices can be compared over time and the percentage of change calculated. This is illustrated in Exhibit 6–1 and the related explanations.

The GNP deflator, the consumer price index, and other indexes such as stock and bond prices, wholesale prices, and export commodity prices all measure and report price changes.

Variations in the purchasing power of money have triggered intense accounting controversy. Some believe that it is essential for accounting to recognize formally and fully the changing purchasing power of money. Other believe equally strongly that more consistent and more objective accounting information is obtained by assuming, for accounting measurement purposes, that the value of money is constant. In countries where hyperinflation prevails, there is no question that changing values of national currencies must be completely recognized in accounting. For instance, the 1989 annual rate of inflation in Argentina was 5,000 percent![1] Thus all Argentine accounting measurements are prive level adjusted.

On the other hand, countries with very low inflation rates usually opt for the constancy-of-money-values assumption as far as accounting is concerned. For example, in the mid-1970s and early 1980s, large U.S. corporations had to report effects of changing prices in their financial reports to the public. As U.S. inflationary pressures subsided, this requirement was rescinded.

Exhibit 6–1 illustrates effects of changing prices. We assume that the five items identified are a representative sample of consumer goods and services in the economy.

The hypothetical numbers in Exhibit 6–1 suggest a period of inflation. In year 2 it takes $1,650 to purchase the same group of goods and services which could have been bought on average for $1,500 in year 1. Then in year 3 it takes $1,750 to buy the same bundle of goods and services. Note that the price of automobile oil doubled over the three-year period while the price of a personal

[1] *Christian Science Monitor*, January 11, 1990, p. 1.

computer declined. Also, the relative relationship between the prices changed. A small personal computer was twice the cost of monthly apartment rental in year 1, whereas the two commanded exactly the same price in year 3.

We can calculate a general inflation rate for years 2 and 3 as follows:

$$\begin{aligned}\text{General inflation rate} \atop \text{Year 2} &= \frac{\text{Year 2 average prices} - \text{Year 1 average prices}}{\text{Year 1 average prices}} \\[6pt] &= \frac{\$1,650 - \$1,500}{\$1,500} \\[6pt] &= 10\%\end{aligned}$$

Similarly the year 3 general inflation rate is 100 (1,750 − 1,650) divided by 1,650 or approximately 6.1 percent. For the entire two-year period we have 250 divided by 1,500 equalling 16.7 percent. This is higher than the sum of the annual rates calculated earlier because in year 3 we had the compounding effect of more inflation in year 3 on top of the earlier year 2 inflation. Indexing helps to represent these effects for statistical and other calculational (including accounting) purposes.

CONSTRUCTING PRICE LEVEL INDEXES

An index is a ratio. It measures a given number in terms of a base number. For our purposes, an index states a year's average prices in terms of some other year's (base year) average prices.

Price Level Index. A price level index is a ratio representing the prices of a particular bundle of goods and services at one point in time relative to the prices of the same bundle of goods and services at some specified reference point in time (usually called base year).

Using the numbers from Exhibit 6–1, let us choose year 1 as the base year and set its index value at 100. This means that the $1,500 on that particular monetary scale is equivalent to 100 on our price level index scale. Now the question is, what index number has the same relationship to 100 as $1,650 has to $1,500? Arithmetically letting i_2 (for year 2) represent the unknown value we have

$$\frac{i_2}{100} = \frac{\$1,650}{\$1,500}$$

$$i_2 = \frac{1,650}{1,500} \times 100$$

$$i_2 = 110$$

Keeping year 1 as the base year, the price level index for year 3 is calculated similarly.

$$i_3 = \frac{1,750}{1,500} \times 100$$

$$i_3 = 116.7$$

In other words, under the assumptions we have made, the general price index for year 3 is 116.7 in terms of average general prices prevailing in year 1. Of course i_3 could have been calculated in terms of i_2; that is, the relative average price change from year 2 to year 3 can be related to the year 2 price level index to reach the same result. Arithmetically,

$$i_3 = \frac{1,750}{1,650} \times 110$$

$$i_3 = 116.7$$

The calculation of index numbers lets us express any set of relative prices (specific or general) in terms of any set of base period prices. Note, however, that index numbers are statistical scores whose validity depends heavily on their underlying assumptions. One assumption is that relative prices can be accurately determined or estimated. Another assumption is that the group of goods and services to be measured remains constant during the time period covered by the index. If these assumptions cannot be sustained, the reliability of the index is called into question.

PRICE-LEVEL-ADJUSTED (P-L-A) FINANCIAL STATEMENTS

One method of recognizing the effects of changing prices for accounting purposes is to prepare P-L-A financial statements. The idea here is to start with conventionally prepared financial statements, based on historical cost measurements, and apply price level index adjustments. *Therefore P-L-A accounting is strictly an extension of historical cost accounting.* P-L-A accounting is generally used throughout South America. It was required of large U.S. corporations from 1979 to 1985. The U.S. requirement was contained in the *Statement of Financial Accounting Standards No. 33* issued in September 1979 by the Financial Accounting Standards Board (FASB). The FASB rescinded this requirement with its *Statement No. 82* issued in November 1984.

Why bother with P-L-A financial statements? The answer is that in periods of inflation, conventional financial statements based on historical cost create money illusions that often lead to suboptimal economic decisions.

Example 6–2 | Weyerhaeuser Company is a large forest products and paper company. In its 1985 Annual Report it reported compliance with SFAS No. 33 by using a mixture of P-L-A and current cost measurements (discussed later in this chapter). Here are the company's explanations of its procedures:

> Changes in prices of product inventories were measured by changes in the Company's own cost of producing and purchasing currently goods held for sale. Changes in specific prices were used to measure property and equipment on a current cost basis.
>
> The Company's timber and timberlands and certain related assets have not been adjusted for changes in specific prices. An acceptable methodology for doing so is still under consideration by the FASB. These assets and leased property under capital leases were measured using the CPI-U [consumer price index—urban].
>
> Materials and supplies and all other assets, net, were not re-measured as their historical cost reasonably approximates current cost.

Application of these procedures showed the following comparisons with conventional accrual accounting results:

Net Assets Adjusted for Changing Prices

At December 29, 1985	As Reported	Current Cost
Product inventories	$ 379,399	$ 561,744
Materials and supplies	167,376	167,376
Property and equipment	3,432,377	4,862,705
Timber and timberlands	645,630	1,880,105
Leased property under capital leases	58,750	103,382
All other assets, net	596,253	596,253
	$5,279,785	$8,171,595
Deduct net monetary liabilities	1,955,734	1,927,026
Net assets	$3,324,051	$6,244,569

Consolidated Earnings Adjusted for Changing Prices

Year Ended December 29, 1985	As Reported	Current Cost
Net sales	$5,205,579	$5,205,579
Real estate and financial services	111,914	111,914
Other income, net	30,419	(7,910)
	$5,347,912	$5,309,583
Operating costs and expenses:		
Other than depreciation, amortization and fee stumpage*	4,583,822	4,602,437
Depreciation, amortization and fee stumpage	350,155	611,530
Interest expense	110,219	110,219
	$5,044,196	$5,324,186
Earnings before income taxes	$ 303,716	$ (14,603)
Income taxes	103,600	103,600
Net earnings	$ 200,116	$ (118,203)
Gain from decline in the purchasing power of net amounts owed		$ 70,401

Fee stumpage is the cost of standing timber and is charged to fee timber disposals as fee timber is harvested, lost as the result of casualty, or sold. (Note 4, 1985 Weyerhaeuser Company Annual Report.)

Reported net earnings of $200 million turned into a net loss of $118 million after effects of changing prices were taken into account. During 1985, Weyerhaeuser Company also paid $198 million in cash dividends to its shareholders. Was this dividend payment a distribution of the company's earnings or was it a partial liquidation of the corporation's owners' equity?

There are many arguments both for and against P-L-A accounting. Those supporting P-L-A financial reports point out that there is great merit in keeping the accounting measurement unit constant; that is, in reporting all financial statement amounts in terms of dollars of the same purchasing power. They also argue that readers of financial reports should be given explicit information on the effects of purchasing power changes so that more informed business and investment decisions can be made.

On the other hand, detractors argue that price indexes are statistical averages which are unlikely to be meaningful in individual personal or company situations, and that the entire P-L-A procedure is too costly and cumbersome to employ when general inflation is relatively moderate. Furthermore, opponents fear that P-L-A financial statements are likely to mislead statement users and therefore impair informed business and investment decisions even more than conventional historical cost financial statements.

P-L-A PROCEDURES

We are now in a position to illustrate how to carry out price level adjustments. Recall that our objective is to produce a balance sheet and an income statement which reflect constant dollar measurements; that is, to adjust all original transaction costs by an index of the price level change since the time of transaction. The necessary procedures are divided into four separate steps.

Step One. First we must obtain conventionally prepared, historical cost-based financial statements, select an appropriate price level index to be used, and classify all items in the financial statements as monetary or nonmonetary.

Monetary Financial Statement Items. Monetary financial statement items include cash, rights to receive fixed amounts of dollars at future dates, and obligations to pay fixed amounts of dollars at future dates. All financial statement items not meeting this definition are classified as nonmonetary. As explained and illustrated later in this chapter, changing prices affect monetary and nonmonetary items in different ways.

For ease of reference we again use the financial statements of Fancy Flavors, Inc., developed in earlier chapters. The July 31, 1991 Statement of Financial Position is based on the information in Example 3–1. The corresponding statement for July 31, 1992, as well as the Income Statement for the year then ended, are new information and are presented in Exhibits 6–2 and Exhibit 6–3, respectively.

Following the guidance provided by *SFAS No. 33*, all amounts in Exhibits 6–2 and 6–3 are classified as monetary or nonmonetary. We assume that the price index stood at 100 at July 31, 1991, and at 110 one year later. This change occurred evenly throughout the year, so that the average index for the year is 105.

Step Two. In the next step we calculate monetary gains and losses.

Monetary gains and losses. Monetary gains (losses) are increases (decreases) in purchasing power that result from holding monetary assets and/or carrying monetary liabilities during a period of changing prices.

Example 6–3 | Dr. Mason borrows $100,000 from her local bank on January 1, 1991 to finance the purchase of some new high-tech diagnostic equipment. At that time the CPI-U (consumer price index—urban) was 210. She pays interest on this loan regularly every quarter. On December 31, 1993, the full $100,000 is paid back to the bank. The CPI-U then was 252.

EXHIBIT 6–2

Fancy Flavors, Inc.

Comparative Statements of Financial Position
(in thousands)

	July 31, 1991	July 31, 1992	M = Monetary N = Nonmonetary
Assets:			
Cash	$ 70	$ 200	M
Accounts receivable	0	80	M
Prepaid rent	60	120	N
Ice cream inventory	30	70	N
Supplies	20	30	N
Equipment	600	720	N
Less accumulated depreciation	0	(120)	N
Total assets	$780	$1,100	
Liabilities and Owners' Equity:			
Accounts payable	$ 30	$ 70	M
Accrued liabilities	0	30	M
Bank loan payable	600	450	M
Owner's equity			
Paid-in capital	150	150	N
Retained earnings	0	400	N
Total liabilities and owners' equity	$780	$1,100	N

EXHIBIT 6–3

Fancy Flavors, Inc.

Income Statement
For the Year Ending July 31, 1992
(in thousands)

		M = Monetary N = Nonmonetary
Revenue from sales of ice cream	$3,500	N
Cost of ice cream sold	1,100	N
Operating expenses		
Rent	240	N
Supplies used	180	N
Salaries and wages	940	N
Equipment depreciation	120	N
Interest on loan	70	N
Miscellaneous (heat, light, etc.)	140	N
Federal income taxes	185	N
Net operating income	$ 525	
Less: Tornado loss	$ 5	N
Net income	$ 520	

If Dr. Mason would have returned the same purchasing power to the bank that she borrowed three years earlier, she would have had to pay $100,000 × 252/210 = $120,000 (i.e., it took $120,000 on December 31, 1993 to purchase the same bundle of goods and services that $100,000 bought on January 1, 1991). Since only $100,000 was paid back, Dr. Mason received a monetary gain of $20,000 ($120,000 − $100,000) from this transaction.

Monetary gains and losses have two components: (1) purchasing power gain or loss for a period on beginning monetary balances; and (2) gain or loss on additions to or subtractions from beginning balances during the period. As illustrated in Example 6–4, Fancy Flavors had a monetary gain on its accounts payable during 1991–1992 because it will be able to pay off its accounts payable obligations with "cheaper" dollars than the money that would have been required when the obligations originally were incurred.

Example 6–4 | **Monetary Gain on Accounts Payable**

	Actual Monetary Amounts	*Index*	*July 31, 1992 Purchasing Power Equivalent*
July 31, 1991 balance	$30,000	110/100	$33,000
1991–1992 additions (change during year)	40,000	110/105	41,900
Totals	$70,000		$74,900
1991–1992 monetary gain			$ 4,900

Calculating the amount of monetary gain or loss for each monetary item of a business can be tedious, especially regarding the many transactions normally occurring in the cash account. Therefore an estimating procedure is typically used to approximate monetary gains and losses. This estimating process combines all monetary assets and liabilities as of a given date into a single amount called *net monetary position*. From Exhibit 6–2 we note that on July 31, 1991, Fancy Flavors had monetary assets of $70,000, and monetary liabilities of $630,000. Hence its net monetary position was a net monetary liability position of $560,000 ($70,000 − $630,000).

To apply the estimating procedure, we follow the same steps as those illustrated in Example 6–4 for accounts payable. First we multiply the net monetary position at the beginning of the year by the ratio of the ending and beginning price indexes and subtract the balance of the beginning net monetary position. This procedure is equivalent to multiplying the beginning net monetary position by the rate of inflation for the year. If a firm had a beginning net monetary asset position and inflation occurred during the year, we would expect a monetary loss. If there was a beginning net monetary liability position, we would expect a monetary gain. (Refer to Example 6–3 for the reasoning involved.)

Next we calculate the increase or decrease in net monetary position over the year, multiply the change by the ratio of the ending and average price indexes, and then subtract the amount of the change. The difference is the monetary gain or loss incurred during the year. Given increasing prices during the year, a change toward a larger net asset position means a monetary loss. If the change is toward a net monetary liability position, we can expect a monetary gain. Example 6–5 presents the calculations for Fancy Flavors for 1991–1992.

Example 6–5 | **Fancy Flavors, Inc.**

Monetary Gains and Losses 1991–1992

	July 31, 1991	*July 31, 1992*	*Change 1991–1992*
Monetary assets	$ 70,000	$ 280,000	$210,000
Monetary liabilities	(630,000)	(550,000)	80,000
Net monetary liability position	$(560,000)	$(270,000)	$290,000

General price-level index:		
	July 31, 1991	100
	Average for 1991–1992	105
	July 31, 1992	110

	Net Monetary Gain (Loss)
Monetary gain on beginning Net monetary liability position $(560,000 \times 110/100) - 560,000$	$ 56,000
Monetary loss on change for 1991–1992 $(290,000 \times 110/105) - 290,000$	(13,800)
Net monetary gain for 1991–1992	$ 42,200

Step Three. We next restate all nonmonetary items in the financial statements by applying an appropriate price level index. All amounts are to appear in purchasing power equivalents as of the end of the year (balance sheet date). Events and transactions occurring relatively evenly throughout the year are restated on the basis of the average price index for the period. This is the case with nearly all items in the income statement.

In general the P-L-A restatement method for nonmonetary items is

$$\text{HISTORICAL COST AMOUNT} \times \frac{\text{PRICE LEVEL INDEX AT BALANCE SHEET DATE}}{\text{PRICE LEVEL INDEX AT TIME OF PURCHASE}} = \text{P-L-A AMOUNT}$$

Exhibits 6–4 and 6–5 contain the restatements of all nonmonetary items earlier identified. The restated amounts are obtained using the following procedures and assumptions. With regard to prepaid rent, two months' rent ($40,000) remained prepaid all year long (as rent security deposit). Thus $40,000 is restated for the entire year by using the ratio 110/100. An additional rental prepayment of $80,000 was made on July 30, 1992. This is restated at 110/110 in recognition of the timing of the additional prepayment.

All of the ice cream remaining in the inventory at July 31, 1992 was purchased during June and July of 1992. It is therefore restated at an index number

EXHIBIT 6–4

Fancy Flavors, Inc.

P-L-A Financial Position
July 31, 1992

	Historical Cost	Ratio	P-L-A Basis
Assets:			
Cash	$ 200,000	Not restated*	$ 200,000
Accounts receivable	80,000	Not restated*	80,000
Prepaid rent	120,000	40,000 × 110/100	44,000
		80,000 × 110/110	80,000
Ice cream inventory	70,000	110/109	70,600
Supplies	30,000	110/105	31,400
Equipment	720,00	510,000 × 110/100	561,000
		210,000 × 110/105	220,000
Less: Accumulated depreciation	(120,000)	102,000 × 110/100	(112,200)
		18,000 × 110/105	(18,900)
Total assets	$1,100,000		$1,155,900
Liabilities and Owners' Equity			
Accounts payable	$ 70,000	Not restated*	$ 70,000
Accrued liabilities	30,00	Not restated*	30,000
Bank loan payable	450,000	Not restated*	450,000
Owners' Equity			
Paid-in capital	150,000	110/100	165,000
Retained earnings	400,000	Reconciliation item	440,900
Total liabilities and owners' equity	$1,100,000		$1,155,900

* Price level change effect already recognized and calculated in step two.

estimated for the last six weeks of the annual index (i.e., we use 109 as the index number at the time of purchase because six weeks are approximately one-tenth of one year).

The supplies on hand at July 31, 1991 were used up during the year and those on hand at July 31, 1992 were acquired evenly throughout the year. Hence the average index for 1991–1992 is appropriate for the P-L-A restatement of this item.

Concerning equipment, we learned in Chapter 5 that $150,000 worth of new equipment was purchased in September 1991. Another $60,000 of new equipment was purchased early in July 1992. Thus $510,000 of the original equipment remains at the end of the year which must therefore be restated for the price level effect of the full year. For convenience, the new additions are restated at the yearly average index. Accumulated depreciation in the balance sheet and the depreciation expense in the income statement are restated according to the same considerations.

With regard to the bank loan payable, even though the principal balance was reduced during the year, we assume that interest was paid evenly throughout

EXHIBIT 6–5

Fancy Flavors, Inc.

P-L-A Income Statement
Year Ending July 31, 1992

	Historical Cost	Ratio	P-L-A Basis
Revenue from ice cream sales	$3,500,000	110/105	$3,666,700
Cost of ice cream sold	(1,100,000)	110/105	(1,152,400)
Rent	(240,000)	110/105	(251,400)
Supplies used	(180,000)	110/105	(188,600)
Salaries and wages	(940,000)	110/105	(984,800)
Equipment depreciation	(120,000)	102,000 × 110/100	(112,200)
		18,000 × 110/105	(18,900)
Interest on loan	(70,000)	110/105	(73,300)
Miscellaneous (heat, light, etc.)	(140,000)	110/105	(146,700)
Federal income taxes	(185,000)	110/105	(193,800)
Net operating income	$ 525,000		$ 544,600
Less: Tornado loss	(5,000)	110/100	(5,500)
Add: Net monetary gain	0		42,200
Conventional net income	$ 520,000		
P-L-A net income			$ 581,300
Cash dividend paid monthly	$ 120,000	110/105	$ 125,700
Retained earnings	$ 400,000		$ 455,600

the year. The tornado loss occurred in August 1991 and is, therefore, restated for a full year's price level effect. The cash dividend was paid to the owners monthly during 1991–1992 and thus restated at the average index for the year.

Step Four. Finally all the information now at hand is combined into a P-L-A income statement for the year and a P-L-A financial position statement at the end of the year. These are also illustrated in Exhibits 6–4 and 6–5.

It is important to note that the monetary assets and liabilities are not restated, since their respective year-end balances already express the then-current purchasing power. We note a discrepancy between the P-L-A retained earnings amounts appearing in the two exhibits. The difference relates to the estimating procedures used for the P-L-A calculations (e.g., net monetary position, equipment purchases, and cost of ice cream sold). In a real-world situation, the difference would be fully analyzed and properly assigned to individual accounts. However, the detail involved in doing this reaches beyond the scope of the present book.

Even though there was a 10% decline in the purchasing power of money for the year under consideration. Fancy Flavors, Inc., managed a net monetary gain under P-L-A accounting. How was this possible? Since they borrowed very heavily at the start of their business oeprations, they benefited greatly from being a debtor during an inflationary period (see Example 6–5).

The P-L-A financial position statement (Exhibit 6–4) shows all year-end balances at dollar amounts reflecting year-end purchasing power (i.e., all were adjusted to the year-end price index). Put differently, a uniform measurement procedure was applied on each item to compensate for the timing effects of the original transactions. Thus we have comparable figures throughout the statement and can quickly determine how changing prices impacted the financial position of the enterprise.

On the P-L-A income statement (Exhibit 6–5) we find the inflation effects on business operations. In the Weyerhaeuser example (6–2), the sales revenue was not restated, which produced a P-L-A net loss in comparison to net income measured on the basis of historical cost. For Fancy Flavors, Inc., we restated all income statement items, which produced a P-L-A gain. In addition, as already mentioned, there was a net monetary gain. Thus Fancy Flavors, Inc. shows a P-L-A net gain for its first year of operations. Whether sales revenues are restated or not is a matter of interpretation only. The key point is that the P-L-A amounts, together with the net monetary gain or loss, provide ready information on how enterprise performance is affected by the impact of changing prices.

CURRENT COST (C-C) ACCOUNTING

The topic of current cost accounting is introduced only briefly. It involves many complex technical procedures which render it most suitable for intermediate and advanced accounting courses. We already mentioned that large U.S. corporations had to report current cost financial statements during the early 1980s (see Example 6–2). One reason for rescinding this requirement was the high preparation cost of the C-C financial statements.

> **Current cost** is the normal business cost to obtain currently an existing product or service of equivalent capability.

The foregoing definition equates C-C with the current replacement cost of an existing asset or liability (e.g., a service contract or guarantee on an item sold to a customer). In the accounting literature, the terms *current value* and *replacement value* are sometimes used to mean the same thing as C-C. For example, Dutch financial statements regularly refer to "replacement value" in connection with C-C reporting.

What sets C-C accounting apart from P-L-A accounting is its complete departure from original transaction costs. C-C accounting is based on a *physical capital* concept. It views a business enterprise as a reservoir of physical productive capacity used to provide products and services to customers. Replacement of these physical resources as needed is what keeps an enterprise in business. Hence the C-C idea involves *current* replacement cost rather than some *past* transaction cost. (Also note the definition used by the Weyerhaeuser Company as reprinted in Example 6–2.)

Following the earlier definition of C-C, we observe that its largest impact occurs on nonmonetary assets like inventory, plant and equipment, and land. These items are stated at their end-of-period C-C *regardless* of their beginning-of-period C-C or their original cost. Therefore, under C-C accounting each individual accounting period is independent of all other accounting periods.

Monetary assets and liabilities are typically not restated for C-C accounting purposes because their end-of-period amounts are effectively the equivalent of their C-C amounts.

Simplified C-C Accounting Illustration

Land Holders Ltd. speculates in parcels of land for real estate development. Its transactions on five parcels of land and their respective year-end C-C values are shown in Example 6–6. For the sake of computational simplicity we assume that all purchases and sales occur near the end of each year indicated.

Example 6–6 | **Land Holders Ltd.**

		Land Parcels			
		1988–1992 Purchases and (Sales)			
Parcel	*1988*	*1989*	*1990*	*1991*	*1992*
A	$30,000			($ 50,000)	
B	80,000		($210,000)		
C		$ 50,000	(20,000)		
D			120,000		
E			60,000		($ 90,000)
		1988–1992 Year-end C-C Values			
Parcel	*1988*	*1989*	*1990*	*1991*	*1992*
A	$30,000	$ 35,000	$ 45,000	$50,000	
B	80,000	155,000	210,000		
C		50,000	20,000		
D			120,000	140,000	$200,000
E			60,000	80,000	90,000

How would these data be reported in financial statements?

Before answering this question, we must introduce the concept of *holding gains or losses* which is central to C-C accounting. We also refer to the definition of realization given in Chapter 3: Realization occurs "when goods or services are exchanged for cash or claims to cash." If the C-C of a nonmonetary asset is higher than its original transaction (historical) cost, the difference is a holding gain. This holding gain is unrealized until the asset is sold or used up in the production of other goods and/or services. Total unrealized holding gains (losses) are reported in C-C statements of financial position.

Unrealized holding gain (loss). An unrealized holding gain (loss) is the difference between end-of-period current (replacement) cost and the original transaction cost of assets and liabilities on hand at the end of the period.

Holding gains or losses become realized when the related asset or liability is sold, exchanged for a claim to cash, or used up in the production of other goods and/or services. Realized holding gains (losses) are reported in C-C income statements.

Returning to Example 6–6, at year-end 1989 the three parcels of land then on hand will be carried at a total value of $240,000 on the C-C statement of financial position: Parcel A at $35,000; B at $155,000; and C at $50,000. These three parcels have a total purchase cost of $160,000. Therefore $80,000 is reported

EXHIBIT 6–6

Land Holders Ltd.

Partial 1990 C-C Income Statement

Revenue from sale of parcels B and C	$230,000
Less: C-C of parcels sold*	(205,000)
C-C operating income before expenses	$ 25,000
Add: Realized holding gains†	75,000
C-C realized income before expenses	$100,000
Unrealized holding gain for 1990 (on parcel A)‡	$ 10,000

* *Valued at 1989 year-end C-C. (Note: C-C determinations are made annually at year-end.)*
† *This is the unrealized holding gain on parcel B for 1989 which is realized by virtue of parcel B's sale in 1990. (Note: Holding gains or losses for parcels B and C for 1990 are not separately recognized since the parcels were sold before the end of the year.)*
‡ *Parcels D and E were just purchased. There was no 1990 holding gain on them.*

as unrealized holding gain among the owners' equity items on the December 31, 1989 statement of financial position.

At year-end 1990 we observe two parcels sold (B and C) and three still in inventory. The three still in inventory are carried at $225,000 in the C-C financial position statement with an unrealized holding gain of $15,000 in owners' equity. The $15,000 of unrealized holding gain relates only to parcel A, with $5,000 gained in 1989 and another $10,000 gained during 1990. Thus the $15,000 of unrealized holding gain is a cumulative total.

The related C-C income statement effect is illustrated in Exhibit 6–6.

At year-end 1991, with parcel A sold and parcels D and E still in inventory, the C-C statement of financial position, as well as the C-C income statement, will show an unrealized holding gain of $40,000 on parcels D and E. The 1991 C-C income statement will report $50,000 in revenue from the sale of parcel A, $45,000 as the C-C of the parcel sold, and $15,000 of realized holding gain on parcel A for the prior years 1989 and 1990.

Concluding Observations

From Exhibit 6–6 we observe that C-C operating income plus realized holding gains equal C-C realized income, which in turn equals conventional accrual accounting income (sales price of parcels B and C of $230,000 less their historical costs of $130,000). Therefore, C-C accounting changes only the periods in which certain gains and losses are reported—but not the eventual totals.

Depreciation accounting is fairly complicated under C-C procedures. The current year's depreciation expense is always proportional to the year-end C-C amounts of the assets being depreciated. If C-C depreciable amounts increase over the years, then prior years' depreciation charges are insufficient to cover the later higher amounts. Hence retroactive depreciation charges are sometimes encountered in C-C financial statements.

Larger companies in Australia, the U.K., and the Netherlands occasionally publish formal C-C financial statements in their regular annual reports.

SUMMARY

In this chapter we have confronted financial accounting with the inflation phenomenon. Various effects of changing prices were considered and construction of price level index numbers explained. Then the idea of price level adjustments in financial accounting was launched. We explained and demonstrated the procedures involved and derived an illustrative set of P-L-A financial statements. The calculation of monetary gains and losses is a central feature of P-L-A accounting. Then current cost accounting was introduced. We noted its complete break from any transaction-based accounting and presented a limited illustration of its application. The concept of holding gains and losses is central to current cost accounting.

Questions for Review and Discussion

6–1. Define

    a. Price level index
    b. Price-level-adjusted net income
    c. Price-level-adjusted operating income
    d. Monetary gain (loss)
    e. Current cost
    f. Realized holding gains
    g. Unrealized holding gains
    h. Current-cost-based net income

6–2. Given that all economic units have unique preferences for different kinds of goods and services, how can we justify adjusting original transaction amounts for changes in the general purchasing power of the dollar?

6–3. Briefly explain how a price level index is constructed. In what way does technological change enter into the construction and use of a general price-level index?

6–4. Suppose you have been asked to construct a price level index for the U.S. consumer:

    a. How would you go about constructing such an index?
    b. What characteristics would you like it to have?
    c. Would you use the same index for the Northwest Computer Manufacturing Company? Explain.

6–5. In preparing a general price-level-adjusted income statement, the revenue recorded under the conventional accounting model should be adjusted for the change in the general level of prices between the date of sale and the end of the period. True or false? Defend your position.

6–6. Explain why debtors gain and creditors lose in times of general inflation.

6–7. **a.** How do we distinguish monetary assets (liabilities) from nonmonetary assets (liabilities)?

    b. Classify each of the following as to whether it is a monetary or a nonmonetary item. Explain, in each case, why you chose the classification you did.

        Cash
        Merchandise inventory
        Marketable securities
        Note payable
        Obligation to deliver goods in the future
        Accounts receivable

Goods purchased but not yet paid for
A note payable secured by a mortgage
U.S. government bonds held by the firm
Taxes owed to the federal government
A parcel of land owned

6–8. When prices generally increase, owners of monetary assets lose while owners of nonmonetary assets gain. True or false? Defend your position.

6–9. When prices generally rise, conventional accounting operating income is clearly irrelevant as a measure of enterprise performance in the long-run cash-generating-ability sense. Do you agree or disagree? Defend your position.

6–10. Price-level-adjusted operating income has all of the properties in times of changing prices that conventional accounting operating income has when prices are static. Do you agree or disagree? Defend your position.

6–11. Barden Corporation, a manufacturer with large investments in plant and equipment, began operations in 1965. The company's history has been one of expansion in sales, production, and physical facilities. Recently some concern has been expressed that the conventional financial statements do not provide sufficient information for decisions by investors. After consideration of proposals for various types of supplementary financial statements to be included in the 1991 annual report, management has decided to present a balance sheet as of December 31, 1991, and a statement of income and retained earnings for 1991, both restated for changes in the general price level.

    a. On what basis can it be contended that Barden's conventional statements should be restated for changes in the general price level?

    b. Distinguish between financial statements restated for general price-level changes and current cost financial statements.

    c. Distinguish between monetary and nonmonetary assets and liabilities, as the terms are used in general price-level accounting. Give examples of each.

    d. Indicate the major similarities and differences between the proposed supplementary statements and the corresponding conventional statements.

    e. Assuming that in the future Barden will want to present comparative supplementary statements, can the 1991 supplementary statements be presented in 1992 without adjustment? Explain.

(AICPA adapted)

6–12. It is asserted that general price-level accounting does not depart in principle from the conventional accounting model, but that the current cost model does. Explain the basis for this proposition.

6–13. Explain the physical capital concept.

6–14. Assume that the income tax law is changed such that holding gains realized by a going concern are excluded from taxable income in order to allow the firm to maintain its physical capital. What tax treatment would you propose for the accumulated holding gains at the time the firm decides to liquidate its operations and distribute all of its assets (presumably in the form of cash after liquidation) to the shareholders?

6–15. Under the current cost model, what values should be assigned to (*a*) monetary assets and liabilities; (*b*) inventory; and (*c*) plant and equipment?

Problems

6–1. Present Value and the Price Level. Mrs. Ann Smith, in looking forward to retirement, invested $10,000 on January 1, 1981, in U.S. government bonds. The bonds paid interest at a rate of 10 percent per year, compounded, with repayment of principal and interest on January 1, 1991. In effect, she postponed consumption in 1981 in favor of consumption during her retirement. At the time she invested, her time preference rate between current and future consumption was 10 percent and she expected no inflation. However, during the 1981 to 1991 time period, the price level moved from a beginning level of 100 to a 1991 level of 140.

Required:

1. In retrospect (i.e., on January 1, 1991), how do you suppose Mrs. Smith felt about her investment? Explain.
2. If she had anticipated the inflation, what is the maximum amount she would have paid for the investment in 1981?

6–2. Present Value and the Price Level. Mr. Al Johnson is considering purchase of a bond with a face value of $5,000 which is to be repaid in six years. It has a coupon interest rate of 6 percent. He realizes that the price level has been rising at an average rate of 3 percent per year during the last two years and expects inflation to continue at that rate for the life of the bond.

Required:

1. How might Mr. Johnson recognize this in considering the investment?
2. What is the maximum amount he would be willing to pay for this bond under these circumstances if his time preference rate is 4 percent for cash flows of constant purchasing power?

6–3. Computation of Price Level Indexes. Suppose the U.S. Bureau of Labor Statistics had been buying what it considered to be a representative "basket" of consumer goods over the last six years with year-end costs as follows:

1985	$2,400
1986	2,700
1987	2,500
1988	3,000
1989	3,300
1990	3,200

Required:

Construct a price level index based on these figures, using 1988 as the base year. What is the rate of inflation (deflation) in each of the years?

6–4. Differential Monetary Gains. On January 2, 1990, a group of wealthy investors formed three separate companies and invested $1 million in each company. Alpha Company invested its entire $1 million in a piece of land zoned for a business park development. Beta Company lent its $1 million to Delta Company. Delta Company in turn invested its own $1 million, the $1 million it borrowed from Beta Company, and an additional $3 million borrowed from a bank, in a money market fund. The general price level stood at 150 on January 2 and 180 on December 31, 1990.

Required:

1. For each company, state how it would carry its assets in its financial position statement as of December 31, 1990 using P-L-A.
2. For each company, calculate the monetary gain or loss appearing in its respective 1990 P-L-A income statements. (Note: a money market fund is a monetary asset.)

6–5. Computation of Monetary Gains (Losses.) The Ace Novelty Company has experienced the following changes in its accounts receivable during the past year:

Beginning balance	$ 23,000
Sales on account January through March	46,000
Sales on account April through June	41,000
Sales on account July through September	33,000
Sales on account October through December	52,000
Payments received (uniformly during year)	160,000

The beginning price-level index was at 100. Average quarterly indexes were 105, 110, 115, and 120, respectively, with an ending price-level index of 125. The average index during the year was 112.5. Compute the monetary gain (loss) from accounts receivable during the year. Is it a gain or a loss? Why?

6–6. Monetary Gains (Losses)—Annual versus Quarterly Data. Suppose you had only the following information concerning the changes in accounts receivable for the Ace Novelty Company during the past year:

Beginning balance	$ 23,000
Sales on account	172,000
Payments received on account	160,000

The beginning price-level index was 100. During the year, the price level index averaged 112.5 and was at a level of 125 at year-end.

Required:

1. Assuming sales and payments on account occurred uniformly during the year, what is the monetary gain (loss) on accounts receivable?
2. Compare this with your answer in problem 6–5. Explain the differences.

6–7. Calculating General Price-Level-Adjusted Values. Calculate the specified values for each of the following independent cases.

Case 1. The conventional accounting balance sheet of the Root company showed the original cost of depreciable assets as $5 million at December 31, 1990, and $6 million at December 31, 1991. These assets are being depreciated on a straight-line basis over a ten-year period with no salvage value. Acquisitions of $1 million were made on January 1, 1991. A full year's depreciation was taken in the year of acquisition.

Root Company presents general price-level financial statements as supplemental information to its conventional accounting financial statements. The December 31, 1990, depreciable assets balance (before accumulated depreciation), restated to reflect December 31, 1991, purchasing power, was $5.8 million. What amount of depreciation expense should be shown in the general price-level income statement for 1991 if the general price-level index was 100 at December 31, 1990, and 110 at December 31, 1991?

Case 2. The Chalk Company reported sales of $2 million in 1990 and $3 million in 1991 made evenly throughout each year. The general price-level index during 1989 remained constant at 100, and at the end of 1990 and 1991 it was 102 and 104, respectively. What approximate amount should Chalk report as sales for 1991, restated for general price-level changes?

Case 3. On January 2, 1991, the Mannix Corporation mortgaged one of its properties as collateral for a $1 million, 9 percent, five-year loan. During 1991 the general price level increased evenly, resulting in a 5 percent rise for the year. In preparing a balance sheet expressing financial position in terms of the general price level at the end of 1991, at what amount should Mannix report its mortgage note payable? What was the amount of the monetary gain or loss that Mannix realized on the outstanding note in 1991 (assuming the interest was paid in 1991)?

(AICPA adapted)

6–8. Price-Level-Adjusted Operating Income. The accountant for the Northern Equipment Corporation, a small manufacturer of camping equipment, has just completed recording all the adjustments for 1991 and has prepared the following list of account balances as of December 31, 1991 (conventional accounting basis):

Cash	$ 52,600	
Accounts receivable	30,000	
Inventory (December 31, 1991)	90,000	
Equipment	36,000	
Accumulated depreciation—Equipment		$ 12,000
Buildings	52,000	
Accumulated depreciation—Buildings		20,000
Land	17,000	
Accounts payable		30,000
Notes payable		28,000
Paid-in capital		100,000
Retained earnings		67,000
Sales		316,000
Wages and salaries	90,000	
Heat, light, etc.	4,000	
Miscellaneous expenses	12,000	
Interest expense	1,400	
Cost of sales	180,000	
Depreciation of equipment	4,000	
Depreciation of building	4,000	
	$573,000	$573,000

The accountant has noted that the firm has experienced serious inflation for the first time during 1991 and is concerned about its impact on operating performance.

In anticipation of making general price-level adjustments to these conventional accounting data, the accountant develops the following information:

1. Price-level indexes for the year were

January 1, 1991	87
December 31, 1991	100
Average index during 1991	91

2. The beginning inventory (with an original transaction value of $70,000), equipment, and buildings were all acquired when the general price-level index was 87. All of the beginning inventory has been consumed during 1991, and its cost is included in cost of sales. Purchases of inventory during 1991 (amounting to $200,000) are assumed to all have been made at the average price-level index for the year.
3. Sales were made uniformly over the year, and all expenses other than depreciation and cost of sales were incurred uniformly over the year.
4. No dividends were paid by Northern during 1991, nor were there any additional investments by owners.

Required:

1. Compute conventional accounting net income for the year.
2. Compute price-level-adjusted operating income for the year. (Carry calculation of adjustment factors to two decimals only.)
3. How are the two income numbers you have computed conceptually different?

6–9. **Estimating Net Monetary Gain or Loss.** Given that Northern Equipment Corporation in problem 6–8 had a net monetary *asset* position at January 1, 1991, of $16,000, estimate the net monetary gain or loss that the company experienced during 1991.

6–10. Estimating Net Monetary Gain or Loss. The following balances were taken from the financial statements of Lasater Company at December 31, 1991:

	January 1, 1991	*December 31, 1991*
Monetary assets	$325,000	$300,000
Monetary liabilities	(125,000)	(150,000)
Net monetary asset (liability) position	$200,000	$150,000

The following general price-level indexes applied to the year:

January 1, 1991	250
Average for 1991	260
December 31, 1991	270

Required:
Assuming that the change in the net monetary position occurred uniformly over 1991, estimate the net monetary gain or loss for Lasater Company during 1991 as a result of the change in the general purchasing power of the dollar.

6–11. Price-Level-Adjusted Operating Income. The conventional accounting income statement of the Fullmer Sales Company for the year ending December 31, 1991 is shown at the bottom of this page.

Prior to 1991 prices had been stable at a price level of 75. However, during 1991 the economy experienced rapid inflation. By the end of 1991 the price level index was at 90. The average index during the year was 82. Merchandise sold was purchased uniformly throughout the year, and wages and commissions were paid as earned, also uniformly throughout the year. Interest was accrued continuously. No new equipment purchases were made during the year.

Required:

1. What is price-level-adjusted operating income for 1991? (Carry calculation of adjustment factors to only two decimals.)

Fullmer Sales Company

Income Statement
For the Year Ending December 31, 1991

Revenue from sales		$1,750,000
Less expenses:		
Cost of goods sold	$1,400,000	
Wages and sales commissions	175,000	
Interest expense	22,000	
Equipment depreciation	43,000	
Total expenses		1,640,000
Net income		$ 110,000

2. In what way does price-level-adjusted operating income differ conceptually from conventional accounting operating income? Is the price-level-adjusted figure a better measure of performance? Explain.

6–12. Distribution of Earnings. The University Student Services Company had the following financial position as of January 1, 1991.

University Student Services Company

Balance Sheet
As of January 1, 1991

Assets:			Liabilities and Owners' Equity:	
Cash		$ 900	Note payable	$2,000
Inventory		3,500	Paid-in capital	2,500
Office equipment	$2,500		Retained earnings	1,900
Less accumulated				
depreciation	(500)	2,000	Total liabilities and	
Total assets		$6,400	owners' equity	$6,400

During 1991, its second year of operation, the company entered into the following transactions:

1. Sold merchandise for a total of $14,000.
2. Purchased additional merchandise for $8,200.
3. All of the beginning inventory was sold.
4. At year-end, $2,800 worth of the merchandise purchased remained.
5. Paid wages to employees totaling $3,000.
6. Recorded depreciation on office equipment for the year totaling $500.
7. Made an annual payment on the note payable totaling $500, of which $100 was interest charges.

All merchandise was sold uniformly throughout the year for cash. Likewise, purchases occurred throughout the year and were paid for with cash. Wages were paid as earned.

Required:

1. Record the previous information in a financial position worksheet.
2. The company is operated as a student cooperative, with all profits distributed to students at the end of each year. During 1991 the price level, after remaining stable for several years, has moved from a January 1 level of 240 to a December 31 level of 264, averaging 251 during the year. The members of the cooperative suspect that the inflation has had an impact on the amount they should distribute to students. They have come to you for help.
   (a) Compute their price-level-adjusted net income for 1991. (Carry calculation of adjustment factors to only two decimals.)
   (b) Is the answer in (*a*) the amount you would recommend distributing in 1991? Why or why not?

6–13. Relationship between Price-Level-Adjusted Net Income, Operating Income, and Net Monetary Gain or Loss. The Regina Stamping Company has been in business for three years. Its operations and other changes in financial position during year three are reflected in the conventional accounting worksheet shown in Exhibit 6–7. For both of the first two years of operations, the general price-level index remained steady at 200. But during year three, the index went from 200 to 242, averaging 220 for the year as a whole.

Required:

1. Determine price-level-adjusted *net* income for the period. The steel was all purchased (line 1) at the beginning of the year, whereas all other external transactions were made at intervals throughout the year. Show your computations.
2. Determine price-level-adjusted *operating income*. Show your computations.

EXHIBIT 6–7

Regina Stamping Company

Financial Position Worksheet, Year Three

Description	Cash	Accounts Receivable	Sheet Steel	Net Equipment	Accounts Payable	Paid-in Capital	Retained Earnings
Beginning Position	$ 3,000	$ 3,000	$ 6,000	$20,000	$ 2,000	$10,000	$20,000
1. Purchased steel			16,000		16,000		
2. Rent and wages paid	(11,000)						(11,000)
3. Sales		43,000					43,000
4. Payments on account	(15,000)				(15,000)		
5. Receipts on account	41,000	(41,000)					
6. Steel used			(17,000)				(17,000)
7. Equipment depreciation				(2,000)			(2,000)
Preliminary Balances	$18,000	$ 5,000	$ 5,000	$18,000	$ 3,000	$10,000	$33,000

3. Calculate the monetary gains and losses from each monetary asset and liability and the *net* monetary gain or loss for the period. Be sure to note whether it is a net gain or a net loss amount.

6–14. Relationship between Price-Level-Adjusted Income Measures. The conventional accounting income statement of Planetary Gears Corporation for 1991 follows. The revenues earned during the year, the wages paid, and the miscellaneous expenses all resulted from transactions taking place throughout the year. The rent was all prepaid at the end of the prior year. The steel used was purchased in part ($300,000) prior to the beginning of the year and in part ($500,000) at regular intervals throughout the year. However, it was used at a fairly even rate during the year. Interest was accrued continuously. No equipment was purchased during the year. During 1991 the price level index rose from 120 to 135, averaging 125 for the year as a whole. All beginning balances in nonmonetary assets had been previously adjusted to beginning-of-year dollars.

Planetary Gears Corporation

Results of Operations (in thousands of dollars)
For the Year Ended December 31, 1991

Revenues		$3,000
Less expenses:		
Steel used	$ 800	
Rent	30	
Wages	1,000	
Depreciation	500	
Interest	70	
Miscellaneous	100	2,500
Net operating income		$ 500

Required:

1. Determine price-level-adjusted operating income. (For convenience round adjustment factors to two decimals.)

2. Assume that price-level-adjusted net income was $400,000. Was there a net monetary gain or a net monetary loss for the period? What amount?

3. Assuming that the company started 1991 with equal amounts of monetary assets and liabilities, what does your answer to number 2 imply about the mix of monetary assets and liabilities during the year? Explain your answer.

6–15. Calculating Price-Level-Adjusted Income Measures. On January 1, 1991, Jones Company was incorporated by the owner, J. J. Jones, with his investment of $95,000 and a bank loan of $75,000 at an interest rate of 10 percent. On the same date, all but $5,000 of the available cash was invested in inventory and the building.

A list of account balances for Jones Company at December 31, 1991, follows:

Cash	$ 15,000	
Accounts receivable	40,000	
Inventory (December 31)	25,000	
Building	100,000	
Accumulated depreciation—Building		$ 5,000
Notes payable		75,000
Paid-in capital		105,000
Retained earnings	20,000	
Sales		90,000
Cost of sales	40,000	
Wages and salaries	20,000	
Interest expense	7,500	
Depreciation on building	5,000	
Miscellaneous expense	2,500	
	$275,000	$275,000

Additional information:

1. Price level indexes for 1991: beginning of the year—100; end of the year—115; average during the year—110.

2. Mr. Jones received a cash dividend of $20,000 from the company when the general price-level index stood at 105, and later in the year had to make an additional cash investment of $10,000 in the company when the general price level index was 110.

3. Sales and collections of accounts receivable occurred evenly over the year. Also, all expenses other than cost of sales and depreciation expense were incurred evenly over the year.

4. After the initial inventory purchase on January 1, no additional purchases of inventory were made during the year.

Required:

1. Determine conventional accounting net income for the year.
2. Determine price-level-adjusted net income for the year.
3. Determine price-level-adjusted net operating income for the year.
4. Determine the net monetary gain or loss for the year.

6–16. Comparing Dividend Distribution Policies. Morriss Enterprises was incorporated on January 1, 1991 with an initial cash endowment of $1 million for the purpose of buying and selling turquoise rings. The rings will be purchased in New Mexico and Arizona and will be sold in New York City. The company's operating expenses will only consist of a sales commission amounting to 20 percent of selling price.

On January 1, 1991, Morriss purchased 50,000 rings at a price of $20 per ring. During the year, the rings were sold at the expected 150 percent markup, or $30 per ring. On January 1, 1992, Morriss replaced its stock of 50,000 rings at the same $20 unit cost. But shortly after this purchase, the replacement cost of the rings increased to $25 per ring, and accordingly the selling price went up to $37.50 per ring. All of the rings were sold during 1992 at the $37.50 price. At the end of 1992, the replacement cost of the rings remained at $25, and no further price changes occurred in 1993. On January 1, 1993, Morriss purchased as many rings as it could with the cash available.

Required:
1. Prepare conventional accounting income statements for 1991, 1992, and 1993, assuming that Morriss Enterprises distributed a cash dividend at the end of each year equal in amount to conventional accounting net income.
2. Prepare current cost income statements for 1991, 1992, and 1993, assuming that Morriss Enterprises distributed a cash dividend at the end of each year equal in amount to current-cost-based curent operating income.
3. Calculate the return on investment (i.e., net income divided by the dollar investment in inventory at the start of the year) for 1993 under the two alternative dividend policies, and relate these calculations to the amounts of net income realized in 1993 in the two different circumstances.

6–17. How Much Dividend Should Be Distributed? Purmer Company is in the business of producing and selling calendars. Because most of the calendars are sold between October and April, the company determines its results of operations on a fiscal year basis running from July 1 to June 30. The company has experienced fairly stable prices over the past few years and thus has been able to operate on a constant financial capital of $500,000. The company has no debt.

During the period July 1 to September 30, 1991, the company produced 1 million calendars for 1992 at a unit cost of $0.50. During this production period, the replacement cost of paper increased dramatically. Fortunately, Purmer had acquired a sufficient supply of paper before the price increase, but Mary Purmer, the president of the company, estimates that the present replacement cost of the calendars (using the current price for paper) is $0.75. Most other companies in the industry were not as fortunate as Purmer Company, and they had to purchase their paper stock for the 1991 production run at the new (higher) price. Accordingly, the selling price for the calendars has increased from $1.00 to $1.25. On June 30, 1992, the company had sold all of the calendars at the $1.25 price, and all of its assets are in the form of cash.

Required:
1. Prepare an income statement for Purmer Company for fiscal year 1992 using current cost accounting.
2. In the past, Mary Purmer has always had the company pay a cash dividend on June 30 equal to conventional accounting net income for the fiscal year. In view of the increase in the price of paper, she asks your advice as to dividend policy for the current year. You may assume that prices have stabilized at the new, higher level, and that no further increases appear imminent.

6–18. Comparing Measurement Alternatives. Ira Corporation purchased the following assets:

January 2, 1989	$100,000	office building site (land)
January 2, 1990	120,000	stock in another corporation (nonmonetary item)
July 1, 1990	200,000	crude oil futures contract (monetary item)

On January 2, 1991, the land was sold for $140,000 and the stock for $125,000. Other information follows:

General Price-Level Indexes

January 2, 1989	100
December 31,1989	115
July 1, 1990	125
December 31, 1990	135
January 2, 1991	135

Current Costs

	Land	Stock	Contract
December 31, 1989	$110,000	$ 0	$ 0
December 31, 1990	140,000	125,000	250,000

Required:
Supply all missing amounts in the following schedules.

Balance Sheet

December 31	Conventional Historical Cost	P-L-A Basis	C-C Basis
1989: Building site	$_____	$_____	$_____
1990: Building site	$_____	$_____	$_____
Stock	$_____	$_____	$_____
Contract	$_____	$_____	$_____

Income Statement

Year Ended December 31	Conventional Historical Cost	P-L-A Basis	C-C Basis
1989 land holding gain	$_____	$_____	$_____
1990 land holding gain	$_____	$_____	$_____
1990 stock monetary or holding gain (loss)	$_____	$_____	$_____
1990 contract monetary or holding gain (loss)	$_____	$_____	$_____

The Financial Accounting Information System

CHAPTER SEVEN

All accounting processes depend upon the availability of relevant data. Such data must reflect financial events and transactions that affect the subject entity. Data must be collected, analyzed, organized, summarized, and stored in some form of data-processing system. In small organizations, the accounting system is manual, or increasingly, on personal computers. In larger, more complex, organizations the systems are usually maintained on computers using specialized software. Because the design and operation of an accounting system, whatever its level of complexity, are important aspects of accounting and management practice, the basic elements of such a system are examined briefly in this chapter.

We restrict our attention to a simplified accounting system for two reasons. First, one can develop an understanding of accounting systems without becoming involved in the technical characteristics of more complex systems. Second, it is possible to draw upon the concepts and methodology developed in this simplified analysis to serve the purposes of other business and accounting courses.

The Financial Accounting Process as a System

When the financial position framework was introduced in Chapter Four, we pointed out that a new financial position of the firm can be computed after analyzing the effects of each transaction. Indeed, by following such a procedure we illustrated that the fundamental equation—assets equal liabilities plus owners' equity—remained in balance at all times. A closer approximation of actual accounting data gathering and processing was then achieved through the introduction of the financial position worksheet. The device enabled us to defer the computation of each new financial position until the end of a chosen time period, whether month, quarter, or year. The financial position worksheet is therefore a means of analyzing, organizing, and storing the transactions of the firm in a form that allows us to apply appropriate accounting principles and generate financial statements at periodic intervals. It is thus an accounting system, albeit a simple one.

However, the financial position worksheet has limitations as a practical accounting system, even for a small firm. One important limitation is the format of the worksheet. Most businesses have a larger variety of resources and obligations than we have used in our simplified examples. To use the worksheet format for a firm with, say, 25 different types of assets and liabilities, the accountant would be confronted with a "wall-to-wall" worksheet. Also, since most companies enter into many transactions each period, their financial position worksheets soon would stretch from "floor to ceiling" as well. To solve these problems the accounting system must be able to accommodate both large numbers of accounts and large numbers of transactions.

Another important limitation is the ease with which the data may later be summarized in financial statements. A principal purpose of a financial accounting information system is to organize and summarize raw economic data into a form that makes the preparation of financial statements relatively convenient. However, the financial position worksheet requires that each transaction in the retained earnings column be reanalyzed so that each can be properly classified and summarized for presentation in the income statement (e.g., the total of all salary and wage payments to be included under the single "salary and wage expense" classification in the income statement). This is inefficient and tedious. It would be useful, therefore, if the system could be modified to perform this accumulation function as individual events are analyzed and recorded.

To avoid the limitations of the simple financial position worksheet mechanism, most businesses employ some variation of general ledger bookkeeping. General ledger bookkeeping uses two interrelated recording devices: the accounting transaction file (i.e., general journal) and the general ledger, in place of the financial position worksheet. It also employs a more elaborate set of procedures than the simplified accounting cycle described in Chapter Four.

GENERAL LEDGER BOOKKEEPING

A modern financial accounting system is abstracted in Exhibit 7–1.

EXHIBIT 7–1

Basic Financial Accounting System

Transactions and events data	Accounting Data Base	Financial statements
Systems and other inputs		Invoices, paychecks, and other financial documents
		Planning and budgeting information

Transaction files and general journals are important components of an accounting data base. Other components contain information on such things as employee personnel records, management analysis projects and tax return filing.

Accounting Transaction File

An accounting transaction file (ATF) is nothing more than a complete diary of an organization's financial activities. It is a chronological record of all transactions. In traditional bookkeeping systems, the ATF is called the general journal. Each entry in the ATF contains the date, the accounts affected, the dollar amounts of the transactions, and explanations of sources (or references) of the transactions. Effects of transactions are conventionally expressed in terms of debits and credits. Exhibit 7–2 represents a typical ATF format.

The first column of the ATF in Exhibit 7–2 contains the dates of the transactions. The second column creates a specific individual reference (i.e., source code) for each ATF entry so that the accounting data base can always identify the origin of every item of data. The third column lists all accounts affected by a transaction. Sometimes a brief explanation is also provided, as in entry AT/7074323 in Exhibit 7–2. Such explanations do not accompany routine, repetitive transactions. They occur only to the extent of direct information needs of users.

The last two columns of the ATF contain the dollar effects of the transactions on the accounts identified. These effects are classified in terms of debit (Dr) and credit (Cr). The Dr and Cr terms have no meaning as arithmetic notations. They are simply effect identifiers.

A debit to an account signifies:

1. An increase in an asset account, or
2. A decrease in a liability or an owners' equity account (because income statement accounts are part of owners' equity, expenses are debits).

In contrast, a credit to an account signifies:

1. A decrease in an asset account, or
2. An increase in a liability or an owner's equity account (including revenue on the income statement).

So long as debits equal credits in recording transactions and events (on an ATF or any other general bookkeeping journal), the balance of the accounting equation is maintained.

EXHIBIT 7–2

Accounting Transaction File (ATF) in Traditional Bookkeeping Format

Date	Source/Reference	Description	Amount	
			Debit	*Credit*
May 1	AT/7074321	Retained earnings (rent expense)	$ 1,200	
		Cash		$ 1,200
May 3	AT/7074322	Merchandise inventory	10,000	
		Accounts payable		10,000
May 4	AT/7074323	Cash	2,500	
		Accounts receivable		2,500
		(To record collection of an overdue receivable from Placer, Inc.)		

We are now in a position to explain more fully the three transactions illustrated in Exhibit 7–2.

Transaction 1. On May 1, the monthly rent of $12,000 was paid in cash. The effect of this transaction is to decrease the asset account, cash; and to decrease the retained earnings account for rent expense. Accordingly, the affected accounts are identified in the third column, and the amount of the decreases in their balances are placed in the appropriate Dr–Cr columns. Cash is an asset, and thus its decrease is placed in the Cr column; the decrease in retained earnings is in the Dr column. After the transaction is recorded, it is immediately apparent that the debits equal the credits. This is equivalent to observing that we have decreased total assets by $1,200 and also decreased the sum of liabilities and owners' equity by $1,200. Therefore the fundamental accounting equation remains in balance: total assets remain equal to the sum of liabilities and owners' equity.

Transaction 2. On May 3, inventory items were purchased at a cost of $10,000 and charged to an account payable with the supplier. The effect of this transaction is recorded by a debit to the asset account, merchandise inventory; and a credit to the liability, accounts payable. Again after this transaction is recorded, total debits equal total credits and the fundamental accounting equation remains in balance. Total assets increased by $10,000, and the sum of liabilities and owner's equity also increased by $10,000.

Transaction 3. On May 4, $2,500 is collected from a customer (Placer, Inc.), to whom the firm had previously sold merchandise on account. The effect of this transaction is to increase the firm's cash balance recorded by a debit to cash; and to decrease the total amount due from customers, recorded by a credit to accounts receivable. The transaction does not affect any liability or owners' equity accounts. Since the net effect of the transaction on total assets is zero, and similarly the total of liabilities and owners' equity is unchanged, the fundamental equation again remains in balance, and the debits still equal the credits.

Entries to the ATF can be made at any time, either individually or in batches. In actual business situations, daily recording procedures are common. Care must be taken that *all* transactions and events are properly recorded. Omissions cause data errors, which adversely affect the entire financial accounting information system. Therefore, a complete and reliable ATF is the mainstay of any effective accounting data base.

Using the ATF, we have a manageable technique for recording all transactions. But how do we then periodically prepare a statement of financial position and an income statement from this chronological record of transactions? The answer is, we do not—financial statements are prepared from the record known as the general ledger.

General Accounting Ledger

The general ledger is a collection of the accounts of the firm. Each account accumulates every transaction affecting it. This is done automatically by an appropriate computer software program as soon as an ATF entry is completed. The file thus created is called the general ledger file (GLF). We have encountered various account titles in Exhibit 7–2 and in the column headings of financial position worksheets covered in prior chapters. A printout of a general ledger account from the GLF is likely to look like the illustration in Exhibit 7–3.

EXHIBIT 7–3

General Ledger Account in Traditional Bookkeeping Format

Acct. Name:	CASH	Acct. No.: XXXX	Year: 1991
Date	*Reference*	*Debit*	*Credit*
April 30	Initial Balance	$ 8,400	
May 1	AT/7074321		$1,200
May 4	AT/7074323	2,500	
	Totals	$10,900	$1,200
	New Balance	$ 9,700	

It is assumed that the cash account illustrated in Exhibit 7–3 has a balance of $8,400 on April 30. This corresponds to the amount of cash the firm has on hand and in the bank on that date. All ATF entries specifying a cash account effect are then transferred to this account, after which column totals and a new balance can be calculated. The transfers from the ATF to individual general ledger accounts create the GLF mentioned earlier.

A simpler representation of a general ledger account known as the *T-account* is often useful. A T-account representation of the same information as that contained in Exhibit 7–3 is shown in Exhibit 7–4. Notice that all that is really needed is an account name and two columns, with convention specifying that the left column contains the debit entries and balances, and the right column the credit entries and balances.

EXHIBIT 7–4

T-Account

		Cash		
April 30	8,400	1,200		May 1
May 4	2,500			
Balance	9,700			

The *balance* of any account is the difference between the Dr and Cr totals. Because most asset, liability, and owners' equity accounts usually contain positive balances, asset accounts normally have Dr balances and liability and owners' equity accounts usually have Cr balances. As a reminder the following table is offered:

Type of Account:	Increases are:	Decreases are:	Balances usually are:
Assets	Debits	Credits	Debits
Liabilities	Credits	Debits	Credits
Owners' equity	Credits	Debits	Credits

The ATF and the GLF taken together constitute an integrated system for recording and summarizing all the transactions of the firm. At any point in time, financial statements may be prepared using the balances indicated for each account in the general ledger.

This system is more redundant than the financial position worksheet because each transaction is necessarily recorded twice. However, the system is a feasible one (whereas the financial position worksheet is not), and it also facilitates such management objectives as good internal control (discussed in Chapter Fourteen).

Use of Temporary (Period-Related) Accounts

The second limitation of the financial position worksheet is the need to reanalyze and summarize each of the revenue and expense entries in the retained earnings account whenever one wishes to prepare an income statement. As the system has been explained to this point, the many different types of revenues and expenses for the period are recorded in the retained earnings account. What we seek now is some means of summarizing the revenue and expense transactions into desired separate categories during the initial recording process.

This objective is accomplished by using a new set of accounts for different revenue and expense items. These accounts are called temporary accounts (or nominal accounts). They are subdivisions of retained earnings and have balances only for specified periods of time (usually one month or one year). At the end of the period, the balance of each temporary account is transferred back (closed) to the retained earnings account.

Temporary accounts are selected categories of revenue and expense items accumulated separately for a period of time. By expanding retained earnings with the temporary revenue and expense accounts, we have immediately available their balances in the general ledger as the information needed to prepare an income statement for the period. When the balances of the temporary accounts are transferred (closed) as net credits or debits to retained earnings, the balance of each temporary account becomes zero. Then we begin a new accumulation for the next period in the new temporary accounts.

In the first sample transaction (May 1) in Exhibit 7–2, the payment of rent for the month was recognized as a debit to retained earnings. Using the temporary accounts, however, it would be recorded as a debit to the "rent expense (retained earnings)" account. Thus the following entry is made in the ATF:

Date	Description	Dr	Cr
May 1	Rent expense (retained earnings)	1,200	
	Cash		1,200

Illustration of General Ledger Bookkeeping

The data for this illustration are taken from the financial position worksheet for Fancy Flavors, Inc., in Chapter Four (Exhibit 4–3). An ATF for all transactions recorded on this worksheet is presented in Exhibit 7–5. The entries are divided into the three categories of the accounting processing function: (1) Entries 1–10 and 17–18 to record the external *transactions*; (2) entries 11–16 to record *end-of-period adjustments*; and (3) entry 19 to close the *temporary accounts* to retained earnings.

EXHIBIT 7–5

Fancy Flavors, Inc.

Date (Entry #)	File I.D. (Description)	Dr	Cr
	Accounting Transaction File (ATF) for August 1991		
	TRANSACTIONS		
(1)	Equipment	$600,000	
	Cash		$600,000
	(To record purchases of equipment)		
(2)	Prepaid rent	60,000	
	Cash		60,000
	(To record prepayment of three months' rent)		
(3)	Supplies inventory	20,000	
	Cash		20,000
	(To record purchase of supplies)		
(4)	Ice cream inventory	30,000	
	Accounts payable		30,000
	(To record purchase of ice cream on account)		
(5)	Ice cream inventory	135,000	
	Accounts payable		135,000
	(To record additional purchases of ice cream on account)		
(6)	Accounts payable	130,000	
	Cash		130,000
	(To record payment (partial) to the ice cream supplier)		
(7)	Supplies inventory	10,000	
	Accounts payable		10,000
	(To record purchase of additional supplies on account)		
(8)	Cash	400,000	
	Accounts receivable	50,000	
	Sales (retained earnings)		450,000
	(To record cash and credit sales)		
(9)	Miscellaneous expense (retained earnings)	10,000	
	Cash		10,000
	(To record payment for miscellaneous services received during the month; e.g., cleaning services)		
(10)	Wages and salaries expense (retained earnings)	150,000	
	Cash		120,000
	Wages and accounts payable		30,000
	(To record salaries and wages expense)		
(17)	Tornado loss (retained earnings)	5,000	
	Ice cream inventory		5,000
	(To record uninsured extraordinary tornado loss)		
(18)	Retained earnings	10,000	
	Cash		10,000
	(To record payment of cash dividend to owners)		
	END-OF-PERIOD ADJUSTMENTS		
(11)	Cost of ice cream sold (retained earnings)	145,000	
	Ice cream inventory		145,000
	(To adjust the ice cream inventory balance to the cost of ice cream on hand at month-end and recognize the cost of ice cream sold)		

EXHIBIT 7–5 (cont.)

Date (Entry #)	File I.D. (Description)	Dr	Cr
(12)	Cost of supplies used (retained earnings)	15,000	
	Supplies inventory		15,000
	(To adjust the supplies inventory balance to the cost of supplies on hand at month-end and recognize the cost of supplies used)		
(13)	Rent expense (retained earnings)	20,000	
	Prepaid rent		20,000
	(To recognize the portion of the rent prepayment that applies to the month of August as an expense)		
(14)	Depreciation expense (retained earnings)	10,000	
	Accumulated depreciation–equipment		10,000
	(To recognize the depreciation of equipment applicable to August 1991)		
(15)	Interest expense (retained earnings)	6,000	
	Accounts payable and accrued liabilities		6,000
	(To accrue interest expense)		
(16)	Income tax expense (retained earnings)	24,000	
	Accounts payable and accrued liabilities		24,000
	(To accrue income tax expense)		
	CLOSING ENTRY		
(19)	Sales	450,000	
	Salaries and wages expense		150,000
	Miscellaneous expense		10,000
	Cost of ice cream sold		145,000
	Cost of supplies used		15,000
	Rent expense		20,000
	Depreciation expense		10,000
	Interest expense		6,000
	Tornado loss		5,000
	Income tax expense		24,000
	Retained earnings		65,000
	(To close the temporary revenue and expense accounts to owners' equity)		

The two most active general ledger accounts affected by these transactions are shown in Exhibit 7–6.

Please note that the ending balances (August 31, 1991) for all general ledger accounts not illustrated in Exhibit 7–6 are exactly as reported under "New Position" in Exhibit 4–3. Of course the two general ledger accounts appearing in Exhibit 7–6 have identical balances with the corresponding worksheet column totals in Exhibit 4–3. This again makes the point that the ATF/GLF system is conceptually exactly the same as the financial position worksheet system. Only their respective procedures differ.

Also note that the nature of entries 1 through 18 is explained item by item in Chapter 4. We have merely put them into a Dr–Cr format in the present chapter. The only new entry is entry 19. It is the periodic (in our case monthly) entry to close the temporary revenue, expense, and gains and losses accounts to

EXHIBIT 7–6

Fancy Flavors, Inc.

Two General Ledger Accounts for August 1991

Acct. Name:	*Cash*	*Acct. No.: XXXX*	*August 1991*

Date (Entry #)	*Reference*	*Debit*	*Credit*
August 1	Initial Balance	$ 750,000	
(1)	ATF		$600,000
(2)	ATF		60,000
(3)	ATF		20,000
(6)	ATF		130,000
(8)	ATF	400,000	
(9)	ATF		10,000
(10)	ATF		120,000
(18)	ATF		10,000
	Totals	$1,150,000	$950,000
August 31	Ending Balance	$ 200,000	

Acct. Name:	*Accounts Payable and Accrued Liabilities*	*Acct. No.: YYYY*	*August 1991*

Date (Entry #)	*Reference*	*Debit*	*Credit*
August 1	Initial Balance		$ 0
(4)	ATF		30,000
(5)	ATF		135,000
(6)	ATF	$130,000	
(7)	ATF		10,000
(10)	ATF		30,000
(15)	ATF		6,000
(16)	ATF		24,000
	Totals	$130,000	$235,000
August 31	Ending Balance		$105,000

the retained earnings account. For example, in Exhibit 7–5 the revenue account "sales (retained earnings)" is used to record operating transactions that increase retained earnings (owners' equity). The month-end balance, $450,000, is a credit balance. To close the sales account, a Dr of $450,000 is made to bring the balance to zero, and a Cr to retained earnings results. All expense accounts are treated similarly. Since expense accounts usually have Dr balances, Cr entries are necessary to close them.

Further note that the single entry to retained earnings (19—a credit of $65,000) represents the net effect of all closing entries to the revenue, expense, and gains and losses accounts. Had expenses and losses been greater than revenues and gain, the net effect would have been a Dr entry to retained earnings (reflecting a net loss for the period).

Preparing Financial Statements

After all appropriate end-of-period adjusting and closing entries have been recorded in the ATF and the GLF, financial statements for the period can be prepared directly from balances in the general ledger accounts. The statement of financial position as of August 31, 1991 collects all assets, liabilities and owners' equity accounts. These (general ledger) accounts are then classified and placed on the statement as shown in Exhibit 4–4.

Similarly, the income statement contains all the temporary account balances which were closed into retained earnings. To reiterate, the temporary accounts mechanism was established in the first place to facilitate periodic income statement preparation. In effect, an income statement is nothing more than the detail of the period's changes in the retained earnings account that stem from ordinary business operations (in our case for the month of August, 1991). Exhibit 4–5 depicts the income statement resulting from the transaction described.

Preparation of the statement of cash flows proceeds as described in Chapter Five. We call attention to the fact that general ledger account balances are used to determine cash flow effects. For noncash accounts, Cr changes generally represent sources of cash (e.g., a decrease in accounts receivable or an increase in notes payable). Dr changes in noncash accounts are typically uses of cash (e.g., an increase in merchandise inventory or a decrease in accounts payable). These effects are illustrated in the statement of cash flows appearing in Exhibit 5–5. (Note that this statement covers the month of September 1991).

Summary: The Accounting Cycle

The set of steps we have followed in the foregoing illustrations is referred to as the *accounting cycle* because it is followed in the same sequence period after period. To summarize, the essential steps of the accounting (general ledger bookkeeping) cycle are as follows:

1. Systematically collect data associated with transactions having a financial effect on the firm, as they take place.
2. Record transactions (external events) with individuals or other business firms in the chronological accounting transaction file (ATF) with automatic transfer of dollar effects to individual general ledger accounts contained in the general ledger file (GLF).
3. Record end-of-period adjustments (internal transactions).
4. Prepare an income statement for the period from balances of the temporary accounts.
5. Record closing entries to transfer the balances of the temporary accounts to retained earnings.
6. Prepare a statement of financial position as of the end of the period and a statement of cash flow for the period from balances of, and changes within, general ledger accounts.

After the sequence of steps is completed for one period (in our case, a month), the cycle begins again at step 1 at the start of the next period, and so on.

As already indicated, various computers and compatible specialized software handle nearly all procedural aspects of the accounting cycle in the present-day business environment. It is important to remember, however, that the decisions of "how to account" for specific transactions and the decisions on unusual adjustments must be made by accountants.

Trial Balance and Financial Statement Worksheet

A tool used widely in general ledger bookkeeping is the trial balance. It is a listing in debit and credit format of all the balances (both permanent and temporary accounts) in a company's general ledger accounts as of a given date. The balances may be as they appear in the general ledger accounts themselves (an unadjusted trial balance), or they may be as they would appear after tentative adjustments are made (an adjusted trial balance). The most obvious advantage of the trial balance over the general ledger itself is that it lists all accounts and their balances on one or, at most, a few pages. Additionally, a trial balance may be used for recording interim adjusting entries and avoiding closing entries altogether in the process of preparing financial statements at intervals less than one fiscal year (say, monthly or quarterly).

A financial statement preparation worksheet is illustrated in Exhibit 7–7. In the two columns headed "Unadjusted Trial Balance" are the debit and credit balances from the general ledger accounts of Fancy Flavors, after all the transactions for August were recorded (entries 1–10 and 17–18) but before any adjusting or closing entries. The next two columns (headed "Adjustments") show the effects of the adjusting entries (11–16) for August. The adjustments are numbered in parenthesis and match items in Exhibit 7–5. The last two columns (headed "Adjusted Trial Balance") show the result of combining the unadjusted trial balance figures for the various accounts with any adjustments to the accounts that appear in the Adjustments columns.

With one exception, the figures in the Adjusted Trial Balance trace into the income statement (Exhibit 4–5) and the balance sheet (Exhibit 4–4) prepared earlier. The exception is that, since the closing entry (19) is excluded from the worksheet procedure, the retained earnings figure in the adjusted trial balance is the same as the unadjusted trial balance figure. To this figure must be added the net effect of closing the temporary accounts (that is, the net income or loss of the period) to arrive at the appropriate ending balance sheet amount. In our case $65,000 in net income is added to the beginning Dr balance of $10,000 (resulting from the dividends payment) to get the appropriate ending balance of $55,000.

THE FINANCIAL ACCOUNTING DATA-PROCESSING SYSTEM

Gathering and Processing Accounting Data

To create the accounting data base depicted in Exhibit 7–1 and to achieve its desired outputs, various processes are used by the business enterprise to record, store, control, and summarize data about individual transactions and events. Such processes are facilitated by systems, called data-processing systems, consisting of the following components:

Source documents are used to record data about individual transactions and other events as they take place. Many businesses have computer-produced doc-

EXHIBIT 7–7

Fancy Flavors, Inc.

Trial Balance and Financial Statement Worksheet
August 31, 1991

Account Name	Unadjusted Trial Balance		Adjustments		Adjusted Trial Balance	
	Dr	Cr	Dr	Cr	Dr	Cr
Cash	$200,000				$200,000	
Accounts receivable	50,000				50,000	
Prepaid rent	60,000			$ 20,000 (13)	40,000	
Ice cream inventory	165,000			150,000 (11, 18)	15,000	
Supplies inventory	30,000			15,000 (12)	15,000	
Equipment	600,000				600,000	
Accumulated depreciation		$ 0		10,000 (14)		$ 10,000
Accounts payable and accrued liabilities		75,000		30,000 (15, 16)		105,000
Bank loan		600,000				600,000
Paid-in capital		150,000				150,000
Retained earnings	10,000				10,000	
Sales		450,000				450,000
Salary and wages expense	150,000				150,000	
Miscellaneous expense	10,000				10,000	
Cost of ice cream sold	0		$145,000 (11)		145,000	
Cost of supplies used	0		15,000 (12)		15,000	
Rent expense	0		20,000 (13)		20,000	
Depreciation expense	0		10,000 (14)		10,000	
Interest expense	0		6,000 (15)		6,000	
Tornado loss	0		5,000 (18)		5,000	
Income tax expense	0		24,000 (16)		24,000	
Total	$1,275,000	$1,275,000	$225,000	$225,000	$1,315,000	$1,315,000

uments. For example, a retail store clerk enters a sales transaction into the point-of-sale terminal (electronic cash register). The terminal produces the sales invoice containing customer information, description and quantity of goods purchased, prices, and total charge. It enters the transaction directly into the accounting system. Alternatively, some systems accumulate transaction data and enter it into the accounting system only periodically.

Subsidiary journals or registers are special records into which transaction data contained on source documents are entered chronologically or periodically. An example of a subsidiary journal is the sales journal. Following the preceding example, each sales transaction is entered into the sales journal file by the point-of-sale terminal. Thus a sales journal can be produced by the computer for any time period. The journal can list details of each sale, such as total amount, amount of cash received, sales tax collected, and the amount receivable.

Other examples of subsidiary journals or registers are the cash receipts and cash disbursements journals, the purchases journal, and the payroll register, all of which generally form parts of an integrated computerized accounting system.

Subsidiary ledger accounts are records of individual components of certain asset, liability, and owners' equity accounts. Subsidiary ledgers also can be maintained on a computerized system. For example, the accounts receivable subsidiary ledger records amounts owed and received from individual customers. When a credit sale is made and entered into the system, the computer software automatically records the amount debited to the customer's account. When a payment is received and the amount entered into the system, it is credited to the customer's account (as well as recorded in the cash receipts journal).

Standardized procedures must be specified such that all transaction data are accurately recorded by the appropriate employee at the time the transaction takes place. The procedures must also give reasonable assurance that only valid transaction data reach the accounting records. While a computer system does not assure proper entry of data, it does automatically carry out all necessary data transfer and summarization. Computer applications have increased the efficiency of accounting data-processing systems.

Charts of accounts, systems flow charts, and operations handbooks are employed to varying degrees by business firms to ensure standard procedures. Standardization within a firm is essential whether manual or computerized data processing is used. Although manual and computerized accounting systems differ in appearance, their substance is very much the same. The basic record-keeping documents (e.g., data files, journals, and ledgers) exist in different forms in the two types of systems, but serve essentially the same functions.

Accounting Subsystems and Related Operations

The use of subsidiary journal and ledger records is expanded in most firms to several subsystems of each total financial accounting system. There are certain natural divisions that center on sets of interrelated activities and events that satisfy specific operational needs as well as accounting needs. Thus accounting subsystems and procedures tend to correspond to and are integrated with the operating subsystems and procedures of the business. An example of a set of subsystems for moderate to large businesses that buy (or produce) products for sale to customers is described next.

The sales and collections subsystem is concerned with filling customers' orders (or authorizing shipment); ensuring that only authorized sales are made (i.e., to approved customers with ability to pay); accurately recording all valid sales and related accounts receivable; maintaining accurate customer accounts; collecting cash from customers and securely depositing it in the bank; and accurately recording all cash receipts and crediting the correct customer accounts. This subsystem ties directly to the cash receipts and sales journals previously discussed.

The acquisitions and payments subsystem is concerned with placing orders for all authorized resource needs other than personnel; ensuring that acquisitions are received; accurately recording all valid liabilities arising from acquisitions; authorizing payment for bona fide acquisitions; remitting payments; and accurately debiting the appropriate liability accounts when payments are made. This system links to fixed asset records and cash disbursement journals.

The payroll subsystem is integrated with both mainline operations and the personnel function and is concerned with accurately recording labor costs in periods in which they are incurred; accurately calculating each employee's gross and net pay, payroll taxes, and fringe benefits; accurately assessing related employer payroll taxes, insurance premiums, pension contributions; properly recording all related liabilities (including wages payable); paying all such liabilities on a timely basis; and debiting the appropriate liability accounts when paid. Once again the cash disbursement journal is directly affected.

The inventory/warehousing subsystem is concerned with safeguarding the raw materials, work-in-process, and finished goods inventories; releasing materials for authorized uses within the company and appropriately deducting them from inventory records; releasing finished goods for authorized deliveries (shipments) to customers and recording reductions in goods on hand; receiving, inspecting, and accurately recording purchases; periodically checking inventory records against physical counts of quantities on hand; periodically summarizing and recording costs of materials on hand (used), costs of work-in-process on hand (transferred to finished goods), and costs of finished goods on hand (sold). This subsystem is relied on for determining inventory levels and cost of goods sold.

The capital acquisitions and repayments subsystem relates primarily to the long-term financing of the business and is concerned with accurately recording capital contributed by owners and proceeds of borrowings from lenders; maintaining accurate shareholder records, dividends payable ledgers, bonds payable ledgers, etc.; accurately recording interest expense in the proper period; and timely payment of interest and principal on debts and dividends declared and payable (to the "owners of record.").

From the accounting perspective, each of these subsystems is made up of the four components discussed earlier: source documents, subsidiary journals, subsidiary ledgers, and sets of procedures tying the components together and integrating them with the operations of the business. Together these elements function as a financial accounting information system.

SUMMARY

In the first section of this chapter we developed the essentials of the general ledger bookkeeping system, the practical counterpart to the financial position worksheet. Although the effects of all transactions and events of a given period on financial position and net income cannot be represented visually as completely as with the worksheet tableau, general ledger bookkeeping is used effectively in practical business applications where the numbers of accounts, transactions, and events are more than trivial.

At the same time, general ledger bookkeeping operates with already-summarized transactions data in most applications. In order to understand the financial accounting system it is therefore necessary to understand the gathering and processing of accounting data by means of source documents, subsidiary journals, subsidiary ledgers, and coordinating procedures to capture, store, control, summarize, and feed transaction data into the general ledger bookkeeping process.

For convenience, efficiency, and effectiveness the data-gathering and processing dimension may be split up into subsystems along functional lines, such as sales-collections, acquisitions-payments, and payroll.

A financial accounting information system functions through integration with a firm's other operating systems. Financial statements and other outputs from the accounting system are only as reliable as the system inputs.

The speed and overall efficiency of computerized financial accounting systems have registered major advances in recent years. Systems design has become a cornerstone accounting activity.

Questions for Review and Discussion

7–1. Define

    a. Accounting transaction file (ATF)
    b. General ledger
    c. T-account
    d. Temporary account
    e. Adjusting entry
    f. Closing entry
    g. Accruals
    h. Accounting cycle
    i. Dr–Cr convention
    j. Subsidiary journal
    k. Subsidiary ledger
    l. Source document
    m. Trial balance

7–2. State concisely the objectives of a financial accounting information system. How does such a system differ from other data-processing systems; for example, those relating to traffic tickets, university course grades, social security payments?

7–3. What four elements constitute a typical ATF entry?

7–4. List 20 general ledger account titles (including temporary accounts) that might be found in the accounting system of a large department store.

7–5. Distinguish between a permanent general ledger account and a temporary account.

7–6. Why are closing entries required? What accounts are normally affected by closing entries?

7–7. What distinguishes a subsidiary journal from the general journal?

7–8. List the advantages and disadvantages of the Dr–Cr convention of traditional bookkeeping.

7–9. Explain the reason behind the often quoted bookkeepers' maxim that debits must equal credits.

7–10. Why do asset accounts normally have Dr balances and liability and owners' equity accounts Cr balances?

7–11. List the components of the accounting data-processing system. What relationship does the data-gathering and processing system bear to general ledger bookkeeping?

7–12. Explain the role of source documents in accounting data gathering and processing in business operations.

7–13. Distinguish between subsidiary ledgers and the general ledger. What relationship exists between these two types of accounting records?

7–14. Explain the advantages of the trial balance as a tool for preparing financial statements.

7–15. Briefly describe the nature and functions of financial accounting subsystems. How do subsystems relate to a total financial accounting information system?

Problems

7–1. Making ATF Entries. Refer to the external transactions listed in problem 4–10. Set up an ATF as illustrated in Exhibit 7–2 and record these transactions (source references are not required).

7–2. Making Transaction and Adjusting Entries. Set up an ATF as illustrated in Exhibit 7–2 and record the following events (source references are not required). Also make appropriate adjusting entries, distinguishing them from transaction entries.

The Antique Weavers Company:
1. Purchased wool from suppliers on credit for $1,000.
2. Purchased weaving machine for $5,000, paying $2,500 in cash with the bank paying the balance.
3. Placed advertisements in the local paper at a cost of $180, payment has not yet been made.
4. Paid rent for the next eighteen months: $1,800.
5. Paid wages owed for work done in the preceding period: $800.
6. Paid $500 to bank in repayment of a loan.
7. Made sales of $3,000 to a major retailer who paid cash of $1,500 and promised payment of the balance within thirty days.
8. One of the owners contributed a delivery van (market value $2,000) to the company.
9. Depreciation of equipment for the period: $150.
10. The retailer in number 7 returned some goods, claiming he was overstocked. Antique Weavers gave him a credit note for $500 (i.e., reduction in the amount payable).
11. Discovered at the end of the period:
    a. Wool supplies used during period cost $300.
    b. Amount of prepaid rent that expired during the period was $500.
    c. Wages owing at end of the period were $250.
    d. Interest owing at the end of the period was $80.
12. Paid a $500 cash dividend to owners.

7–3. Identifying ATF Entries. Briefly explain the following ATF entries. As a guide, this has already been done for the first entry.

| 1. Merchandise inventory | 8,234 | | 4. Retained earnings | 147,312 | |
| Accounts payable | | 8,234 | Cost of goods sold | | 147,312 |

To record a credit merchandise purchase.

2. Rent expense	1,073		5. Dividends (Ret. earn.)	23,411	
Prepaid rent		1,073	Dividends payable		23,411
3. Cash	835		6. Dividends payable	20,709	
Accounts receivable		835	Cash		20,709

Complete the following entries with the most likely account title.

1. Notes payable	3,600		4. Accrued expenses	2,077	
_____		3,600	_____		2,077
2. Advances from customers	1,910		5. Insurance expense	810	
_____		1,910	_____		810
3. Advances to suppliers	2,500		6. _____	8,902	
_____		2,500	Wages payable		8,902

7–4. Dr–Cr Analysis. Since the accounting equation has only three elements, there can be no more than nine possible *pairwise* changes of equation elements. For each of the following changes, specify a corresponding business event or transaction that could give rise to it:

1. Dr Asset = Cr Liability
2. Dr Asset = Cr Asset
3. Dr Asset = Cr Owners' equity
4. Dr Liability = Cr Asset
5. Dr Liability = Cr Liability
6. Dr Liability = Cr Owners' equity
7. Dr Owners' equity = Cr Asset
8. Dr Owners' equity = Cr Liability
9. Dr Owners' equity = Cr Owners' equity

7–5. General Ledger Bookkeeping. Refer to problem 4–7. Set up an ATF format like the one in Exhibit 7–2, and general ledger accounts in T-account format.

Required:

1. Record the listed transactions.
2. Make any necessary adjusting entries.
3. Transfer entries to individual general ledger accounts. Use T-account format.
4. Prepare an income statement for the Record Center for the month of July.
5. Prepare an entry to close the temporary accounts.
6. Prepare a balance sheet as of the end of July.

7–6. Account Analysis. The inventory account of Schilthorn Enterprises has a Dr balance of $32,000 at December 31, 1991. At the end of the 1991 accounting cycle, *a closing entry* was made debiting $142,000 to cost of goods sold. Inventory transactions during 1991 included

1. Purchases of $145,000 of inventory.
2. $6,000 of unacceptable inventory items were returned to a supplier.
3. $12,000 was added to the account because some inventories were discovered in a warehouse which had not been included in the inventory count of December 31, 1990.

Required:
Determine the balance in the inventory account of Schilthorn Enterprises at January 1, 1991. Support your calculations.

7–7. Preparing Transaction, Adjusting, and Closing Entries. Kennedy Corporation rents its land and buildings. Here are some, but not all, of its 1991 transactions, including all those to be reflected on its 1991 income statement (amounts in thousands).

1. All sales were on account; they totaled $600.
2. The firm bought all its merchandise on account, for $233.
3. Its December 31, 1990 and December 31, 1991 merchandise inventories were $48 and $43, respectively.
4. It issued $89 of notes payable for new equipment.
5. Interest accruals totaled $7; all were made at year end.
6. Rent expense was $170; the firm prepays rent once per year.
7. It incurred $50 of miscellaneous operating expenses: $23 for cash and $27 on account.
8. Equipment depreciation was $103.
9. The firm sold equipment with a $12 net book value for $15, cash.
10. It paid $15 of dividends.
11. Its December 31, 1990 and December 31, 1991 dividends payable balances were $5 and $3, respectively.

    a. Insofar as the previous data allow, prepare the firm's 1991 ATF entries.
    b. Insofar as the previous data allow, prepare the firm's 1991 adjusting entries.
    c. Prepare a single 1991 closing entry.

7–8. **Account Analysis and Closing Entry.** The retained earnings account of Luft Corporation had credit balances of $830,000 on January 1, 1991 and of $785,000 on December 31, 1991 after closing entries had been made. Net sales revenue for the year 1991 was $1.85 million and $25,000 in dividends was paid. Except for operating expenses and the foregoing events, no other items affected retained earnings during 1991.

Required:

1. Calculate total operating expenses of Luft Corporation for 1991.
2. On a Dr–Cr basis, make the appropriate closing entry as of December 31, 1991, using the information available to you.

Hint: *Assume that only one temporary account was used to accumulate all expenses of the period.*

7–9. **General Ledger Bookkeeping.** The financial statements of the NJW Art Shop at November 30, 1991, follow:

NJW Art Shop

Statement of Financial Position
As of November 30, 1991

Cash	$ 4,200	Accounts payable		$ 1,800
Accounts receivable	2,000	Accrued salaries payable		200
Merchandise inventory	4,000	Paid-in capital		1,000
Fixtures	3,500	Retained earnings:		
Accumulated depreciation—		Balance, January 1	$1,000	
Fixtures	(1,000)	Net income for		
Prepaid rent	300	11 months	9,000	10,000
	$13,000			$13,000

NJW Art Shop

Income Statement

For November 1991 and 11 Months Ended November 30, 1991

	Month of November 1991	*Eleven Months Ended November 30, 1991*
Sales	$4,500	$51,000
Expenses:		
Cost of merchandise sold	$2,300	$26,000
Salaries expense	900	10,450
Rent expense	300	3,300
Advertising expense	150	1,700
Depreciation expense	50	550
	$3,700	$42,000
Net (operating) income	$ 800	$ 9,000

The NJW Art Shop engaged in the following transactions in December:

Dec. 2	Purchased frames (inventory) on account for $1,500.
Dec. 5	Paid salaries (including those accrued at the end of November) of $350.
Dec. 7	Paid $200 for a special Christmas advertising supplement put out by the local Junior Achievement.
Dec. 10	Collected $1,500 on account.
Dec. 15	Recorded sales for the first half of the month: cash sales, $4,000; credit sales, $1,000.
Dec. 15	Paid salaries of $500.
Dec. 17	Paid $2,200 to suppliers.
Dec. 18	Purchased art supplies (inventory) for $1,000 cash.
Dec. 24	Paid salaries of $800.
Dec. 28	Collected $1,200 on account.
Dec. 30	Paid $150 for advertising in the local newspaper for the month.
Dec. 31	Paid rent in advance for the first six months of 1992, $1,800.
Dec. 31	Recorded sales for the last half of the month: cash sales, $5,000; credit sales, $800.

The information for the end-of-period adjustments follows:

1. When the fixtures were purchased, it was estimated that they would have a five-year life and a salvage value at the end of the five years of $500.
2. The prepaid rent at the end of November was for the month of December.
3. The cost of merchandise (frames and other art supplies) on hand at the end of December was $1,500.
4. As of December 31, the total earned but unpaid wages amounted to $100.

Required:

1. Assuming the temporary (revenue and expense) accounts are only closed to retained earnings at the end of the calendar year, construct a general ledger (set of T-accounts) for NJW Art Shop with appropriate balances as of November 30, 1991. (Note: The balance of the retained earnings account will be a credit of $1,000, since the temporary accounts have not yet been closed to it.)
2. Record the transactions for December in an ATF, and transfer dollar amounts to the general ledger.

3. Record the end-of-period adjustments in the ATF, and transfer dollar amounts to the general ledger.
4. Prepare an income statement for the month of December 1991 and for the year ended December 31, 1991.
5. Make a closing entry in the ATF and the general ledger.
6. Prepare a statement of financial position as of December 31, 1991.

7–10. General Ledger Bookkeeping. The financial statements of the Modern Sound Shop at November 30, 1991 follow:

Modern Sound Shop

Statement of Financial Position
As of November 30, 1991

Cash	$ 12,000
Accounts receivable	5,000
Records and tapes	65,000
Furniture and fixtures	30,000
Accumulated depreciation—	
Furniture and fixtures	(6,000)
Prepaid rent	8,000
	$114,000
Accounts payable	$ 10,000
Accrued salaries payable	5,000
Paid-in capital	30,000
Retained earnings:	
Balance, January 1 $10,000	
Net income for 11 months 59,000	69,000
	$114,000

Modern Sound Shop

Income Statement
For November 1991 and 11 Months Ended November 30, 1991

	Month of November 1991	Eleven Months Ended November 30, 1991
Sales	$60,000	$720,000
Expenses:		
Cost of sales	$40,000	$480,000
Salaries expense	10,000	126,000
Rent expense	4,000	44,000
Advertising expense	1,000	8,250
Depreciation expense	250	2,750
	$55,250	$661,000
Net (operating) income	$ 4,750	$ 59,000

The Modern Sound Shop engaged in the following transactions in December:

Dec. 3 Paid $2,000 for advertising in the local paper for the month.
Dec. 4 Received a special order of records and tapes for the Christmas season. The total cost was $32,000 (purchased on account).

Dec. 5 Paid salaries accrued at the end of November. (The pay period is semi-monthly; however, salaries are not paid until five days after the end of each pay period.)

Dec. 12 Collected $4,500 on account.

Dec. 15 Recorded sales for the first half of the month: cash sales, $40,000; credit sales, $2,000.

Dec. 20 Paid salaries of $6,000 for the December 1 to December 15 pay period.

Dec. 20 Paid $10,000 to suppliers.

Dec. 21 Paid $1,000 for spot advertising over a local radio station.

Dec. 31 Recorded sales for the last half of the month: cash sales, $44,000; credit sales, $4,000.

The information for the end-of-period adjustments follows.

1. The cost of records and tapes on hand at December 31, 1991 was $36,000.
2. Salaries for the December 16 to December 31 pay period totaled $6,500.
3. The prepaid rent at the end of November was for December and January.
4. The original estimated life of the furniture and fixtures was ten years; the salvage value was estimated to be zero.

Required:

1. Construct a general ledger (set of T-accounts) for the Modern Sound Shop with appropriate balances as of November 30, 1991. Assume that the revenue and expense accounts are closed to retained earnings only at the end of the calendar year.
2. Record the transactions for December 1991 in an ATF and transfer dollar amounts to the general ledger.
3. Record the end-of-period adjustments in the ATF and transfer dollar amounts to the general ledger.
4. Prepare an income statement for the month of December 1991 and the year ended December 31, 1991.
5. Make a closing entry in the ATF and the general ledger.
6. Prepare a statement of financial position as of December 31, 1991.

7–11. Making Adjusting Entries. For each of the following *independent* situations, prepare an entry or entries to record appropriate end-of-period adjustments. Record all entries, using the Dr–Cr ATF format. Select descriptive account titles. Assume that December 31 is the end of the accounting period and that no previous adjustments have been made during the year unless otherwise specified.

1. The inventory on January 1 totaled $35,000. Purchases of inventory during the year totaled $200,000. The inventory on hand at December 31 totaled $25,000.
2. Rent was prepaid for four months on November 1. The total amount of the prepayment was $2,000. Rent payments for months prior to November have already been debited to the appropriate retained earnings temporary account.
3. Equipment costing $10,000 and having an estimated life of five years with $1,000 salvage value was purchased on January 1.
4. The supplies inventory on January 1 totaled $4,000. Purchases of supplies during the year totaled $8,000. Calculations at year-end showed that $7,000 of supplies were consumed during the year.
5. A monthly magazine publisher received ten thousand annual subscriptions at $12 each, totaling $120,000 during the year. The liability account "subscription deposits" was credited upon receipt of the subscriptions; cash was debited. For five thousand of the subscriptions, eight issues were mailed during the year. For the remaining five thousand subscriptions, six issues were mailed.

6. On January 1, the company had wages payable of $10,000. During the year it paid employees $200,000. However, just before year-end employees had earned $11,500 of wages as yet not paid.

7–12. Preparing and Adjusting Trial Balances. Stu Notes was founded in the summer of 1989 by three graduate students who had just completed their first year at State University. The firm offers a note-taking service. When instructors of large lecture sections are willing, it hires graduate students to take notes which the three founders then type, duplicate, and make available to subscribers at the beginning of the next lecture. The firm charges a $2.50 subscription fee for each one-semester course, payable in advance.

The first year was successful. Here's the firm's August 16, 1990 balance sheet, prepared at the end of its first fiscal year:

Stu Notes
Balance Sheet
August 16, 1990

Assets		*Owners' Equity*	
Cash	$140	Paid-in capital	$300
Paper and supplies	50	Retained earnings	120
Prepaid advertising	100		
Duplicating machine	130		
Total assets	$420	Total owners' equity	$420

At August 16, 1990, the firm estimated that its duplicating machine offered two more years of service, after which it would have a $30 scrap value. The firm initially recorded all subscriptions and amounts owed note takers as liabilities, in the accounts "*prepaid subscriptions*" and "*due note takers*," respectively.

1. Here's a summary of its 1990–1991 transactions. Record them in appropriate ATF entries and T-accounts.

   a. The firm sold 5,000 subscriptions, for $12,650.
   b. It bought paper and supplies for $3,620, cash.
   c. Note takers earned $3,800.
   d. Prepaid advertising cost $500.
   e. The firm paid all note takers in full.
   f. The founders withdrew $4,500 of dividends.
   g. On February 16, 1991, the firm bought a second used duplicating machine for $420, cash, expecting it to have a total service life of four years and a $100 scrap value upon retirement.
   h. On February 16, 1991, the firm brought up to date the depreciation on its old duplicating machine, then sold it for $120 cash.

2. Prepare the firm's August 16, 1991 unadjusted trial balance.
3. In adjusting its books prior to preparing its August 16, 1991 financial statements, the firm determined the following:

   a. $90 of paper and supplies remained on hand at August 16, 1991.
   b. $70 of advertising remained prepaid at August 16, 1991.
   c. Depreciation is to be taken on the new duplicating machine.
   d. All subscription contracts had been fulfilled.

   Prepare and enter the firm's August 16, 1991 adjusting entries.
4. Prepare the firm's August 16, 1991 adjusted trial balance.

5. Prepare and enter appropriate August 16, 1991 closing entries.
6. Prepare the firm's August 16, 1991 final trial balance.
7. Prepare its 1990–1991 income statement and August 16, 1991 balance sheet.

7–13. Preparing Financial Statements from a Trial Balance.   Exhibit 7–8 is the December 31, 1991, *unadjusted* trial balance drawn up from the balances in the general ledger accounts of BAC Corporation. All transactions for the year 1991 and adjusting entries for the first three fiscal quarters had been recorded before drawing up the trial balance. BAC Corporation follows the practice of making quarterly and year-end adjustments on a financial statement worksheet (see Exhibit 7–7) before actually making adjusting entries in the ATF and general ledger and (annually only) closing its temporary accounts. Its quarterly and annual financial statements are prepared from the worksheets.

EXHIBIT 7–8

BAC Corporation

Unadjusted Trial Balance
December 31, 1991

Account	*Dr*	*Cr*
Cash	400,000	
Accounts receivable	900,000	
Inventories	750,000	
Prepaid expenses	90,000	
Buildings and equipment	2,000,000	
Accumulated depreciation		700,000
Land	1,000,000	
Accounts payable		750,000
Interest payable		0
Wages payable		0
Taxes payable		0
Bank loan		1,500,000
Paid-in capital		1,000,000
Retained earnings (balance December 31, 1990)		275,000
Revenues		5,000,000
Cost of sales	1,400,000	
Wages and salaries expense	2,200,000	
Depreciation expense	300,000	
Interest expense	135,000	
Income tax expense	50,000	
	9,225,000	9,225,000

Information on which December 31, 1991, adjusting entries are to be based is as follows:

1. A physical count and subsequent pricing (from purchase invoices) indicate that inventory costing $350,000 is actually on hand at December 31.
2. The December payroll (not yet included in expense), totaling $200,000, will not be paid until the end of the first week in January 1992.
3. Depreciation expense is recognized at $400,000 per year. The first three quarters' depreciation has already been recognized.

4. Interest is payable at 12 percent per year in four installments, on the first days of January, April, July and October, on the bank loan of $1.5 million.
5. Income tax expense for the year as a whole is estimated at $82,000. Three quarterly installments totaling $50,000 had been paid through December 31.

Required:

1. Prepare a trial balance and financial statement worksheet as of December 31, 1991, for BAC Corporation (see Exhibit 7–7) and enter the unadjusted balances given in Exhibit 7–8.
2. Make the necessary adjustments in "adjustment" columns and derive an adjusted trial balance.
3. Prepare an income statement for 1991 and a statement of financial position as of December 31, 1991.
4. Write the general entry that would properly close the temporary accounts of BAC Corporation as of December 31, 1991, assuming that *all* adjusting entries have already been recorded in the general ledger accounts.

7–14. Preparing Financial Statements from a Trial Balance. The December 31, 1991 unadjusted trial balance of Trigor Corporation is shown in Exhibit 7–9. It is drawn up from the corporation's general ledger account balances prior to adjusting entries. The corporation follows the practice of preparing year-to-date financial statements monthly using a trial balance and financial statement worksheet. After the financial statements are prepared each month, the adjustments in the worksheet are entered into the ATF and the general ledger accounts. Therefore at the end of the year, all that is required to prepare financial statements for the year are adjustments for December.

Information on which December adjustments are to be based is as follows:

1. A physical count (and pricing) of inventory showed that inventory costing $450,000 was actually on hand at December 31, 1991.
2. Wages and salaries totaling $250,000 for the last two weeks of December would not be paid until January 1992. They had not yet been recognized as expenses at December 31.
3. The unadjusted prepaid expenses balance consists of three months' rent ($300,000) and three months' insurance ($60,000), each paid on December 1 and due to expire on February 28, 1992.
4. Depreciation on the equipment is recognized monthly on an assumed useful life of ten years and zero salvage value.
5. Interest expense on the bank loan is recognized at 1 percent per month—with the next quarterly payment of $66,000 due on February 1, 1992.
6. Income tax expense for December 1991 is estimated to be $20,000.

Required:

1. Prepare a trial balance and financial statement worksheet as of December 31, 1991 for Trigor Corporation (see Exhibit 7–7) and enter the unadjusted balances from Exhibit 7–9.
2. Make the necessary adjustments on the worksheet and derive an adjusted trial balance.
3. Prepare an income statement for 1991 and a December 31, 1991 statement of financial position for Trigor.

EXHIBIT 7–9

Trigor Corporation

Unadjusted Trial Balance
December 31, 1991

Account	Dr	Cr
Cash	$ 450,000	
Accounts receivable	1,050,000	
Inventories	900,000	
Prepaid expenses	360,000	
Equipment	3,000,000	
Accumulated depreciation		$ 575,000
Accounts payable		250,000
Wages and salaries payable		0
Interest payable		22,000
Taxes payable		32,000
Bank loan		2,200,000
Paid-in capital		1,000,000
Retained earnings		504,000
Revenue		9,500,000
Cost of sales	3,000,000	
Wages and salaries expense	3,300,000	
Rent expense	1,100,000	
Insurance expense	220,000	
Depreciation expense	275,000	
Interest expense	242,000	
Income tax expense	186,000	
	$14,083,000	$14,083,000

4. Write entries to correspond to your adjustments in number 2.
5. Write an ATF entry to close Trigor's *adjusted* temporary accounts at December 31, 1991.

7–15. Trial Balance Analysis. Merkur Stores prepares financial statements once per quarter. Its December 31, 1990 final trial balance and March 31, 1991 adjusted trial balance appear on the next page, together with certain additional data about its January 1 through March 31, 1991 activities. Answer the following questions:

1. What was the firm's net loss for the quarter?
2. What amount of merchandise did the firm buy during the quarter?
3. What amount of store equipment did it buy during the quarter?
4. How much did it pay its employees during the quarter?
5. How much interest did it collect on the 8 percent notes receivable during the quarter?
6. How much cash did it collect from customers during the quarter?
7. How much interest did it pay during the quarter?
8. How much dividends did the firm pay during the quarter?
9. What will be the total credits on the firm's March 31, 1991 final trial balance?

	December 31, 1990 Final Trial Balance		March 31, 1991 Adjusted Trial Balance	
	Debit	*Credit*	*Debit*	*Credit*
Accounts payable		$ 65,100		$ 84,000
Accounts receivable	$ 80,000		$ 63,000	
Buildings	75,600		74,844	
Cash	21,000		22,470	
Paid-in Capital		200,000		200,000
Cost of merchandise sold	0		179,676	
8% Notes receivable	4,200		4,200	
Interest payable		1,575		0
Interest receivable	0		84	
Interest expense on mort-gage	0		1,575	
Interest income on 8% notes		0		84
Land	56,700		56,700	
Merchandise inventory	88,000		92,400	
Retained earnings		43,600		43,600
6% Mortgage payable, due December 31, 1995		105,000		105,000
Sales		0		210,000
Selling and administrative expenses	0		57,750	
Store equipment	94,500		92,610	
Taxes expense	0		3,150	
Utility bills payable		0		2,100
Wages payable		4,725		3,675
Total	$420,000	$420,000	$648,459	$648,459

1. Out of all sales, 20 percent were for cash and 80 percent on account.
2. All purchases of merchandise and equipment were on account.
3. Selling and administrative expenses include all depreciation of store equipment ($2,520) and all costs of employee services ($46,200).
4. The firm acquired the 8 percent notes at issue on December 31, 1990.
5. It sold no store equipment.
6. All accounts receivable are paid within 75 days.

Revenue Recognition and Measurement Issues

CHAPTER EIGHT

The accrual basis of accounting was introduced in Chapter Three as the conventional measure used to assess the enterprise's performance. Revenues and expenses were depicted as the measure of accomplishment and sacrifice, respectively. This chapter addresses the judgmental and complex issues involved in determining revenue and their accounting treatment. These issues include revenue recognition (deciding the time period in which the revenue has been earned) and measurement (determining the amount of the revenue which has been earned). The specific topics covered regarding revenue recognition include accounting for sales at the receipt of an order or point of production; long-term contracts; value accretion, appreciation, and discovery; and credit sales. The specific topics which relate to revenue measurement include goods and future services (e.g., warranty services); and discounts, returns, and allowances.

REVENUE RECOGNITION

In Chapter Three we said revenue is realized or earned when goods or services are exchanged for cash or claims to cash. This usually occurs when the price to be received is reasonably certain and the enterprise does not face any substantial production barriers or steps. Simply stated, we treated revenue as earned when the products are delivered or the services are performed. This is the time of sale, when title to the goods or services has passed to the buyer and the seller has a legally enforceable claim for the amount of the price agreed upon in the sales

EXHIBIT 8–1

Revenue Recognition in the Production-Sale-Collection Sequence

Production–Sale–Collection Sequence	Receipt of Order		Point of Production			
	Raw Materials Purchased	Work in Process	Finished Goods	Value Accretion, Appreciation, Discovery	Sales	Cash Collection
UNCERTAIN INCOME	⊢—————————⊣————————⊣————————⊣————————⊣————————⊣—————— CERTAIN INCOME					
Revenue Recognition Method		Percentage of Completion	Completed Contract		Credit Sales	Installment Sales
						Cost Recovery

transaction. In this circumstance, no major earning effort takes place following the sale. Therefore, this is the time period when the revenue is recognized, or included in the current period's net income.

However, determining when revenue has been earned is not always as straightforward as implied in Chapter Three. Significant uncertainties may exist, or the firm may not have completed its performance in the production or delivery cycle. As a result, complications arise which necessitate alternative accounting treatments.

Alternative revenue recognition methods are depicted in Exhibit 8–1 along with the stages of production, sales and collection typically experienced by a firm. Income is most uncertain when an enterprise first purchases materials and other resources to be used to create a salable product or service. At this stage no value has been added or customer identified. Income becomes more certain as the product or service is created and a purchaser identified. Cash collection from sale of the firm's output establishes income with certainty. However, from Chapter Three we know that on the accrual basis it is usually inappropriate to wait until ultimate cash collection to recognize revenue. Thus we must discuss the alternative revenue recognition techniques and the general business circumstances under which they are most appropriately used. We should note, however, that such methods are more subjective than the cash basis, oftentimes leading to debate even among experienced accounting professionals over their use.

Receipt of Order

Occasionally a firm will receive orders for goods or services and a time period may elapse between the order and delivery. Products may have to be secured from suppliers; services may await the availability of the firm's staff. The central question is whether this situation justifies recognition of revenue at a time prior to delivery of the ordered goods or services. An argument might be made that the securing of an order is an important part of the earning process (particularly in industries such as magazine publishing). However, present accounting policy does not permit recognition of revenue at such a time, primarily because of the practical difficulty in separating the total price into that associated with securing the order from that associated with producing and/or delivering the goods or services. Therefore, no accounting recognition is given to the receipt of an order. If an advance payment is received, the receipt of cash and the associated obligation to provide goods or services in the future are recognized, but no revenue is recognized.

Example 8–1 | The Abbott Magazine Company was recently formed to sell the new magazine *Scan*. The price of the magazine on the newsstand is $1 per copy. Individuals can subscribe to the magazine for one year for a price of $10. During the first month of operations the company sold 12,000 new annual subscriptions, accompanied by total advance payments of $120,000.

If the obtaining of orders were interpreted as satisfying the criteria for recognition of revenue, the company would recognize $120,000 revenue in the first month of operation. But unless it can be argued that the order-getting process is the major part of the overall earning process, leaving only minor services yet to be performed, it would not be appropriate to recognize all the revenue at this point in time. Although no revenue is recognized at this time, the advance payment must be given accounting recognition as an obligation (liability) of the firm either to provide future services or, failing to do so, to return the money. For the Abbott Magazine Company, a liability entitled advance payments on subscriptions would be recorded.

The appropriate journal entry follows:

Cash	120,000	
Advance payments on subscriptions		120,000

Since production and delivery on orders can be associated in this case with identifiable and separable units (i.e., individual magazines), the realization principle is presumed to be satisfied with each partial delivery, and a proportional amount of the total price is recognized as revenue. Thus, in the first month that magazines are produced and distributed, the company recognizes revenue of $10,000 (1/12 × $120,000). This is accomplished by reducing the liability, advance payments on subscriptions, by $10,000 and increasing revenue by a similar amount. The journal entry is as follows:

Advance payments on subscriptions	10,000	
Subscription revenue earned		10,000

This revenue recognition process continues each month until the company has provided each subscriber with 12 copies of the magazine and earned the total revenue of $120,000. Note this accounting treatment was originally discussed in Chapter Four as an internal adjustment.

Point of Production

In Exhibit 8–1, the finished goods stage represents the state of production where a marketable good exists. In some cases this results in an unquestionable salable commodity, such as gold or silver. These goods may meet the conditions of the realization principle during their production or creation if their prices are certain

period is a function of (1) the costs incurred during the period; (2) the revised estimate of costs yet to be incurred to complete the project; (3) the estimated profit earned to date; and (4) the amount of profit recognized in prior periods. In the first year (1989), it is estimated that 40 percent of the total work on the project was completed, based on the ratio of costs incurred in that year ($400,000) to the end-of-year estimate of total costs on the project ($1,000,000 = $400,000 + $600,000). Based on the presently estimated total profit of $500,000, $200,000 is recognized as income in 1989. The journal entry to recognize the expense accumulations during 1989 is as follows:

December 31, 1989	Cost of contract completed (expense)	400,000	
	Various assets and liabilities		400,000

Then the revenue earned on the percentage-of-completion basis is recognized:

December 31, 1989	Accounts receivable—contract	600,000	
	Contract revenue earned		600,000

The difference between contract revenue earned and research contract expenses at December 31, 1989 is profit of $200,000 for the year 1989.

In 1990 the same procedure is applied. But in this year, the sum of the costs incurred to date and the revised (as of December 31, 1990) estimate of costs to complete produce a new estimate of total profit from the project, $450,000. This new estimate of profit is the basis for the allocation of projected accomplishment to past and future periods. The income to be recognized in 1990 is the difference between profit allocated to work done to date and the amount of profit from the project already recognized in 1989. Thus the profit recognized in 1990 reflects both the estimate of accomplishment in the period and the correction of amounts reported in prior periods that were based on an earlier estimate of total income on the project.

The journal entries are

December 31, 1990	Cost of contract completed	350,000	
	Various assets and liabilities		350,000
December 31, 1990	Accounts receivable—contract	471,429	
	Contract revenue earned		471,429

Comparing the effects of these journal entries with the arithmetic analysis shown in Exhibit 8–2, we note that total contract revenue earned to December 31, 1990 is $1,071,429. Total project costs incurred to the same point in time are $750,000. The difference is the total profit recognized on the contract for 1989 and 1990, namely $321,429 ($1,071,429 − $750,000 = $321,429), which is allocated $200,000 to 1989 and $121,429 to 1990.

In 1991, the project is completed and the total income from it becomes known. Profit recognized in 1991 is the difference between the actual total income and the cumulative income recognized in the two prior years (see Exhibit 8–2 for details). The journal entries are

December 31, 1991	Cost of contract completed	275,000	
	Various assets and liabilities		275,000
December 31, 1991	Accounts receivable—contract	428,571	
	Contract revenue earned		428,571

Unrealistic Assumption

A long-term production project accounted for under the percentage-of-completion method is reflected as an asset in the statement of financial position while still in progress. At any point in time, the value assigned to the project is the account receivable related to the contract less any progress billings made by the customer. In our example, assuming no progress billings had been made, the research project would be valued at $600,000 at the end of 1989, and $1,071,429 at the end of 1990.

Completed Contract Method. The completed contract method recognizes revenue in accordance with the point-of-sale interpretation of the realization principle. That is, no revenue is recognized until the production is completed and accepted by the customer. All costs incurred in the production activity are accumulated in a construction-in-process asset account until delivery is made. At that time, the total sales price is recognized as revenue, and the accumulated costs of production are recognized as an expense. By deferring the recognition of revenue until the period in which the project is completed, the total accomplishment (revenue and profit) is associated only with this period. No amount of accomplishment is attributed to prior periods, even though substantial productive activity may have occurred. Hence, if long-term projects represent a significant part of the contracting firm's operations, the revenue recognition pattern produced by the completed contract method significantly distorts the performance (net income) reported by the firm over time.

Using Example 8–2 to illustrate this method, the following journal entries would be made to record the work performed on this contract during 1989 and 1990:

December 31, 1989	Contract in process (asset)	400,000	
	Various assets and liabilities		400,000
December 31, 1990	Contracts in process	350,000	
	Various assets and liabilities		350,000

In 1991, when the contract is completed, Ecology, Inc., would record the revenue and related expenses. Thus the entire amount of the profit on the contract would be included in 1991 net income.

December 31, 1991	Cost of contract completed (expense)	1,025,000	
	Contract in process		750,000
	Various assets and liabilities		275,000
December 31, 1991	Accounts receivable—contract	1,500,000	
	Contract revenue earned		1,500,000

Any payments received from the customer during the production of the contract (progress billings) would be recorded as a liability representing deferred revenue. This revenue is treated as earned in the year the contract is completed.

Percentage-of-Completion and Completed Contracts Methods Compared. Whenever the production period is significantly long and the customer's eventual payment is relatively certain, the percentage-of-completion method is used so as to better associate the recognition of revenue (and profit) with the period in which it is earned. Using Example 8–2, we have the following contrast between the completed contract method and the percentage-of-completion method:

	Profit Recognized under:	
	Percentage-of-Completion Method	*Completed Contract Method*
1989	$200,000	0
1990	121,429	0
1991	153,571	475,000
	$475,000	$475,000

The percentage-of-completion method in this case clearly traces the productive activities of the firm better than does the completed contract method. But since the percentage-of-completion method introduces a much greater degree of uncertainty into the income measurement process, it should be used only when the estimates required can be made with an acceptable degree of accuracy. These estimates involve the price to be received when the project is completed, the costs to be incurred on the project, and periodic assessments of the percentage of completion achieved. Where these estimates are believed to be reasonably dependable, the percentage-of-completion method is preferred. However, if the uncertainties associated with a long-term project are so great as to render the estimates of doubtful validity, the completed contract method should be used.

Value Accretion, Appreciation, and Discovery

The case of long-term contracts raises the question of whether the sale transaction per se earns revenue, or if revenue is earned by the prior effort to ready goods or services for sale. Of course, we probably would not wish to recognize revenue on the basis of production alone, especially when the items produced simply pile up in warehouse possibly because they have limited or no salability.

Many economic commodities are subject to accretion growth and enhancement of economic value during a period of time. For instance, timber on tree farms grows with the passage of time and is typically worth more at the end of an accounting period than at the beginning. Appreciation produces similar results but without any physical changes. For example, corporate stocks or bonds may appreciate in value due to rises in market prices over and above the rate of inflation. Paintings in art collections sometimes appreciate, as do rare stamps and coins. Even though there is no physical change involved, economic value may grow through passage of time, through changes in people's tastes and preferences, and the like. Relatedly, valuable resources may be discovered. Mineral deposits or natural resources may be found as additions to known reserves or as new reserves altogether. Application of the realization principle precludes the recognition of revenue on the basis of accretion, appreciation, or discovery. The monetary amounts (prices) in any such economic value enhancements are typically not reasonably certain enough to warrant their recognition as revenue.

Credit Sales

Upon completion of a sale transaction, the seller either receives cash or a legally enforceable claim against the buyer. However, a legally enforceable claim is not a guarantee that payment will be received. Whether short term or long term, all receivables have a common characteristic—there is some uncertainty about their ultimate collectibility. When the uncertainty is judged to be low, or reasonably measurable, revenue is recognized at the date of sale. Normally there is concurrent recognition of the estimated losses expected from accounts that will ultimately be uncollectible. However, when the degree of uncertainty regarding the final collection of cash is high (e.g., when the collection period extends over a long period of time), recognition of revenue may be deferred beyond the point of sale. In this case, the installment sales or cost recovery method might be used.

Estimating Bad Debts. When a customer is unable to pay an account, the loss incurred by the business is a bad debt loss. These losses could be recognized as an expense of the period in which it is determined that the account is uncollectible. However, this treatment violates the matching principle since the extension of credit and the related acceptance of the risk that some accounts will ultimately be uncollectible represent costs directly related to the generation of the revenue recognized. Thus the bad debt is recognized in the same period that the sale giving rise to the account is recognized as revenue.

The question then is how to associate future bad accounts with the related current sales revenues. Firms generally do not make specific credit sales that they expect to prove uncollectible. But they do have historical evidence of their experience with bad accounts. Using this experience they can estimate the amount of bad debts that they ultimately can expect from the current period's sales. This estimate provides the measure of the bad debt expense to be assigned to the current period.

The recognition of bad debt expense also involves an adjustment to accounts receivable. The balance of accounts receivable is reduced to the net amount estimated to be ultimately collected from the group of claims against customers for current sales. This adjustment to accounts receivable is made using a contra-asset account, similar to the accumulated depreciation account, entitled allowance for doubtful accounts. Each time that estimated bad debts are recognized as an expense, the negative balance of the account increases. Note that the expense account is an income statement account; the allowance account appears in the financial position statement as a contra account to accounts receivable.

When an individual account included in accounts receivable is determined to be bad, the balance of the uncollectible account is deducted from both accounts receivable and allowance for doubtful accounts. There is no change in the net amount estimated to be collectible, nor is an expense recorded, since one was recognized in the period of the sale.

Actual experienced losses influence the net receivable amount reported on the financial statement only if an end-of-period review suggests that such losses were substantially different than originally estimated. In this case an additional adjustment to expense and the contra-asset account is required. Example 8–3 illustrates the journal entries.

Example 8–3 | Easy Sales Company makes many of its sales to customers on credit. The treasurer's staff screens the credit application of each new customer before delivery of the first order. If the customer is judged credit-worthy, the goods are delivered and the customer billed by mail. If the customer is judged not credit-worthy, the goods are delivered COD. As a result of this policy, only about 2 percent of total credit sales turn out in the long run to be uncollectible. Sales and collection data for Easy Sales for 1990 and 1991 are as follows:

Year	Sales		Collections of Accounts Receivable	Actual Accounts Determined Uncollectible
	Cash	Credit		
1990	$50,000	$300,000	$245,000	$5,000
1991	40,000	360,000	370,000	9,000

Easy Sales records the estimated uncollectible portion of new accounts receivable as a bad debt expense each year for income measurement purposes. At the end of the year, all unpaid customer balances are reviewed for their estimated collectibility. If the balance in the allowance account is deemed inadequate to absorb the estimated uncollectible accounts receivable, an additional adjustment is made. On January 1, 1990, the balances of accounts receivable and allowance for doubtful accounts were $40,000 and $1,500, respectively. At the end of 1991, it is discovered that a customer who owed the company $3,000 at the beginning of the year has unexpectedly gone bankrupt.

During 1990, Easy Sales would make the following journal entries to record the cash and credit sales and collection of accounts receivable:

Cash	50,000	
Accounts receivable	300,000	
Sales revenue		350,000
Cash	245,000	
Accounts receivable		245,000

At the end of 1990, Easy Sales estimates 2 percent of 1990 credit sales will be uncollectible, and $5,000 of existing accounts will never be collected. The following entries record the estimated bad debt expense due to current period sales and the actual bad debt experience due to prior periods' sales, respectively:

Bad debt expense	6,000	
Allowance for doubtful accounts		6,000
Allowance for doubtful accounts	5,000	
Accounts receivable		5,000

Accounts receivable in Easy Sales' December 31, 1990 balance sheet would appear as follows:

Accounts receivable	$90,000
Less: Allowance for doubtful accounts	(2,500)
Net accounts receivable	$87,500

At the end of 1991, Easy Sales estimates 2 percent of 1991 credit sales will be uncollectible, and $9,000 of existing accounts will never be collected. Entries are made in 1991 to reflect cash and credit sales, collection of accounts receivable, estimated bad debt expense, and actual uncollectible account:

Cash	40,000	
Accounts receivable	360,000	
Sales revenue		400,000

Cash	370,000	
Accounts receivable		370,000
Bad debt expense	7,200	
Allowance for doubtful accounts		7,200
Allowance for doubtful accounts	9,000	
Accounts receivable		9,000

On December 31, 1991 an additional adjustment of $3,000 is needed to reflect the discovery that one of Easy Sales' credit customers had gone bankrupt. However, since this customer had not yet failed to pay Easy Sales, the adjustment represents an increase to the allowance for doubtful accounts (rather than reduction in accounts receivable).

Bad debt expense	3,000	
Allowance for doubtful accounts		3,000

Accounts receivable in Easy Sales' December 31, 1991 balance sheet would appear as follows:

Accounts receivable	$71,000
Less: Allowance for doubtful accounts	(3,700)
Net accounts receivable	$67,300

Bad debt allowances may be arithmetically determined in a number of different ways. Generally accepted accounting principles only stipulate that appropriate calculations be (1) systematic; (2) related to actual bad debts experience; and (3) consistent from period to period. In our example we used a percentage of the period's credit sales as the bad debts estimator. Some firms employ a percentage of total receivables outstanding at year-end as the appropriate adjustment. Still other firms prepare elaborate aging schedules which classify all of their receivables according to the length of period for which they have remained unpaid. Then, on the basis of such classifications, they assign uncollectibility ratios to different age groups of accounts receivable. The objective of all the methods is an appropriate matching of revenue and expense in the income statement, and an appropriate statement of collectibility of the receivables in the statement of financial position.

Installment Sales Method. Estimating bad debts is used in most situations involving credit sales, regardless of the period of time over which the accounts are to be collected. However, there are circumstances where the uncertainty regarding ultimate collection is so great that using an allowance for doubtful accounts is insufficient. In such cases it may be more appropriate to use a revenue recognition basis that is tied directly to the collection of cash, such as the installment sales method.

Example 8–4 | The Frontier Land Company develops and sells lots in West Texas. The company's objective is to create a retirement community similar to those in Arizona and Florida. While the owners of the company believe that the climatic conditions are well suited to this type of development, they realize that many potential customers may have reservations about the viability of the project. Under these circumstances it will be difficult to sell the lots on a cash basis, or even on credit if the terms of sale provide for full payment to be made within a fairly short time. Yet some lots must be sold and building initiated in order for this potential customer apprehension to be overcome. Therefore the developers decide to offer the lots for sale for $99 down, and $400 at the end of each year for the next five years. If a customer fails to make a payment on a contract within 60-day grace period after each annual due date, title to the land reverts to the developer.

Under conditions such as those described in Example 8–3, it is difficult to determine at the time of sale the amount of cash that will ultimately be realized from any single customer. Previous experience on projects of this type indicates that many customers will default, often early in the life of the contract. If a reasonable estimate of the potential losses from the installment contracts can be made, the total revenue can be recognized in the period of sale along with the estimated bad debt expense. However, the management of Frontier may decide that it is not possible to make a reasonably dependable estimate of the number of land contract accounts that will default. Therefore it might decide to recognize the profit from the transaction in relation to actual collections of cash using the installment sales method.

If the cost of each lot to Frontier was $1,099, the total profit to be recognized when the cash is ultimately collected will be $1,000 ($2,099 − $1,099). Under the installment sales method, the profit to be recognized in any period is determined by multiplying total potential profit times the ratio of cash collections in that period to the total cash collections to be made from the sale. This method is illustrated in Exhibit 8–3.

The journal entry made at the time of sale represents several aspects of the transaction. The account containing the cost of the item sold is reduced by that cost with a credit to inventory (in this case $1,099). The cash account is increased by the amount of the down payment ($99). The account, installment contracts receivable, is increased by the total amount of the installment payments ($2,000). A contra-asset account, deferred income on installment contracts, is credited for the profit on the uncollected installments ($950). A revenue account is credited for the portion of the total profit related to the down payment ($50). For Frontier, the journal entry is as follows:

Cash	99	
Installment contracts receivable	2,000	
Lot inventory (West Texas)		1,099
Deferred income on installment contracts		950
Realized income on installment contracts		
(retained earnings)		50

As each installment payment is received, cash is increased and installment contracts receivable is decreased by the amount of the installment ($400 per year), and the deferred income on installments is reduced and income is realized for the portion of the total profit related to the installment ($190 for each installment). For Frontier the journal entries are as follows:

Cash	400	
Installment contracts receivable		400
Deferred income on installment contracts	190	
Realized income on installment contracts		190

EXHIBIT 8-3

Revenue Recognition Pattern for Frontier Land Company Under Installment Sales Method

Year	Cash Collection	Ratio of Cash Collected to Selling Price	Profit Recognized
1	$ 499	$499/$2,099 = 24%	$ 240(24% × $1,000)
2	400	400/ 2,099 = 19	190(19 × 1,000)
3	400	400/ 2,099 = 19	190(19 × 1,000)
4	400	400/ 2,099 = 19	190(19 × 1,000)
5	400	400/ 2,099 = 19	190(19 × 1,000)
	$2,099	100%	$1,000

Cost Recovery Method. An even more conservative approach than the installment sales method to account for a high degree of uncertainty regarding ultimate collection is to defer recognition of income altogether until the cost of the product sold has been fully recovered. In Example 8–3, no income would be recognized until cash of $1,099, equal to the cost of the land, had been collected. After the total cost had been recovered, all subsequent collections would be recognized as profit. While the installment sales method of recognizing revenue is applied in current financial reporting by some companies, the cost recovery method is rarely used.

REVENUE MEASUREMENT

Even when there is no question as to the time period for recognizing revenue, issues may arise as to the amount of revenue to be recorded. Typically this occurs when the price of the product includes future services to be provided, when discounts to the selling price are granted, or when merchandise is returned.

Goods and Future Services

Occasionally a single sales price may include goods that are delivered at the date of sale and the promise to provide future services. Such additional services may involve the provision of financing, warranty, or franchising services. It is inappropriate to recognize the total sales price as revenue of the current period when the company has not earned the revenue related to the future services. Thus the single price must be allocated separately to the goods and the future services. The portion allocated to the goods may be recognized as revenue in the period of sale, while the portion allocated to future services should be recognized as revenue concurrent with the delivery of these services. We will illustrate this procedure for financing, warranty, and franchising services.

Financing Services. In many instances, the period of time between the date of sale and the collection of cash is of short duration. However, when the length of the collection period is substantial, recognition should be given to the opportunity cost incurred by the seller to wait to collect his or her money. This

EXHIBIT 8–4
Calculation of Present Value of a Westlake Used Car Sales Contract

Year	Cash Flow	PV$_{(n,0.10)}$	Present Value of Cash Flows
0	$1,000	1.0	$1,000
1	1,000	0.909	909
2	1,000	0.826	826
3	1,000	0.751	751
4	1,000		683
	$5,000		$4,169

opportunity cost represents the price of the financing services provided to the buyer. To measure the price related to the financing service, the price for the delivered good to be paid in the future by the customer should be discounted at the time of the sale to determine the cash equivalent value of the credit sale. The difference between the total price which will eventually be collected and the cash equivalent (present value) of the future payments represents the price paid for the financing services. Thus financing revenue is recognized as earned over the collection period of the receivable.

Example 8–5 | Westlake Used Cars offered a customer a car for $1,000 down and $1,000 at the end of each year for four years. Westlake had paid $3,000 for the car. The total price charged to the customer of $5,000 represents compensation for two services: selling the car and providing services. The present value of the sales contract is determined to measure the portion of the total price attributable to the car and financing. Assuming Westlake has an opportunity rate of 10 percent, the present value is calculated in Exhibit 8–4.

The calculation of the present value of the sales contract in Exhibit 8–4 implies Westlake Used Cars would be willing to accept $4,169 today in lieu of the contract terms of $1,000 down and $1,000 per year for four years. The price associated with the sale of the car is more properly stated at $4,169. The difference of $831 is the amount of revenue that will be earned from providing a financing service.

The journal entries to record this type of contract involve first recognizing an asset contracts receivable for the present value of the future cash payments and crediting revenue related to the sale of the good. At the end of each year the amount in contracts receivable is increased by the imputed interest, calculated as the opportunity rate times the beginning balance in contracts receivable. Interest income realized is credited for an equal amount. Contracts receivable is reduced each time a cash collection is received. At the end of the life of the contract, the balance of the receivable will be reduced to zero.

Returning to the facts given in Example 8–5, Westlake Used Cars would make the following journal entries to record the sale of the car:

Cash	1,000	
Contracts receivable	3,169	
Revenue from car sales		4,169
Cost of cars sold	3,000	
Car inventory		3,000

Note that contracts receivable has been reduced by the $1,000 down payment received by Westlake. The amount of revenue from the financing service and related amount assigned to contracts receivable each year is summarized in Exhibit 8–5. These amounts are recorded at the end of each year, along with the $1,000 payment made by the customer. Thus, at the end of year 1 Westlake would make the following journal entry:

Contracts receivable	317	
Interest income realized		317
Cash	1,000	
Contracts receivable		1,000

This method has two advantages. First, it separates the total contract price of $5,000 into the amount related to the sale of the car ($4,169) and the amount related to providing financing services ($831). Second, it associates the interest income recognized with the time period in which it is earned (namely, the length of the contract period). Additionally, it measures the earned interest income based on how much has been loaned to the customer during the time period (note the decline in the contracts receivable account).

Warranty Services. When merchandise is sold with a warranty or service guarantee, the total selling price is again composed of two elements: a price for the product itself and a price for the warranty on the product. The amount of the selling price that is attributable to the product itself is earned in the period of sale. However, the portion of the selling price that represents compensation for the guarantee is not earned until the services are provided over the life of the warranty. Example 8–6 illustrates these points.

EXHIBIT 8–5

Interest Revenue and Contracts Receivable for Westlake Used Cars

	Year			
	1	*2*	*3*	*4*
Contracts receivable, beginning of year	$3,169	$2,486	$1,735	$ 909
Interest income (10% times beginning balance)	317	249	174	91
Cash collection	(1,000)	(1,000)	(1,000)	(1,000)
Contracts receivable, end of year	$2,486	$1,735	$ 909	$ 0

Example 8–6 | The Modern TV Company sells 27-inch color television sets at a price of $495. This includes a warranty on all parts and labor for a two-year period. In establishing the selling price, Modern assumed that the average cost per customer of servicing defective units would be $45 in the first year of the warranty and $80 in the second year of the warranty. Since Modern wishes to earn a 20 percent profit on its warranty cost, it increased the price of the TV by $150 (120 percent × $125). Therefore it would be willing to sell the TV without a service warranty at a price of $345.

Based upon these facts, revenue should be recognized at the time of sale for $345 per unit. The additional $150 received at the time of sale represents payment for undelivered services; its recognition is deferred to future periods, as it is earned throughout the warranty period.

Assuming a credit sale based on the facts of Example 8–6, the following journal entry is made at the point of sale:

Accounts receivable	495	
Sales revenue		345
Warranty service liability		125
Deferred income on future warranty services		25

Assume that during the first year after the sale, warranty service expenses were $45 as estimated. This prompts the following journal entries:

Warranty service liability	45	
Cash (or other assets or liabilities)		45
Deferred income on future warranty services		
(45/125 of $25)	9	
Realized income on warranty services		9

Application of this method depends upon the ability to separate the total sales price into the portion applicable to the product and the portion applicable to the warranty. Except in cases where it is impossible to measure the costs involved in providing goods and future services, the total sales price should be separated into its component parts and each part included in income in the time period when it is earned.

Franchising Services. Fast-food operations, car and equipment rental agencies, computer service bureaus, hotels, and motels are oftentimes operated as franchises. Franchising occurs when the holder of a patent or the owner of a unique product or service (the franchisor) permits someone else to sell the good or service (the franchisee) in exchange for payment of fees. Normally an initial fee is required when the franchise contract is signed, and subsequent payments are made for continued use of the franchise and purchase of franchise-related items. For example, a franchise restaurant might purchase food, menus, and restaurant furniture. Although the initial contract payments are often large, the franchisor usually delivers relatively little product when the franchising operation begins. As illustrated by Example 8–7, this presents a difficult revenue recognition situation.

Example 8–7 | The Photo Lab franchise was set up to sell film for amateur photographer use and to provide quick photo developing services. Since little physical space is required for each Photo Lab sales outlet (supplies are reordered biweekly from central warehouses, and developing is done in central processing laboratories), franchise holders occupy small counter spaces in shopping malls or drive-up booths in parking lots.

The franchise contract requires a $12,000 initial payment for which Photo Lab paints and equips the interior of a small shopping center location or installs a drive-up parking lot sales booth. Space rentals, utility costs, taxes, insurance, and the like, are the responsibility of the franchisee. Costs to individual franchisees of supplies and processing are at a discount of 25 percent from the published prices. The franchisee is obligated to pay Photo Lab 10 percent of all gross receipts. For this 10 percent fee, Photo Lab supplies credit, bookkeeping services, advertising in local news media, sales personnel training, and management consulting.

In this example, the initial payment of $12,000 by the franchisee exceeds the value of the product delivered by Photo Lab (interior furnishings of a small sales outlet). The portion of the fee which represents these costs plus a reasonable markup for profit should be recognized as revenue when the contract is signed. The remainder of the initial fee should be allocated in equal amounts to periods covered by the initial contract, assuming it is earned ratably over that period. The subsequent sale of supplies and film-developing services by Photo Lab to its franchisees is revenue earned by Photo Lab in the period of sale. However, the yearly fee charged of 10 percent of gross receipts presents problems similar to the initial payment. The services provided in exchange for this fee are likely to occur unevenly from year to year. Advertising and bookkeeping services probably vary little, but sales training and consulting services may vary greatly. Additionally, a part of the fee relates to the continuing use of the franchise. As a practical matter, therefore, the annual franchise fee is recognized as revenue in the year it is assessed.

Discounts, Returns, and Allowances

Determining the amount of revenue to recognize may be complicated when the seller reduces the normal selling price for volume or cash discounts, accepts merchandise returns, or grants allowances.

Price Discounts. In some industries, it is common to have a series of discounts from standard prices granted to customers based on the volume of products they purchase. Sometimes these price discounts are stated in terms of a single percentage reduction from the list price, say 10 percent. The price would then be 90 percent of the stated list price. Other times the price discounts are stated as a series of percentage discounts from the list price, say 10/10/5. In this case, the first discount is applied against the list price, and succeeding discounts are applied sequentially to the price established after taking into account the previous discount.

Example 8–8 | The Globe Steel Company sells a wide range of steel products. It maintains a standard set of list prices for these products, together with a series of price discounts based on the volume a customer orders. When the Globe Steel Company sells 1,000 units to a customer at a price of $20 per unit with price discounts of 20/10/10, the actual selling price is computed as follows:

List price (1,000 units @ $20)	$ 20,000
Less: 20% price discount	−4,000
	$ 16,000
Less: 10% price discount	−1,600
	$ 14,400
Less: 10% price discount	−1,440
	$ 12,960

In this example, the selling price is not the list price of $20,000, but rather the $12,960 the customer is obligated to pay. The revenue to be recognized by Globe Steel in the year of the sale is $12,960.

In general, where price discounts are made available to customers, revenue is recognized for each sale in the amount of the net price to the customer after the price discounts are deducted. The price discounts are not expenses; rather, they are means of adjusting the set of list prices to prevailing or competitive prices.

Cash Discounts. Sellers also grant discounts for prompt payments, as inducement to customers to pay as soon as possible. Such discounts may also reduce the risk of bad debt losses if they induce payment by otherwise delinquent customers. Cash discounts are normally stated as: terms 2/10, net/30. This means that the customer is entitled to a 2 percent discount for paying the account in ten days; or obligated to pay the full balance in thirty days. If these terms were applied to a sale for $1,000 on July 1, the customer would have the option of paying $980 within the ten-day period following the sale, or the full $1,000 by July 31.

Two different treatments of cash discounts are found in accounting practice. In the first method, the seller might recognize the discount (when taken by the buyer) as an expense or as a reduction to revenue in that period. In the previous example the seller would report revenue of $1,000 and then deduct the $20 cash discount as either an offset against revenue or as a cash discounts expense. A weakness in this treatment is that it does not recognize revenue at the cash equivalent price when the customer fails to take the discount. In the previous example, if the customer fails to take the discount, $1,000 sales revenue would be recognized. However, the cash equivalent price of the sales transaction was $980—the amount at which the merchandise could have been purchased with a cash payment during the first ten days. Recording the sale at the full $1,000 ignores the financing service being provided by the seller.

The second method of recording cash discounts is to record the revenue and the accounts receivable at the cash equivalent price at the date of sale—in the example, $980. If the discount is taken, no further adjustments are required. However, if the customer fails to take the discount, the seller receives $1,000 and accounts receivable is reduced by $980. The $20 difference is reflected by the seller as income from discounts allowed but not taken by the buyer, or revenue from the short-term credit or financing service the seller has provided.

Merchandise Returns. Many business enterprises, especially retail stores, allow customers to return recently purchased merchandise which is either left unopened in original packages or found defective. Unopened merchandise is typically returned to the seller's inventory and later sold to another customer. The journal entries are of the following form:

Sales returns
    Accounts receivable (or cash)
Merchandise inventory
    Cost of merchandise sold

At the end of the period, the sales returns account is subtracted from the total in the sales revenue account, leaving the net sales figure that appears in the income statement. Maintaining the sales returns in a separate account (rather than reducing sales revenue) allows management to accumulate a record of the volume of sales being returned.

Sales Allowances. Allowances on items sold usually result from defective or otherwise unusable merchandise. The item cannot be returned to the regular inventory. Instead it is either sent out for repair, returned to the manufacturer, sold at a discount, or destroyed. Allowances are reductions in revenue and the customers' payments. No changes are made to the inventory account. The appropriate journal entry is

Sales allowances
    Accounts receivable (or cash)

As in the case of merchandise returns, the balance in sales allowances is treated as a direct reduction from the sales revenue shown in the income statement.

SUMMARY

This chapter explored some of the more common situations which give rise to difficulties in determining when to recognize revenue and how to measure revenue. The timing of revenue recognition becomes a problem when the time period for the earning process is long (percentage of completion versus completed contract) and the ultimate collection of the sales price is uncertain (credit sales, installment sales, or cost recovery). Measurement questions arise when goods are sold along with future services (financing, warranty, and franchising services); and when price and cash discounts, merchandise returns, and sales allowances are granted. This chapter has discussed and illustrated the accounting procedures used in these various situations.

Questions for Review and Discussion

8–1. Define

    a. Revenue
    b. Realization
    c. Recognition
    d. Percentage of completion
    e. Completed contract
    f. Value accretion
    g. Credit sale
    h. Bad debts
    i. Installment sale
    j. Cost recovery
    k. Financing services

    l. Warranty
    m. Franchising
    n. Price discount
    o. Cash discount
    p. Merchandise return
    q. Sales allowance

8–2. State the two criteria for revenue recognition required by the realization principle. When is this principle usually considered satisfied in current financial reporting?

8–3. Why is revenue usually not recognized when a firm order is received from a customer?

8–4. What are the three circumstances when revenue is recognized as progress is made on the production of ordered goods or services rather than at the point of sale? Which criterion of the realization principle is emphasized in this case?

8–5. Explain why the realization principle might be relaxed when revenue is recognized as silver and gold are produced.

8–6. When the percentage-of-completion method is used for recognizing revenue from a long-term production project, what amount is assigned to the inventory related to the project on the statement of financial position?

8–7. Even though long-term construction contracts are typically negotiated for a fixed price, the estimated costs to complete a given contract often vary from period to period. Explain how the percentage-of-completion method accomodates varying contract completion cost estimates.

8–8. One of the issues in a court case involving the propriety of the reported income of Four Seasons Nursing Centers of America, Inc., was the method used to determine the percentage of completion on the construction of nursing homes. The initial estimate of income under the percentage-of-completion methods was based on architects' physical estimates of completion. The auditors tested these estimates by comparing costs incurred to total estimated costs and insisted that the percentage completion to date (and therefore income recognized) be reduced. Nevertheless, the auditors were criticized for having included $2 million in costs incurred for special-order components and subcontract work done "off site" for which no deliveries had been made. Under what conditions, if any, do you believe that such off-site costs should be included in the calculation of percentage-of-completion achieved?

8–9. Suppose you own a surfboard manufacturing shop in Hawaii. You manufacture surfboards on an assembly-line basis for 6 months, then close your operation for the following 18 months while your surfboard inventory is sold. The same cycle repeats itself every 2 years. What are the shortcomings of the conventional revenue recognition procedure in this case? Would financial reporting be improved if financial statements were prepared only every two years?

8–10. Discuss the pros and cons of permitting large oil companies to recognize discovery values of oil reserves as revenues in their published income statements.

8–11. Some uncertainty exists as to the ultimate collectibility of all receivables, but the accounting treatment varies depending upon the degree of uncertainty. Describe two alternative approaches to uncertainty. Which of the two criteria of the realization principles is emphasized under each approach?

8–12. Why are bad debts that may be incurred in future periods estimated and reflected as expenses in the period of the sale, rather than in the period in which they are determined uncollectible?

8–13. What effect does the write-off of a bad account receivable have on the net value of accounts receivable and bad debt expense of the current period?

8–14. In published financial statements, should estimated bad debt losses be reported as reductions from sales revenue or as a separate expense item? What difference does it make, if any, how bad debt losses are reported in financial statements?

8–15. Arithmetically, there are at least four different ways of estimating future bad debt losses. Which of these four methods do you think yields the most acceptable results? Give the reasons for your conclusion.

8–16. The installment sales method of accounting for very risky installment accounts receivable is described in this chapter. An alternative to that method is one in which (1) the present value method is used to value the accounts receivable, with an appropriately high discount rate which recognizes the high opportunity cost for such risky credit granting; and (2) a substantial allowance is created for bad debts. Contrast the pattern of income recognition and asset valuation under this alternative with the installment sales method. Make up an example to illustrate your explanation. Which method do you prefer? Defend your position.

8–17. Not every installment sales contract is accounted for by the installment sales method of revenue recognition. Why? Describe a business situation where point-of-sale revenue recognition is appropriate for an installment sales contract.

8–18. When a single sales price includes goods that are delivered at date of sale, as well as the promise to provide future services, describe in general terms the modification that is made to the point-of-sale interpretation of the realization principle. Indicate which criterion of the realization principle is given more weight in this modification.

8–19. Financing, warranty, and franchising activities are all identified in the text as future service elements encountered in some business operations and as posing special revenue recognition challenges. Identify three critical dimensions on which these three types of future services (1) differ from each other; and (2) are similar or alike. Be specific.

8–20. Existing financial accounting policies require that the present value method be employed in financial statement reporting of certain receivables. Why are some accounts receivable stated at actual transaction values and others at present values? Is revenue recognition affected by the choice between these two measurement methods?

8–21. Why is it so difficult to account for future services such as warranties included in the price of a physical product? What are the key accounting problems encountered in recognizing both revenues and expenses related to warranty services?

8–22. One of the booming industries in recent years is the franchising industry—partly, say some critics, because of the accounting methods employed. Describe alternative revenue recognition methods that might be used to account for the initial franchise fee. Which method would you prefer? How would it affect your answer if large initial fees are required but continuing franchise fees are small in relation to future services?

8–23. For each of the following events (1) describe the economic effects involved; and (2) write a representative accounting journal entry or entries to record it.

    a. Merchandise sold on credit by a department store is returned in resalable condition.

    b. A piece of furniture is returned to a furniture store after it is damaged by a customer opening the packing crate at home. The store refunds the full cash purchase price and plans to resell the item at a coming sale at 50 percent of its usual price.

    c. A box of stereo equipment was mislabeled and returned by a customer to the store where it was purchased. From there it was returned to the manufacturer. Full-price credit is allowed in each instance. Take the point of view of the store.

8–24. When prompt payment discounts are offered, both the seller and the buyer have the option of recording the transaction either at the gross amount (before any discount is taken), or at the cash equivalent (net) amount. Is the same transaction-recording procedure appropriate for both seller and buyer? Which of the two methods do you recommend and why?

Problems

8–1. Timing of Revenue Recognition. Discuss (1) the time of likely revenue recognition; and (2) any special problems related to such recognition for each of the following types of business enterprises:

1. Grocery store
2. Broker securing motion picture rights for television networks from film studios
3. Forest products company (growing and selling fir logs)
4. Land developer building office parks and selling completed projects to groups of doctors, dentists, and lawyers
5. Computer software firm selling computer programs and computer time to small-business clients
6. Winery producing champagne typically aged three years
7. Travel agency
8. Full-service bank with trust, mortgage, and international divisions
9. Engineering firm building hydroelectric power dams and bridges; typical contract completion time: three years
10. Art gallery
11. Private telephone company serving customers on an island chain of summer resort communities
12. Cattle ranch
13. Savings and loan association lending money for home mortgages
14. Leather shop producing custom-order western saddles
15. Automobile-leasing company
16. College professor receiving royalties on textbook
17. CPA firm providing income tax advice to corporate client
18. Veterans Administration Hospital
19. Gourmet restaurant
20. Municipal museum
21. Life insurance company
22. Ice follies road show
23. Toll Bridge Authority

8–2. Journalizing Revenue Transactions. The West Gate Toll Bridge Authority has established the following rates for passenger automobile crossings: (1) 50¢ cash for cars with one or two occupants; (2) 15¢ cash for cars with three or more occupants; and (3) $6 for commuter ticket books containing twenty coupons.

Required:

Prepare journal entries for the following transactions:

1. Sale of 500-ticket books for cash
2. Daily report from a toll booth showing cash collections of tolls of $875 plus 315 commuting coupons

Enumerate whatever special problems you perceive in recognizing and reporting bridge toll revenues.

8–3. Motion picture rights are typically sold for television exhibition under a contract that covers a package of several films and permits one or more exhibitions of each film during specified license periods. A representative license agreement might include the terms shown next.[2]

---

[2] Adapted from American Institute of Certified Public Accountants, *AICPA Industry Accounting Guide on Accounting for Motion Picture Films*, copyright © 1973 by the American Institute of Certified Public Accountants, Inc., and amended by *Statement of Position 79-4*, 1979.

Contract execution date: July 31, 1991
Number of films and telecasts permitted: 4 films, 2 telecasts each
Fees, license periods, and print delivery dates:

		License Periods		
Film	Total Fee	From	To*	Print Delivery
A	$ 800,000	Oct. 1, 1991	Sept. 30, 1993	Sept. 1, 1991
B	500,000	Oct. 1, 1991	Sept. 30, 1993	Sept. 1, 1991
C	375,000	Sept. 1, 1992	Aug. 31, 1994	Dec. 1, 1991
D	225,000	Sept. 1, 1993	Aug. 31, 1995	Dec. 1, 1993
	$1,900,000			

* The actual license periods expire at the earlier of (1) the second telecast or (2) the end of the stated license period.

Payment schedule: $100,000 at contract execution date, $50,000 per month for 36 months commencing January 1, 1992.

The AICPA committee studying this subject identified four methods in use for financial reporting of revenue from the licensing of films for television:

1. *Contract method.* Total revenue recognized on date the contract is executed.
2. *Billing method.* Revenue recognized as installment payments become due.
3. *Delivery method.* Revenue recognized at date the prints are delivered to licensee.
4. *Deferral or apportionment method.* Revenue spread evenly over the period of the license.

After deliberating the problem, the committee concluded that a licensing agreement should be considered as the sale of a right, and that revenue should be recognized "when a film may be shown for the first time under a licensing agreement" but not until all the following conditions have been satisfied:

1. The sales price for each film is known.
2. The cost of each film is known or reasonably determinable.
3. Collectibility of the full license fee is reasonably assured.
4. The film has been accepted by the licensee in accordance with the conditions of the license agreement.
5. The film is available; i.e., the right is deliverable by the licensor and exercisable by the licensee.

Required:

1. What amount of revenue would be recognized each year from 1991 to 1995 under each of the four methods in use at the time the committee studied the problem?
2. Assuming that the first four of the five conditions promulgated by the committee are satisfied, what pattern of revenue would be recognized from 1991 to 1995 under this present accounting policy?
3. Would you adjust the revenue computed under present accounting policy for the time value of money?
4. Do you believe present policy is an improvement over the four methods the committee found in use in 1973?

8–4. Accounting for Rental Revenues. Video-X Company has developed a videotape library that is continually being updated and further developed. These tapes can be used in connection with several hundred integrated training courses. Video-X

Company rents access to the tape library for a minimum annual fee, plus additional charges for usage above the level covered by the minimum fee.

The basic accounting policy question faced by the company's financial vice-president is whether the contracts constitute completed sales and thus permit the recognition of revenue at the dates of the contracts.

After careful study and deliberation, the vice-president proposes that 50 percent of the economic contribution (defined as total contract revenues less commissions and estimated royalties and servicing costs, all discounted at appropriate interest rates) be recognized at the date a contract is signed, and that the remaining 50 percent be recognized on a straight-line basis over the life of the contract. His principal reasons for proposing this accounting treatment are

1. The AICPA *Motion Picture Films Guide* applies to the Video-X Company (see Problem 8–3).
2. All uncertainties with respect to collection of revenues and determination of related costs (as contemplated in the *Motion Picture Films Guide*) have been substantially removed.

Required:

1. As you understand the facts presented, does the *AICPA Industry Accounting Guide on Accounting for Motion Picture Films* apply?
2. Assume you are the independent CPA of the Video-X Company and are asked to review this particular accounting proposal. State whether you will or will not accept it and give appropriate reasons.
3. Irrespective of existing authoritative financial accounting rules and policies, take a position on how Video-X Company's revenues should be accounted for in the interest of external investment decision makers. Defend your answer.

8–5. Subscription Contracts. The Sports Forecasting Company was formed in 1988 to sell the sports newsletter *We-Pick-Em*. The newsletter is published weekly from August through December, and sold by subscription only. The subscription price for one year is $50.

The newsletter predicted the results of games correctly 80 percent of the time during 1988–1989. Therefore the company expects an increase in subscriptions for 1990. To take advantage of the current seller's market, the company is offering a three-year subscription for $135. The entire amount must be paid before the customer is placed on the mailing list.

The company received total payment for the following number of subscriptions in 1990–1991. (Subscriptions fell off in 1991 because the newsletter was correct only 60 percent of the time in 1990.)

	One-Year Subscriptions	*Three-Year Subscriptions*
1990	5,000	3,000
1991	4,000	1,000

Required:

Prepare a worksheet for 1990–1991 that shows the effects of the listed receipts in all the appropriate accounts, assuming that revenue is recognized in the year in which the service is provided. Assume that revenue is recognized at the end of each year. Ignore beginning balances. Also, prepare appropriate journal entries for 1991.

8–6. Financial Statement Effects of Subscriptions Received. The Local Top Executive Newsletter was started on June 1, 1991. Cash was received each month for yearly subscriptions to this monthly letter, the service to start at the beginning of the month following cash receipt. The following amounts of cash subscriptions were received from subscribers:

June (subscriptions to start July 1)	$5,400
July	6,000
August	4,100
September	4,800
October	7,500
November	6,400
December	4,500

All the foregoing amounts were recorded in a current revenue account labeled newsletter subscription revenue.

Required:

1. Make appropriate adjusting journal entries as of December 31, 1991.
2. Identify all applicable account titles and amounts in the December 31 statement of financial position and income statement.

8–7. Timing of Revenue Recognition for Professional Services. On October 1, 1991, Dr. John Collins, a dentist specializing in orthodontia, initiated teeth positioning treatment and bite correction on Kent Moyer. After previous examination and a consultation with Kent's parents, Dr. Collins had estimated that the corrective treatment would take approximately 20 months. Kent's parents have agreed to pay $400 in cash at the time treatment is initiated and the make 24 monthly payments of $35 each. Dr. Collins has agreed to provide as many treatment sessions and as much mechanical equipment as is needed for the desired corrections. His expected revenue flow from the Moyers is roughly proportionate to the volume of professional services he expects to provide.

Required:

1. How would Dr. Collins recognize revenue from his contract with the Moyers under the realization principle?
2. Assume that you are a banker and that Dr. Collins has applied for a substantial loan to move his offices and purchase additional equipment. Would you treat the value of the contract with the Moyer family for credit evaluation purposes the same as it is interpreted under generally accepted accounting principles? What additional information would be helpful to you as a banker evaluating an appropriate loan limit for Dr. Collins?
3. Enumerate three other economic fact situations in which similar revenue recognition problems occur.

8–8. Completed Contract versus Percentage-of-Completion Revenue Recognition Methods. Free Form Construction Company was awarded a contract in 1988 by The Big University to build a new library. The contract price was $8 million, and Free Form expected to complete the job in 1991. At the time construction begin (early 1989), Free Form estimated that the total costs on the job would be $6 million.
  During the construction period, the following financial data were compiled:

Date	Total Costs Incurred to Date	Estimated Additional Costs to Complete Project
December 31, 1989	$1,500,000	$4,500,000
December 31, 1990	3,900,000	2,600,000
December 31, 1991	6,600,000	0

Required:

Determine the net income that would be reported for each of the three years and in total under (1) the completed contract method; and (2) the percentage-of-completion method. Also, present appropriate journal entries for both accounting methods for 1991.

8–9. Income from Long-Term Construction Contracts. Tower Construction Company builds high-rise office buildings in areas of the Midwest. In 1989 the company won the contract on the Life Insurance Building. The contract price of the building was $10 million. The construction of the building was to be started in July 1989 and completed in June 1991. The Life Insurance Company, the client, agreed in the contract to pay the Tower Construction Company on a limited-percentage-completion basis. Every six months a team of independent consulting engineers paid by Life would inspect the building and Tower's cost records to determine the percentage completion on the project. Life would then be billed by Tower for the percentage toward completion that occurred during the six-month period times the contract price, less 20 percent retainage to be due upon completion (to ensure Tower's interest in completing the building). Payment would be made within 30 days.

During the period July 1, 1989, to June 30, 1991, the engineers judged the project

15 percent complete by December 31, 1989
35 percent complete by June 30, 1990
65 percent complete by December 31, 1990
and complete by June 30, 1991.

During that period of time, the following financial data were assembled by Tower's accountant:

Date	Costs Incurred to Date	Estimated Costs to Complete Project
December 31, 1989	$2,125,000	$6,375,000
June 30, 1990	3,825,000	4,675,000
December 31, 1990	6,300,000	2,700,000
June 30, 1991	9,100,000	0

In measuring income under the percentage-of-completion method, Tower Construction Company uses the cost data (costs incurred and estimated costs to complete the project) rather than the engineering estimates as an indicator of percentage completion.

Required:

1. As of the end of each six-month period, determine the amounts called for below under the completed contract method, and under the percentage-of-completion method of accounting for long-term construction contracts:

(a) Cash collected to date, assuming that Life paid each billing in the 30 days following the date of billing

(b) Income for the six-month period

(c) Balance in construction-in-process (or unbilled contracts in process) account

2. Appropriate journal entries for both accounting methods for 1989 and 1990.

8–10. Recognition of Discovery Values.   The Great Western Gold Mining Company has just completed a particularly significant year because, in the course of its regular mining operations, it discovered at midyear a large and rich vein of gold ore on its holdings. Independent consultants confirmed that the size, content, and purity of the gold in this vein means that it will eventually yield salable gold worth more than $200 million at the current government minimum purchase price of $200 an ounce.

As the executive assistant to the firm's management committee, you are aware that you could also sell gold at various retail markets in Europe at prices in excess of $350 per ounce. Management of the company believes that the value of this gold ore net of production costs should be included in its current annual reports to shareholders as a revenue item for the current year. Since the company has significant experience in gold mining, getting the metal out of the ore is a routine operating matter.

Required:

1. Does currently applicable financial accounting policy permit recognition of revenues from gold ore discoveries? Be specific in supporting your answer.
2. Assume that authoritative conventional financial accounting rules permit revenue recognition of gold ore discoveries. How would the current discovery appear in this year's financial statements of the Great Western Gold Mining Company?
3. State whatever you deem to be the most appropriate financial accounting rule in relation to discovery of independently proven reserves of gold ore and defend the position taken.

8–11. Bad Debts Adjustments.   In the recent past, Columbine Corporation has annually debited bad debts expense and credited allowance for doubtful accounts at 1.5 percent of credit sales for the year. Pertinent data are as follows:

	1989	*1990*	*1991*
(1) Sales on account	$300,000	$350,000	$320,000
(2) Cash collections on these sales:			
In 1989	$200,000	—	—
In 1990	80,000	$300,000	—
In 1991	14,000	45,000	$260,000
(3) Amounts written off as uncollectible:			
In 1989	500	—	—
In 1990	4,800	600	—
In 1991	700	4,400	300
	$300,000	$350,000	
(4) Accounts receivable balance, December 31, 1991			59,700
			$320,000

As indicated in the table, all balances due from customers arising from sales of 1989 and 1990 have, by December 31, 1991, either been collected or written off.

The bookkeeper has made no entries or adjustments beyond those necessary to reflect the sales, the collections from customers, the annual addition to allowance for doubtful accounts, and the write-off of individual accounts against the allowance.

Required:
Assume that all beginning balances at January 1, 1989, were zero.

1. Prepare T-accounts that show the effects of the foregoing transactions as the bookkeeper would have recorded them in the records of the Columbine Corporation.
2. In journal entry form, present whatever adjusting entry or entries you deem necessary as of December 31, 1991. State any assumptions you make to accomplish this requirement.
3. Suppose that on January 15, 1992, after appropriate adjustments as of December 31, 1991, a recovery of $1,000 cash is made on an account receivable that was recorded in 1989 and written off as worthless in 1990. Present an appropriate journal entry to record the recovery as of January 15, 1992.

8–12. Write-off and Recovery of an Account.   During 1991, Clyde Hill Wholesalers experienced the following chain of events:

1. On January 15, Redmond Suppliers, a customer whose overdue account for $2,900 was included in accounts receivable at December 31, 1990, offered a 60-day note in settlement of the account. The face value includes interest for the overdue period. The note, with a face value of $3,000, is non-interest-bearing. It was accepted on the terms offered.
2. The note from Redmond Suppliers was sold to (discounted at) King County State Bank at a discount of 2 percent on January 20, 1991. The proceeds from this discounting were added to Clyde Hill Wholesalers' checking account with the bank.
3. Redmond Suppliers failed to pay the note at maturity. Accordingly, the amount of the note was charged to (i.e., subtracted from) the checking account of Clyde Hill Wholesalers at the note's face value of $3,000.
4. On July 1, 1991, Clyde Hill Wholesalers wrote off the note as worthless. At this time it had determined, through a small-claims court process, that the note was in fact uncollectible.
5. Two years later, on January 15, 1993, Redmond Suppliers paid off the previously defaulted note with compound interest at 10 percent for the intervening two-year period.

Required:

1. Prepare journal entries to record all the foregoing events on the books and records of Clyde Hill Wholesalers.
2. Discuss the revenue recognition implications arising from the chain of events as described.
3. Why would Redmond Suppliers wish to satisfy an obligation that had been written off two years earlier? Were there any special recording problems on the part of Clyde Hill Wholesalers when restitution on the defaulted note was made in 1993?

8–13. Recognition of Bad Debts.   The Buy Now–Pay Later Department Store makes approximately half its sales to customers on credit. The customer obtains credit by completing an application for a credit card. After the application is checked by the credit department and approved by the credit manager, the customer is issued a credit card which he or she must present when purchasing merchandise on credit.

The store sends a balance forward statement (showing beginning balance due, new purchases, payments, and ending balance due) to each customer having a nonzero ending balance at the end of each month. Payment is due when the customer receives the statement. An account becomes past due if the total balance due is not received before the next month's statements are prepared. A list is maintained of accounts with a past-due balance more than 90 days old so that no further credit sales to those accounts will be made.

A study of collections on credit sales for 1985–1989 indicated that approximately 1 percent of credit sales proved to be uncollectible. Also, a study of account balances at year-end showed that differing percentages of year-end balances were ultimately uncollectible, depending on the age of the account. The percentages were as follows:

Current accounts	$\frac{1}{2}\%$
Accounts past due, 1–30 days	1
Accounts past due, 31–60 days	5
Accounts past due, 61–90 days	20
Accounts past due, over 90 days	30

The store follows the practice of matching the estimated uncollectible portion of credit sales against recognized sales revenue (i.e., an allowance for doubtful accounts is used). Whenever a customer account is determined to be uncollectible, the balance of that account is written off against the balance of the allowance account. Also, at year-end the store applies the appropriate percentages (by age category) to customer balances to determine if the balance in the allowance account is sufficient to cover estimated losses in the year-end customer receivable balance. If not, an additional adjustment is made.

The store used the percentages developed in the 1985–1989 study for its accounting adjustments in 1990–1991. Sales and collection data for 1990–1991 follow:

Year	Cash Sales	Credit Sales	Collections on Account	Accounts Determined Uncollectible
1990	$800,000	$ 800,000	$774,000	$ 6,000
1991	800,000	1,000,000	889,000	11,000

The age distribution of customer accounts at year-end for 1990–1991 follows:

Year	Total A/R Balance	Current Accounts	1–30 Past Due	31–60 Past Due	61–90 Past Due	Over 90
1990	$140,000	$120,000	$10,000	$ 6,000	$ 2,000	$ 2,000
1991	240,000	180,000	20,000	20,000	10,000	10,000

Account balances at the end of 1989 were as follows:

Accounts receivable	$120,000
Allowance for doubtful accounts	(4,000)

Required:

1. Prepare a financial position worksheet that shows the effects of the sales, collections, and bad debts experience for 1990–1991. Provide columns for the ef-

fect on cash, accounts receivable, allowance for doubtful accounts, and owners' equity.

2. What are the implications of the analysis of the customer balances at the end of 1991?

8–14. Installment Sales Method. On June 30, 1991, Wilson Corporation sold a parcel of land to Deakin, a developer, for $4 million. Wilson received 10 percent down, and a three-year, 12 percent (per annum) note for the balance. The terms of the note provide that every three months Deakin is to pay $300,000 principal, plus interest on the unpaid balance. The land cost Wilson Corporation $1.2 million five years ago.

The officers of Wilson Corporation are not sure that Deakin will be able to meet his payment obligations on the note. However, they completed the deal because they believed that the price agreed upon was a very favorable one to them; $400,000 was received as a down payment. If Deakin defaults, title to the land reverts to Wilson.

Because of the uncertainty regarding the collectibility of the note, this transaction is recorded using the installment sales method of recognizing revenue.

Required:
Assuming that Deakin makes all payments as they come due, prepare a schedule showing the income that would be recognized by Wilson Corporation each year from 1991 to 1994.

8–15. Journal Entries for Installment Sales Transactions. Office Music Systems, Inc., started business on January 1, 1991. It sells high-quality stereo music systems to businesses and professional firms. If requested to do so, it will also install stereo music systems in new office buildings. The stereo systems and components it carries are sold on regular 30-day open accounts or 24-month installment contracts. Business activities for 1991 can be summarized as follows:

30-day regular sales	$620,000
Installment sales	740,000
Installation revenues (all cash)	120,000
Cost of 30-day open account sales	380,000
Cost of installment sales	370,000
Cost of installation services	140,000
General administrative, sales, and operating expenses	200,000
1991 collections on 30-day open account sales	550,000
Collections on installment sales	260,000

Required:
Prepare journal entries to record all the listed transactions. Assume that the installment sales method of recognizing revenue is employed to account for all sales made on the installment basis. (For expense-recording entries, assume that resources used are represented by various asset and liability accounts.)

8–16. On July 1, 1991, Local Speculation Company sold a parcel of land it had acquired ten years ago (at a cost of $500,000) to Giant Manufacturing Company for $1.8 million. Local received a non-interest-bearing note due July 1, 1994, in payment.

Required:
1. Assuming 12 percent is the appropriate time preference rate for Local, indicate how Local would record the sale transaction on July 1, 1991.

2. Calculated the value at which the note receivable would be carried in the statement of financial position at the end of 1991, 1992, and 1993.

3. Prepare a schedule of revenue that Local would recognize for each year from 1991 through 1994.

8–17. Joint Sale of Product and Installment Financing Services. The Reliable Equipment Company buys construction equipment from heavy-equipment manufacturers and in turn sells the equipment to small to medium-sized construction contractors. The contractors buy from Reliable rather than from the equipment manufacturer because Reliable sells equipment on the installment basis. All of the company's sales are made on an installment basis involving 20 percent down and the remainder in two equal annual installments.

The earnings of the company are composed of (1) profits from the sale of equipment, and (2) the interest on installment sales contracts. The explicit rate is stated to be 12 percent in the sales contracts. Sales prices are set so that if the required payments are discounted at 12 percent, the present value is equal to the list price the customer would have to pay if he or she bought directly from the manufacturer. Reliable makes a profit because it only pays 90 percent of the list price (due to volume discounts).

The company began operations at the start of 1989. Following are the total contract sales prices of the equipment sold each year for 1989–1991.

Year	Contract Sales Price
1989	$1,000,000
1990	1,600,000
1991	2,000,000

Required:

1. Compute the cost to Reliable of the equipment sold for each of the three years. Assume that all purchases and sales occur at the first of the year and that installment payments are made at the end of the year.

2. Prepare all necessary journal entries for 1989–91 to reflect sales, costs, and collection experience, assuming the sale-with-financing method of recognizing income. Be sure to recognize the effects of the time value of money.

8–18. Joint Services and Normal Uncertainty Combined. Computer Sales Company buys and sells small standardized computer systems. All the company's sales are made on an installment plan involving one-third down, and remainder in two equal annual installments.

Computer Sales Company's long-run earnings are composed of two major components: (1) profits from the sale of the computers; and (2) the implicit interest on the installment sales contracts that the customer signs. No explicit interest charge is included in the installment sales contracts. But the company has designed the contract so that when the required payments are discounted at 10 percent, the present value is approximately equal to the market value of the computers in a cash sale. The 10 percent interest rate also approximates the market rate of interest on installment loans of equal risk (considering the contract terms, the class of clientele, etc.).

Computer Sales Company started operations at the beginning of 1989. Since that time, it has had the following sales and collection experience:

Year	Sales	Collections	
		Down Payments	Installment Payments
1989	$ 600,000	$200,000	$ 0
1990	900,000	300,000	200,000
1991	1,200,000	400,000	500,000

The costs of the computers sold each of these three years were:

1989	$480,000
1990	720,000
1991	960,000

Required:

1. Record, in T-account form, all the effects of the company's sales and collection experience according to the sale-with-financing method of recognizing income from installment sales, taking into account the time value of money. For convenience assume the following:
    (a) All sales are made and all collections received at the end of each year.
    (b) The cost of computers sold is paid in cash by Computer Sales to the manufacturers at the time it sells the systems to its own customers (the manufacturer then delivers direct to Computer Sales' customers).
    (c) The company began business in 1989 with $1.6 million cash and $1.6 million owners' equity.
    (d) The company experiences no other expenses or revenues except the ones described.
2. Suppose now that Computer Sales Company recognized income under the strict point-of-sale method, taking into account expected bad debts but ignoring the time value of money. The industry experience has been that approximately 5 percent of the total value of the accounts receivable at the time of sale proves to be uncollectible. During the past years, the actual collection experience of the company was as follows:

	Collections		Amounts Determined to Be Uncollectible	
Year	Down Payments	Installment Payments	From 1989 Sales	From 1990 Sales
1989	$200,000	$ 0	$ 0	$ 0
1990	300,000	192,000	16,000	0
1991	400,000	467,000	5,000	40,000

Using the point of sale income recognition method with recognition of estimated bad debts, record in worksheet form the effects of the sales, expenses, and revised collection experience for Computer Sales Company.
3. Suppose now that Computer Sales Company recognized income under the sale-with-financing method, taking into account both time value of money and expected bad debts. Under this income recognition method, prepare all necessary journal entries to record the effects of Computer Sales Company's transactions for the first two years only.

8–19. Warranty Contracts. The Waterfall Appliance Company assembles washing machines and dryers (using components purchased from other manufacturers) and retails the appliances through its own appliance stores. To maintain a competitive position, the company offers a two-year warranty (the industry average) on parts and labor. The appliance store provides a repair service for warranty and general repairs. The repair service is considered to be a revenue-producing function.

Price-cost data that apply to 1989, 1990, and 1991 for washers and dryers are as follows:

	Washers	*Dryers*
Unit sales price	$225	$150
Unit total cost (includes components and labor)	110	90
Average unit cost of warranty service in the first year of warranty	10	5
Average unit cost of warranty service in the second year of warranty	30	5

Sales data for 1990 and 1991 are as follows:

	Washers		Dryers	
Year	*Units*	*Dollars*	*Units*	*Dollars*
1990	1,000	$225,000	800	$120,000
1991	1,200	270,000	1,000	150,000

Required:
1. **(a)** Calculate the markup percentage (on cost including average unit warranty cost) for both appliances.
   (b) Assuming that the percentages calculated in (a) are appropriate for determining revenue from sales and revenue from warranty repairs, what portion of the selling price (for each appliance) should be recognized in the year of sale?
2. Prepare for 1990 and 1991 appropriate journal entries that show the effects of these sales and costs. Use the preferred method of deferring revenue from warranty sales until it is earned. You may assume the following:
   (a) Beginning balances are irrelevant and may be ignored.
   (b) All purchases, sales, and wages are for cash.
   (c) In a given year, the company produces only the units that it expects to sell (i.e., no year-end inventories).
   (d) If a part is required for a warranty repair, the part is purchased for cash at the time of the repair.
   (e) All claims for first-year warranty service for units sold in 1990 are made in 1991, and so forth.
3. Calculate the expected effects of 1992–1993 warranty repair transactions (as a result of 1990–1991 sales and ignoring other 1992–1993 transactions). What

are the balances of the warranty service liability and deferred income on future warranty services accounts at the end of 1993 (as a result of 1990–1991 sales)?

4. **(a)** Prepare a schedule showing revenue and net income for 1990 and 1991 for the following alternative revenue-expense recognition methods:

    (1) Defer warranty service income until earned

    (2) Recognize total selling price as revenue in period of sale, and accrue expected future warranty expenses

  (b) Under what set(s) of circumstances might each of the above alternatives be appropriate?

8–20. Effect of Price and Prompt Payment Discounts on Revenue Recognition. The Swivel Equipment Company sells office equipment. The company maintains a catalog which contains standard list prices, product descriptions, and sales terms. Sales terms include allowance of price discounts (depending upon dollar volume of an order), and prompt payment discounts (for payment of an invoice within ten days).

Some transactions of the company during July and August are as follows:

1. Sold equipment with a list price of $200 to the Handy Office Supplies store. No price discount was allowed, but prompt payment discount terms were 2/10, net/ 30.

2. Sold equipment having a list price of $15,000 to the Globe Steel Company. A price discount of 20/10 was allowed, and prompt payment discount terms were 1/10, net/30.

3. Sold equipment having a list price of $6,000 to the Downtown Office Equipment Company. A price discount of 20 percent was allowed, and prompt payment discount terms were 1/10, net/30.

4. Received payment from Handy Office Supplies after ten days. The store had deducted the prompt payment discount, even though it was not entitled to do so.

5. Received payment from the Globe Steel Company. All allowable discounts had been deducted.

6. Received full payment from the Downtown Office Equipment Company after ten days. The company had not deducted the prompt payment discount.

Required:

1. **(a)** What revenue would be recognized from sales for transactions 1 through 3, assuming that prompt payment discounts are recognized at the time of sale?

  (b) What additional revenue would be recognized at a later time, if any?

2. **(a)** What revenue would be recognized from sales for transactions 1 through 3, assuming that prompt payment discounts, if any, are recognized when payment is received?

  (b) What revenue offsets would be recognized at a later time, if any?

3. Prepare a table contrasting sales revenue, discounts taken, discounts allowed but not taken, and total net revenue for the two alternative methods of recognizing prompt payment discounts.

8–21. Alternative Methods of Recording Transaction Discounts in Journal Entry Form. Refer to transactions 1 through 6 described in Problem 8–20.

Required:

Prepare journal entries for each of the six transactions described by showing, side by side:

1. The method of recognizing discounts at the time of sale

2. The method of recognizing discounts when payments are received

(Hint: *You should have two sets of journal entries, one for each transaction.*)

8–22. Journal Entries for Sales Discount and Return Transactions. Elegant Office Interiors, Inc., sold a set of office furniture and equipment to Coast Menu Company on September 3. The sales price is $2,500 with terms 2/10, net/60. On September 4 the furniture is delivered to Coast Menu Company. Four days later, on September 8, an invoice totaling $125, terms net/30, is received by Coast Menu Company from Custom Transport Service for delivery of the merchandise.

Immediately on receipt of the furniture (September 4), the office manager of Coast Menu Company notified Elegant Office Interiors, Inc., that one executive chair costing $250 contained flaws that rendered it worthless. The next day, Office Interiors issued a credit memo covering the worthless chair and asked that it be returned at company expense. The freight on this merchandise return was $25, paid by Coast Menu Company on September 10. Coast Menu Company paid the balance due (net of the $25 freight) on September 12 to Elegant Office Interiors, Inc.

Required:

1. Prepare journal entries on the books of Elegant Office Interiors, Inc., to record each of the foregoing events, assuming that revenue is recorded net of allowable discounts.
2. Repeat the journal entry made to record the invoice payment from Coast Menu Company to Elegant Office Interiors, Inc., under the assumption that payment is not made until October 30, without the prompt payments discount.

Asset Measurement and Expense Recognition

CHAPTER NINE

This chapter addresses the two major categories of assets which present complex measurement issues: inventories and long-lived assets. The approach used to quantify inventory and long-lived assets in dollar terms affects both the balance sheet and income statement through the related expense (cost of goods sold and depreciation, respectively). Issues regarding measurement and expense recognition as well as the most commonly used approaches to resolve them are discussed in this chapter.

ASSET MEASUREMENT

In Chapter Four we stated that assets, liabilities, and owners' equity are recognized at their historical cost, or the amount originally exchanged when the assets are acquired, liabilities incurred, or owners' equity originated. This concept was defined as the cost principle, and the original cost was the basis for all accounting for the components of the financial statements. It is necessary to establish the appropriate amount for an asset prior to determining the corresponding expense. Up to this point the cost of an asset has been fairly straightforward: the amount of cash paid. The amount to be recognized for the asset becomes more complicated when noncash resources are exchanged. In general, the measure of the cost of acquiring an asset is established by applying one of the following criteria, in order of priority:

1. Cash or other monetary consideration paid.
2. Cash or other monetary consideration paid, plus the current market value of any nonmonetary consideration given.
3. Current market value of monetary and nonmonetary consideration received.
4. Cash or other monetary consideration paid, plus the unexpired cost of nonmonetary consideration given.

Example 9–1 | The Data Processing Service Company has made a study of its future computer needs and has decided to trade in its present computer for a larger computer. The new computer, with a list price of $850,000, is acquired in exchange for the old computer plus a cash payment of $500,000. The estimated current market value of the old computer at the present time is $325,000. The original cost of the old computer is $500,000 and accumulated depreciation to date is $240,000.

Applying asset measurement criteria 2 through 4 to the facts of this case (criterion 1 is inapplicable), we arrive at the following alternative costs and related journal entries:

Criterion 2: $500,000 + $325,000 = $825,000

Computer equipment	825,000	
Accumulated depreciation:		
Computer equipment	240,000	
Computer equipment		500,000
Cash		500,000
Gain on trade-in of computer equipment		65,000

Criterion 3: $850,000

Computer equipment	850,000	
Accumulated depreciation:		
Computer equipment	240,000	
Computer equipment		500,000
Cash		500,000
Gain on trade-in of computer equipment		90,000

Criterion 4: $500,000 + $260,000 = $760,000

Computer equipment	760,000	
Accumulated depreciation:		
Computer equipment	240,000	
Computer equipment		500,000
Cash		500,000

Notice that in each of the journal entries the debit of $240,000 to accumulated depreciation and the credit of $500,000 to computer equipment together remove the unexpired cost ($260,000) of the old computer from the company's accounts. The difference between the cost established for the new computer and the cash paid determines the imputed proceeds of the trade-in. The imputed proceeds minus the unexpired cost equals the gain (if any).

Choice of the appropriate criterion in Example 9–1 depends upon the order or priority of the asset measurement criteria and the relative reliability of the estimated current market values. In determining the amount to recognize using criterion 2, the estimated current market value of the old computer is used in conjunction with the cash payment of $500,000 to arrive at a cost of $825,000. Under criterion 3, the estimated current market value of the new computer (for this example, list price) is used to establish a cost of $850,000.

The choice between these two alternative amounts will depend upon the facts of the particular case. In some instances, because of the wide prevalence of discounts, list prices are not good estimates of the market value of an asset. If there is no reason to believe that the estimated market value of the consideration given (the $325,000 value of the old computer) is biased, criterion 2 would be used to establish the amount to be recognized for the new computer. However, if the estimated market value of the old computer is lacking in objectivity and reasonableness, the list price ($850,000) of the new computer might be used in accordance with criterion 3.

If both these market values are suspect, criterion 4 would be used to arrive at an amount of $760,000: the cash paid ($500,000) plus the unexpired cost ($260,000) of the asset given in the exchange. This last method implicitly assigns proceeds of $260,000 to the disposition of the old computer, and thus results in no gain or loss on the disposition.

In addition to its purchase price, the cost of an asset includes all outlays to acquire, transport, transform, and install the asset. These expenditures are included in the amount recorded for the asset.

Example 9–2	Returning to the facts of Example 9–1, assume that The Data Processing Service Company has decided that the cost of its new computer was $825,000, in accordance with criterion 2. But, in addition to this outlay, they also paid $5,000 to transport the new computer from the manufacturer's place of business to their operating facilities, and incurred a $1,000 installation cost. Given these facts, the total cost of the new computer is $831,000 ($825,000 + $5,000 + $1,000), and the following journal entry would record the acquisition:

Computer equipment	831,000	
Accumulated depreciation:		
Computer equipment	240,000	
Computer equipment		500,000
Cash		506,000
Gain on trade-in of computer equipment		65,000

If Data Processing Service Company has been required to make any outlays for the removal of the old computer, this expenditure would not be treated as an additional cost of the new computer. Rather it would be incorporated into the calculation of the gain or loss on the disposal of the old computer.

Just as the cost of a purchased item should include all costs of acquiring the item and putting it in service, the cost of finished products resulting from a manufacturing process is the sum of all the outlays made to acquire the raw material inputs and transform these into resources for ultimate sale.

Example 9–3	Walker Art Wholesalers, Inc., assembles oil painting for distribution in large shopping centers. Its manufacturing process involves the purchase of oil paintings and frames from different suppliers, and the assembly of the canvases and frames for sale at local shopping centers. Walker purchased

a canvas at a cost of $16, and the frame used on this canvas for $12. These two separate costs provide the basis for the amount recognized for the items in the two types of inventory—canvas inventory and frame inventory—before they are used in the assembly process. The labor cost to assembly a finished painting is $3 per painting. Thus, when this painting has been assembled, the cost of the new, finished goods inventory (framed oil paintings) is $31 ($16 + $12 + $3).

EXPENSE RECOGNITION

As we noted in Chapter Three and Chapter Four, there is a measurement linkage between the statement of financial position and the income statement. Given the amount assigned to the ending balance of an asset or a liability, the related expense measure is a derivative calculation of that amount. Conversely, if an expense is measured independently, the related asset or liability amount is altered by this expense measurement process. The two related measures—expense and asset or liability—are not independent calculations.

For the case of asset measurement and the related expense recognition, this duality principle is expressed by the following basic relationship:

BEGINNING ASSET AMOUNT + ACQUISITION − EXPENSES
= ENDING ASSET AMOUNT

For any given accounting period, the beginning asset measure was established at the end of the prior period. The new acquisitions of the period are a matter of record; that is, the result of observable business transactions. The fundamental problem is to determine how to allocate the pool of costs associated with resources acquired and available for use between expense of the period and asset amount at the end of the period. This allocation problem is resolved by matching or associating the costs of the resources used with the revenues they generate in the same time period. Alternatively, the asset can be valued at the end of the period as to its future service potential, or ability to generate additional revenue. The expense is then deduced as the change in asset value from the beginning to the

EXHIBIT 9-1

The Duality Principle for Asset Measurement and Expense Recognition

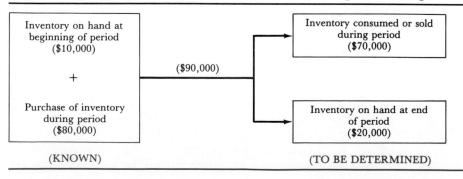

end of the period. Thus, once a decision is made on the expense, the ending amount of the asset is produced as a residual calculation, and vice versa.

Example 9–4 | Audio Dealers, Inc., had an inventory of high-fidelity equipment at the start of the year measured at $10,000. During the year, the company purchased merchandise in the amount of $80,000. Thus the total amount of inventory available for sale during the period is $90,000. Audio Dealers determines that the amount left in its ending inventory is $20,000. The related expenses for the period, cost of sales, is a derivative calculation: $70,000. The duality relationship for this case is schematically depicted in Exhibit 9–1 on page 216.

INVENTORY

In Chapter Four we discussed the internal adjustments made at the end of each accounting period to recognize the cost of inventory sold during the period as an expense. There we assumed that we know either the cost of the inventory on hand at the end of the period, or the cost of the inventory sold or used. However, the way in which these amounts are determined is an important accounting issue, involving many physical and clerical tasks and some important assumptions. We will now explore the inventory measurement problem in greater detail, with particular emphasis on the alternative assumptions from which the accountant may choose in arriving at these amounts.

Physical Quantities

The first problem in assigning dollar amounts to inventory on hand at the end of the period and cost of sales for the period is to determine the physical quantities applicable to these two categories. That is, we must allocate the total quantity of inventory available for sale during the period (the sum of inventory on hand at the start of the period and the purchases of inventory during the period) between the quantities on hand at the end of the period and the quantities that were used or sold during the period. This allocation problem can be resolved by independently determining either of these two variables, and then inferring the measure of the other variable based on the total number of units to be allocated.

To independently determine the quantity of units consumed or sold during the period, the firm may choose to maintain some type of record system that is continuously updated throughout the period. This is a perpetual inventory system, and it will be discussed separately. More common is a periodic inventory system, in which the quantity of units on hand at the end of the period are determined by means of a physical count.

Example 9–5 | Wholesale Steel Co. buys rolled sheet steel and steel bars in large quantities and sells smaller quantities to its customers. For 1988, the beginning inventory quantity of #2006 cold-rolled steel bar was 451 linear meters. The company's purchase records show that 6,000 meters were purchased during the period. At year-end, employees counted 349 meters of #2006 on hand. Thus, a total of 6,102 meters of #2006 were presumed to have been sold during 1988.

Assignment of Cost

Having determined the quantity of units of inventory allocable to units on hand and units sold or consumed, the next task is to associate cost data with the quantities. The assignment is accomplished by electing one of several alternative pricing, or costing, assumptions. The objective is to match the cost of the inventory sold with the revenues earned from the sale of those units during the time period. Theoretically, the method used to assign costs should mirror the actual flow of inventory during the period. This is accomplished by using the specific identification method. In practice, maintaining records regarding the cost of specific units as they are purchased and sold is very costly. Therefore, alternative cost flow assumptions are discussed in this section as well.

Specific Identification. One method of assigning costs to the quantities of inventory on hand or consumed is to identify the specific costs of each particular item consumed and/or on hand. This method is feasible only when the inventory items are uniquely identifiable and of sufficient market value to justify maintaining such detailed records. For a business such as a jewelry shop, the individual inventory items are often uniquely identifiable. And because of the high market value per item, the jewelry shop may maintain the necessary detailed records to aid in such activities as setting or negotiating selling prices, or in providing evidence should insurance claims be filed. If this is the case, the specific identification method of assigning costs to units sold and on hand is feasible.

Example 9–6 | Aesthetic Arts Limited buys copies, signed by artists, of multiple-copy, limited edition art objects. At the present time it holds in inventory 150 copies of a 200-copy signed, limited edition print of a painting by a famous painter. Eight years ago, 30 copies were acquired at a price of $200 each. A second block of 80 copies was purchased three years ago at $550 each. Aesthetic Arts therefore began the current year with an inventory of 110 prints having a total cost of $50,000. This year, 40 more copies were purchased at $1,000 each, including shipping, packaging, and insurance costs. Aesthetic Arts launched an advertising campaign offering 100 of the prints to the public at $1,500 each. All 100 were sold.

Aesthetic Arts recorded the current year's purchases of the prints with the following journal entry:

Inventory	40,000	
Accounts payable		40,000

This establishes a total cost of goods available for sale of $90,000.

Aesthetic Arts is able to use the specific identification method to measure its inventory because each print can be identified by its serial number and a specific cost associated with it. Aesthetic Arts determines that of the 100 prints sold, 24 were ones acquired during the current year at a price of $1,000 each, 50 were ones acquired three years ago for $550 each, and 25 were ones acquired eight years ago at a price of $200 each. The following journal entry would be made to record the cost of the prints sold:

| Cost of goods sold | 57,500 | |
| Inventory | | 57,500 |

This leaves 50 prints in the ending inventory with a total dollar amount of $32,500 (35 at $200 each, 30 at $550 each, and 15 at $1,000 each).

Average Cost Method. A second method of assigning cost to inventory is to use an average cost. We can calculate a weighted average cost per item of inventory by adding the cost of the inventory on hand at the beginning of the period to the cost of inventory purchased during the period, and then dividing by the total number of units of inventory available for sale. The single weighted average cost calculated in this manner is then assigned both to the units of inventory sold during the period and to the units on hand at the end of the period. The average cost method to measure inventory is relatively easy to apply. To use it, we need only know the total cost and total units of inventory on hand at the start of the period and acquisitions of inventory during the period.

Example 9–7

Using the data for Aesthetic Arts in Example 9–6, we would apply the average cost method (assuming 100 copies were sold) as follows:

Inventory, beginning of period		
30 copies @ $200	$ 6,000	
80 copies @ $550	44,000	$50,000
Purchases during period		
40 copies @ $1,000		40,000
Total cost of inventory		
available for sale		$90,000
Weighted average cost		
per copy = $900,000/150		
= $600 per copy		
Total cost of inventory available		
for sale allocated:		
To cost of goods sold		
100 copies @ $600	$60,000	
To ending inventory		
50 copies @ $600		30,000
		$90,000

The following journal entry would be made to record the cost of the prints sold:

| Cost of goods sold | 60,000 | |
| Inventory | | 60,000 |

First-in, First-out (Fifo) Method. Fifo assumes that the earliest inventory items purchased are the first inventory items sold. Thus, in measuring cost of goods sold, the first unit in is assumed to be the first unit out. Oftentimes, this assumption about cost flows is justified by normal business practices since many businesses try to maintain an orderly flow of product so they do not have old merchandise on hand.

Example 9–8 | Again using the data of Example 9–6 and assuming the 100 prints sold were from the earliest acquisitions, we can assign amounts to either cost of goods sold or ending inventory in the following manner:

	Units	Unit Cost	Total
Cost of goods sold:	30	$ 200	$ 6,000
	70	550	38,500
	100		$44,500
Ending inventory:	10	$ 550	$ 5,500
	40	1,000	40,000
	50		$45,500

The following journal entry would be made to record the cost of the prints sold:

Cost of goods sold	45,500	
Inventory		45,500

In applying the first-in, first-out method to establish the amount for the ending inventory, the unit cost of the latest purchase is assigned to the ending inventory. If there are more units in the ending inventory than were acquired in the latest purchase (as there are in Example 9–8), the unit cost from the next latest purchase is applied in a similar manner. We continue in this fashion until all the units in the ending inventory have been assigned costs. If we wish to assign an amount to cost of sales rather than to the ending inventory, the same procedure is followed except that we begin with the unit cost associated with the first purchase (which is assumed to be sold first). Of course, once either one of the amounts (inventory or cost of goods sold) has been established, the other can be deduced.

Last-in, First-out (Lifo) Method. Under the Lifo method, it is assumed that items sold come from the latest acquisitions. Thus the cost flows associated with the items sold are based upon the latest costs incurred. For example, if the physical units represent an inventory of coal and each new acquisition is placed on top of the coal pile, the quantities used are drawn from the latest units acquired.

Example 9–9 | Using the Lifo method of inventory measurement for Aesthetic Arts' prints, we arrive at the following allocation of costs:

	Units	Unit Cost	Total
Cost of goods sold:	40	$1,000	$40,000
	60	550	33,000
	100		$73,000
Ending inventory:	20	$ 550	11,000
	30	200	6,000
	50		$17,000

The following journal entry would be made to record the cost of the prints sold:

Cost of goods sold	73,000	
Inventory		73,000

Summary of Costing Methods. Exhibit 9–2 reflects the allocation of costs under each of the inventory costing methods examined. The data for Aesthetic Arts illustrates the potential differences in the allocation of costs between cost of goods sold and inventory, depending upon the method adopted. Only the specific identification method results in an exact matching of costs with the specific items sold and, thus, the revenue they produce. During periods of changing prices for the inventories, the income statement and balance sheet are affected by the costing method used. The average cost method associates the effect of changing prices with both the cost of goods sold and ending inventory. When prices are rising, as in the Aesthetic Arts example, Fifo assumes the more recent (and thus more expensive) units remain in the ending inventory. Cost of goods sold reflects the lower prices paid for the older units acquired. Lifo, on the other hand, assumes the more recent purchases are sold. Thus the ending inventory is valued at the cost of the less expensive units, while cost of goods sold is measured at the higher price. Note that despite the costing method used, the same number of physical units is assumed to have been purchased and sold. But the different pricing assumptions can have significant effects on the financial statements, as seen in Exhibit 9–2. Because of the effect on cost of goods sold, during periods of rising prices profits are lower, using Lifo as compared to Fifo.

EXHIBIT 9–2

Aesthetic Arts Limited

Comparative Summary of Alternative Costing Methods		
Costing Method	*Cost of Goods Sold*	*Inventory, End of Period*
Specific identification	$57,500	$32,500
Average cost	60,000	30,000
First-in, first-out (Fifo)	44,500	45,500
Last-in, first-out (Lifo)	73,000	17,000

Departure from Cost Basis

Although inventories are normally measured at historical cost, there are two general exceptions to this rule: the lower-of-cost-or-market test and the measurement of obsolete or damaged merchandise.

Lower-of-Cost-or-Market Rule. Inventory is initially quantified at the cost of the inventory using one of the alternative costing methods previously discussed. The cost-based measurement (using individual inventory items, categories of inventory, or the total inventory) is then compared with the current replacement cost or market value of the inventory. If cost exceeds market value, the inventory is measured at market value. If market exceeds cost, the inventory is kept at the original cost.

Lower-of-cost-or-market measurement reflects conservatism in accounting. This method assumes that a drop in the replacement cost of inventory portends a drop in future selling prices, and thus the potential loss should be recognized as soon as possible. Note that the opposite situation is not recognized; that is, potential gains are not recognized prior to sale of the inventory since they have not yet been realized. Note too that as a consequence of measuring inventory at the lower of cost or market, the inventory amounts on the balance sheet are also conservatively stated. The journal entry to record the decrease in inventory would be a debit to loss from decline in inventory market value (included on the current period's income statement), and a credit to inventory (to reduce the balance sheet account).

Obsolete or Damaged Merchandise. When inventory items have suffered damage or obsolescence, the original cost of the items must be decreased so that the amount shown for the inventory represents no more than the amount for which it can be sold.

Manufacturing Costs

The discussion to this point has focused on companies that purchase inventory and resell the items without modification. The measurement of the inventories of a manufacturing firm involve additional problems. A manufacturing firm has three basic classes of inventory: raw material inventory, work-in-process inventory, and finished goods inventory. These categories correspond to the major forms in which the manufacturing firm holds inventory: units not yet placed into the production process (raw material); partially completed units at some stage in the production process (work in process); and completed units held prior to shipment to customers (finished goods).

No new problems arise by the need to assign amounts to raw material inventories. The beginning inventory is increased by purchases of raw material made during the period and decreased by raw material used in production to yield the ending inventory. Measurement of the work-in-process inventory involves adding the cost of the raw material used to the cost of labor employed in the manufacture of products plus a pro-rata share of the general overhead costs of the factory. The cost of units completed during the period are removed from work-in-process inventory and transferred to finished goods. Thus the ending work-in-process inventory is equal to the beginning inventory plus raw materials used (i.e., transferred out of raw materials inventory), plus labor used, plus a share of general overhead, minus goods brought to completion. The finished goods inventory is increased during the period by the inventory transferred in from work in process, and decreased by the units sold during the period. The effect of these changes on the beginning inventory amount yields the ending finished goods inventory.

Periodic and Perpetual Methods

The periodic method of inventory measurement was illustrated in the above methods whereby the allocation of cost to ending inventory and cost of sales is made at the end of the period. Thus, the inventory was quantified based upon

EXHIBIT 9–3

Periodic versus Perpetual Inventory Measurement

	Basic Data:	Units	Unit Cost	Total Cost
January 1	Inventory on hand	100	$10	$ 1,000
3	Sale	(100)		
5	Purchase	500	12	6,000
10	Sale	(300)		
18	Purchase	200	15	3,000
25	Sale	(100)		
	On hand, end of period	300	Cost of goods available	$10,000

Fifo:

Periodic Method			Perpetual Method				
Units	Unit Cost	Total		Units	Unit Cost	Inventory	Cost of Goods Sold
Inventory on hand:							
200	$15	$ 3,000	January 1	100	$10	$1,000	
100	12	1,200	3	(100)	10	(1,000)	$1,000
300		$ 4,200		0		0	
			5	500	12	6,000	
				500	12	$6,000	
Cost of goods sold:							
100	$10	$ 1,000	10	(300)	12	(3,600	3,600
400	12	4,800		200	12	$2,400	
500		$ 5,800	18	200	15	3,000	
				400		$5,400	
Total cost allocated		$10,000	25	(100)	12	(1,200)	1,200
				300		$4,200	$5,800

the number of units on hand at the end of the period, and the number of units sold during the period was inferred.

An alternative approach is to use the perpetual method, whereby the cost of goods sold is assessed throughout the period as sales are made. These two methods will produce different amounts for inventory and cost of goods sold only if there are purchases and sales that are intermingled throughout the period. (Note that the specific identification method produces identical results under both the periodic and the perpetual techniques.) Exhibit 9–3 illustrates these points.

In Exhibit 9–3 we see that the Fifo method is unaffected by the application of the periodic or the perpetual techniques. Both techniques assign $4,200 to the ending inventory and $5,800 to cost of goods sold. However, the Lifo and the average cost methods produce different results. In the average cost method, the reason for the different result under the perpetual method is that the average cost per unit of inventory is changed each time a new purchase is made. If units sold are then assigned costs at the time they are sold, the average cost is a function of the aggregate costs of units on hand at that time. When the periodic method is used, however, the average cost per unit is determined on the basis of all

EXHIBIT 9–3 (cont.)

Lifo:

Periodic Method				Perpetual Method			
Units	Unit Cost	Total		Units	Unit Cost	Inventory	Cost of Goods Sold
Inventory on hand:							
100	$10	$ 1,000	January 1	100	$10	$1,000	
200	12	2,400	3	(100)	10	(1,000)	$1,000
300		$ 3,400		0		0	
			5	500	12	6,000	
				500	12	$6,000	
Cost of goods sold:							
200	$15	$ 3,000	10	(300)	12	(3,600)	3,600
300	12	3,600		200	12	$2,400	
500		$ 6,600	18	200	15	3,000	
				400		$5,400	
Total cost allocated		$10,000	25	(100)	15	(1,500)	1,500
				300		$3,900	$6,100

Average Cost:

Periodic Method				Perpetual Method			
	Units	Cost	Total	Units	Cost of Inventory	Average Unit Cost	Cost of Goods Sold
Inventory beginning of period	100	$ 1,000	January 1	100	$1,000	$10	
Purchases	700	9,000	3	(100)	(1,000)	10	$1,000
	800	$10,000		0	0		
Average cost/item			5	500	$6,000		
= $10,000/800 = $12.50				500	6,000	12	
			10	(300)	(3,600)	12	3,600
Allocated to:				200	2,400	12	
Cost of goods sold			18	200	3,000		
(500 @ $12.50)		$ 6,250					
Inventory				400	5,400	13.50	
(300 @ $12.50)		3,750	25	(100)	(1,350)	13.50	1,350
Total cost allocated		$10,000		300	$4,050	13.50	$5,950

acquisitions during the period, and thus one weighted average cost is applied uniformly to all units sold and all units remaining in the inventory.

In the Lifo method, the difference under the perpetual method arises when some of the older acquisitions of inventory are sold before new acquisitions are made. Under the perpetual method, some of these older costs will be assigned to cost of goods sold, and thus they cannot be later assigned to the ending inventory. Applying the periodic method, however, inventory on hand at the end of the period is based first upon units on hand at the start of the period and then upon the earliest acquisitions during the period.

As with the differences which arise using different cost methods, the effect on inventory and cost of goods sold using periodic versus perpetual measurements does not relate to the physical flow of the units, but rather assumptions as to the specific units flowing and thus the cost to be associated with those units.

LONG-LIVED ASSETS

Long-lived assets represents a second major class of assets that creates problems of measurement and related expense recognition. The chief differences between long-lived assets and inventories are that: (1) the long-lived assets are acquired for use rather than sale; and (2) the benefits to be derived from the long-lived assets generally extend over a much longer period of time than for inventories. This latter attribute gives rise to unique problems in determining the time period in which to recognize the cost of the asset.

Long-lived assets are divided into two categories: tangible and intangible. Tangible assets include items such as buildings, machinery, equipment, vehicles, and natural resources like land and mineral rights. Intangible assets consist principally of rights acquired under law which do not themselves have physical substance, such as patents, copyrights, franchises, and trademarks.

Three difficult problems in accounting for long-lived assets will be discussed in this section:

1. Determination of the appropriate treatment of expenditures made over the life of the asset to maintain and/or improve it.
2. Measurement of benefits that have been consumed in the production of revenue.
3. Recognition of gain or loss on the disposal of the assets.

Although not in the list, quantifying the amount to be recognized for long-lived assets at acquisition is also an important issue. This topic was discussed at the beginning of the chapter where we broadly construed the cost principle to include all expenditures made to acquire and install the asset such that it is ready to use.

Maintenance and Improvements

After an asset has been acquired, additional expenditures will often be made over its life to maintain or improve its operating capability. If these expenditures maintain the asset's operating efficiency, they are regarded as normal repairs and maintenance and reported as expenses of the period in which the outlays are made. Other expenditures are made to increase the level of benefits to be derived from the asset. Expenditures of this type are added to the unexpired cost of the asset and then matched against revenue in future periods as the additional benefits are derived.

Often times it is difficult to distinguish between an expenditure that improves the asset and one that maintains it in proper operating order. In these situations, the accountant must exercise judgment in properly classifying the expenditure. In making this judgment, the significance (materiality) of the expenditure is an important consideration. If the expenditure is considered relatively immaterial, it will normally be treated as an expense of the period, even though it may in fact be a minor improvement. However, if the potential financial statement impact of the expenditure is relatively large, the accountant must assess more carefully the effect of the expenditure on the services to be derived from the asset in future periods.

Depreciation Expense

Use of long-lived assets represents a consumption of the benefits (service potential) inherent in the asset. This use of resources contributes to the production of revenue of the period. In accordance with the matching principle, the cost of the benefits consumed should be reflected as an expense of the current period. Yet, it is often difficult to ascertain precisely the benefits derived in a particular period.

One of two approaches to matching the cost of the asset with the revenue it generates is commonly used. The first approach is based upon the output of the asset. Where benefits potentially available from an asset can be expressed in terms of a maximum potential output, the total cost of the asset can be allocated to periods based upon the output produced in a period.

Example 9–10 | The Jones Company acquired a machine that is expected to have a total output of 25,000 units over its life. The cost of the machine is $50,000, and Jones does not anticipate any salvage value at the end of the machine's useful life. Applying an output measure, we recognize as an expense of the period a cost of $2 ($50,000/25,000) for each unit produced on the machine. Therefore, if the company produced 4,000 units of product on this machine during the current period, the depreciation expense for the period would be $8,000 (4,000 × $2). The journal entry each period would be as follows:

Depreciation expense	8,000	
Accumulated depreciation		8,000

(This form of journal entry is always used to record depreciation, with the amount changing to reflect the different methods.)

The output method is the preferable approach when we can determine fairly accurately an identifiable output from a long-lived asset and estimate the total potential output over its life. However, there are a number of different types of long-lived assets for which we are not able to identify the specific output; for example, an office building. This leads to the second approach for measuring current period expense: an assessment of the benefits consumed from the use of the asset based upon the passage of time. The service potential of many tangible assets (such as buildings) is influenced primarily by the passage of time (e.g., from effects such as the weather). In this case, unused capacity in one period is not usable in future periods. Thus, the time-based method of determining expense is appropriate. Three determinations must be made when time is used as the basis for determining the services derived from the use of an asset, and thus the related expense measure: the useful life of the asset; the market value of the asset at the end of its useful life (salvage or residual value); and a method of depreciation.

In our previous discussions of the depreciation of long-lived assets we have

EXHIBIT 9–4

Sum-of-the-Years'-Digits Depreciation Method

Year	Book Value, Beginning of Year	Depreciation Rate	Depreciation Expense	Book Value, End of Year
1	$16,000	5/15	5/15 × $15,000 = $ 5,000	$11,000
2	11,000	4/15	4/15 × 15,000 = 4,000	7,000
3	7,000	3/15	3/15 × 15,000 = 3,000	4,000
4	4,000	2/15	2/15 × 15,000 = 2,000	2,000
5	2,000	1/15	1/15 × 15,000 = 1,000	1,000
		1.00	$15,000	

Sum-of-the-years' digits = 1 + 2 + 3 + 4 + 5
$$= 15$$

selected a depreciation method that allocates an equal portion of the depreciation cost (cost less estimated salvage value) of the asset to each period of time in its useful life. This method is called the straight-line method of depreciation. Other methods commonly in use produce larger measures of expense in the early years of the asset's life, and correspondingly smaller expense measurements in the later years. Two of these accelerated methods of expense recognition in current practice are the sum-of-the-years'-digits method and the declining-balance method. These methods are approximations of the asset's service potential which has been used. They are allocation schemes devised to measure income on the accrual basis.

Sum-of-the-Years'-Digits Depreciation Method. The sum-of-the-years'-digits method produces larger measures of depreciation expense in the early years in the life of the asset by applying decreasing depreciation rates to the depreciable cost.

Example 9–11 | The Longhorn Manufacturing Company was formed on January 1, 1991, to manufacture various types of gift items with Longhorn emblems embossed on them. Embossing machinery was purchased on January 1 at a cost of $16,000. Longhorn estimated that the machinery would have a life of five years and that the residual value would be $1,000. Exhibit 9–4 illustrates the amount of depreciation recognized under the sum-of-the-years'-digits method.

The depreciation rate to be used in the sum-of-the-years'-digits method is determined by first summing the digits from 1 to "n," where "n" is the number of years of useful life that the asset is expected to be productive. In Example 9–11, the asset has an expected useful life of 5 years, and the sum of the digits from 1 to 5 is 15 (1 + 2 + 3 + 4 + 5 = 15).[1] This sum is placed in the denominator in determining the depreciation rate. The numerator of the depreciation rate changes each year, starting with the largest number in the sum (i.e., 5), and decreasing by 1 each year until, in the last year, the numerator is

[1] For larger numbers of years, it is useful to know that the sum of the years' digits is always equal to [n (n + 1)] ÷ 2, where n is the number of years. For example, for n = 5 the formula is 5 (6) ÷ 2 = 15.

1. Therefore the depreciation rate for the first year is 5/15, and when this rate is applied to the depreciable cost of $15,000 we obtain depreciation expense of $5,000. In the second year, the numerator of the depreciation rate is reduced by 1 to 4, and the rate is 4/15. Applying this rate again to the depreciable cost of $15,000, the depreciation expense for the year is $4,000. This modification of the depreciation rate continues until the last year, when the depreciation rate is 1/15. At the end of the 5-year life of the asset, book value of the asset (original cost less accumulated depreciation) is $1,000—the amount of the estimated salvage value.

Declining-Balance Depreciation Method. Under the declining-balance depreciation method, a fixed percentage is applied to the book value of the asset at the beginning of each year to determine depreciation expense for that year. Commonly, 150 percent and 200 percent of the straight-line rate are the percentages used. For the data of Example 9–11, the straight-line depreciation rate, give a five-year life, is 20 percent; that is, we allocate 20 percent of the total depreciable cost of the asset to each year. Therefore, using a 150 percent declining-balance depreciation method, the rate would be 30 percent (20 percent × 150 percent). Using the 200 percent, or double-declining-balance depreciation method, the depreciation rate is 40 percent (20 percent × 200 percent).

There are two important differences between the straight-line and sum-of-the-years'-digits method, and the declining-balance method. The depreciation for the year under the declining-balance method is determined by multiplying the depreciation rate times the asset book value at the beginning of each year. The first difference is that no estimate of salvage value is used in the calculation. Secondly, the depreciation rate is applied to the book value of the asset at the beginning of the year, not its total depreciable cost. Exhibit 9–5 applies the double-declining-balance depreciation method to the facts of Example 9–11.

To review the procedures followed in Exhibit 9–5, we note that in the first year, depreciation expense is calculated by multiplying the double-declining-balance depreciation rate (40 percent) by the original cost of the asset ($16,000), yielding $6,400 depreciation expense. The book value of the asset at the end of the year is the original cost ($16,000) less the accumulated depreciation ($6,400), or $9,600. This amount at the end of year 1 is the book value at the beginning of year 2, and it is the basis for the calculation of depreciation expense in the second year. We therefore multiply the 40 percent rate times the $9,600 book value of the asset at the beginning of the second year to compute the $3,840

EXHIBIT 9–5

Double-Declining-Balance Depreciation Method

Year	Book Value, Beginning of Year	Depreciation Rate	Depreciation Expense		Book Value, End of Year
1	$16,000	40%	$16,000 × 40% =	$ 6,400	$9,600
2	9,600	40	9,600 × 40 =	3,840	5,760
3	5,760	40	5,760 × 40 =	2,304	3,456
4	3,456	40	3,456 × 40 =	1,382	2,074
5	2,074	40	2,074 × 40 =	830	1,244
				$14,756	

depreciation expense for the second year. Continuing in this fashion, at the end of year 5 we have an ending asset value of $1,244 (which appropriately is not less than the estimated salvage value of $1,000), and total depreciation expense for the five-year period amounts to $14,756.

In general, the total depreciation expense recognized under the declining-balance depreciation method will not equal the total depreciable cost, although the difference will usually be fairly small. One way of handling the difference is to follow the double-declining-balance method until the last year in the life of the asset. In that year, depreciation expense can be recognized as the difference between beginning book value and expected salvage value. For Example 9–11, this would lead to year 5 depreciation expense of $1,074 and total five-year depreciation of $15,000, as with the other methods.

Summary of Depreciation Methods. The different amounts of depreciation expense that would be recognized each year for the data of Example 9–11 under the alternative depreciation methods we have considered are summarized in Exhibit 9–6. As noted earlier, the straight-line method allocates the depreciable cost equally over the asset's life, while the two accelerated methods allocate larger amounts to the early years of the asset's life. As Exhibit 9–6 illustrates, the three methods result in different net incomes and asset values on the balance sheet in each year of the asset's life.

The disparity in the amounts allocated to the different periods using alternative time-based approaches raises the question of what factors the accountant considers in choosing a depreciation method. One consideration may relate to the pattern of related costs associated with the long-lived asset. Some normal pattern of expenditures for repairs and maintenance over the life of the asset is to be expected. If it is anticipated that these costs will increase as time passes, we may conclude that a larger portion of the asset's service potential is consumed in the early years of its life. Thus a depreciation method should be selected that allocates a larger amount of the depreciable cost to the early years. If repairs and maintenance expenditures are increasing over time, a combination of this expense pattern with a decreasing depreciation expense will result in a fairly uniform pattern of total expense (depreciation expense plus repairs and maintenance expense) recognized each period over the life of the asset.

EXHIBIT 9–6

Comparison of Depreciation Expense Determined under Alternative Depreciation Methods

Year	Straight Line	Sum of the Years' Digits	Double Declining Balance
1	$ 3,000	$ 5,000	$ 6,400
2	3,000	4,000	3,840
3	3,000	3,000	2,304
4	3,000	2,000	1,382
5	3,000	1,000	1,074*
	$15,000	$15,000	$15,000

* Year 5 depreciation equals the amount necessary to ensure the asset is fully depreciated by the end of year 5.

Alternatively, the decision regarding the depreciation method to be selected may be based upon the expectation as to revenue patterns. For example, if the revenue to be derived from the asset is expected to remain fairly uniform over the life of the asset, the straight-line depreciation method might be appropriate. However, if there is an expectation of decreasing productivity over the life of the asset, this might suggest that a larger percentage of services would be consumed in the early years of the asset's life. Thus one of the two methods that produce decreasing depreciation expense over time should be adopted.

Land and Natural Resources

Our discussion of the measurement of benefits received from long-lived assets and related expense recognition has focused on constructed physical assets such as buildings or machinery. Certain other types of long-lived tangible assets have a finite reservoir or service potential. These nonconstructed assets include natural resources that are exploited by a company, such as mineral deposits or stands of timber. In many cases the production or output method of recognizing the expense of consuming such resources is used. The first step is to estimate the total quantity of the resource available (e.g., number of tons of iron ore). Dividing the total cost of the asset by this estimate of total units available yields a cost per unit. Then as the resources are extracted or otherwise consumed, the expense to be recognized is calculated by multiplying the cost per unit by the number of units consumed. The allocation of the cost of natural resources to time periods is referred to as depletion expense (as distinct from depreciation expense, the term used for constructed physical assets).

Land that is acquired by a company for use as a site for its manufacturing, marketing, or administrative operations represents a special case. We assume that the service potential of such land is unaffected by the passage of time or the degree of use. Accordingly, none of the cost of land is allocated to periods or otherwise matched against revenue. Land owned for these purposes is measured at its original cost, with no accumulated depletion. However, land held because of the natural resources it contains is accounted for at original cost less accumulated depletion.

Intangible Assets

Intangible assets include such resources as patents, copyrights, trademarks, franchises, and goodwill. Their unique characteristic is that they lack physical substance. The treatment of intangible assets is similar to the treatment of long-lived tangible assets. The cost incurred to acquire an intangible is allocated to expense over the expected useful life of the asset. In many cases the life of the intangible is reasonably well defined by the legal right that the company holds (for example, the 17-year life of a patent).

Example 9–12 | The Meyer Company manufactures a product which uses a unique finishing process. A newly registered patent on this process was acquired from the inventor several years ago at a cost of $51,000. The patent is legally binding for 17 years.

The patent is shown as a long-lived intangible asset in Meyer's statement of financial position. At the date of acquisition, the asset is recorded at $51,000 and a portion of this cost is allocated to expense each year. If the useful life of the patent were expected to be equal to its legal life, $3,000 ($51,000/17) would be recognized as amortization expense each year. (Note the change in terminology from depreciation and depletion. Also observe no accumulated amortization account is used. Instead the amortization expense is a direct reduction to the original cost of the intangible.)

In other cases, however, the estimated useful life of an intangible is not apparent from legal or other criteria, and a more arbitrary judgment must be made.

Disposal of Long-lived Assets

Oftentimes, a gain or loss must be recognized at the time of disposal of long-lived assets. This gain or loss is measured as the difference between the book value of the asset and the sales proceeds. If there are additional expenses incurred to dispose of the asset, these expenses are deducted from the proceeds in determining the gain or loss. Gains and losses on disposal of long-lived assets (net of the related tax effects) are a component of income from continuing operations.

A similar accounting treatment is also used when the asset is traded in to acquire a new asset of the same kind. The gain or loss to be recognized is the difference between the book value of the old asset and its market value. The new asset is then recorded as the total of any cash paid plus the market value of the traded-in asset. Alternatively, the new asset could be recorded at the sum of the cash payment plus the unexpired cost of the traded-in asset. This treatment results in no gain or loss being recognized on the disposition of the old asset.

Example 9–13 | Baker Corporation disposed of a piece of equipment with an original cost of $50,000 and accumulated depreciation of $30,000. Cash of $25,000 was received in return. The journal entry to record the disposal is as follows:

Cash	25,000	
Accumulated depreciation:	30,000	
Equipment		50,000
Gain on disposition		5,000

If instead, Baker had sold the equipment for $15,000, the journal entry would be as follows:

Cash	15,000	
Accumulated depreciation:	30,000	
Loss on disposition	5,000	
Equipment		50,000

This example illustrates the journal entries when the equipment is sold for more or less than its book value, respectively.

SUMMARY

This chapter has considered complex issues related to asset measurement. First, the general principles underlying the recording of assets in the balance sheet and the related expense recognition were explained. Two specific asset categories were considered: inventories and long-lived assets. The complications presented by inventories revolve around assumptions about the physical flow of units (whether merchandise or manufacturing-related) and how to assign costs to these units. The most common inventory accounting methods were illustrated: specific identification; average cost; first-in, first-out; and last-in, last-out. Departures from the cost basis are necessary when market value falls below the original cost paid for the units or when merchandise becomes damaged or obsolete. The periodic and perpetual approaches to the physical flow were contrasted.

Long-lived assets include both tangible, physical assets as well as intangible assets. The major issues revolve around recognizing a portion of the cost of such assets over their useful life. Alternative methods for recognizing depreciation expense were illustrated: straight line, sum of the years' digits, and declining balance. Disposal of long-lived assets and recognition of any gain or loss were also explained.

Questions for Review and Discussion

9–1. Define or briefly explain the following terms:
   a. Specific identification inventory method
   b. Average cost inventory method
   c. First-in, first-out inventory method
   d. Last-in, last-out inventory method
   e. Lower-of-cost-or-market inventory valuation rule
   f. Periodic inventory method
   g. Perpetual inventory method
   h. Depreciable cost of an asset
   i. Straight-line depreciation method
   j. Sum-of-the-years'-digits depreciation method
   k. Declining-balance depreciation method
   l. Book value of an asset
   m. Depletion expense
   n. Intangible asset
   o. Amortization expense

9–2. What are the criteria to be applied (in order of preference) in determining the cost of acquiring nonmonetary assets?

9–3. The cost of an asset includes more than merely the price of the item. Explain what is included in cost.

9–4. Express in equation form the relationship between asset measurement and expense recognition.

9–5. Explain briefly the major inventory costing methods used in accounting.

9–6. Identify the major exceptions to measuring inventory at cost in accounting. What is the justification for each exception?

9–7. In applying the lower-of-cost-or-market rule for recording inventories, "market" typically refers to the current replacement cost of the inventory. What amount would you choose for replacement cost if a series of prices was quoted, depending on the size of the order?

9–8. Many firms account for their operations on a calendar-year basis; however, some adopt what is called a natural business year. The natural business year for a firm is usually defined as a year ending on a date when operations (and usually inventory) have reached the lowest point in their annual cycle. For example, retail department stores often choose a fiscal year for accounting for their operations that ends on February 28—presumably their natural business year. How might the choice of a natural business year reduce the potential for the significant differences in net income that may result solely from firms' arbitrary choices of different (but acceptable) inventory methods?

9–9. When it was formed in 1947, Jonathan Corporation adopted the Lifo method for measuring its inventory of flour used in making its special brands of spaghetti. Since that time, the quantity of flour normally maintained in inventory has increased only slightly because the volume of operations has been fairly constant. The price of flour has increased an average of 5 percent per year since 1947. At the end of previous fiscal years, the number of tons of flour on hand has usually been within 10 percent of the normal inventory level. However, during the last few months of 1991, the corporation encountered substantial difficulties in purchasing flour and, at the end of the year, its inventory had been depleted to approximately 20 percent of its normal level.

   a. What effect would this temporary inventory reduction have on net income for 1991?

   b. Would the effect be the same if the company used Fifo?

   c. If the inventory stock-out is regarded as a temporary, abnormal phenomenon, do you believe that some modification of the Lifo method might be justified? If so, what modification might be suitable?

9–10. Each year the Abbott Corporation purchases merchandise which increases in market value with age. They store the merchandise for eight years and then sell the aged product. In preparing their financial statements, Abbott asks you if it would be appropriate to include the interest costs they have incurred on money borrowed to finance the inventories as an addition to the purchase cost of the merchandise rather than as an expense of the period in which paid.

   a. How would you respond (giving specific attention to the cost and matching principles)?

   b. Would your answer change if Abbott provided the financing from invested rather than borrowed funds?

9–11. Identify and discuss the major issues involved in accounting for long-lived assets.

9–12. What factors should be considered when choosing a depreciation method?

9–13. An investor purchases a motel in Florida for $550,000. The motel is situated on land that has been leased for ten years. At the end of the ten-year period, ownership of all structures thereon reverts to the owner of the land (there is no option for renewal of the lease).

   a. What factors would you consider in deciding how to recognize the purchase price of the motel as an expense over the life of the venture?

   b. If the average occupancy rate was 80 percent from November to May, and 40 percent from June to October, would this affect your measurement of expense for annual income statements? For monthly income statements? How?

Problems

9–1. **Comparative Inventory Measurement.** Pryor Data Terminals compiled the following data on one of its principal products, the Datapoint 6000, for the month of August:

Date Purchased	Units	Price per Unit	Cost
Beginning inventory	20	$400	$ 8,000
August 5	40	375	15,000
August 13	50	340	17,000
August 25	40	350	14,000

At the end of August, a physical inventory count indicated that Pryor had 50 units of the Datapoint 6000 on hand.

Required:

1. Write a journal entry to record the new Datapoint 6000 acquisitions of the month in the purchases account.
2. Calculate the amount for the ending inventory and the cost of sales for August under each of the three inventory costing methods:

   a. Fifo
   b. Lifo
   c. Weighted average

3. Write adjusting journal entries to establish the appropriate month-end balances in the inventory and cost of goods sold accounts under the three costing methods listed in number 2.

9–2. Comparative Inventory Measurement. Jones Electronics Wholesalers, Inc., has compiled the following data on one of its principal products, the XT-100, for the month of May:

Date Purchased	Units	Price per Unit	Cost
Beginning inventory	100	$5.00	$ 500
May 3	600	4.50	2,700
May 16	800	5.50	4,400
May 25	500	6.00	3,000

At the end of May, a physical inventory indicated that Jones had 400 units of the XT-100 on hand.

Required:

1. Calculate the amount for the ending inventory and the cost of sales for May under each of the three costing methods:

   a. Fifo
   b. Lifo
   c. Weighted average

2. Write all the journal entries, beginning with recording May purchases, required to ultimately establish the appropriate month-end balances in the inventory and cost of goods sold accounts for each of the three costing methods.

9–3. Inventory Measures: Physical Flows and Cost Flows. The Stanley Steel Company is a metals service center. The company buys metal sheets, bars, and rolls in large quantities from the producers and sells in smaller quantities to local manufacturers. One of the company's most popular items is 24-by-⅛-inch rolled sheet steel that it buys in 200-foot rolls and then cuts (to order) for customers in smaller lengths.

During February 1991 the company had the following amounts of this particular rolled sheet steel available:

Date Received	Number of Rolls Purchased	Price per Roll	Total Price
Beginning inventory	10	$100	$1,000
February 7	20	110	2,200
February 15	12	112	1,344
February 24	10	116	1,160
	52		$5,704

The company uses the periodic inventory method for establishing the levels of inventory and number of rolls of steel sold. At the end of February, a count showed that $15\frac{1}{2}$ rolls of the 24-by-$\frac{1}{8}$-inch steel were on hand.

Required:

1. Determine the ending inventory and the cost of sales for February with respect to the 24-by-$\frac{1}{8}$-inch steel based on each of the following cost flow alternatives:

   a. Fifo
   b. Lifo
   c. Weighted average

2. Suppose that the company had kept perpetual inventory records. Indicate for each of the cost-flow assumptions whether the cost of sales and inventory amounts under the perpetual inventory method would have been greater than, equal to, or less than the amounts recognized under the periodic method. Support your conclusion logically. You may assume that sales took place relatively evenly over the whole month.

(Note: *Because specific sales data are not provided, it is not possible to make actual calculations of the perpetual inventory amounts.*)

9–4. Inventory Measures: Physical Flows and Cost Flows (Perpetual Method). Refer to the data presented in problem 9–3. Assume that the sales of rolled sheet steel (in terms of 200-foot rolls) were made throughout February as follows:

Sale Date	Number of Rolls
February 4, 1991	5
February 12, 1991	15
February 22, 1991	8
February 27, 1991	$8\frac{1}{2}$
	$36\frac{1}{2}$

Required:

Determine the ending inventory and the cost of sales in February for each of the cost-flow alternatives listed. Assume that the company uses the perpetual inventory method.

1. Fifo
2. Lifo
3. Weighted average

(Note: *Use of a schedule such as the following may be helpful in developing your answers.*)

	Purchases			Sales			Balance		
Date	Quantity	Unit Cost	Total Cost	Quantity	Unit Cost	Total Cost	Quantity	Unit Cost	Total Cost

9–5. Whirlpool Corporation's 1988 Annual Report shows the following inventory balances:

December 31 (millions of dollars)	1988	1987
	536.8	615.6

Note 1 to Whirlpool's financial statements explains that inventories are stated at last-in, first-out (Lifo) cost, except nonproduction and non-U.S. inventories which are stated at first-in, first-out (Fifo) cost.

Note 4 contains the following additional information:

(4) Inventories December 31 (millions of dollars)	1988	1987
Finished products	$543.0	$603.6
Work in process	56.7	61.3
Raw materials	157.2	155.2
Total Fifo cost	756.9	820.1
Less excess of Fifo cost over Lifo cost	220.1	204.5
	$536.8	$615.6

Lifo inventories represent approximately 79 percent and 80 percent of total inventories at December 31, 1988 and 1987.

Required:

1. Did the replacement cost of Whirlpool's inventories increase or decrease during 1987 and 1988? How can you tell?
2. Estimate the effect on cost of goods sold and net income for the year ending December 31, 1988 if Whirlpool used Fifo rather than Lifo.

9–6. Measurement of Assets at Time of Acquisition. The Acme Leasing Company leases passenger cars on a two-year basis. At the end of the lease period, the customer can either purchase the car at a price specified in the original lease contract, or return the car to Acme. Cars returned to Acme are traded in on new cars. If necessary, Acme purchases new cars for cash to compensate for cars purchased by customers.

For 1991 the following data apply:

Number of leases expiring	20
Number of cars purchased by customers	10

Number of cars returned to Acme (and traded in on new cars)	10
Number of new cars purchased by Acme	20
List price of new cars purchased	$4,800
Trade-in allowance (on list price) per car received by Acme on cars traded in	$2,000
Total cash price per car for cars purchased for cash by Acme	$4,700
Average wholesale price per car for cars returned by customers	$1,900
Average retail price per car for cars returned by customers	$2,300
Lease contract selling price	$2,200
Original cost of cars returned to Acme by customers	$4,400

Acme depreciates the total price of cars over an estimated five-year life using the sum-of-the-years'-digits method, even though Acme never owns the cars for more than two years.

Required:

1. What amount should be recorded for the ten cars Acme purchased for cash alone? Write the journal entry to record their acquisition. Assume that the market value of the ten cars purchased for cash is independent of the market value of the cars acquired by trade-in.
2. Identify several alternative approaches that might be used in determining the recorded value of the ten cars acquired by trade-in, and determine the total amount that would be assigned to the ten cars for each alternative. Write the journal entry to record the transaction for each alternative.
3. Comment briefly on the propriety (or relative desirability) of each of the alternative approaches you developed in number 2.

9–7. **Treatment of Repairs and Maintenance.** In December 1987 the Stevens Company purchased a secondhand portable conveyor line for use in loading trucks from various inventory areas. The conveyor line was composed of four independent sections, with each section having its own electric motor. The original (new) price of the conveyor line was $6,000, but the company paid only $4,000. At the time of purchase, the company estimated the salvage value to be $800 and the remaining useful life to be four years.

During 1988 the company performed only routine maintenance on the conveyor line, at a total cost of $200.

In 1989 two motors burned out because of overloading and had to be replaced. The cost of the motors was $600. Other maintenance expenditures in 1989 totaled $300. Also, in December 1989 the company purchased an additional section of conveyor line to serve as a backup if another section broke down and to increase the length of the conveyor line. The acquisition cost of the additional section was $1,200, and the estimated increase in salvage value was $400.

During 1990 repairs and maintenance totaled $900 because of recurrent breakdowns. As a result, in December the company stopped using the conveyor line and reverted to manual loading of the trucks. The conveyor line was put up for sale, but it was not sold until April 30, 1989 for a cash price of $1,500.

Assume that depreciation is calculated on a straight-line basis.

Required:

1. What amount should be assigned to the conveyor line at the date of acquisition?
2. How should the acquisition of the additional section of conveyor line in 1989 be treated (i.e., is it an expense)? Why?
3. How much depreciation should be recorded in 1991? Why?
4. Prepare a schedule showing the expense in total and by categories (depreciation

expense and repairs and maintenance expense) associated with the conveyor line for each year of its life.

5. Calculate the gain or loss incurred in 1991 when the conveyor line was sold.

9–8. Comparative Depreciation and Asset Disposition. On January 1, 1989, Demkon Corporation acquired a new machine for producing its product, at a cost of $175,000. The machine is expected to have a useful life of five years, and a salvage value at the end of the five years of $25,000.

Required:

1. Calculate the depreciation expense for 1990 (the second year) under each of three depreciation methods:

   a. Straight line
   b. Sum of the years' digits
   c. Double declining balance

2. Suppose that Demkon had actually used the straight-line method and on December 31, 1991 sold the machine for $95,000. Write the journal entry to record the sale. Assume a tax rate of 33 percent.

9–9. Asset Acquisition and Comparative Depreciation Methods. The Cruse Company acquired a new machine on January 1, 1991 for $125,000 cash plus the trade-in of an old machine having an original cost of $150,000, accumulated depreciation to date of $90,000, and a market value of $95,000. Costs of installation totaled $5,000, all paid in cash. The company estimates that the new machine will have a useful life of six years, and a salvage value at the end of the six years of $15,000.

Required:

1. Write the appropriate journal entry to record the acquisition of the new machine. Ignore income taxes.

2. Calculate the annual depreciation expense for 1991 through 1997 under the following alternative depreciation methods:

   a. Straight line
   b. Sum of the years' digits
   c. Double declining balance

3. Assuming the Cruse Company had revenue of $800,000 and expenses (exclusive of depreciation expense) of $600,000 for each of the next six years, determine the net income that Cruse would report in the first and the sixth year under each of the three alternative depreciation methods. Assume the machine was sold for $15,000 at the end of the sixth year.

9–10. Comparative Depreciation Methods. The Skyline Construction Company purchased new construction equipment at the beginning of 1991 for $300,000. The company estimated that the useful life of the equipment would be ten years and that the net salvage value would be $25,000.

Required:

1. Prepare a depreciation schedule indicating (*a*) the annual depreciation expense and (*b*) the net asset amounts at the beginning of the year for each year of the estimated ten-year life under the following alternative depreciation methods:

   a. Straight line
   b. Double declining balance
   c. Sum of the years' digits

2. Assume the equipment is sold at the end of the eighth year for $50,000. Write a separate journal entry recognizing the disposition, assuming each of the listed depreciation methods has been used. Ignore taxes.

3. Assume the equipment is traded in on new equipment at the end of the sixth year. The net cash paid for the new equipment is $200,000. If no gain or loss is to be recorded, what initial amount should be assigned to the new equipment for each alternative depreciation method?

9–11. Calculation of Depletion. In 1987 the Black Gold Company acquired an option to purchase a five-year lease on a block of acreage. The option included the right to perform seismographic surveys on the land. A survey was performed and indicated the presence of strata with oil-producing potential. Therefore the company exercised its option to acquire the lease (for 1987 through 1991).

A well was drilled during 1987, and oil was found. The total recoverable barrels were estimated to be 100,000. Production was scheduled to begin in 1988.

At the end of 1987, the total of the expenditures made in 1987 subject to depletion (option price, survey costs, and cost of lease) was $20,000. The total expenditures made in 1987 subject to depreciation (tangible well costs) amounted to $30,000. The company planned to depreciate the depreciable costs over the remaining life of the lease. The salvage value of depreciation equipment was estimated to be $2,000.

Production figures for 1988 through 1991 are as follows:

Year	Barrels of Oil Produced and Sold
1988	15,000
1989	25,000
1990	40,000
1991	40,000
Total	110,000

Operations were discontinued at the end of 1991, and the lease was not renewed. The company received $2,000 for the salvageable wellhead equipment and pipe.

Required:

Prepare a schedule showing cost depletion and depreciation for each year of the well's life. Assume that the company did not change its estimate of recoverable barrels until 1991.

9–12. Acquisition of a Copyright. The Carroll Hardback Press published a book that became a best seller. Because of short-term cash considerations, the author and the Carroll Hardback Press sold the copyright rights to the Smith Paperback Company for a lump sum of $130,000.

The copyright has 26 years remaining out of its 28-year life and can be renewed for an additional 28 years. The Smith Paperback Company expects to make sales of the book only during the next 5 years, after which the book will probably be out of print.

Required:

1. What is the expected useful life of the copyright acquired by the Smith Paperback Company? Why?

2. What portion of the initial amount of the copyright should be recognized as expense each year of the copyright's useful life?

9–13. Development and Start-up Costs. The accounting treatment of the costs of development and/or start-up of a major new program has been a controversial issue. Late in 1974, the FASB modified accounting policy to require companies to recognize these costs as expenses of the period in which the expenditures are made. Prior to this time the costs could be capitalized as assets and matched against revenues from the project in future periods. The problem with the previously acceptable alternative is that the assets and net income of the early periods would be overstated if the project were not ultimately successful. This problem was illustrated in a report on Lockheed Aircraft Corporation (*The Wall Street Journal,* June 3, 1974):

> A huge write-down of its financially troubled L1011 "TriStar" commercial aircraft program, probably totaling at least $600 million, is the key element in a complex plan for a far-reaching financial restructuring of Lockheed Aircraft Corp., sources close to Lockheed said.
>
> . . .
>
> Some Lockheed critics have long contended the company was engaging in "fantasy accounting" in its handling of the books for the L1011 program and doubtless will say, in the wake of one of the biggest writeoffs in American corporate history, that the company and its auditors should have "bitten the bullet" some time ago. The auditing firm . . . has regularly qualified its opinions of the extensively footnoted Lockheed financial statements because of uncertainties over "realization of the L1011 inventories" and the maintenance of financing arrangements.
>
> At the end of 1973, Lockheed was carrying $1.16 billion of its total assets of $1.85 billion (and current assets of $1.56 billion) in the form of net inventories in the TriStar program. This unrecovered TriStar investment comprises the plane's development costs, initial tooling and other nonrecurring costs and production costs, less payments for planes delivered to date and customer advances on future deliveries.
>
> Lockheed said in its latest annual report that it expected to recover this inventory through the anticipated sale of 300 TriStars, though it cautioned this could take into the early 1980s and was subject to certain variables and uncertainties. Although it had delivered 56 TriStars through 1973, Lockheed said it didn't expect to reach the point at which current production costs of each plane will be less than the sales price of planes then being delivered until mid-1974. It said the inventory at the end of 1974 would be only slightly less than a year earlier and eventual recovery of about $900 million of gross inventory depended on firm orders beyond the 129 in hand at year-end 1973.
>
> A write-down of the L1011 inventories of about $600 million without a new cash infusion wouldn't drop Lockheed into a negative working-capital position but also wouldn't leave much room between current assets, which would drop to less than $1 billion based on the year-end $1.56 billion figure, and current liabilities, which stood at $718 million at year-end. It would, apparently, wipe out the company's retained earnings, which totaled $192.8 million at year-end.
>
> Lockheed hasn't recorded any loss (or profit) on its L1011 deliveries to date, posting those delivered at the full sales price ($730 million in 1973 and $302 million in 1972). It has charged to income slightly over $300 million to date in general administrative expenses, however. The current sales price of an L1011 is about $20 million.
>
> Currently, Lockheed has firm orders, including those already delivered, for 135 TriStars and second buys, or options, for 67 more, or a total of 202. Airline industry sources say, however, that prospects for substantial additional orders in the next few years are almost nonexistent and, except for a few instances, airlines holding the L1011 options aren't likely to convert options to firm orders during 1974.
>
> Lockheed posted 1973 net income of $16.8 million, or $1.48 a share. This result includes an operating profit on programs other than the TriStar and new ship construction of $165.8 million and a loss of $69.7 million from

general and administrative costs on the TriStar program. Sales of $2.76 billion included the $730 million from TriStars, on which zero profit or loss was recorded, as noted earlier.[2]

Required:

1. In capitalizing the development and startup costs of its TriStar program, do you believe that Lockheed was engaging in "fantasy accounting" as alleged by some of its critics? Would your answer have been different at the outset of the program than it is now with the benefit of hindsight?

2. Assuming it is appropriate to capitalize development and start-up costs:

   a. Do you believe that the investment in the TriStar program was properly classified as a current asset—that is, inventory? Why might a corporation wish to reflect development and startup costs as a current asset rather than a noncurrent asset such as "other assets"?

   b. What justification might be offered for the policy of capitalizing the net production costs (the excess of current production costs over the sales proceeds from this production) of early production (at a minimum, at least the first 60 to 70 planes based on Lockheed's statement that "it didn't expect to reach the point at which current production costs of each plane will be less than the sales price of planes then being delivered until mid-1974")?

   c. In view of the policy of capitalization adopted by Lockheed, why do you suppose that it did not elect to capitalize the general administrative costs (presumably related to the program) rather than recognizing them as expenses of the period in which incurred?

   d. After capitalizing the plane's development costs, initial tooling, and other nonrecurring costs, what system of matching these costs against future revenues was adopted by Lockheed? Do you believe this results in a proper matching of these costs with related revenue?

3. What do you suppose was the basis for the proposed $600 million write-down of an inventory carried at a cost of $1.16 billion (i.e., why was the proposed write-down not some larger or smaller amount)?

4. While a major program is still in the development stage, do you believe that an auditor's qualification (or caveat) that the fairness of the financial statement presentation depends upon the "ability to realize capitalized development costs" is adequate for external investors? If not, what alternative financial data and/or auditor actions would you suggest?

---

[2] *The Wall Street Journal*, June 3, 1974. Reprinted with the permission of the Wall Street Journal, © Dow Jones & Company, Inc., 1974.

Liability Measurement and Expense Recognition

CHAPTER TEN

Corporations have two major sources of funds for use in acquiring assets: monies obtained from borrowing and from selling ownership interests. Borrowing gives rise to liabilities which must be repaid at a stated time in the future. Complications related to liabilities usually deal with measuring the interest expense to be recorded each period. Liabilities such as leases, income taxes, and pensions involve additional complexities due to the need to account for the substance of the transaction as opposed to the legal form (i.e., determining whether economically the transaction represents debt). This chapter concerns the issues which arise in measuring a corporation's liabilities and the related expenses.

LIABILITIES

As defined in Chapter Four, liabilities are obligations of the firm to external parties other than the owners. There is usually a specified date by which the liability must be repaid. While many liabilities require a future cash payment to discharge the obligation, some may be fulfilled through the provision of products or services, as in the case of advance payments by customers. Obligations may be incurred by acquiring resources and postponing payment (e.g., accounts payable arising from credit purchases of merchandise), as well as by borrowing cash from individuals or institutions (e.g., a note payable to a bank). The time value of money concept discussed in Chapter Two is central to understanding the accounting for liabilities. Because time elapses between the acquisition of the money or resource and ultimate repayment of the liability, the value of the loan to the borrower is equal to the present value of the future payments to be made.

Example 10–1 | The treasurer of a company signed a note payable to a bank which calls for payment of $10,000 one year from the date of signature. The bank's charge for interest is 12 percent per year, but the note does not call for separate interest payments. Hence the proceeds of the loan were $8,928.57, the present value of $10,000 to be paid in one year at 12 percent. The total cost of funds is $1,071.43—the difference between the total proceeds, $8,928.57, and the total payments, $10,000. This is equal to 12 percent, the bank's interest rate, on the $8,928.57 of funds provided.

The cost of funds may be ignored when the time period between the acquisition of resources or money in a credit arrangement and its ultimate repayment is short, usually less than one year. Other times, there is an explicit charge for the use of the funds provided for as a rate of interest in the contractual agreement. In all cases there are two primary issues which arise when accounting for liabilities: (1) allocating the cost of using the funds to the proper time periods over the life of the liability; and (2) measuring the value of the liability to be disclosed on the balance sheet.

Interest Expense

Our first thought might be that the periodic cost of using borrowed funds should be measured by the stated interest rate times the amount to be repaid. For example, if a firm borrows $5,000 for three years and is required to pay interest annually at the rate of 10 percent, it would seem that the annual cost is $500 interest expense. However, transactions giving rise to the creation of a liability typically involve more complex circumstances.

For example, a corporation might issue a series of bonds with a face value (principal) of $1,000 per bond and a stated interest rate of 8 percent. This means that the holder of each bond will receive $80 per year in interest, and $1,000 repayment of principal at the maturity date of the bond. If, however, the prevailing market rate of interest for bonds of equal risk is greater (or less) than the 8 percent rate stated on the bond, the market will adjust the actual interest cost to the borrower by paying less (or more) than $1,000 for each bond. If the amount paid for the bond is more than the face amount, the difference is called a premium. If it is less than the face amount of the bond it is called a discount. The existence of premiums or discounts on the original issue of corporate bonds gives rise to the need for more involved approaches to the recognition of liabilities and measurement of the related expense.

Example 10–2 | On January 1, 1991, Holland Corporation decided to issue 100 five-year bonds with a stated interest rate of 8 percent and a face value per bond of $1,000. At the time of issue, the prevailing interest rate was higher than 8 percent, and the investors compensated for this difference by paying only $950 per bond. Thus, Holland Corporation received $95,000 for bonds with a face value of $100,000 and it had the additional obligation of making $8,000 cash interest payments each year. Note that interest payments are based on the face amount, not the proceeds received.

The $5,000 discount is a reduction in proceeds of the bond issue to compensate the lenders (bondholders) for the fact that the 8 percent interest rate paid on the face amount of the bonds is not an adequate interest rate to warrant loaning the company the full face amount. By loaning less than the face value, the bondholders earn an effective interest rate over the life of the bonds that is greater than 8 percent. We must therefore devise some means of taking the $5,000 original discount into account over the life of the bonds as we assess the interest cost of each period.

Effective Interest Rate Method.

Effective Interest Rate.   The effective interest rate of a liability at the time it is issued is that interest rate at which the present value of the principal and interest payments to be made over the life of the liability exactly equals the proceeds to the borrower.

What this definition says is that to find the effective interest rate, we must try different interest rates (r) until the following relationship is satisfied:

$$\text{Proceeds} = \frac{\text{First payment}}{(1 + r)} + \frac{\text{Second payment}}{(1 + r)^2} + \ldots$$

Unfortunately, in most cases there is no shortcut to the trial-and-error method for finding the right interest rate. However, the following steps can make the search process more efficient:

1. If the liability is issued at a discount (premium), start the search at an interest rate above (below) the stated rate.
2. After selecting a trial interest rate, calculate the total present value of all payments (principal and interest).
3. Compare the present value computed in step 2 with the proceeds of the liability. If the present value and proceeds are approximately equal, stop—the rate selected is the effective rate. If the present value of the payments is greater (smaller) than the proceeds, select a higher (lower) trial rate and repeat steps 2 and 3.

Example 10–3 | Holland Corporation's bonds described in Example 10–2 were issued at a discount, presenting the following implicit interest problem (to be solved for r):

$$\$95,000 = \frac{\$8,000}{(1 + r)} + \frac{\$8,000}{(1 + r)^2} + \frac{\$8,000}{(1 + r)^3} + \frac{\$8,000}{(1 + r)^4} + \frac{\$108,000}{(1 + r)^5}$$

The discount implies that the trial rate should be greater than the 8 percent rate of interest payments (on face value). Arbitrarily selecting 10 percent, the search process proceeds as follows:

Trial 1 (at 10 percent)[1]

$$PV = \frac{\$8,000}{1.10} + \frac{\$8,000}{1.10^2} + \frac{\$8,000}{1.10^3} + \frac{\$8,000}{1.10^4} + \frac{\$108,000}{1.10^5}$$

[1] Recall that for whole (integer) interest rates, present value factors are given in the present value tables corresponding to $1/(1 + r)^n$ for various rates and numbers of periods.

$$PV = \$8,000 \, (.909) + \$8,000 \, (.826) + \$8,000 \, (.751) + \$8,000 \, (.683) \\ + \$108,000 \, (.621)$$

$$PV = \$92,420$$

Since the present value of the payments at 10 percent is less than the proceeds, 10 percent is higher than the actual effective rate. We continue with trial interest rates until we find that at 9.3 percent the present value of the interest and principal is $94,982, which approximately equals the proceeds received by Holland Corporation.

The implicit interest to be earned by the creditors over the life of a liability as represented by the effective interest rate determines the interest expense to be recognized by the borrower. This will be illustrated with the following example.

Example 10–4   On January 1, 1987, the Escola Company issued five-year bonds with a total face value of $50,000 and a stated interest rate of 8 percent. Based upon the market determination of the value of the bonds at the prevailing interest rate, Escola Company received $46,210. Therefore it had a discount on the issuance of the bonds of $3,790 ($50,000 − $46,210). Using the trial-and-error method just described, the effective interest rate is determined to be 10 percent.

For the buyers of the Escola bonds, the ownership of the bonds is equivalent to having $46,210 cash invested at 10 percent, since $46,210 is the present value at 10 percent of the set of payments to be received from the Escola Company. We therefore conclude that the bondholders' effective interest earned and Escola Company's interest expense for the year 1987 must be 10 percent of $46,210, or $4,621. However, according to the terms of the bonds, the first cash interest payment on December 31, 1987 is only $4,000 (8 percent times the face amount of $50,000). In effect, the difference between the interest earned by the bondholders ($4,621) and the cash paid ($4,000) is like an additional loan of $621 to Escola Company at the end of 1987. It should therefore be added to the $46,210 original proceeds to get a new balance for the liability of $46,831.

Another way of arriving at the same conclusion is to recognize that the liability of $46,210 earned interest for the bondholders, and therefore caused Escola Company to incur expense of $4,621. If no payment was called for at the end of 1987, the $4,621 would be added to the original liability of $46,210 to get a balance of $50,831. However, since a $4,000 payment was made, the balance is reduced as of December 31, 1987 to $46,831.

An important feature of this reasoning is that $46,831 is equal to the present value as of December 31, 1987 of the remaining payments from the bonds at the original 10 percent effective rate. This is shown in Exhibit 10–1. Therefore, in effect, the remainder of the bond contract is equivalent to a new loan of $46,831 at 10 percent interest as of December 31, 1987. The interest expense for 1988 should be 10 percent of this new balance of $46,831, or $4,683. If no payment was made on December 31, 1988, this full amount would be added to the liability, giving a balance of $51,514. Subtracting the actual December 31, 1988 payment of $4,000 gives an actual balance of $47,514, which is the present value at 10 percent of the remaining payments as of December 31, 1988.

EXHIBIT 10–1

Escola Company

Present Value of Bonds at December 31, 1988

		Remaining Payments			
Date	Interest	Repayment of Principal	Total	Present Value Factor (10% rate)*	Present Value
December 31, 1988	$ 4,000		$ 4,000	0.90909	$ 3,636
December 31, 1989	4,000		4,000	0.82645	3,306
December 31, 1990	4,000		4,000	0.75113	3,004
December 31, 1991	4,000	$50,000	54,000	0.68301	36,883
Totals	$16,000	$50,000	$66,000		$46,830*

* Note that more accurate present value factors are used here than the decimal factors appearing in Table A–1. This reduces the rounding error when working with large numbers (in this case the result is a rounding error of $1 rather than $5).

The critical element in this calculation of interest expense is the rate of interest that was established by the market at the time the funds were borrowed. This rate determines the borrower's interest expense in any given period in the following manner:

INTEREST EXPENSE = EFFECTIVE RATE OF INTEREST × CARRYING VALUE OF LIABILITY AT THE BEGINNING OF THE PERIOD

For Example 10–4, the effective rate of interest is 10 percent. Therefore, the interest expense equals 10 percent times the carrying value of bonds at the beginning of the period.

Using this effective interest approach, the total interest expense recognized over the period of time the obligation is outstanding is equal to the excess of cash payments over the proceeds received from the loan. This expense is allocated to the periods of time benefiting from the effective amount of funds on loan, using the rate of interest established implicitly in the transaction when the liability was originally created. Although the market rate of interest for liabilities of equal risk and stated terms may vary over time, the original loan transaction established the effective rate of interest, and the total interest cost, that the borrower must pay over the life of the bonds.

Carrying Value of Liability. The amount of the liability to be reflected on the borrower's balance sheet is inextricably tied to the periodic effective interest expense in the following manner:

ENDING BALANCE OF LIABILITY = BEGINNING BALANCE OF LIABILITY + INTEREST EXPENSE − CASH PAYMENTS

This is demonstrated in Exhibit 10–2 using the data from Example 10–4.

The original effective interest rate is used for all subsequent measurement of the liability and expense allocations, notwithstanding subsequent variability in market rates of interest. As a consequence, the carrying value of the liability at any point in time reflects the present value of the remaining cash payments to

EXHIBIT 10–2

Escola Company

		Carrying Value of Liability of Bonds			
Year Ended	Proceeds	*(1)* Carrying Value Beginning of Year	*(2)* Interest Expense for Year 10% × (1)	*(3)* Cash Payment, End of Year	Carrying Value End of Year (1) + (2) − (3)
December 31, 1987	$46,210	$46,210	$ 4,621	$ 4,000	$46,831
December 31, 1988		46,831	4,683	4,000	47,514
December 31, 1989		47,514	4,751	4,000	48,265
December 31, 1990		48,265	4,826	4,000	49,091
December 31, 1991		49,091	4,909	54,000	0
Totals	$46,210		$23,790	$70,000	

Note: Check on total interest expense:

$$\text{TOTAL COST (INTEREST EXPENSE)} = \text{SUM OF CASH PAYMENTS} - \text{PROCEEDS OF LOAN}$$
$$= \$70,000 - \$46,210$$
$$= \$23,790$$

be made, at the original effective rate of interest. If the market rate of interest also remains at this rate, the carrying value of the liability will equal the amount at which the bonds can be traded in the market (sold by holders or redeemed by the borrower). But if the prevailing market rate of interest is not equal to the effective rate, the market value of the bonds will not be the same as the carrying value. A higher (lower) market rate of interest will cause the market value of the bond to be less (greater) than its carrying value.

Recording Interest Expense. The journal entries required to recognize interest expense and the related liability under the effective interest method, applied to the facts of Example 10–4 as analyzed in Exhibit 10–2, are as follows:

January 1, 1987	Cash	46,210	
	Bonds payable		46,210
December 31, 1987	Interest expense	4,621	
	Bonds payable		4,621
	Bonds payable	4,000	
	Cash		4,000

Alternatively, the two transactions recorded on December 31, 1987 could be recorded in one compound entry:

December 31, 1987	Interest expense	4,621	
	Bonds payable		621
	Cash		4,000
December 31, 1988	Interest expense	4,683	
	Bonds payable		683
	Cash		4,000
December 31, 1989	Interest expense	4,751	
	Bonds payable		751
	Cash		4,000

December 31, 1990	Interest expense	4,826	
	Bonds payable		826
	Cash		4,000
December 31, 1991	Interest expense	4,909	
	Bonds payable		909
	Cash		4,000
	Bonds payable	50,000	
	Cash		50,000

Note that we have separated the recognition of the final year's interest expense and interest payment from the retirement of the bonds to show how the carrying value of the liability finally equals the principal amount just before retirement of the debt. The discount together with the annual interest payments equals the total cost of funds incurred over the life of the liability. Under the effective interest method, the discount portion of the total cost of funds is automatically allocated to the appropriate period in the life of the liability.

Many accountants prefer to record the issuance of a bond at its face value and any difference between the proceeds received and face value in a separate premium or discount account. Subsequently, recording interest expense involves reducing the premium or discount account rather than changing the amount in bonds payable. Using the facts of Example 10–4, the issuance of the bonds and first interest expense entry following this approach would be as follows:

January 1, 1987	Cash	46,210	
	Discount on bonds payable	6,790	
	Bonds payable		50,000
December 31, 1987	Interest expense	4,621	
	Discount on bonds payable		621
	Cash		4,000

The carrying value of the bond at any time is the face value of the bonds as recorded in the bonds payable account, minus the unamortized discount on bonds payable. After recording the interest expense on December 31, 1987, the balance in the discount account is $6,169 ($6,790 − $621). When subtracted from the bonds payable account, this yields a carrying value on that date for the bonds of $43,831.

Note that this is the same amount as found on line 2 of Exhibit 10–2, where the bonds payable account is credited directly. At the maturity date of the bond, after recording the last interest payment, the balance in the discount account is zero and the carrying value of the bonds equals their face value; i.e., the amount in the bonds payable account.

When the bonds are sold for more than their face value, this approach requires crediting premium on bonds payable for the excess of the proceeds over the principal amount. Subsequent interest payments are a reduction (debit) of the premium for differences between the cash payment and interest expense determined using the effective interest rate method. The carrying value of the bonds at any date is the bonds payable account plus the unamortized premium on bonds payable. When the bond matures and all interest payments have been made, the balance in the premium account is 0 and the carrying value equals the bond's principal amount.

Installment Liabilities

The terms of some liabilities may call for regular payments that include both principal and interest, rather than waiting until the maturity date for full repayment of the face amount. Measuring such liabilities and recognizing interest expense presents no special problems. The principal repayment serves to reduce the total amount borrowed. This establishes a new carrying value for the liability, and the effective interest rate is multiplied by that amount to determine the interest expense.

Retirement of Debt Before Maturity

At the maturity date of a debt instrument, the carrying value of the liability is equal to the face amount of the debt. When repayment of the principal is made, cash and the liability are decreased by equal amounts. However, at times prior to maturity, the carrying value of the liability may not be equal to either the face value or the current market value of the debt. Therefore, if the corporation elects to retire, or extinguish, debt prior to its maturity, a difference may exist between the repurchase price and the carrying value of the liability. If the repurchase price is less than (exceeds) the carrying value of the liability, an extraordinary gain (or loss) is recognized in determining net income in the period in which the debt is retired.

Disclosure of Liabilities

The balances in various liability accounts will appear opposite appropriate captions in the statement of financial position. For long-term liabilities it is particularly useful to disclose the terms of the liabilities, such as the rates at which interest is paid on face amounts, the dates that interest and principal (or combined installment) payments are due, and so forth. If a company has relatively few, uncomplicated liabilities, such facts can be given parenthetically in the statement of financial position itself. Otherwise a lump-sum amount can be shown opposite the caption of each major category of liabilities in the statement of financial position, with details disclosed in notes to the financial statements.

LEASES

A business enterprise can acquire and finance long-lived assets for its operations in a number of different ways. One way is to rent assets on a period-by-period basis. An advantage of such short-term rental arrangements is that, at any one time, the enterprise only has to pay for a fraction of the asset's cost. Disadvantages include the possible lack of availability of rental assets, the abrupt withdrawal by the owner of the assets, and the fact that the renter does not obtain ownership of the assets. No special problems exist in accounting for such operating leases. The procedures for these leases are illustrated later in this section.

Another way to acquire resources is by outright purchase. A popular alternative to outright ownership and periodic rental is a long-term noncancelable lease. A long-term noncancelable lease is a contract between a lessor (owner) who agrees to provide use of the assets for a specified number of periods, and a lessee (renter) who agrees to pay a specified schedule of rent payments in exchange. Neither party can unilaterally fail to perform without being held liable for damages to the other. In this sense, a long-term noncancelable lease is an executory contract. This means that although neither party is free to withdraw from the contract, if one party does fail to perform its obligation, the other party need not continue to perform. The appropriate accounting treatment for long-term noncancelable leases is a major issue of debate, with some accountants viewing such leases as similar to outright purchases of assets.

Capital Lease

The Lessee. A long-term noncancelable lease may be considered a purchase of an asset by the lessee, in which the seller (lessor) extends credit to the buyer. The lease agreement is then recognized by the lessee as a liability valued at the present value of the lease payments at the time the lease agreement is made. Simultaneously, the related asset received in exchange for the liability is recognized (the rights to use the leased assets for the term of the lease), also at the present value of the lease payments. Thereafter, the expense to the lessee of using the leased assets is recognized as depreciation of the initial asset value over the term of the lease. In addition, interest expense is recognized each period on the present value of the remaining lease payments.

. The Lessor. If a lease is judged a purchase of the asset by the lessee, it is then considered an installment sale by the lessor. This means that in the period that the lease agreement is consummated, the present value of the lease payments is recognized as revenue, and the unexpired cost of the leased asset is recognized as expense. The lessor recognizes a new asset, lease payments receivable, valued at the present value of the lease payments. During the term of the lease, the lease receivable balance is reduced by payments received from the lessee and increased by interest on the present value of the remaining payments. The interest is recognized as financing income from the lease in that period. This accounting treatment recognizes that the lessor has in effect sold the assets to the lessee and financed the purchase by extending long-term credit.

Example 10–5 | Sumner Company has entered into a six-year lease agreement with Elipse Equipment Company. According to the lease agreement, Elipse will provide Sumner, for a six-year period, with heavy equipment that Elipse manufactures. Sumner has agreed to payments of $300,000 at the end of each of the six years. The retail price of the equipment acquired by Sumner is $1,233,422. Based on this price, the effective interest rate (the rate at which the present value of the lease payments approximates that value received) is 12 percent, which is also equal to the market rate of interest for secured loans of risk equal to the lease agreement.

Assuming that Sumner recognized the lease rights as an asset and the lease obligation as a liability at the time of signing the lease, and assuming that the company felt that straight-line depreciation of the asset was appropriate, all of the accounting effects of capitalizing the lease agreement over its six-year life are summarized in Exhibit 10–3.

The journal entries in Sumner's accounts to record (1) the acquisition of the equipment; (2) the first year's depreciation; (3) the first year's interest expense; and (4) the first year's lease payment are as follows:

1.	Leased equipment	1,233,422	
	Long-term lease liability		1,233,422
2.	Depreciation expense	205,570	
	Lease equipment		205,570
3.	Interest expense	148,011	
	Long-term lease liability		148,011
4.	Long-term lease liability	300,000	
	Cash		300,000

Looking at Exhibit 10–3, several important relationships are worth noting. The initial amount of both the liability and the asset recognized, $1,233,422, is equal to the discounted value of the lease payments at the effective interest rate of 12 percent. Thereafter, the asset balance is adjusted downward by the amount of depreciation expense recognized each year. The amount of the liability is increased by the interest expense recognized each year and reduced by the annual payment. Note that the leased asset and related obligation appear as if Sumner had acquired the same asset by purchase and financed it with a loan involving an identical schedule of payments.

The sum of the depreciation plus interest expense recognized over the six-year term (see the last column of Exhibit 10–3) equals the total of the lease payments (see the Less Lease Payment column). The capitalization method allocates the total cost of leasing the equipment to the various periods in the life of the lease. The portion of this total cost that is related to the use of the resource in operations (depreciation) is separated from the portion that is related to financing the acquisition of the resource (interest).

EXHIBIT 10–3

Sumner Company

Lease-Related Asset, Liability, and Expense
Capitalization Treatment

	Asset and Related Expense		Liability and Related Expense				Total Expense
Year	Depreciation Expense	Year-end Balance	Beginning Liability Balance	Add 12% Interest Expense	Less Lease Payment	Year-end Liability Balance	Depreciation Plus Interest
Lease signed		$1,233,422				$1,233,422	
1	$ 205,570	1,027,852	$1,233,422	$148,011	$ 300,000	$1,081,433	$ 353,581
2	205,570	822,282	1,081,433	129,772	300,000	911,205	335,342
3	205,570	616,712	911,205	109,344	300,000	720,549	314,914
4	205,570	411,142	720,549	86,466	300,000	507,015	292,036
5	205,571	205,571	507,015	60,842	300,000	267,857	266,413
6	205,571	0	267,857	32,143	300,000	0	237,714
	$1,233,422			$566,578	$1,800,000		$1,800,000

Example 10–6 | Assume that the lease described in Example 10–5 is judged to be a sale for Elipse. Suppose that Elipse's cost to manufacture the leased asset was $1 million and Elipse expects zero recoverable (salvage) value after six years. The equipment was included at the $1 million cost in Elipse's financial position at the time the lease agreement was consummated. Elipse now recognizes a lease receivable from Sumner equal to the present value of the lease payments, $1,233,422, and includes that amount in its revenue in the current period. At the same time, the cost of the leased asset, $1 million, is expensed, and the asset itself no longer appears on Elipse's balance sheet. The difference between the present value of the lease payments and the cost of the leased assets, $233,422, is recognized in full as income in the period of inception of the lease. In addition, interest income will be recognized each year. Elipse will recognize the same amount for lease receivable and interest income that Sumner recognizes as its liability and interest expense, respectively. Thus, from the Interest Expense column of Exhibit 10–3 we see that Elipse has interest income of $148,011 in year 1; $129,772 in year 2; and so forth. A schedule showing the lease receivable balance, interest income, and lease payment recorded by Elipse according to the capitalization method appears in Exhibit 10–4.

The journal entries in Elipse's accounts to record (1) the delivery (sale) of the equipment to Sumner; (2) the cost of the equipment as an expense associated with the sale; (3) the first year's interest income on the lease receivable; and (4) the first year's payment from Sumner are as follows:

1. Lease payments receivable	1,233,422	
Revenue		1,233,422
2. Cost of equipment sold	1,000,000	
Manufactured equipment		1,000,000
3. Lease payments receivable	148,011	
Interest income		148,011
4. Cash	300,000	
Lease payments receivable		300,000

Exhibit 10–4 makes several important points in connection with the capitalization method for the lessor. The accounting treatment is the same as the sale-with-financing method for dealing with any long-term installment sales contract. That is, initially, a receivable is recognized as the present value of the set of payments to be received in the future. Thereafter the receivable is increased by the amount of interest income recognized in each period (at the original effective rate) and reduced by payments received. Note the total income from the lease recognized over its term is equal to the sum of the income recognized in the period of inception plus all the interest on the lease receivable recognized each period. In the previous example, this total is equal to $233,422, the income recognized at the time the lease is signed; plus $566, 578, the total of the Interest Income column of Exhibit 10–4. The sum of these two amounts, $800,000, is also equal to the difference between the total of the six lease payments, $1.8 million, and the cost of manufacturing the equipment, $1 million. The capitalization method is one means of allocating this total income to the different periods in the life of the lease.

EXHIBIT 10–4

Elipse Equipment Company

	Lease-Related Asset and Income Capitalization Treatment			
Year	Beginning Receivable Balance	Add 12% Interest Income	Less Lease Payment	Year-end Receivable Balance
1	$1,233,422	$148,011	$ 300,000	$1,081,433
2	1,081,433	129,772	300,000	911,205
3	911,205	109,344	300,000	720,549
4	720,549	86,466	300,000	507,015
5	507,015	60,842	300,000	267,857
6	267,857	32,143	300,000	0
Total		$566,578	$1,800,000	
Income recognized at time lease is signed		233,422		
Total income		$800,000		

Operating Leases

Operating leases are equivalent to the short-term rental of an asset. As noted in the introduction to this section, no particularly complex issues arise in accounting for operating leases. The periodic payment is recognized as expense by the lessee and revenue by the lessor in the period for which it covers use of the assets. The leased assets continue to be included in the financial position of the lessor at their unexpired cost, reduced each period by the depreciation expense that is matched against the recognized rental revenue. No assets or liabilities are recognized by the lessee.

Example 10–7 Reconsider the lease between Sumner and Elipse and assume it will be accounted for as an operating lease. Elipse depreciates the leased assets on a sum-of-the-years'-digits basis over the six-year term of the lease, with no salvage value. Exhibit 10–5 shows the schedule of rent expense for Sumner; and for Elipse, it shows the schedules of the declining unexpired leased asset balance, the depreciation expense, the rental revenue, and the rental income that would be recognized over the term of the lease, according to the operating method.

Unlike the capitalizing method, the operating method does not call for any recognition of the signing of the lease or delivery of the equipment in the accounts of either the lessor or the lessee. Instead, the lessee, Sumner, merely recognizes each annual rent payment as rent expense for the year:

Rent expense	300,000	
Cash		300,000

Elipse correspondingly recognizes lease revenue equal to the payment received each year and matches the related depreciation expense on the equipment against the lease revenue. For the first year of the lease, the entries for Elipse are as follows:

Cash	300,000	
Lease revenue		300,000
Depreciation expense	285,714	
Accumulated depreciation		285,714

Two observations can be made about Exhibit 10–5 as compared to Exhibits 10–3 and 10–4. First, the total income recognized by the lessor (Elipse) over the term of the lease is the same under both the capitalization and operating methods. But the timing and nature of the amounts recognized in each period differ. This illustrates that the capitalization and operating methods are two alternative ways of allocating total income from the lease to the different periods in the life of the lease. Second, the nature and the amount of the lease-related asset recognized under the two methods differ. Under the capitalization method, the leased assets are exchanged by the lessor for another asset, lease payments receivable.

In the case of the lessee (Sumner) the schedule of rent expense is all that is necessary under the operating method. Note that the capitalization method requires the recognition of the leased asset and related depreciation expense as well as the lease liability and related interest expense. Again it is important to recognize that the sum of the periodic depreciation and interest expenses recognized by the lessee under the capitalization method is equal to the sum of the periodic rent expense under the operating method. This again illustrates that the two methods are alternative ways of allocating total cost to the periods in the life of the lease.

Distinguishing Capital and Operating Leases

The previous discussion and example assumed it was appropriate to apply either the capitalization or operating method to a given situation. As was seen, the two alternative accounting methods can produce substantially different revenue, expense, asset, and liability recognition in each period for both the lessor and the

EXHIBIT 10–5

Sumner and Elipse Equipment Companies

		Operating Method			
Sumner (Lessee)		Elipse Equipment (Lessor)			
Year	Rent Expense	Year-end Balance Leased Assets	S-Y-D Depreciation	Rental Revenue	Rental Income
Lease signed		$1,000,000			
1	$ 300,000	714,286	$ 285,714	$ 300,000	$ 14,286
2	300,000	476,190	238,096	300,000	61,904
3	300,000	285,714	190,476	300,000	109,524
4	300,000	142,857	142,857	300,000	157,143
5	300,000	47,619	95,238	300,000	204,762
6	300,000	0	47,619	300,000	252,381
Total	$1,800,000		$1,000,000	$1,800,000	$800,000

lessee. Determining which method is appropriate to use for a given lease has been an issue of debate among accountants. Resolution of the issue has focused on identifying criteria which indicate whether the lease was in substance a sale. The FASB has identified these criteria to be as follows:

1. Title passes to the lessee,
2. The lessee can purchase the leased asset at the end of the lease term for substantially less than its fair market value (a bargain purchase option),
3. The lease term is at least 75 percent of the economic life of the leased asset, and
4. The present value of the lease payments is at least 90 percent of the fair market value of the leased asset.[2]

The presence of any one of these criteria in a specific lease causes it to be construed a sale and both the lessee and lessor must use the capitalization method. In the absence of these factors, the operating method is used.

INCOME TAXES

Income taxes are a genuine expense of doing business. The amount of income tax to be paid each period is determined by the special provisions of the Internal Revenue Code, as well as by the entity's revenue and expense. Management is usually motivated to minimize the corporation's taxable income and thus the amount of taxes the corporation pays. Complications arise when we attempt to measure the periodic tax expense related to financial accounting income.

Financial Accounting Income versus Tax Accounting Income

In the United States, the federal income tax is levied on taxable income as determined by the Internal Revenue Code. Taxable income is largely based on conventional accounting principles; that is, the difference between revenue realized matched with the expenses incurred. However, certain kinds of revenue (e.g., interest received on municipal obligations) and certain kinds of expenses (e.g., amortization of goodwill) are not included in taxable income as a matter of national tax policy. These items are called permanent differences because they will never become a part of taxable income.

In the absence of permanent differences, the sum of taxable income will equal the sum of financial accounting income over the life of the entity. In any given period, taxable income may differ from financial accounting income because different measurement rules are oftentimes used for tax and financial accounting purposes. For example, management may elect to use straight-line depreciation for equipment in determining financial accounting income. The selection of measurement rules for financial accounting purposes reflects management's intention to best represent the financial status and activities of the entity. Yet management may elect to use sum-of-the-years'-digits depreciation for depreciating the same equipment in determining taxable income. This accounting

[2] Financial Accounting Standards Board, *Statement No. 13* "Accounting for Leases" (Stamford, Conn.: FASB, 1975).

procedure choice reflects management's intention to minimize taxable income, and thereby minimize the taxes paid by the corporation.

Note that two different purposes motivate the selection of measurement rules. Thus it is quite common, as well as legally and morally acceptable, for a corporation to maintain two separate sets of books: one for financial accounting purposes and another for tax purposes. As will be seen, differences which come from the selection of measurement rules arise from timing the recognition of revenue and expenses. These are called timing differences because they eventually reverse and cancel each other.

Income Tax Expense

If financial accounting income and taxable income differ in a given period, an issue arises about how to measure income tax expense. Some accountants contend that the income taxes paid represent expenses because they are assessed and payable according to the taxable income of a given period. The income tax expense recognized is then equal to the amount of tax calculated based on taxable income.

Example 10–8 | Vending Machine Company owns and operates a large number of vending machines. The company buys a complete new set of machines every three years from the manufacturer, who allows 40 percent of the original cost of three-year-old machines as a trade-in allowance on new machines. The company purchased its first set of machines in 1989 for $1 million. All of its sales are for cash, and all expenses incurred other than depreciation are cash expenditures at the time incurred (for both tax and accounting purposes). The supplies in the company's vending machines are the property of the suppliers, who bill the company only for the supplies sold. The company's sales for each of its first three years of operation were $1 million for both financial accounting and tax purposes. Expenses other than depreciation for both purposes were $600,000 each year. However, the company used straight-line depreciation for financial accounting purposes and sum-of-the-years'-digits depreciation for tax purposes. Exhibit 10–6 shows the company's before-tax financial accounting income and taxable income for 1989 through 1991.

If Vending Machine Company is subject to a 33 percent tax rate and considers tax expense to be a period expense, after-tax financial accounting income would be determined as in Exhibit 10–7.

Using the period-cost approach, the journal entries made by Vending at the end of each year to record income tax expense (assuming the taxes are not yet paid) are as follows:

December 31, 1989	Income tax expense	33,000	
	Income taxes payable		33,000
December 31, 1990	Income tax expense	66,000	
	Income taxes payable		66,000
December 31, 1991	Income tax expense	99,000	
	Income taxes payable		99,000

Note that if Vending had used straight-line depreciation for tax purposes, taxable income would have been the same as financial accounting income,

EXHIBIT 10–6

Vending Machine Company

<table>
<tr><td colspan="5" align="center">Comparative Income Statements
1989–1991
Before-Tax Financial Accounting Income</td></tr>
<tr><td></td><td align="center">*1989*</td><td align="center">*1990*</td><td align="center">*1991*</td><td align="center">*Total*</td></tr>
<tr><td>Revenues</td><td>$1,000,000</td><td>$1,000,000</td><td>$1,000,000</td><td>$3,000,000</td></tr>
<tr><td>Less expenses:</td><td></td><td></td><td></td><td></td></tr>
<tr><td> Depreciation</td><td>200,000</td><td>200,000</td><td>200,000</td><td>600,000</td></tr>
<tr><td> Other expense</td><td>600,000</td><td>600,000</td><td>600,000</td><td>1,800,000</td></tr>
<tr><td>Before-tax income</td><td>$ 200,000</td><td>$ 200,000</td><td>$ 200,000</td><td>$ 600,000</td></tr>
</table>

<table>
<tr><td colspan="5" align="center">Taxable Income</td></tr>
<tr><td></td><td align="center">*1989*</td><td align="center">*1990*</td><td align="center">*1991*</td><td align="center">*Total*</td></tr>
<tr><td>Revenues</td><td>$1,000,000</td><td>$1,000,000</td><td>$1,000,000</td><td>$3,000,000</td></tr>
<tr><td>Less expenses:</td><td></td><td></td><td></td><td></td></tr>
<tr><td> Depreciation</td><td>300,000</td><td>200,000</td><td>100,000</td><td>600,000</td></tr>
<tr><td> Other expense</td><td>600,000</td><td>600,000</td><td>600,000</td><td>1,800,000</td></tr>
<tr><td>Taxable income</td><td>$ 100,000</td><td>$ 200,000</td><td>$ 300,000</td><td>$ 600,000</td></tr>
</table>

EXHIBIT 10–7

Vending Machine Company

<table>
<tr><td colspan="4" align="center">After-Tax Financial Accounting Income
1989–1991</td></tr>
<tr><td></td><td align="center">*1989*</td><td align="center">*1990*</td><td align="center">*1991*</td></tr>
<tr><td>Before-tax financial accounting income
  (based on S-L depreciation)</td><td>$200,000</td><td>$200,000</td><td>$200,000</td></tr>
<tr><td>Income tax expense
  (based on S-Y-D depreciation)</td><td>33,000</td><td>66,000</td><td>99,000</td></tr>
<tr><td>After-tax financial accounting income</td><td>$167,000</td><td>$134,000</td><td>$101,000</td></tr>
</table>

$200,000. Tax expense in each year is then $66,000 (33 percent × $200,000). The sum of the three-year tax bill (i.e., over the life of the equipment) is $198,000, irrespective of which depreciation method is used for tax purposes. However, under the sum-of-the-years'-digits method, less tax is paid initially and more tax is paid later. Because money has a time value, such postponement is preferable for the company.

Interperiod Tax Allocation

Critics of the period-cost interpretation of income taxes argue that income taxes are a function of the revenues and expenses of the entity. Accordingly, the income tax implications of the various revenue and expense transactions belong in the period in which the revenues and expenses are recognized for financial accounting purposes. This approach of matching the tax effects to their time period of occurrence is called interperiod tax allocation. The timing of recognition of those same revenues and expenses for tax purposes is relevant only insofar as it determines when the taxes actually become payable.

Example 10–9 | Returning to Vending Machine Company, recall that before-tax financial accounting income was $200,000 in 1989, 1990, and 1991. To be matched properly with related revenue and expense of the period, the company's income tax expense should be $66,000 in each of the years (assuming the tax rate is 33 percent). However, with taxable income based on sum-of-the-years'-digits depreciation, the actual assessed taxes (taxes payable) for the three years were $33,000, $66,000, and $99,000, respectively.

An account is needed to handle the discrepancy between income tax expense measured related to financial accounting income (as required for interperiod tax allocation), and income taxes payable measured related to taxable income. This account is a liability entitled deferred income taxes. It is credited whenever financial accounting income exceeds taxable income such that income tax expense exceeds income taxes payable. It is debited in the journal entries made for the reverse situation. Using the interperiod tax allocation method, the journal entries to be made by Vending Machine Company at the end of each year to record income tax expense (assuming the taxes are not yet paid) are as follows:

December 31, 1989	Income tax expense	66,000	
	Income taxes payable		33,000
	Deferred income taxes		33,000
December 31, 1990	Income tax expense	66,000	
	Income taxes payable		66,000
December 31, 1991	Income tax expense	66,000	
	Deferred income taxes	33,000	
	Income taxes payable		99,000

In 1989, the discrepancy between income tax expense and income taxes payable is caused by the excess of the sum-of-the-years'-digits depreciation over straight-line depreciation. It is known that in some future period (in this case 1991), the relationship will reverse because the lifetime depreciation of the assets (and hence, lifetime income) must be equal under the two methods. Thus the difference between the income tax expense recognized in 1989, and the tax that must be paid in 1989, is recognized as a liability: deferred income taxes. This liability is eliminated in 1991 when the relationship reverses and sum-of-the-years'-digits depreciation exceeds straight-line depreciation. After-tax financial accounting income using interperiod tax allocation is determined as in Exhibit 10–8.

Income Tax Accounting Controversies

Only one controversial issue has been discussed in this section: whether to recognize income tax expense based on the matching concept (interperiod tax allocation) or as a period expense. Some accountants suggest income taxes should be allocated to future periods only when they are expected to reverse, as in the

EXHIBIT 10–8

Vending Machine Company

After-Tax Financial Accounting Income 1989–1991			
	1989	*1990*	*1991*
Before-tax financial accounting income (based on S-L depreciation)	$200,000	$200,000	$200,000
Income tax expense (based on S-L depreciation)	66,000	66,000	66,000
After-tax financial accounting income	$134,000	$134,000	$134,000

case of Vending Machine Company. However, it is difficult to know with certainty whether such differences will reverse since they are based on unknown future events such as the rate at which the business purchases new assets.

A second controversy arises concerning the appropriate tax rate to use in establishing the credit to deferred taxes. Note that 33 percent (the current tax rate) was used for all three years in the Vending Machine Company example. However, if tax rates were expected to decrease in future years, Vending Machine might argue that a lower amount should be credited to the deferred income taxes account in 1989. This would be consistent with the fact that lower taxes payable would be due in 1991 if tax rates were lower than 33 percent. (For example, if tax rates were 25 percent in 1991, tax expense in that year would be $50,000, taxes payable would be $75,000, and the offsetting debit to deferred taxes would be $25,000.) Of course, it is difficult to know with certainty what will happen to future tax rates.

Current accounting policy requires interperiod tax allocation using the tax rate of the period when the timing difference arises. A recent accounting standard[3] makes notable changes to current income tax accounting practice. Most significant is that deferred income taxes are determined using enacted tax rates applicable to future years. Changes in these rates cause changes in the deferred tax liability balance. Because of significant corporate opposition to this standard, due largely to the complexities involved in applying the procedures, the FASB has delayed the effective date of the new standard to fiscal years beginning after December 15, 1990 and retained current procedures while they study the issues further.

PENSIONS

Corporations frequently grant their employees pension benefits as a part of their total compensation package. The specific benefits are detailed in a pension plan contract. Pension plans in general are intended to provide employees with income payments when they retire from the firm. The amount of the payments or benefits to be received by any one individual employee is usually a function of the terms of the contract; the employee's age, compensation, and length of employment

[3] FASB, *Statement No. 97*, "Accounting for Income Taxes" (Stamford, Conn.: FASB, 1987).

with the company; and the amount of contributions made to the pension plan by the employer and employee.

In recent years, pension plans have become a major component of employee compensation. As a result, they represent significant expenditures and obligations on the part of most corporations. The accounting profession has been concerned about the adequacy of the disclosures about firms' pension plans and the disparate treatment of pension costs by corporations. As a result, the FASB has established requirements intended to improve employers' accounting for pensions.[4] The complexities which arise in understanding pension plans and the accounting for their specific provisions are beyond the scope of an introductory book. However, a brief discussion of this topic is needed due to the economic magnitude of pensions in the United States.

Pension Assets and Liabilities

Each year companies typically segregate and restrict a portion of their cash to be used to pay future pension benefits to their employees at retirement. They do this by making annual deposits of cash with a pension fund trustee (a person independent of the company) who is responsible for investing the cash in earning assets (e.g., stocks and bonds) and paying retirees their benefits.

At any point in time, the balance in the pension plan assets is equal to the cash contributions made by the employer (and in many cases, the employees as well), plus the earnings from investing the contributions minus the benefits paid to the retirees. These plan assets have a fair market value which may be different from the cash deposited with and withdrawn from the pension plan fund. This fair market value equals the market value of the specific securities the trustee has purchased for the pension fund as an investment of the cash deposits not currently needed to pay benefits.

In addition to the pension plan assets, a company also has a pension liability which can be measured at any point in time. This liability arises from the obligation to pay current and former employees the pension benefits promised in the pension plan contract. As noted earlier, specific amounts to be paid are a function of several future events such as the employees' tenure with the firm, longevity, salary at retirement, and the like. While the pension obligation is theoretically the present value of all the future payments to be made under the retirement plan, a number of assumptions must be made to quantify this liability. The FASB requires two measures of the pension liability: (1) the accumulated benefit obligation, based on current and past compensation levels; and (2) the projected benefit obligation, based on assumed future compensation levels.

Pension Cost

The pension expense to be recognized in the current period is measured independent of the cash deposits made to the pension fund or the cash payments made from the pension fund to retirees. The intent is to measure pension cost over the time period the employee is in active service to the company. The cost of these benefits is to be associated with the individual years of service the employee renders while actively working. As a means of accomplishing this objective, the

---

[4] FASB, *Statement No. 87*, "Accounting for Pensions" (Stamford, Conn.: FASB, 1985).

FASB has identified six components to the net pension cost to be recognized for a given period:

1. Service cost: the benefits attributed by the pension plan to employee service during the period.
2. Interest cost: the increase in the present value of the pension liability (measured as the projected benefit obligation) due to the passage of time.
3. Actual return on plan assets: the change in the fair market value of the plan assets during the period. Gains (losses) reduce (increase) net pension cost.
4. Prior service cost: a portion of the cost of retroactive benefits given in plan amendments to current and former employees for increased benefits based on services rendered in prior periods.
5. Gains or losses due to changes in the assumptions underlying the valuation of the plan assets or pension liability.
6. A portion of the transition amount, or the initial pension asset or pension liability that was recognized when SFAS No. 87 was first adopted.

Balance Sheet Recognition

The components of the net pension cost determine the amount debited by the employer to pension expense, while the contributions to the pension fund determine the amount credited to cash. If the cash contributions exceed the pension expense in a given period, the company records an asset entitled prepaid pension cost. If the expense recognized exceeds the cash contributions, the company records a liability entitled unfunded accrued pension cost. Additionally, if at the end of the period the pension liability (measured as the accumulated benefit obligation) exceeds the fair value of the plan assets, the employer is required to recognize a liability equal to the net unfunded liability (i.e., the excess of the accumulated benefit obligation over the plan assets). On the other hand, no asset is recognized (other than prepaid pension cost) if the fair market value of the plan assets exceeds the pension liability.

Example 10–10 | Corl Company has a pension plan in place which it funds each year by depositing $80,000 with a pension fund administrator. On December 31, 1989, Corl determines the fair market value of the plan assets to be $575,000. On December 31, 1988, Corl determined the accumulated benefit obligation was $540,000 and the projected benefit obligation was $585,000. On December 31, 1989, these amounts were $590,000 and $640,000, respectively. The pension fund administrator reported that the actual return on the plan assets for 1989 was income of $65,000. The terms of the pension contract specify that the employees in service to Corl during 1989 earned $75,000 in pension benefits during the year. Corl had amended its pension plan in 1985, granting employees retroactive benefits with a present value of $99,000. Corl is amortizing this prior service cost over 12 years. Corl uses an 8 percent interest rate to measure its liabilities.

The determination of Corl's net pension cost is illustrated in Exhibit 10–9. On December 31, 1989 Corl would record pension expense for $76,750. Because the contributions to the pension fund exceed this amount, Corl would also record

EXHIBIT 10–9

Corl Company

<table>
<tr><td colspan="2" align="center">Net Pension Cost
1989</td></tr>
<tr><td>*Pension Cost Component*</td><td align="right">*Amount*</td></tr>
<tr><td>Service cost: benefits earned during 1989</td><td align="right">$75,000</td></tr>
<tr><td>Interest cost: increase in the present value
  of projected benefit obligation during 1989
  (.08 × $585,000)</td><td align="right">58,500</td></tr>
<tr><td>Actual return on plan assets</td><td align="right">(65,000)</td></tr>
<tr><td>Prior service cost: amortization of retroactive
  benefits granted in plan amendment
  ($99,000 ÷ 12)</td><td align="right">8,250</td></tr>
<tr><td align="center">Net pension cost</td><td align="right">$76,750</td></tr>
</table>

an asset prepaid pension cost. Assuming the deposit is made with the pension fund trustee on December 31, the following journal entry would be made:

December 31, 1989	Pension expense	76,750	
	Prepaid pension cost	3,250	
	Cash		80,000

On December 31, 1989, Corl would also assess the need to recognize a liability in its statement of financial position based on the fair market value of the plan assets and the accumulated benefit obligation. At this date the plan assets have a market value of $575,000 while the accumulated benefit obligation is measured at $590,000. Thus Corl would need to include a pension liability on its balance sheet for the difference of $15,000.

SUMMARY

This chapter considered the complexities which arise in accounting for liabilities. We began by observing that interest expense must be measured related to market rates of interest rather than the stated rate for the debt. Further, we saw that certain agreements were in substance liabilities even though not formally labeled as such. These include leases which in essence are financed purchases of assets, income taxes which arise from timing difference in computing financial accounting and taxable income, and the pension benefits which must eventually be paid to employees. The measurement and related expense recognition issues which arise for leases, income taxes, and pensions were addressed.

Questions for Review and Discussion

10–1. Define or describe

    a. Face value or principal of a bond

    b. Maturity date of a bond

    c. Stated rate of interest
    d. Bond premium and discount
    e. Effective interest rate
    f. Periodic interest expense
    g. Carrying value of liability
    h. Installment liability
    i. Long-term noncancelable lease
    j. Executory contract
    k. Capital lease
    l. Operating lease
    m. Taxable income
    n. Income tax payable
    o. Income tax expense
    p. Interperiod tax allocation
    q. Pension plan assets
    r. Accumulated benefit obligation
    s. Projected benefit obligation
    t. Service cost
    u. Prior service cost

10–2. What two attributes are generally common to all liabilities?

10–3. In what ways are liabilities typically created? How are liabilities usually discharged?

10–4. What two measurement problems are associated with liabilities?

10–5. Explain how to calculate the effective rate of interest of a liability at the time it is incurred (issued).

10–6. How is interest expense calculated using the effective interest approach?

10–7. Explain the relationship between (a) the stated and effective rates of interest; and (b) the face amount of bonds and the proceeds that will be received when the bonds are issued.

10–8. In what sense may a long-term noncancelable lease be considered equivalent to long-term debt? In what sense does it differ?

10–9. Describe the two kinds of accounting treatments that may be used by lessors and lessees for measuring the assets and liabilities and recognizing the expenses and revenues associated with leases.

10–10. Under the capitalization method of accounting for leases, what assets, liabilities, expenses, and revenues (if any) are recognized by (a) lessors; and (b) lessees?

10–11. Under the operating method of accounting for leases, what assets, liabilities, expenses, and revenues (if any) are recognized by (a) lessors; and (b) lessees?

10–12. Explain why income taxes present problems in asset and liability measurement and expense recognition.

10–13. In what ways are conventional financial accounting and taxable income calculations similar? In what ways do they differ?

10–14. Do you believe it is deceptive or unethical for a company to keep two sets of books, one for financial accounting purposes and one for tax purposes?

10–15. Explain the nature of the account entitled deferred tax liability that appears on many corporate balance sheets as a liability.

10–16. Identify and describe the components of net pension cost.

10–17. What are the events that cause the amount in the pension plan assets to change during the year?

10–18. What are the events that cause the amount of the pension liability to change during the year?

10–19. When a company's pension liability (accumulated benefit obligation) exceeds the fair market value of the plan assets, it is required to recognize a liability on its balance sheet equal to the net difference. However, companies are not permitted to record an asset when the reverse situation occurs. Why do you suppose this is true?

Problems

10–1. Calculation of Selling Price of Bonds—Present Value Method. A company plans to sell $100,000 worth of bonds immediately. The stated interest rate of the bonds is 8 percent, and the bonds will mature in four years. Interest will be paid annually.

Required:

1. Calculate the selling price of the bonds, using the present value method, for each of the following market (effective) rates of interest:

   a. 6 percent
   b. 8 percent
   c. 10 percent

2. What is the relationship (greater than, equal to, or less than) between the market rate of interest and the stated rate of interest for each of the following situations?

   a. Bonds are sold at a discount.
   b. Bonds are sold at a premium.
   c. Bonds are sold for face value.

10–2. Effective Interest Rates and Liability Measurement. On July 1, 1991, Paymore Corporation sold 1,000 negotiable notes payable, each promising four annual payments of $300 beginning June 30, 1992. The notes were sold to a major insurance company for $911,205.

Required:

1. Determine the effective rate of interest (to the nearest whole percent) on the notes.
2. Suppose that a pension fund was also interested in buying the notes but had submitted a late bid. If the pension fund had offered an effective interest cost (rate) of 11 percent, would it have been willing to pay more or less for the notes than the insurance company? Explain your reasoning.

10–3. Interest and Liability Measurement. Bonds with a face value of $50,000 were issued by a company on January 1, 1991. The stated interest rate was 7 percent. However, the bonds sold for $46,269. Interest is paid annually on December 31. The bonds mature on December 31, 1993 (three years after issue).

Required:

1. Determine the effective rate of interest at issuance of the bonds.
2. Prepare journal entries to recognize the issuance of the bonds, the annual interest expense, and annual cash payments for each year over the life of the bonds and the retirement of the bonds.
3. Set up a T-account for the bonds payable and record the effects of these entries, noting the balance at each year-end.

10–4. Journal Entry Treatment of Bond Liability. Bonds with a face value of $100,000 were issued on January 1, 1990, for $92,420. The stated interest rate is 8 percent, and the effective rate of interest at issue is 10 percent. The interest is payable each year on December 31.

Required:

1. Calculate the following amounts for 1990 and 1991:

   a. Cash interest payment for the year
   b. Interest expense for the year
   c. Carrying value of the liability at the end of the year

2. Set up a T-account for bonds payable. Prepare journal entries to record (*a*) issue of the bonds; and (*b*) interest paid and interest expense for 1990 and 1991. Post the changes in the bonds payable account due to each of these journal entries and clearly label the balance in the account as of December 31, 1990 and 1991.

10–5. Calculation of Interest Expense and Liability Amounts. On January 1, 1990, Gammon Corporation issued five-year bonds with a total face value of $10,000 and a stated interest rate of 10 percent. Cash interest payments to bondholders are to be made annually on December 31. The market rate of interest at the date of issue was 12 percent. Based upon the market determination of the value of the bonds at the prevailing interest rate of 12 percent, Gammon Corporation received $9,275 for the bonds.

Required:

1. Using the effective interest method of accounting for liabilities, calculate the interest expense for 1992 and the carrying value of the bonds (the amount at which they will be shown in the financial statements) at December 31, 1992. (Note that calculations are for the second year the bonds are outstanding.)
2. Write the journal entry or entries to record the 1992 interest expense.

10–6. Interest Measurement and Liability Measurement. On January 1, 1987, the Acme Manufacturing Company issued five-year bonds with a face value of $100,000 and a stated interest rate of 10 percent. On that date the market rate of interest was 9 percent, and the bonds were sold at a price equal to the present value of future payments discounted at 9 percent. Interest is payable on December 31 of each year.

Required:

1. Prepare a schedule to support the calculation of the amount that Acme received on January 1, 1987. Write the journal entry to record the issue of the bonds.
2. Set up a bonds payable T-account and post the account to record the issue of the bonds. Calculate the annual interest expense and the carrying value of the liability at the end of each year over the life of the bonds. Prepare journal entries for annual interest payments and interest expense and for the final payment on the bonds, and post the changes in the liability to the T-account. Calculate the balance in the account and label it for each December 31.

10–7. Interest Measurement and Liability Measurement. On December 31, 1985, a company issued six-year bonds with a face value of $50,000. The stated interest rate was 9 percent; interest is payable on December 31 of each year. The market rate of interest was 10 percent, and the bonds were sold at a price equal to the present value of future payments discounted at the market rate of interest.

Required:

1. Calculate the selling price of the bonds.
2. Calculate the annual interest expense and carrying value of the liability at the end of each year over the life of the bonds.

10–8. Measurement and Interest Expense—Installment Debt. On March 31, 1990, Locker Corporation signed a note payable to Hemp Bank. The note calls for three annual payments to the bank of $1.5 million on March 31, the end of Locker's fiscal year. The rate of interest charged by the bank on the loan is 11 percent. The bank paid Locker the proceeds of the loan on April 1, 1990.

Required:

1. Determine the proceeds of the note and make a journal entry recording the proceeds and the liability.
2. Set up a notes payable T-account and record the note payable at April 1, 1990.
3. Present journal entries recording the 1991 interest expense and payment on the note and post the related changes in the liability to the T-account.
4. Trace the remaining history of the note payable by making the remaining annual entries in the T-account (no journal entries required).

10–9. Gain or Loss on Early Retirement of Debt.   Refer to the facts in the previous problem. Suppose that on April 1, 1991, Locker Corporation's management wants to reduce its total debt. The note payable to Hemp Bank contains a clause permitting early retirement of the note at any time for 101 percent of the present value of the remaining payments based on the original 11 percent effective interest rate.

Required:

1. Calculate the loss that Locker would experience if it retired the note on April 1, 1991.
2. Assuming management proceeded with the early retirement, write a journal entry to record the transaction.

10–10. Retiring Debt before Maturity.   Debtor Corporation issued 20-year bonds with an aggregate par value of $10 million on January 1, 1988. The bonds pay 9 percent interest, or $900,000 each year, on December 31. At the time the bonds were issued, the market rate for bonds of equal risk was above 9 percent. Thus the proceeds from issuing the bonds were only $9.15 million, giving an effective interest rate of 10 percent.

By December 1991 the market rate of interest was 7 percent on bonds of equivalent risk to Debtor Corporation's bonds. A provision in the original bond indenture agreement provided that at any time after January 1, 1991, but before maturity, the original bonds could be retired at 105 percent of par value. Management of Debtor Corporation is considering retiring the original bonds on January 1, 1992, and reissuing on the same date $10 million in bonds paying 7 percent, or $700,000 annually (on December 31). The administrative costs of the retirement of the old bonds are expected to be $300,000.

The management of Debtor Corporation has asked you to provide it with advice on this matter.

Required:

1. Assuming that Debtor Corporation can earn an average 12 percent return on assets employed in the business, should management retire the bonds? Support your position with appropriate calculations.
2. At what amount will the present bonds be recognized on the corporation's December 31, 1991 balance sheet? How much expense will be recognized with respect to long-term debt in 1994?
3. Assuming that the corporation does not retire and reissue the bonds, how much expense will be recognized with respect to the long-term debt in 1992–93?
4. Assuming that the corporation does retire the old bonds and reissue new ones on January 1, 1992, what total effect on income (interest expense and gain or loss, if any) with respect to long-term debt will be recognized in 1991, 1992, and 1993? Assume (*a*) that the new bonds are issued for net proceeds (after costs of issuing) equal to the par value of $10 million; and (*b*) that the cost of retiring the old bonds was $300,000, as expected. Is the contrast between this pattern of expense and the expense amounts called for in numbers 2 and 3 consistent with your answer to number 1?

10–11. Accounting for a Lease by the Lessor. Central Property Company purchased a building for $10,000 on January 1, 1991. The building was immediately leased to a highly credit-worthy former customer for 20 years at $12,265 per year, payable January 1 of each year. The company expects that the building will have zero salvage value at the end of the lease period. The company is trying to decide whether to use the capitalization method or the operating method to account for the lease. The interest rate implicit in the lease payments is 8 percent. The present value of the lease payments is therefore approximately $130,000. If the company uses the operating method, it will use straight-line depreciation on the building.

Required:

1. How much income will be recognized in connection with the lease under each of the two methods of accounting

    a. For 1991?
    b. Over the whole duration of the lease?

    Discuss any significant differences and similarities in the amounts.

2. What assets and liabilities (if any) will be recognized by Central in connection with the lease under each of the two accounting methods

    a. Immediately after the inception of the lease?
    b. At December 31, 1991?
    c. At January 2, 1992?

3. What considerations should enter into the selection of an accounting method for the lease?

10–12. Accounting for a Lease by the Lessee. Assume the same facts as in the previous problem.

Required:

1. How much of each type of expense will be recognized by a lessee under the operating and capitalization methods

    a. In 1991?
    b. Over the life of the lease?

2. What assets and liabilities will be recognized, if any, under each of the two methods

    a. Immediately after inception of the lease?
    b. At December 31, 1991?
    c. At January 2, 1992?

3. Which method should be used by the lessee? Defend your position.

10–13. Lessor and Lessee Accounting for the Same Lease. At the beginning of 1991, Shipping Company leased a large warehouse on Pier 67 in Port City from the owner of the warehouse, Storage Company. The lease agreement extends for five years and calls for payments as follows:

Initial Payment	Payment at the Beginning of:			
	1992	*1993*	*1994*	*1995*
$100,000	$50,000	$50,000	$30,000	$30,000

Storage Company would have accepted a lump-sum payment of $225,000 at the outset for the same five-year occupancy. The lease payments therefore include a 12 percent effective interest charge.

Shipping Company accounted for the lease over its duration according to the capitalization method, using straight-line amortization of the leasehold asset. Storage Company, on the other hand, has accounted for the lease according to the operating method. The unexpired cost at the time the lease was signed was $150,000. The warehouse was then expected to be demolished at the end of the five years. Its salvage value was expected to equal the cost of demolition and removal. Storage Company depreciated the warehouse on a sum-of-the-years'-digits basis.

Required:

1. Prepare a schedule showing the annual expense to Shipping Company recognized in connection with the use and financing of the warehouse, along with the year-end balances in the related asset and liability accounts, for the years 1991 through 1995.

(Note: *The leased asset and the lease liability will not start out equal in this case because of the initial payment of $100,000.*)

2. Prepare a schedule for Storage Company of the lease-related revenue and expense recognized and contribution to net income, along with the year-end asset balances, for 1991 through 1995.
3. At the 1992 annual meetings of both Shipping Company and Storage Company, a representative of the Stockholders Protection Association accused both companies' managements and auditors of fraud and deception. In support of his charge he pointed out that both companies recognized the warehouse facility as an asset. Since it was impossible for the same building to belong to both companies, the companies were obviously misleading their stockholders. Can you defend the practice of the two companies? What explanations of the situation, if any, can you give that might counter the criticism?

10–14. Allegis Corporation (United Air Lines) shows the following in its December 31, 1987 Statement of Financial Position:

Operating property and equipment:
Owned:

Flight equipment	$5,374,809
Advances on flight equipment purchase contracts	168,541
Other property and equipment	1,670,678
	$7,214,028
Accumulated depreciation and amortization	(3,534,297)
	$3,679,731

Capital leases:

Flight equipment	$ 541,944
Other property and equipment	101,190
	$ 643,134
Accumulated amortization	(316,981)
	$ 326,153
	$4,005,884

The notes to the financial statements contain additional information about the lease obligations:

Lease Obligations:

As of December 31, 1987, United leased 55 of its aircraft, 30 of which were capital leases. The majority of these leases have terms of 18 years, and expiration dates range from 1988 through 2008. Under the terms of leases for 48 of the aircraft, United has the right of first refusal to purchase, at the end of the lease term, certain aircraft at fair market value and others at either fair market value or a percentage of cost. Other leases include airport passenger terminal space, aircraft hangars and related maintenance facilities, cargo terminals, flight kitchens, real estate, office and computer equipment and vehicles.

Future minimum lease payments as of December 31, 1987, under capital leases and under noncancelable operating leases having initial or remaining lease terms of more than one year are shown below:

(*In Thousands*)	*Operating Leases*	*Capital Leases*
Payable during		
1988	$ 232,325	$ 63,222
1989	242,173	59,831
1990	236,414	62,958
1991	235,067	64,887
1992	222,919	66,235
After 1992	3,064,580	457,139
Total minimum lease payments	$4,233,478	$774,272
Imputed interest (at rates of 5.3% to 12.2%)		323,565
Present value of minimum lease payment		$450,707
Current portion		(19,965)
Long-term obligations under capital leases		$430,742

Amounts charged to rent expense, net of minor amounts of sublease rentals, were $211,021,000 in 1987, $172,447,000 in 1986, and $94,553,000 in 1985.

Required:

1. What are the amounts shown for capital leases on the Statement of Financial Position and the related lease liability in the footnote? Explain in words why these two amounts are different or the same.
2. Prepare the journal entry to record the change in the lease obligation expected during 1988. Make the following assumptions: lease payments made at the beginning of the year, no new capital leases added, and a weighted-average interest rate of 8.8 percent.

10–15. Effects of Income Tax Allocation. Because of differences in timing of recognition of certain items of expense, Longhorn Corporation reported the following for 1989 through 1991.

	1989	*1990*	*1991*
Taxable income per tax return	$30,000	$55,000	$65,000
Financial accounting net income before taxes	50,000	50,000	50,000

Assuming that the company's income is taxed at a 40 percent rate and that interperiod tax allocation is used, answer the following questions for each of the three years:

1. What is the income tax payable for the year?
2. What is the income tax expense for the year?
3. What is the net income for the year?
4. What is the balance of the deferred tax liability account at the end of each year, assuming a zero balance at the beginning of 1991?

10–16. Effects of Income Tax Allocation. Because of differences in timing of recognition of certain items of income, Finegan Corporation reported the following for the fiscal years 1989 through 1991:

	1989	1990	1991
Taxable income per tax return	$90,000	$45,000	$30,000
Financial accounting net income before taxes	40,000	65,000	60,000

Assuming that the company's taxable income is taxed at 40 percent, answer the following questions for each of the three years:

1. What is the income tax payable for the year?
2. What is the income tax expense for the year?
3. What is the net income for the year?
4. What is the balance of the deferred tax liability account at the end of each year? (Assume that the balance is zero at the beginning of 1989.)

10–17. Selecting Tax Accounting Measurement Rules and Interperiod Tax Allocation. Computer Services Company began business on January 1, 1991. Its balance sheet on that date follows:

Balance Sheet
As of January 1, 1991

Assets:		Liability and Owners' Equity:	
Cash	$ 100,000	Accounts payable	$ 50,000
Supplies inventory	50,000	Long-term debt	1,000,000
Computer equipment	2,000,000	Owners' equity	1,100,000
	$2,150,000		$2,150,000

Computer Services supplies small businesses with computer assistance for their inventory control, payroll accounting systems, and the like. The computer equipment on the balance sheet is new. It is expected to be traded in four years later. The manufacturer has agreed to take it back at $400,000 cash or trade-in allowance at that time.

With the exception of depreciation on the computer equipment, the company recognizes all revenues and expenses on the same basis for financial accounting and tax purposes. The company has selected straight-line depreciation for financial accounting purposes but has not yet selected a method for tax purposes. Its options for tax purposes are straight line, sum of the years' digits, and declining balance at double the straight-line rate.

Required:

1. Assuming that (a) the company has an after-tax opportunity rate of 8 percent; (b) taxes will be paid at the end of the year for which they are assessed; and (c) the tax rate is 40 percent: Which depreciation method should be used for tax purposes? Defend your choice.

(Hint: *Consider the differential effects of the methods on the tax bill in each year, assuming all other things are constant and that there is sufficient revenue such that taxable income will be positive in every year regardless of the method selected.*)

2. Assuming that the sum-of-the-years'-digits method is selected for tax purposes, give the year-end balance, if any, in the deferred tax liability account for each of the years 1991 through 1994. Assume that the tax rate is 40 percent.

10–18. Tax Allocation Inferences from Partial Information. An excerpt from the income statement of Taxpayers Corporation follows:

Before-tax income		$150,000
Income tax expense:		
Taxes currently paid or payable	$100,000	
Decrease in deferred tax liability	(25,000)	75,000
After-tax income		$ 75,000

Which of the following conditions could definitely be true of Taxpayer Corporation based on the statement excerpt? Which are not necessarily true but might be true? Assume that the tax rate is 50 percent. Explain your answers.

1. Taxpayer Corporation uses straight-line depreciation for tax purposes.
2. Taxpayer Corporation's taxable income is less than or equal to $150,000.
3. Taxpayer Corporation uses straight-line (S-L) depreciation for accounting purposes and sum-of-the-years digits (S-Y-D) depreciation for tax purposes, and its depreciable assets are all past the midpoint in their useful lives.
4. Same as number 3, only S-L depreciation is used for tax purposes and S-Y-D for accounting purposes.
5. Taxpayer Corporation's taxable income is greater than $150,000.
6. Taxpayer Corporation uses S-L depreciation for tax purposes and double-declining-balance depreciation for accounting purposes.

10–19. Tax Allocation Inferences from Income Statement Data. Following is the statement of earnings from the 1991 annual report of Johnson, Inc. In the summary of accounting policies included in the annual report, the company noted that it recognizes deferred taxes on earnings to provide for the tax effect of timing differences between components of financial accounting income and taxable income—primarily arising from use of accelerated depreciation methods for tax purposes (straight-line for financial reporting purposes).

Johnson, Inc.

Statement of Earnings
Years Ended December 31
(amounts in thousands)

	1991	*1990*
Revenues:		
Sales	$919,123	$779,586
Other income	5,430	4,903
Gain on sale of assets	1,007	3,500
Earnings before taxes of unconsolidated		
subsidiaries	15,632	16,712
	941,192	804,701
Costs and expenses:		
Costs of operations	775,248	670,579
Selling and administrative	63,841	53,648
Depreciation and amortization	14,339	13,495

Interest	16,108	17,851
Estimated losses of discontinued facilities	2,000	5,250
	871,536	760,823
Earnings before taxes and extraordinary items	69,656	43,878
Taxes on earnings		
Current	18,600	12,700
Deferred	10,200	4,150
	28,800	16,850
Earnings before extraordinary items	40,856	27,028
Extraordinary items, net of tax	1,334	3,697
Net earnings	$ 42,190	$ 30,725

Required:

1. Based on what you observe in Johnson's 1991 statement of earnings, at approximately what stage of their useful lives were Johnson's fixed assets (on the average) during 1990 and 1991?
2. Estimate the amount of depreciation and amortization expense recognized for tax purposes in 1991 by Johnson. (Assume that depreciation and amortization expense accounted for virtually the total difference between financial accounting and taxable income and that costs of operations contained no depreciation costs.) For this purpose assume a tax rate of 48 percent.
3. Within the concepts and principles of accounting practice, what justification (if any) is there for interperiod allocation (deferral in this case) of income tax expense?

10–20. Pension Cost and Disclosures. You are given the following facts concerning three independent pension plans:

	A	B	C
Service cost	$ 615,000	$ 39,700	$ 182,600
Actual return on plan assets			
gain (loss)	857,000	32,720	91,690
Prior service cost (total)	702,000	0	384,250
Amortization period	6 years		10
Accumulated benefit obligation:			
January 1	4,379,000	252,800	787,030
December 31	4,982,000	282,944	824,974
Projected benefit obligation:			
January 1	6,357,000	317,612	921,700
December 31	7,111,000	358,290	1,001,300
Plan assets fair market value:			
December 31	6,590,000	315,670	797,300
Interest rate used to measure liabilities	10%	8%	12%
Contributions made to pension fund	480,000	50,000	240,000
Payments made to beneficiaries	450,000	29,780	239,100

Required:

1. Calculate the net pension cost for each situation.
2. Prepare the journal recorded on December 31 for each situation, assuming contributions to the pension fund are made at the end of the year.
3. Explain whether an asset and/or liability would be shown on the balance sheet in each situation.

10–21. Interpretation of Pension Disclosures. The following information is taken from Note 15, Employee Benefit Plans, in Chrysler Corporation's 1988 Annual Report.

Pension Plans

Chrysler's retirement programs include pension plans providing noncontributory benefits and contributory benefits. The noncontributory pension plans cover substantially all of the hourly and salaried employees of Chrysler Corporation and certain of its consolidated subsidiaries. Benefits are based on a fixed rate for each year of service. Additionally, contributory benefits and supplemental noncontributory benefits are provided to substantially all salaried employees of Chrysler Corporation and certain of its consolidated subsidiaries under the Salaried Employees' Retirement Plan. This plan provides contributory benefits based on the employee's cumulative contributions and a supplemental noncontributory benefit based on years of service and the employee's average salary during the consecutive five years in which salary was highest in the fifteen years preceding retirement.

Annual payments to the pension trust funds for U.S. plans are in compliance with the Employee Retirement Income Security Act (ERISA) and the plans' funding requirements. All pension trust fund assets and income accruing thereon are used solely to administer the pay pension benefits. Chrysler's total pension fund contributions in 1988 totaled $774 million, including $300 million in Chrysler common stock (see Note 14).

Effective January 1, 1987, Chrysler adopted the statement of earnings provisions of Statement of Financial Accounting Standards (SFAS) No. 87, "Employers' Accounting for Pensions," for its pension plans. As permitted by SFAS No. 87, Chrysler will adopt the related balance sheet provisions on January 1, 1989. Adoption of SFAS No. 87 had the effect of increasing 1987 net pension cost of $146.0 million and decreasing 1987 consolidated net earnings by $86.4 million, or $0.40 per share of common stock.

The components of net periodic pension cost are as follows:

| | Year Ended December 31 | |
| | 1988 | 1987 |
	(In millions of dollars)	
Service cost—benefits earned during the year	$127.9	$118.3
Interest cost on projected benefit obligation	647.6	521.5
Actual (gain) loss on plan assets	(363.2)	165.0
Net amortization and deferral	196.4	(328.6)
Pension expense included in plant closing provision (see Note 20)	(23.4)	—
Net pension cost	$585.3	$476.2

Pension cost is determined using the interest assumptions as of the beginning of the year. The funded status is determined using the assumptions as of the end of the year. Interest assumptions used for 1988 and 1987 were:

| | December 31 | | January 1 |
	1988	1987	1987
Discount rate	9.72%	10.18%	9.25%
Rate of increase in future compensation levels	6.00%	6.00%	6.00%
Long-term rate of return on plan assets	9.92%	9.92%	9.90%

The following table presents a reconciliation of the funded status of the plans with amounts recognized in the Consolidated Balance Sheet.

| | December 31 | |
| | 1988 | 1987 |
	(In millions of dollars)	
Actuarial present value of benefits:		
Vested	$ 6,107.5	$ 5,473.5
Nonvested	1,220.8	979.3
Accumulated benefit obligation	7,328.3	6,452.8
Effect of projected future salary increases	77.6	59.1
Projected benefit obligation	7,405.9	6,511.9
Plan assets at fair value	4,358.3	3,706.3
Projected benefit obligation in excess of plan assets	3,047.6	2,805.6
Unrecognized net loss	(313.8)	(20.8)
Unrecognized prior service cost	(589.8)	(382.9)
Tax effect on AMC unfunded pension obligation recognized in purchase accounting	(179.2)	(168.1)
Unamortized net obligation at date of adoption being recognized over 15 years	(1,865.3)	(2,007.7)
Net pension liability recognized in the Consolidated Balance Sheet	$ 99.5	$ 226.1

Plan assets are invested in a diversified portfolio that consists primarily of equity and debt securities. Plan assets include 13,289,162 shares of Chrysler common stock, including 12,972,973 shares contributed to the plans in 1988 (see Note 14).

During 1988 and 1987, Chrysler offered voluntary early retirement opportunities to certain salaried employees. These early retirement opportunities increased 1988 and 1987 pension expense by $34.5 million and $46.5 million, respectively.

Required:

Assume you are the president of the union which represents Chrysler's employees. What information and/or concerns would you offer to the union members based on this footnote? You might consider the pension benefits granted to employees, implications about future wage increases, apparent return on the plan assets, and the likelihood current employees will receive benefits when they retire (especially if Chrysler were to become bankrupt).

Recognition of Ownership Interests

CHAPTER ELEVEN

Ownership interests represent the third major element of the statement of financial position. This component arises from investments in the corporation by its owners through the original sale of stock (paid-in capital) and by the retention of corporate profits (retained earnings). This chapter focuses on distinguishing among and accounting for the several types of ownership interests common to corporations. Also discussed is the distribution of earnings as cash and stock dividends, stock splits, treasury stock, and stock options. Finally, ownership interests are affected by the purchase of one company's stock by a different and previously unrelated company. The accounting techniques used to depict such intercorporate investments are also a topic of this chapter.

OWNERS' EQUITY

In Chapter Four, owners' equity was defined as the residual interest in the assets of an entity that remains after deducting liabilities. It thus represents the ownership interests of the shareholders. Within owners' equity we distinguished between paid-in or contributed capital (the assets contributed by the owners for their ownership interests), and retained earnings or earned capital (cumulative excess of net income over dividend distributions or withdrawals). The claims of nonowners (e.g., creditors) are legally protected by restricting the dividends paid to owners to the balance in retained earnings. This restriction ensures the original capital contributed by owners remains intact. Further distinctions are made within owners' equity based on the sources of the contributed capital. This section discusses these classifications as well as several types of transactions between the corporation and its shareholders.

Classifications of Paid-in Capital

Paid-in capital is often subdivided into additional categories based on the type of ownership interests (the various classes of stock issued by the corporation) and/ or the specification of legal values for shares of stock.

Classes of Stock. Each share of stock of a corporation conveys certain rights to owners of the share. Owners of shares of common stock generally have the following rights:

1. Right to vote for members of the board of directors and, subject to applicable state laws, to vote on certain types of major corporate decisions (e.g.: merging with another corporation).
2. Right to share proportionally in dividends declared by the corporation.
3. Right to share proportionally in the net assets of the firm if the corporation is liquidated.

A corporation may issue other classes of stock which are explicitly given preference over common stock on certain of these rights, but which may also forfeit one or more of the other rights. One such class of stock is preferred stock. Typically, owners of preferred stock have a preference as to dividend or liquidation distributions over common shareholders, but sacrifice voting rights.

Example 11–1 | Hindley Corporation has two classes of stock outstanding: 1,000 shares of preferred stock, which are entitled to an annual dividend of $5 per share; and 5,000 shares of common stock. No dividends can be paid to the common shareholders in any year unless the holders of the preferred stock also receive a total dividend distribution that year of $5,000 (1,000 × $5).

Oftentimes the preferred stock dividend preference is cumulative, meaning any annual dividends of prior periods that the preferred shareholders were entitled to receive but were not paid, must be paid before any dividend distributions can be made to common shareholders. The preferred stock is noncumulative if its owners are entitled only to its annual dividend and forfeit any right to past dividends not declared or paid. Preferred stock may be participating, in which case preferred shareholders share ratably with common stockholders any distributions of earnings exceeding the preferred shareholders' stipulated dividend rate. Some issues of preferred stock also possess a conversion right. This privilege entitles the preferred shareholder to convert each share of preferred stock owned into a specified number of shares of common stock.

Legal Values for Stock. Many states require corporations to specify a value for each share of stock, referred to as the par value or stated value of the stock.[1] Par value and stated value stock cannot be sold by the corporation for an amount less than this value. This requirement was intended to provide a specified capital

---

[1] The difference between par value and stated value stock is largely a legal distinction which does not affect the accounting for such stock issuances.

buffer to protect the legal claims of nonowners against the corporation. However, the par value of stock can be set by a corporation at any arbitrary amount, ranging down to $1 or less per share. Thus the effective buffer provided by par value stock is often negligible and many states now permit the issuance of no-par stock. The real security for creditors is provided by the actual asset values and related earning power of the corporation—not by an arbitrary amount of capital specified by law. The use of no-par stock recognizes this fact.

The par value or stated value of shares of stock creates an additional accounting classification in the owners' equity section. The total proceeds from the sale of shares of stock are divided into two categories of paid-in capital: (1) the amount of the par (or stated) value of stock issued; and (2) the excess of the paid-in proceeds over the par (or stated) value of stock issued.

Example 11–2 | Hunt, Inc., issues 10,000 shares of $5 par value stock to shareholders in exchange for $170,000. The journal entry to record the transaction shows the paid-in capital divided between the two categories:

Cash	170,000	
Common stock, par value		50,000
Paid-in capital in excess of par value on		
common stock		120,000

Dividends

Cash Dividends. Cash dividends (preferred and common stock) must be formally authorized by the board of directors of a corporation. Three dates are important for cash dividends: cash dividends are declared at a given point in time (declaration date); payable to stockholders of record as of a specific future date (date of record); and actually paid on a third date (payment date). At the date of declaration, the total dividend to be paid becomes a binding liability on the corporation. Therefore, on this date, the retained earnings of the corporation are reduced and a liability, dividends payable, is recognized. Payment of the dividend at the later date results in a decrease in cash and a reduction in dividends payable.

Example 11–3 | The board of directors of Boston Corporation declared a cash dividend of $1.20 per share on November 28, 1991 (declaration date). The dividend is payable to shareholders registered as legal owners of the shares as of December 6, 1991 (record date); and it will be paid on December 14, 1991 (payment date). Suppose that the Boston had 1.34 million shares of common stock outstanding on November 28, 1991, and there were no changes in this amount during December 1991. The following journal entries would be used to record the 1991 dividend:

November 28, 1991	Retained earnings	1,608,000	
	Dividends payable		1,608,000
December 14, 1991	Dividends payable	1,608,000	
	Cash		1,608,000

Stock Dividends. Occasionally a corporation will declare a dividend, usually on common stock, which is payable in shares of the same stock. This type of dividend is called a stock dividend. Although each shareholder has more shares of stock after the stock dividend, each individual's proportionate ownership in the corporation is unchanged. Following the declaration of a small stock dividend (less than 25 percent of the outstanding shares), the market price of each share of stock seldom adjusts downward sufficiently to offset the increase in the number of shares outstanding. In this situation the shareholders have received income equal to the market value of the stock received in the dividend. Accordingly, the firm reduces retained earnings by the market value of the number of shares issued to all shareholders. The corresponding credit is to the common stock par value or stated value account for the par or stated value of the new shares issued, and to paid-in capital in excess of par for the amount by which the market value of the stock issued exceeds its par or stated value.

Example 11–4 | Wright, Inc., had 10,000 shares of $1 par-value common stock outstanding. The board of directors of Wright decided not to pay a cash dividend on these shares, but instead authorized a 10 percent stock dividend. This action means that Wright issues 1,000 new shares of $1 par value common stock, and each shareholder receives 1 new share for each 10 shares now owned. Assuming the market value of Wright's stock is $15 per share at the time of the stock dividend, the following journal entry would be made:

Retained earnings	15,000	
Common stock, par value		1,000
Paid-in capital in excess of par value		14,000

The rationale supporting this accounting treatment is that issuing a stock dividend rather than a cash dividend is analogous to the corporation paying out cash dividends and the owners reinvesting the proceeds in new shares of the corporation's stock. Thus the accounting treatment has the effect of capitalizing some portion of the firm's retained earnings.

When a corporation issues a stock dividend greater than 25 percent of the shares outstanding, it is likely that the market price of all the shares will adjust downward to reflect the greater supply of stock. In this case the accounting treatment is limited to reducing retained earnings and increasing common stock par value for the total par or stated value of the stock issued. The market price of the stock (and thus the paid-in capital in excess of par value account) is not relevant in accounting for large stock dividends.

Example 11–5 | Assume that Wright, Inc. issued a 25 percent stock dividend. The journal entry would record only the par value of the 2,500 shares issued:

Retained earnings	2,500	
Common stock, par value		2,500

Stock Splits

In a stock split, the old shares of stock are called in by the corporation. New (usually more) shares of stock with a different par value (proportionately less than the old par value) are issued to the shareholders. The total amount of legal capital is unchanged by a stock split. Therefore, the par value of the new shares must be adjusted in accordance with the number of new shares that the board of directors wishes to issue. Stock splits are often used as a means of increasing the number of shares outstanding in order to reduce the market price per share, presumably making the company's stock more easily purchased by investors with less to invest.

Example 11–6 | Archer Corporation has 100,000 shares of $10 par value stock outstanding. The board of directors wishes to double the number of shares outstanding and declares a two-for-one stock split. As a consequence of this action, each shareholder receives two new shares of $5 par-value stock of Archer Corporation for each old share of $10 par-value stock held.

Before the stock split, the total legal capital of Archer Corporation was $1 million (100,000 shares with a par value of $10 per share). After the split, Archer's legal capital still remains at $1 million (200,000 shares with a par value of $5 per share). Because the legal capital is unchanged, no accounting recognition or journal entries are required for this stock split.

Treasury Stock

Corporations occasionally repurchase some of their outstanding shares of stock in the open market or directly from shareholders. This action is taken for a number of reasons, including the need for shares to be issued to executives under stock option plans, or perhaps because management believes the stock is undervalued in the market. If the stock is not legally retired or canceled following reacquisition, but rather is held by the corporation for possible reissue in the future, the stock is called treasury stock.

The basic principle underlying the accounting for treasury stock is that a corporation cannot own a part of itself. Thus shares repurchased and held for future resale are not considered assets. Nor does the corporation pay itself dividends and record dividend revenue. Instead, the total cost of the treasury stock is treated as a reduction in owners' equity. This effectively reduces the number of shares which are outstanding. If the treasury shares are subsequently sold, any difference between the proceeds from the sale and the cost of the treasury stock is included in paid-in capital. The corporation does not record a gain or loss from buying and selling its own stock.

Example 11–7 | McGraw Company has 25,000 shares of its $5 par value common stock outstanding. The stock had been sold originally for $12 per share. McGraw Company purchased 1,000 shares, paying $10 per share. The following journal entry is made to record this purchase:

Treasury stock	10,000	
Cash		10,000

The paid-in capital section of owners' equity would be reduced by the cost of the treasury stock owned by the company.

Common stock, $5 par; authorized and issued 25,000 shares	$ 125,000
Paid-in capital in excess of par value on common stock	175,000
Less cost of treasury stock (1,000 shares)	(10,000)
Total paid-in capital	$ 290,000

If McGraw Company later resells this stock for $11 per share, the following journal entry is made:

Cash	11,000	
Treasury stock		10,000
Paid-in capital in excess of par value on common stock		1,000

Stock Options

A popular form of senior executive compensation used by corporations in recent years is the stock option. A stock option is a legal instrument permitting the holder to acquire a specified number of shares of stock of the issuing corporation at a specified price. The options typically are valid for a limited period of time (usually up to five years) and they are not transferable. Stock options have been popular as a form of compensation because of the potential tax benefits to the executive (although current tax rules restrict this benefit) and the linking of the executive's compensation to the fortunes of the company.

The potential number of new shares of stock that may be issued if options are granted and exercised must be disclosed so that present shareholders are apprised of how their proportionate ownership may change if the options are exercised. This disclosure is accomplished by adding supplementary information to the financial statements that indicates the general provisions of the stock option plan, the number of options granted and exercised during the period, and the number of options outstanding at the end of the period.

A more complicated issue arises related to (1) measuring the amount of compensation (to the executive) which accompanies the issuance of the stock options; and (2) determining the period(s) in which the expense should be recognized. The total compensation expense is measured by the difference between the price that the executive must pay for the shares if the options are exercised and the fair market value of the stock on the date the options are granted. This compensation expense is then recognized in the period(s) in which the employee performs the services for which the options were granted. Since options are generally assumed to be issued for future rather than past services, the cost will usually be recognized as an expense of several periods in the future.

Example 11–8

On January 1, 1991 the Dravus Corporation granted its president, Janet Rhone, an option to purchase 1,000 shares of Dravus' common stock. Ms. Rhone could exercise this option for five years after it had been granted. The common stock carried a $5 par value and was selling for $30 per share on January 1, 1991. The option stipulated Ms. Rhone was to pay $25 per share when she decided to purchase the stock.

On the date option was granted, Ms. Rhone received something of value: the right to pay $25,000 for stock with a market value of $30,000. Dravus Corporation must record this $5,000 difference as deferred compensation expense, to be recognized as compensation expense in the future periods believed to be of benefit from granting Ms. Rhone this option. The following entry was made on January 1, 1991:

| Deferred compensation expense | 5,000 | |
| Paid-in capital from issuance of stock option | | 5,000 |

If Ms. Rhone exercises the option and acquires the common stock, the journal entry records the issuance of stock at the amount paid, $25 per share.

INTERCORPORATE INVESTMENTS

Many corporations own common stock in one (or more) companies, thereby creating a relationship between (among) the entities. These investments may be intended as temporary depositories of excess cash and thus appear as marketable securities on the balance sheet of the investor (the corporation owning the stock). Or they may represent investments made to obtain ownership control over another entity, which thus becomes a consolidated subsidiary. These distinctions are usually based on the degree of ownership control held by the investor.

Degree of Ownership

A case of minimal ownership interest in one corporation by another implies the need for an accounting technique which recognizes the investment as a temporary use of excess cash. A situation of larger ownership interest requires an accounting procedure which reflects the permanent investment intent of the investor corporation. Accountants use three distinct classes of intercorporate investments to distinguish between minimal and significant degrees of ownership and to guide them in accounting for the investment. These categories are summarized in Exhibit 11–1, and the accounting procedures are described in subsequent sections. (Using percentage ownership in another corporation to indicate the investor's purpose is admittedly arbitrary, and special circumstances may warrant alternative treatment.)

Ownership of less than 20 percent of the stock of a corporation—the investee—is considered insufficient to justify any special treatment beyond an investment in marketable securities. The investment is recorded at its cost or market value, whichever is lower, and dividend income is recognized as received.

When one corporation owns more than 20 percent of the common stock of another corporation, there is assumed to be a relationship in which the investor exerts a significant influence on the investee. While the 20 percent cutoff is admittedly arbitrary, it is clear that as an ownership interest increases to succes-

EXHIBIT 11–1

Intercorporate Ownership and Accounting Treatments

Degree of Ownership	Accounting Treatment
0 to 20%	Lower-of-cost-or-market method
20 to 50%	Equity method
50 to 100%	Equity method plus consolidation

sively larger percentages, the owner gains greater influence through greater voting power. Of course, the percentage at which a specific owner becomes influential depends on conditions such as the number of other shareholders and the size of their ownership interests. In the absence of special circumstances, ownership interest of 20 percent requires using the equity method of accounting for the investment.

If the degree of ownership extends beyond 50 percent and thus to a majority position, the investor now has a controlling voting power. This cutoff is less arbitrary since now the two corporations are as one entity. The accounting treatment reflects this reality by treating the investor and investee as a parent and subsidiary, respectively, and requiring consolidation of the financial statements.

Lower-of-Cost-or-Market Method

When a corporation buys a relatively small percentage of the common stock of another corporation, it is usually considered an investment in marketable securities made for the best use of excess cash. For such purposes it is wise to obtain a small percentage ownership in any one company and to invest only in the stock of large, publicly traded companies whose shares can be sold with little difficulty. Thus no special relationship necessarily develops between the corporations.

These investments receive the same accounting treatment as investments in government securities and corporate bonds. Thus, they are originally recorded at the cost paid to acquire the stock. However, complications arise because there is no guarantee of a specific amount of proceeds to be received from sale of these investments (as there is for the redemption value of bonds). As a result, portfolios (one or more shares) of investee stock are measured at their aggregate acquisition cost unless their aggregate market value is lower.

If the market value of the portfolio is lower than its cost, the portfolio is shown at market and a loss is recorded. If the marketable securities are current assets (held for resale within the next year), the difference between cost and a lower market value (or the change in this difference from year to year) is a loss of the current period recognized in the income statement. If the portfolio is a noncurrent asset (expected to be held for more than one year), the difference between cost and a lower market value (or the change in this difference from year to year) is recognized in a debit-balanced, owners' equity account entitled unrealized loss on noncurrent marketable securities. This account appears on the balance sheet as part of the owners' equity section whenever aggregate market value is less than the cost of the portfolio. For both current and noncurrent assets, an allowance account (contra-asset) is recorded to reduce the balance in the intercorporate investment on the balance sheet.

Dividends are recognized as income at the time they are declared by the investee. When the investment shares are ultimately sold, the difference between their original cost (or carrying value if a loss has been recorded) and the proceeds from sale is recognized as a gain or a loss.

Example 11–9 | During 1990, Acme Corporation invested in a portfolio of marketable equity securities (common stocks) with a total cost of $1.4 million. Although Acme intended to occasionally add to or sell off some of the securities acquired, the general intent was to maintain the portfolio for several years. Dividends received during 1990 were $110,000. By December 31, 1990, the aggregate market value of the portfolio was as follows:

Stock of Company	Aggregate Cost	Aggregate Market Value	Gain (Loss)
A	$ 600,000	$ 570,000	($30,000)
B	400,000	410,000	10,000
C	400,000	400,000	
Portfolio totals	$1,400,000	$1,380,000	($20,000)

The following journal entries would be used to account for Acme's marketable securities transactions for 1990 (ignoring taxes):

Marketable securities	1,400,000	
Cash		1,400,000
Cash	110,000	
Dividend income		110,000
Unrealized loss, noncurrent marketable securities	20,000	
Allowance for decline in value of marketable securities		20,000

In the 1990 balance sheet, the accounts related to the marketable securities would be disclosed as follows:

Asset:	
Marketable securities	$1,400,000
Less: Allowance for decline in market value	(20,000)
	$1,380,000
Owners' equity:	
Unrealized loss, noncurrent marketable	
securities	($20,000)

During 1991, Acme sold half its holdings of A Company shares for $290,000 and received $80,000 in dividends. At year-end, the cost and market value of the portfolio were as follows:

Stock of Company	Aggregate Cost	Aggregate Market Value
A	$ 300,000	$ 280,000
B	400,000	480,000
C	400,000	400,000
Portfolio totals	$1,100,000	$1,160,000

The following journal entries would be required for 1991 (ignoring taxes):

Cash	290,000	
Loss on sale of marketable securities	10,000	
Allowance for decline in value of marketable securities	15,000	
Unrealized loss, noncurrent marketable securities		15,000
Marketable securities		300,000
Allowance for decline in value of marketable securities	5,000	
Unrealized loss, noncurrent marketable securities		5,000

Both the allowance and the unrealized loss accounts are eliminated since the securities have recovered their market value and must be revalued at their cost. Thus, marketable securities will appear on the end-of-1991 balance sheet at their $1.1 million aggregate cost (which is less than aggregate market value at December 31, 1991). Since market value exceeds cost in the aggregate, the contra-asset allowance account and the contra-equity unrealized loss accounts would have zero balances and thus would not appear on the balance sheet at December 31, 1991.

Had these securities been current assets—rather than recording the unrealized loss, noncurrent marketable securities—a realized loss would have been debited and included in the 1990 income statement. If they were current assets, by definition they would have been sold in 1991, possibly giving rise to a realized gain or loss.

Equity Method

Ownership interest greater than 20 percent requires use of the equity method. When the investor initially acquires the stock of the investee, the investment is recorded at cost. At that time a comparison is made between the amount paid for the stock and the investor's percentage ownership of the investee's net assets. Oftentimes more is paid for the investment than the investor's proportional share of the book value of the acquired company's assets. This is because the investee's assets are undervalued and/or there is unrecognized goodwill. This difference will affect the accounting for the investment, as we want to reflect the market value of the assets at the time they are acquired by the investor. In each subsequent accounting period, the amount of the investor's original investment is altered as follows:

1. The investment account is increased by an amount equal to the investor's percentage ownership in the investee's net income. This accounting treatment recognizes the belief that the increase in the investment account is income to the investor and thus reflected by an increase in owners' equity (retained earnings) and in the investment account. Losses are given opposite treatment.
2. The investment account and owners' equity (retained earnings) are reduced through amortization of any excess cost of the investment over the investor's share in the net assets of the investee at the time of acquisition. This reduction of the investment account is considered an expense to the investor associated with its share in the earnings of the investee. The amortization reflects the fact that the market value of the assets exceeded their book value when the investment was made.
3. As dividends are declared by the investee, the investment account is reduced by the amount of the dividends and the dividend receivable (or cash) account is increased. This step is taken because the investee's earnings have already been recognized by the investor as income and an increase in the value of the investment. Now a portion of that investment is being returned to the investor in the form of cash.

EXHIBIT 11–2

Investor Company

Balance Sheet
As of January 1, 1991
(in thousands)

Assets		Liabilities and Owners' Equity:	
Cash	$ 4,000	Accounts payable	$ 1,200
Accounts receivable	500		
Inventory	2,500		
Net plant and equipment	7,200		
Investment in stock of		Paid-in capital	10,000
Investee Co.	2,500	Retained earnings	5,500
Total	$16,700	Total	$16,700

Investee Company

Balance Sheet
As of January 1, 1991
(in thousands)

Assets		Liabilities and Owners' Equity:	
Cash	$ 100	Accounts payable	$ 200
Accounts receivable	100	Bonds payable	1,000
Inventory	1,200	Paid-in capital	4,000
Net plant and equipment	4,800	Retained earnings	1,000
Total	$ 6,200	Total	$ 6,200

Example 11–10 | On January 1, 1991, Investor Company purchased 40 percent of the ownership shares of Investee Company for $2.5 million. The purchase is recorded by the following journal entry:

Investment in Investee Co.	2,500,000	
Cash		2,500,000

Immediately after the investment by Investor, the balance sheet of the two companies appeared as shown in Exhibit 11–2. The 1991 income statement for Investee Company appears in Exhibit 11–3. Notice that the only effect of the initial investment evident in any of the statements is the recognition of the investment account (at cost) on Investor Company's January 1, 1991, balance sheet.

Exhibit 11–3 indicates that Investee Company's net income for 1991 is $1,250,000. Since Investor Company owns 40 percent of Investee Company's stock, it is presumed that its equitable interest in the company is increased by 40 percent of the net income. This reasoning calls for the following entry:

Investment in Investee Co.	500,000	
Equity in income of Investee Co.		500,000

EXHIBIT 11–3

Investee Company

	Income Statement For 1991 (in thousands)	
Revenue (all from sales)		$5,500
Less expenses:		
Cost of sales	$3,100	
Interest	50	
Depreciation	600	
Other expense	500	4,250
Net income		$1,250

In this entry, an increase in the investment asset is offset by an equal increase in retained earnings. This is a manifestation of the central theme of the equity method: that an investor company records, as income, its equitable share of any earnings recognized by its investee companies.

When Investor Company acquired 40 percent of the ownership shares of Investee Company on January 1, it paid $2.5 million. That amount is $500,000 more than 40 percent of Investee's net assets of $5 million at January 1, 1991 (paid-in capital of $4 million plus retained earnings of $1 million—see Exhibit 11–2). In essence, this means that Investor Company paid an amount greater than 40 percent of the unexpired cost of the net assets of Investee Company in order to obtain the rights to a 40 percent equitable share in the benefits to be generated by those assets. This is not surprising, since the unexpired cost of assets is not purported to represent their current value in generating future benefits. However, in representing the income to Investor Company resulting from its equitable interest in the revenue of Investee Company, it is not sufficient to recognize as expense only the original cost of the assets of Investee Company used in producing its revenues (the expense recognized by Investee). Some recognition should also be given to the additional cost incurred by Investor Company to acquire its equitable interest in the revenues of Investee.

To recognize this additional cost, Investor Company would make an entry of the following form:

Amortization expense	50,000	
Investment in Investee Co.		50,000

With this entry, Investor Company will have reduced its investment account and retained earnings (via amortization expense) by one-tenth ($50,000) of the original excess of the cost of the investment over 40 percent of the net asset value of Investee Company at the time of acquisition. The use of one-tenth implies a ten-year total expiration period and was selected for illustrative purposes only. In practice, the period selected for amortization of the differential cost would depend on the individual circumstances regarding the nature of the undervalued assets or expected life of the implied goodwill (but in no case may it exceed 40 years, according to current accounting policy).

Finally, during 1991 Investee Company declared and paid in total $500,000 of dividends. Rather than being income to Investor Company, its share of the

EXHIBIT 11–4

Investor Company

Income Statement
For 1991
(in thousands)

Revenue		$15,500
Less expenses:		
Cost of sales	$9,500	
Depreciation	900	
Other expense	2,100	12,500
Investor Co. operating income		$ 3,000
Income from Investee Co.:		
Equity in income of Investee Co.	$ 500	
Less amortization of excess of cost of investment over net assets of Investee Co. at acquisition	(50)	450
Net income		$ 3,450

total dividends ($200,000) represents a transfer of cash from Investee to Investor Company. We recognize a $200,000 increase in Investor Company's cash and a concurrent decrease in its investment in Investee Company, reflecting the Investor's equitable share of the total decrease in Investee's cash (i.e., 40 percent of $500,000). This is accomplished with the following journal entry:

Cash	200,000	
Investment in Investee Co.		200,000

With this journal entry, the December 31, 1991, balance in the investment in Investee Co. account is $2,750,000 (cost of $2,500,000 plus equity in earnings of $500,000 less amortization of $50,000 less dividends received of $200,000). Exhibit 11–4 illustrates the Investor Co.'s 1991 income statement. Note that the Investor's interest in Investee's earnings and the additional amortization are recognized in the income statement, but the dividends received are not.

Consolidation

Once the investor has acquired a 50 percent ownership interest in an investee company, consolidated financial statements are prepared for the combined entities. (Note that the financial statements of the parent company are still prepared according to the equity method prior to or in the absence of consolidation.) The process of consolidating balance sheets and income statements consists of substituting the subsidiary's balance sheet for the parent's investment account (allowing for recognition of minority interests). The assets and liabilities of the two entities are then added together. Similarly, the revenues and expenses of the parent and subsidiary are aggregated to obtain the consolidated income statement. This accounting treatment represents the two entities as one, inseparable economic unit.

EXHIBIT 11–5

Parent Company

Balance Sheet
As of January 1, 1991
(in thousands)

Assets:		Liabilities and Owners' Equity:	
Cash	$ 1,500	Accounts payable	$ 1,200
Accounts receivable	500		
Inventory	2,500		
Net plant and equipment	7,200		
Investment in stock of		Paid-in capital	10,000
Investee Co.	5,000	Retained earnings	5,500
Total	$16,700	Total	$16,700

Consolidated Balance Sheet at Acquisition.

Example 11–11 Reconsider the Investor Company–Investee Company example introduced in Example 11–7. Suppose that Investor Company (Parent) and Investee Company (Subsidiary) continued to be identical to Investor and Investee Companies except that on January 1, 1991, Parent Company acquired 80 percent (instead of 40 percent) of the outstanding ownership interest in Subsidiary Company for $5 million (instead of $2.5 million). All other facts remain as assumed in the earlier example.[1] The effects of these facts on the financial position of Parent Company as of January 1, 1991, are depicted in Exhibit 11–5.

The 1991 income statement for Parent Company under the revised set of facts is shown in Exhibit 11–6. Notice that down to the Parent Co. operating income figure of $3 million, Exhibit 11–6 is identical to the income statement illustrating the earlier example of 40 percent stock ownership (Exhibit 11–4). The only differences are the doubling of Parent Company's equity in Subsidiary's earnings and the amount of additional cost amortization. The higher amortization expense comes from the Parent's payment of $5 million to acquire 80 percent of the Subsidiary's net asset value of $5 million, equal to $4 million. Thus the $1 million difference is amortized over ten years.

Parent Company's investment account balance in the subsidiary company at the end of 1991 is $5.5 million ($5 million cost, plus $1 million equity in earnings, less $100,000 amortization and $400,000 in dividends).

Exhibit 11–7 depicts the consolidation of the January 1, 1991, balance sheets (in worksheet format) of Parent and Subsidiary Companies. The first two columns of data contain the separate balance sheets of the two companies. (The amounts are traceable back to the balance sheet in Exhibit 11–6 for Parent Company and back to the balance sheet in Exhibit 11–2 for Investee Company). The most significant feature of Exhibit 11–7 is in the third column entitled Eliminations

---

[1] Note that the assumed increase in the share of Subsidiary Company owned by Parent Company has no effect on Subsidiary's separate financial statements for 1991. They would be identical to Investee Company's statements illustrated in Exhibits 11–2 and 11–3.

EXHIBIT 11–6

Parent Company

Income Statement
for 1991
(in thousands)

Revenue		$15,500
Less expenses:		
Cost of sales	$9,500	
Depreciation	900	
Other expense	2,100	12,500
Parent Co. operating income		$ 3,000
Income from Subsidiary Co.		
Equity in earnings of Subsidiary Co.	$1,000	
Less amortization of excess of cost of		
investment over net assets of Sub-		
sidiary Co. at acquisition	$ (100)	900
Net income		$ 3,900

and Reclassifications. It contains debit and credit adjustments related to the combined figures of the first two columns. The entries in this column are necessary to avoid a double counting of assets and ownership interests, and to reclassify certain amounts that should be captioned differently in the consolidated balance sheet than in the related companies' separate balance sheets.

Since a single entity (the combined Parent–Subsidiary, in this case) cannot own itself, we must eliminate the asset representing Parent Company's ownership of Subsidiary stock. This is accomplished by a credit to this account equal to its full balance of $5 million—the entry labeled (1) in Exhibit 11–7. A portion of the total balance in this account is not a claim by Parent Company against the net assets of Subsidiary Company as represented by the latter's paid-in capital and retained earnings. The reason is that Parent Company paid $1 million more for Subsidiary's stock than its 80 percent share in Subsidiary's recognized net assets. Thus in entry (2) we reclassify the $1 million by debiting the new asset account entitled excess of investment cost over equity acquired in net assets of Subsidiary Company (which does not exist on the separate balance sheets). This is the amount which is amortized as an additional expense when the investor (Parent) recognizes its proportionate share of the investee's (subsidiary's) net income. The combined effect of entries (1) and (2) is to eliminate from consolidated assets only Parent's equity in the net assets of Subsidiary, that is, $4 million.

To the extent that they represent Parent's equity in Subsidiary Company, the Subsidiary's paid-in capital and retained earnings must also be eliminated. Entries (3) and (4) actually eliminate all of Subsidiary Company's paid-in capital and retained earnings by debiting the respective accounts in amounts equal to their full balances. However, this overelimination is offset by entry (5), which credits the new account entitled minority interest, in the amount of $1 million. This amount represents Subsidiary's minority shareholders' 20 percent interest in its combined paid-in capital (0.20 × $4,000,000 = $800,000) and retained earnings (0.20 × $1,000,000 = $200,000). Thus the combined effect of entries (3), (4), and (5) is to eliminate Parent Company's 80 percent interest in Subsidiary's

EXHIBIT 11–7

Parent Company–Subsidiary Company

Consolidation of Balance Sheets
As of January 1, 1991
(in thousands)

Accounts:	Parent Company		Subsidiary Company		Eliminations and Reclassifications		Consolidated	
	Dr	Cr	Dr	Cr	Dr	Cr	Dr	Cr
Assets:								
Cash	1,500		100				1,600	
Accounts receivable	500		100				600	
Inventory	2,500		1,200				3,700	
Net plant and equipment	7,200		4,800				12,000	
Investment in stock of Subsidiary Co.	5,000					5,000 (1)		
Excess of investment cost over equity acquired in net assets of Subsidiary Co.					(2) 1,000		1,000	
Total assets	16,700		6,200				18,900	
Liabilities and Owners' Equity:								
Accounts payable		1,200		200				1,400
Bonds of Subsidiary Co.				1,000				1,000
Paid-in capital:								
Parent Co.		10,000						10,000
Subsidiary Co.				4,000	(3) 4,000			
Retained earnings:								
Parent Co.		5,500						5,500
Subsidiary Co.				1,000	(4) 1,000			
Minority interest						1,000 (5)		1,000
Total liabilities and owners' equity		16,700		6,200				18,900
Total eliminations and reclassifications					6,000	6,000		

combined paid-in capital (0.80 × $4,000,000 = $3,200,000) and retained earnings (0.80 × $1,000,000 = $800,000). The combined amount is $4 million, which equals the net amount of Parent's investment eliminated in entries (1) and (2).

After all appropriate eliminations have been recognized in the elimination and reclassification columns, the first columns are summed across to arrive at the balances in the consolidated balance sheet column for the combined entity. Those amounts appear in the Consolidated column of Exhibit 11–7.

Consolidation of Balance Sheets and Income Statements Subsequent to Acquisition. Consolidation of balance sheets subsequent to the date of acquisition does not differ in principle from consolidation at acquisition. Hence Exhibit 11–8, which shows the consolidation of balance sheets for Parent and Subsidiary Companies as of December 31, 1991, needs no great elaboration. In fact, the same eliminations and reclassifications are made, with only the amounts differing ap-

EXHIBIT 11–8

Parent Company–Subsidiary Company

Consolidation of Balance Sheets
As of December 31, 1991
(in thousands)

Accounts:	Parent Company		Subsidiary Company		Eliminations and Reclassifications		Consolidated	
	Dr	Cr	Dr	Cr	Dr	Cr	Dr	Cr
Assets:								
Cash	5,850		1,450				7,300	
Accounts receivable	750		300				1,050	
Inventory	2,000		1,100				3,100	
Net plant and equipment	6,300		4,200				10,500	
Investment in stock of Subsidiary Co.	5,500					5,500 (1)		
Unamortized excess of investment cost over interest in net assets of Subsidiary Co.					(2) 900		900	
Total assets	20,400		7,050				22,850	
Liabilities and Owners' Equity:								
Accounts payable		950		300				1,250
Bonds of Subsidiary Co.								1,000
Paid-in capital:								
Parent Co.		10,000						10,000
Subsidiary Co.				4,000	(3) 4,000			
Retained earnings:								
Parent Co.		9,450						9,450
Subsidiary Co.				1,750	(4) 1,750			
Minority interest						1,150 (5)		1,150
Total liabilities and owners' equity		20,400		7,050				22,850
Total eliminations and reclassifications					6,650	6,650		

propriately. We might note, however, that the Parent Company equity in the net assets of Subsidiary Company, which is eliminated by entries (1) and (2), is now $4.6 million, an increase of $600,000 over the beginning-of-the-year figure of $4 million. This is due to (a) an increase due to the Parent's equity in the earnings of Subsidiary (80 percent of $1.25 million, or $1 million); and (b) a decrease due to dividends received of $400,000. Notice too that the balance in the account representing the excess of Parent's investment cost over its equity in the net assets of Subsidiary, which is reclassified in column four, is $100,000 less than at the beginning of the year ($900,000 instead of $1 million) due to amortization of $100,000 during the year.

Since a year has passed from the date of acquisition and the companies have operated for that period as related companies, it is necessary also to consolidate their income statements for 1991. Again the process is one of summing the amounts in the separate statements after some appropriate eliminations and adjustments. The process is illustrated for the 1991 income statements of Parent and Subsidiary companies in Exhibit 11–9. Notice that, as in the consolidation of balance sheets, we first array the separate income statements of Parent and Subsidiary companies in the first two columns.

The first column of Exhibit 11–9 is the separate 1991 income statement of Parent Company (from Exhibit 11–6). Looking at the second column we observe that (a) the top portion consists of the 1991 income statement of Subsidiary Company (from Exhibit 11–3); and (b) the lower portion of the column consists of adjustments needed to arrive at consolidated net income.

The first adjustment, labeled (1), eliminates double counting. Since all of Subsidiary's revenue and expenses are brought into the consolidated statements through its separate statement, the Parent's equity in Subsidiary's earnings appearing in Parent Company's separate statement (first column) is redundant. Hence the elimination labeled (1) offsets and eliminates the redundancy.

Next it must be recognized that the earning ability of the combined entities would be overstated by simply aggregating the separate income statements of the companies without giving recognition to the minority shareholders' interest in the separate earnings of Subsidiary Company. Thus we have inserted in the second column a $250,000 reduction (2) representing the 20 percent minority interest in the 1991 earnings of Subsidiary.

The entry in the third column is a reclassification. The $100,000 amortization of Parent's excess of cost over its interest in Subsidiary's net assets should not be eliminated from the consolidated income statement for the same reason that the

EXHIBIT 11–9

Parent Company–Subsidiary Company

Consolidation of Income Statements
For 1991
(in thousands)

	Parent Company	Subsidiary Company	Eliminations and Reclassifications	Consolidated
Revenue	$15,500	$5,500		$21,000
Less expenses:				
Cost of sales	$ 9,500	$3,100		$12,600
Interest		50		50
Depreciation (and amortization)	900	600	$ 100 (3)	1,600
Other expense	2,100	500		2,600
Total expense	$12,500	$4,250	$ 100	$16,850
Operating income	$ 3,000	$1,250	$(100)	$ 4,150
Income from Subsidiary Co.:				
Equity in earnings	1,000	1,000 (1)		
Less amortization of excess of cost of investment over interest in net assets of subsidiary	(100)		100 (3)	
Less minority interest in subsidiary net income		250 (2)		(250)
Net income	$ 3,900	0	0	$ 3,900

unamortized portion of the excess is not eliminated from the consolidated balance sheet. However, with the elimination of Parent's equity in Subsidiary's earnings (the first elimination in the second column), the amortization is best classified with the depreciation and amortization of other assets of the combined companies. This is accomplished by the adjustments labeled (3) in the third column.

With all appropriate eliminations, reclassifications, and adjustments, the consolidated income statement results from summing across the first three columns of Exhibit 11–9. An important feature of the consolidated net income figure arrived at in this way ($3,900,000) is that it equals the separate net income figure arrived at earlier for Parent Company under the equity method (see Exhibit 11–6). Under the equity method, the income of the parent is combined with only its ownership share of subsidiary earnings. In consolidated statements, an attempt is made to portray the earnings of all assets under the control of the parent company shareholders (the same ownership group in both cases) by combining the net income of parent and subsidiaries (eliminating double counting) and then deducting from the total the ownership interests in subsidiary earnings not attributable to the parent shareholder group (the minority interests). The final figure should be the same in either situation,

The Purchase versus Pooling Controversy. The pooling-of-interests method of accounting is used for parent companies and subsidiaries whose stock is acquired from former shareholders by issuing stock of the parent company in exchange—rather than by cash or other consideration. A controversy arises because such stock-for-stock transactions can be interpreted two different ways.

One view is that if the parent company's stock was readily marketable, the transaction could be considered to be a purchase in substance. That is, it is presumed that the parent company could have issued the stock for cash and then traded the cash to the former shareholders of the subsidiary for their stockholdings. Under this interpretation, a stock-for-stock acquisition is accounted for as was described above for a cash purchase of subsidiary stock. The investment in subsidiary stock is recorded at the market value of the parent's stock issued in exchange for it.

The second view of a stock-for-stock acquisition is that it represents a mere coming together (i.e., a pooling) of the interests of the original parent corporation shareholders and the shareholders who give up their ownership in the subsidiary to become shareholders of the parent corporation. This view argues for using the pooling-of-interests method of accounting whereby the investment is recorded at an amount equal to the equity acquired by the parent in the subsidiary's net assets. Thus the subsidiary's assets continue to be carried at their book value. Even when the acquisition price exceeds the book value of the acquired equity, no additional amortization expense is offset against the postacquisition combined income of the parent and subsidiary. Thus the combined income will be higher subsequent to acquisition under pooling of interests than under the purchase method of accounting. It is this latter feature that critics of the pooling-of-interest approach feel has led to widespread abuses of the method.

SUMMARY

This chapter has considered the issues which arise surrounding the recognition of ownership interests in an entity. Owners' equity represents the investment funds obtained through selling ownership interests. It is important to maintain the legal distinctions in owners' equity: preferred and common stock, par or stated value and paid-in capital in excess of par, and retained earnings. Additionally, dividends require careful attention such that cash dividends are accounted for differently from stock dividends. The accounting for large stock dividends, stock splits, stock options, and treasury stock which has been reacquired was also addressed in this section.

A second class of complications related to the ownership structure of the corporation arises when the entity's owners consist of another corporation. The complex procedures in accounting for these intercorporate investments were addressed. The corporate-investors' ownership must first be described in terms of the percentage of the investees' common stock which has been acquired. A 20 percent or less ownership interest necessitates using the lower-of-cost-or-market valuation method. Ownership between 20 percent and 50 percent of the investee indicates the equity method must be used. Once the investor has at least a 50 percent ownership interest, the investor and investee financial statements must be combined into consolidated financial statements. These procedures were illustrated in the second section of this chapter.

Questions for Review and Discussion

11–1. Define or briefly explain the following terms:

    a. Common stock
    b. Preferred stock
    c. Cumulative preferred stock
    d. Convertible preferred stock
    e. Par value
    f. Stock dividends
    g. Stock split
    h. Treasury stock
    i. Stock options
    j. Intercorporate investment
    k. Marketable securities
    l. Lower-of-cost-or-market method for marketable securities
    m. Equity method
    n. Consolidated financial statements

11–2. Name and explain the three dates that are important for cash dividends. How do you think the market price of a publicly traded stock would react at each of these dates?

11–3. Explain the two alternative ways of accounting for a stock dividend, and indicate the circumstances when each is appropriate under current accounting policy.

11–4. Explain the similarities and differences (including the accounting treatment) between a stock dividend and a stock split.

11–5. Why is no gain or loss recognized when a corporation buys and sells its own stock?

11–6. There are three significant degrees of ownership of one corporation by another recognized in accounting for the investor's investment. Describe them and give the reasoning for the distinction drawn between each of them. Name the accounting treatment for each degree of ownership.

11–7. Describe the lower-of-cost-or-market method of accounting for an investment by one corporation in the stock of another. Discuss (a) how the investment is originally recorded; (b) what increases and decreases are recognized; and (c) what income is recognized each period.

11–8. Describe the equity method of accounting for intercorporate investments. Discuss (a) how the investment is originally recorded; (b) what increases and decreases are recognized; and (c) what income is recognized each period.

11–9. Explain the principles involved in consolidating the financial statements of parent and subsidiary companies.

11–10. Discuss the reasoning behind recognizing as an expense a portion of the excess of cost to an investor company over its proportional ownership in the net assets of an investee company.

Problems

11–1. Recognizing Cash Dividends. On October 15, 1991, Fremont Company's board of directors declared a dividend of $1.10 per share for 1991. The dividend is payable to stockholders of record on November 30, 1991, and will be paid on December 15, 1991. On November 30, 1991, 453,000 shares were outstanding.

Required:

1. Write journal entries to record the declaration and payment of the dividend.
2. All other things being equal, what would probably happen to the price per share of the company's stock after November 30 relative to the price before that date? Explain your answer.

11–2. Cash Dividends on Preferred and Common Stock. The Acorn Company was incorporated in 1988. The company was authorized to issue 100,000 shares of $10 par-value common stock and 10,000 shares of 8 percent, cumulative preferred stock (par value $100).

In December 1988, the company sold 10,000 shares of the common stock at a price of $15 per share and 1,000 shares of the preferred stock at par. Operations began in January 1989.

Net income for 1989, 1990, and 1991 was $30,000, $2,000, and $40,000, respectively.

The board of directors adopted the policy of paying out 50 percent of the net income for the year in dividends on December 31. This policy was followed in 1989 and 1991, but because of the low earnings in 1990 dividends were not paid in that year.

Required:

1. Prepare a schedule that shows the following for each year of the three-year period:

   a. Net income
   b. Total dividends paid on preferred stock
   c. Total dividends paid on common stock
   d. Dividends paid per common share
   e. Total owners' equity

2. Prepare the owners' equity section of the statement of financial position as of December 31, 1991.

11–3. Cash Dividends, Stock Splits, and Stock Dividends. Following is the stockholders' equity section of the December 31, 1990, statement of financial position of Wiltsie Corporation:

Common stock:		
$2 par-value stock:		
1,000,000 shares authorized		
547,000 shares issued	$1,094,000	
Paid-in capital in excess of par value	6,206,000	$ 7,300,000
Retained earnings		4,700,000
Total shareholders' equity		$12,000,000

Required:

1. Write journal entries (where applicable) to record each of the following events occurring during 1991.

   a. On April 1 Wiltsie declared a cash dividend of $1.30 per share which it paid on June 1 to stockholders of record on May 15.

   b. On July 1 the company split its stock two for one and reduced the par value to $1.

   c. On September 1 the company issued a 10 percent stock dividend. On that date the market value of the stock was $21 per share.

   d. Net income for the year was $1,310,000. (Assume that all individual expense and revenue accounts already have been closed to a single temporary account entitled income summary, whose balance equals net income.)

   e. On December 31 the company purchased 14,000 of its own previously issued shares for the treasury at $24 per share.

2. Based on these events, prepare the stockholders' equity section of Wiltsie Corporation's 1991 statement of financial position.

11–4. Cash Dividends, Stock Dividends, and Stock Splits. The owners' equity section of Miller Corporation's statement of financial position on December 31, 1991, follows:

Common stock:		
$10 par value stock:		
500,000 shares authorized,		
100,000 shares issued	$1,000,000	
Amount received in excess of par value of stock	1,500,000	$2,500,000
Retained earnings		4,500,000
Total shareholders' equity		$7,000,000

Required:

Determine the balances of each of the components of Miller Corporation's owners' equity at the end of 1990 and 1991, taking into account the following events:

1. On March 15, 1990, Miller Corporation paid a cash dividend of $10 per share.
2. On September 15, 1990, Miller Corporation paid a 50 percent stock dividend. The fair market value of Miller Corporation's stock on this date was $150 per share.
3. Net income for 1990 was $1.6 million.
4. On March 15, 1991, Miller Corporation paid a cash dividend of $8 per share.
5. On June 30, 1991, Miller Corporation paid a 20 percent stock dividend. The fair market value of Miller Corporation's stock on this date was $100 per share.
6. On December 15, 1991, Miller Corporation split its stock four for one.
7. Net income for 1991 was $2 million.

11–5. Recognition of Stock Options and Compensation. On November 1, 1988, Wright Corporation put into effect a stock option for its executives. On December 31, 1988, options for 40,000 shares of the company's $2 par-value common stock were granted to its executives. The options could be exercised any time after December 31, 1990, at a per-share purchase price of $25. The market value per share on December 31, 1988 is $31. The board of directors intended the spread between the exercise price and the market value at date of grant to be additional compensation to the executives over the two-year eligibility period. All of the options were exercised during 1991.

Required:

1. Calculate the total executive compensation expense to be recognized in connection with the options.
2. Prepare journal entries to record the granting of the options and the expense allocated to 1989 and 1990.
3. Make the journal entry to record the exercise of the option.

11–6. Recognizing Changes in Owners' Equity. Shown next is the stockholders' equity section of the balance sheet presented in the 1991 annual report of Wallingford, Inc., in which the 1991 balances in the stockholders' equity accounts have been removed.

	1991	1992
Shareholders' Equity:		
Preferred stock, no par value		
Authorized 5,000,000 shares; none issued	—	—
Common stock, $.625 par value		
Authorized 30,000,000 shares; issued 12,952,891		
and 12,815,916 shares, respectively	—	$ 8,010,000
Paid-in in excess of par	—	44,647,000
Retained earnings ($99,022,000 available for		
dividends)	—	143,412,000
	—	$196,069,000
Less cost of reacquired common stock		
(455,144 shares)	—	2,875,000
Total shareholders' equity	?	$193,194,000

Additional information about 1991:

1. Stock options were exercised during 1991 resulting in purchase by executives of 34,200 common shares for a total of $596,000. Assume that no previous paid-in capital had been recognized with respect to the options.
2. Convertible notes payable in the amount of $1,843,000 were converted (exchanged for) 102,775 shares of common stock.
3. Net income of $52,500,000 was recognized.
4. Cash dividends of $10,836,000 were paid.

Required:
Based on the 1990 balances and the additional information, determine the end-of-1991 stockholders' equity account balances (to the nearest $1,000).

11–7. Owners' Equity–Statement Presentation. Prepare the owners' equity section of the statement of financial position as of December 31 from the following information:

Retained earnings at beginning of year	$1,209,000
Number of 8%, cumulative, $100 par-value preferred shares authorized	100,000
Premium on bonds payable at issue	$27,000
Total proceeds received from original issue of 100,000 common shares	$4,000,000
Net income for the year	$600,000
6% bonds payable, due at end of 2000	$500,000
Number of no-par common shares authorized	1,000,000
Dividends in arrears at the beginning of the year	$100,000
Cost of treasury stock (1,000 common shares)	$35/share
Number of preferred shares issued (all at par)	20,000
Total amount of dividends on common shares declared on December 31 ($1/share)	$99,000
Stated value of no-par stock	$10/share

11–8. Marketable Equity Securities. In 1989, Big Industrial Company (BIC) began to accumulate surplus cash that was not needed until its next major plant expansion, planned for 1992. The company therefore began investing in marketable equity securities to utilize the funds effectively in the meantime. Its transactions and year-end portfolios for 1989, 1990, and 1991 were as follows:

1989. Purchased securities costing $1,800,000. Dividends were received in the amount of $90,000. Year-end portfolio:

Company	Cost	Market Value
X	$ 800,000	$900,000
Y	1,000,000	870,000

1990. Sold half of X holdings for $500,000. Purchased shares of Z for $1,500,000. Dividends of $130,000 were received. Year-end portfolio:

Company	Cost	Market Value
X	$ 400,000	$ 450,000
Y	1,000,000	950,000
Z	1,500,000	1,550,000

1991. Sold all Y holdings for $950,000. Purchased additional X shares for $1,200,000. Dividends of $50,000 were received. Year-end portfolio:

Company	Cost	Market Value
X	$1,600,000	$1,630,000
Z	1,500,000	1,420,000

Required:
Prepare the appropriate journal entries to record all of BIC's 1989, 1990, and 1991 transactions related to marketable securities and to recognize the appropriate year-end aggregate amount in the marketable securities account. Ignore income taxes.

11–9. Equity Method Accounting. On January 1, 1991, Ranger, Inc., purchased 8,000 shares of San Juan, Inc., common stock for $180,000. The shareholders' equity accounts of San Juan, Inc., as of January 1, 1991, were: common stock ($10 par), $100,000; retained earnings, $50,000.

The assets of San Juan were reviewed in order to determine the source of the excess of Ranger's cost over the equity acquired in San Juan's net assets. It was determined that $20,000 is applicable to a building with five years of remaining life. (Such assignable differences are amortized over the lives of the related assets.) The remainder of the differential could not be identified with any specific tangible or intangible asset, and Ranger elects to amortize it over 40 years.

For the year 1991, the following information on operations and dividends is available:

	Ranger	*San Juan*
Net income	$15,000*	$15,000
Dividends paid	5,000	8,000

* Not including any effects of subsidiary operations or dividends for 1991.

Ranger uses the equity method of accounting for its investment in San Juan.

1. What was the balance of Ranger's investment in San Juan account at December 31, 1991?
2. What income did Ranger report for 1991?

11–10. Inferences Based on Partial Consolidation Information. Following are some excerpts from the December 31, 1991, balance sheets of Big and Small Corporations.

Assets of Big Corporation	
Cash	$ 1,500,000
Accounts receivable	2,500,000
Inventory	3,500,000
Net plant and equipment	4,500,000
Investment in Small Corporation:	
75% stock ownership	3,500,000
Total assets	$15,500,000

Liabilities and Owners' Equity of Small Corporation:	
Accounts payable	$ 500,000
Note payable	1,500,000
Paid-in capital	3,000,000
Retained earnings	1,000,000
Total liabilities and owners' equity	$ 6,000,000

Required:

1. What amount should appear in the consolidated financial statements to represent the minority interests? Support your answer.
2. Will any amount show up on the consolidated financial statements opposite the caption: Unamortized excess of cost of investment over equity in net assets of subsidiary? If so, what amount? Support your answer.
3. What will be the total amount of consolidated assets as of December 31, 1991?

11–11. Consolidation of Financial Statements. Following are the 1991 balance sheets and income statements (before consolidation) of Super Sales, Inc., and its 80-percent-owned subsidiary, Tiny Toys, Inc., along with certain supplemental information.

Required:

1. Prepare a consolidated balance sheet as of December 31, 1991.
2. Prepare a consolidated income statement for 1991.
3. What was the balance in Super Sales' investment account in Tiny Toys at December 31, 1990? (The equity method is used by Super Sales.)

Supplemental information:

1. Super Sales purchased its share of Tiny Toys on January 1, 1990, at which time it was decided that the excess of its cost over its equity in the net assets of Tiny Toys should be amortized over the maximum period allowed under accounting policy (40 years).
2. Tiny Toys paid total dividends to its stockholders of $500,000 in 1991.

Super Sales, Inc.

Balance Sheet
As of December 31, 1991

Assets:		Liabilities and Stockholders' Equity:	
Cash	$ 5,000,000	Accounts payable	$ 3,000,000
Accounts receivable	4,000,000	Wages payable	1,000,000
Inventory	5,000,000	Taxes payable	1,000,000
Prepaid expenses	1,000,000		
Property, plant, and equipment (net)	18,200,000	Paid-in capital	25,000,000
Investment in Tiny Toys, Inc.	11,800,000	Retained earnings	15,000,000
	$45,000,000		$45,000,000

Super Sales, Inc.

Income Statement
For the Year Ended December 31, 1991

Revenue		$20,000,000
Less expenses:		
Cost of sales	$12,000,000	
Depreciation and amortization	3,000,000	
Other expense (including taxes)	3,000,000	18,000,000
Income from Super Sales' operations		$ 2,000,000
Equity in earnings of Tiny Toys less amortization of excess of cost over equity in net assets		700,000
Net income		$ 2,700,000

Tiny Toys, Inc.

Balance Sheet
As of December 31, 1991

Assets:		Liabilities and Stockholders' Equity:	
Cash	$ 500,000	Accounts payable	$ 2,000,000
Accounts receivable	2,000,000	Wages payable	750,000
Inventory	2,000,000	Taxes payable	250,000
Prepaid expenses	500,000		
Property, plant, and		Paid-in capital	8,000,000
equipment (net)	8,000,000	Retained earnings	2,000,000
	$13,000,000		$13,000,000

Tiny Toys, Inc.

Income Statement
For the Year Ended December 31, 1991

Revenue		$10,000,000
Less expenses:		
Cost of sales	$6,000,000	
Depreciation	1,000,000	
Other expense (including taxes)	2,000,000	9,000,000
Net income		$ 1,000,000

Policy Making

CHAPTER TWELVE

This chapter deals with the broad economic and social contexts of financial accounting. In previous chapters we have explained what financial accounting is, how it measures financial information, and why various procedural steps are necessary to produce financial statements.

Now we shift emphasis to a broader context. How is financial accounting used in making economic decisions in complex market economies? What does accounting information contribute to the effective and efficient functioning of marketplaces? How does accounting standard setting work and what are some of its economic consequences? To what extent is governmental accounting different from enterprise accounting? Why is accounting information as important in the international economy as it is domestically? Answers to these questions will illustrate the broad setting or context of financial accounting.

MARKET ECONOMY

An economy is a system for allocating available resources to various uses. The system may be as large as the world economy or as small as a family or a village. Our point of reference is the national economy. There are large national economies like those of the United States or the Soviet Union, and small national economies like those of Monaco or Liechtenstein.

By political choice, economic systems are organized differently. In a centrally controlled system, the national government directs virtually all uses of economic resources. An example is the Soviet Union. In a free market economy, supply and demand in the marketplace determine prices for economic goods and services.

The party offering the highest price for a given resource typically can acquire (and thus use) it. Switzerland comes close to a free market system.

Most national economic systems fall somewhere between these two extremes. Some, like those of the Scandinavian countries, New Zealand, and many developing nations in Africa and Asia tend toward central control. Others, like the U.S. economy, tend toward the market system. Sometimes the U.S. economic system is identified as an "administered" market system.

Of course the organization of a national economic system changes over time. At present the mood in the United States appears to favor "deregulation"—which means more reliance on the competitive forces of market supply and demand. Within the last decade we have experienced deregulation of entire industries, such as trucking and air travel. As a generalization, free (or open or unregulated) markets tend to be strongly competitive and thereby provide goods and services to consumers at relatively lower prices. Airline tickets, personal and pocket computers, and auto and textile imports to the United States illustrate this point. On the other hand, controlled or manipulated markets often increase the price of resources which in turn results in relatively higher costs to consumers. The OPEC cartel is a case in point.

Market forces play an important role in the U.S. economy. While a fair bit of governmental control and regulation exists, market forces appear to have greater influence than control forces. We therefore refer to the U.S. economy as a market economy.

Capital Formation in a Market Economy

The material standard of living of an individual or a whole society is dependent on how many goods and services can be produced in any period of time with the available supply of resources. The only way to improve the standard of living of a population without increasing the hours of labor required is to improve the level of output per hour of labor. The efficiency of labor is improved by augmenting it with physical, technical, and human capital. In order for a high standard of living to be sustained, a high level of capital must be built up and maintained.

Consumption Postponement. The prerequisite to capital formation is a sacrifice of current consumption. Hence, to form capital, some of the currently available supply of productive resources must be diverted from current production of final consumer goods and services to the production of capital.

In a modern market economy the relationship between sacrificed consumption and capital formation is not simple. Consumption is postponed through direct or indirect savings. Direct saving takes place when an individual, a family, or some other consumption unit does not spend all the funds it currently receives from employment of its factors of production. Indirect saving takes place when business enterprises distribute cash to their owners in amounts less than the current income of the enterprises. In both cases, some of the cash flow from current production of goods and services is not spent for current consumption.

Demand for Capital. By itself, however, direct or indirect savings is not enough. The funds that savers have not spent on current consumption must be spent on new capital or replacements for capital used up in current production. Savings devoted to capital formation result in employment of some of the productive resources of the economy.

But balance is important. Just as an excess of savings can lead to unemployment, an excess in the other direction means that the combined demand for both consumer and capital goods and services will exceed the productive capacity of the economy, leading to inflation.

Transfer of Funds Between Economic Units. If a market economy is to avoid serious unemployment or inflation, there must be some systematic way of transferring funds from savers to those interested in using such funds. Furthermore, if the economy is to maintain (or increase) its standard of living, a sufficient amount of the funds saved must be spent to replace worn-out capital. In a market economy the capital market serves these purposes.

Capital Market. The capital market consists of all the individuals and institutions that together accomplish the transfer of funds from savers to economic units that wish to spend additional funds on capital goods and services.

Capital Market Participants and Transactions. The capital market of an economy like that of the United States has many participants, many types of transactions, and many places of exchange. However, the relationships between market participants are quite simple, as seen in Exhibit 12–1.

Capital Market Intermediaries. Direct transfers would satisfy the needs of only a small fraction of the total savers and users of funds. Thus there are many types of capital market intermediaries working to satisfy demand initiated by either savers or users of funds.

On the savings side, there exist commercial banks, savings banks, savings and loan associations, mutual funds, insurance companies, and pension funds. All of these types of financial intermediaries exist as outlets or opportunities for vast numbers of consumers to put their funds to work as they save. Thus capital savers do not have to worry about who will actually use the funds and for what purpose. In exchange for control over the savings, the financial intermediaries pay interest, dividends, or deferred payments (in the case of insurance companies and pension funds) to savers. The intermediaries, in turn, lend large blocks of pooled savings or invest them in ownership shares in various kinds of users of funds.

From the other side, a potential user of funds, such as a large corporation whose management wants to expand its operations, may find it difficult, time consuming, and costly to seek out the savings of individuals. But, fortunately, it can call upon the services of financial intermediaries to secure the use of saved capital.

Sources of Funds for Business Enterprises—The Corporate Securities Markets. Since our concern is society's regulatory interest in accounting for business enterprises,

EXHIBIT 12–1

Capital Market Relationships in New Capital Formation

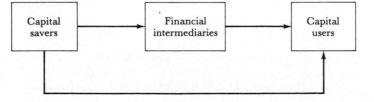

we need only consider that portion of the capital market in which significant numbers of business enterprises raise the funds with which they acquire capital goods and services. We call this segment the markets for corporate securities. From this point on we will ignore other segments of the capital market, such as the markets for mortgage loans and government securities.

Social Demands on the Corporate Securities Markets

In a market economy, public interest demands that the markets for corporate securities include the following characteristics:

1. For economic stability, it is necessary that the supply of funds from savers be matched against the demand for funds from potential users.
2. Businesses must have access to a sufficient supply of funds at a low enough cost to ensure that they can replace worn-out capital and add new capital to the total stock of capital in the economy. This in turn is dependent on two additional requirements:

    a. The markets must be operationally efficient.
    b. The markets must be reasonably fair; that is, free from fraud, deception, and manipulation by any participants. This requirement is the principal motivation for the *public interest in* (and related regulation of) *corporate financial reporting*.

Matching Supply and Demand for Funds in the Corporate Securities Markets. The two major aspects of matching supply and demand for funds in the corporate securities markets are *size* and *time*. Businesses are often interested in investing in capital goods that cost enormous amounts and last many years. Savers, on the other hand, are usually interested in committing relatively small amounts and maintaining flexibility with respect to when they may recover funds committed. Financial intermediaries make available opportunities for savers to save in small amounts. Hence the intermediaries balance saver and user needs and thereby solve the size problems.

Financial intermediaries also balance the duration of savings relative to the duration of investment in capital goods: the time preferences of capital savers and capital users.

But what about individual savers who prefer not to save through intermediaries, and what about the intermediaries themselves? Will they not want to commit funds for intervals less than the duration of business enterprises' investments in capital goods? The answer is clearly yes. For them there exist the opportunities provided by the secondary market in corporate securities.

Primary and Secondary Securities Markets. The markets for corporate securities may be separated into primary and secondary markets.

Primary Corporate Securities Market. The primary corporate securities market consists of all transactions in which the money capital of business enterprises is expanded through the issue of new securities or reduced through the redemption, retirement, or liquidation of previously outstanding securities.

Secondary Corporate Securities Market. The secondary corporate securities market consists of all trades of corporate securities *not* involving the business enterprise whose securities are bought or sold.

It is only in the primary market that business enterprises can acquire the new funds for capital formation. This does not mean that the secondary market (including national securities exchanges like the New York Stock Exchange) is unimportant. On the contrary, if it were not possible to buy and sell corporate securities in the secondary market, the securities would be less attractive at the time of issue, thus making it more difficult for enterprises to raise new funds.

The Operational Efficiency of the Securities Markets. In order for the economy to generate a high level of investment opportunities between savers and capital users, the securities markets must be operationally efficient.

> **Operational Efficiency.** A securities market is operationally efficient when all the intermediaries and others who participate in the transfer of funds from savers to users earn no more than is necessary to induce them to provide their services.

This type of efficiency involves primarily the commissions and fees earned by market makers (intermediaries). Full-service brokers earn higher fees than discount brokers. Large transactions command lower fees per dollar exchanged than small-lot transactions. If the level of fees turns higher than necessary to induce the intermediaries to perform their services, it will unnecessarily inhibit the flow of funds between savers and capital users. In turn, this will inhibit the formation of new capital.

Presumably, the best insurance against excessive fees for intermediaries in either the primary or the secondary market is the rigor of competition. Provided no intermediary or group of intermediaries can bar entry of competitors or otherwise monopolize a part of the market, fees will be competitively low. But in the absence of rigorous competition, there is a definite social interest in regulating or supervising the activities and fee structures of corporate securities markets intermediaries.

Role of Financial Accounting in Corporate Securities Markets

How do a market economy, capital formation, and social demands on corporate securities markets relate to financial accounting? The answer is that financial accounting information drives a significant portion of the decisions made in corporate securities markets. Financial accounting information is a critical link between savers and users of financial capital. Exhibit 12–2 illustrates this link by expanding the earlier Exhibit 12–1.

Principal-Agent Relationship Established

When investors entrust their capital to the managers of a business enterprise, an "agency" relationship is established. The investors invest their funds with the expectation that the returns they will receive in the future are higher than the value of the funds they give up now. To judge the likelihood of future returns and the various risks associated with them, the investors need reliable information to make their decisions. Financial accounting information provides a major source of this information.

Why would business managers provide reliable information to the investors, particularly when the news is bad? Because a legally recognized and *enforceable* agency relationship exists. A manager cannot build a firm and earn compensation without an adequate supply of capital. Capital availability is part of the lifeblood

EXHIBIT 12-2

Financial Accounting Role in Corporate Securities Markets

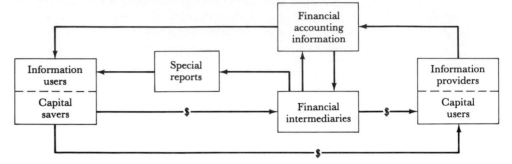

of business in a market economy. Thus managers are willing to act as agents of the investors (investors = principals). As agents they have legal and ethical duties to render faithfully periodic reports about their activities—in the corporate case, periodic financial accounting reports.

Fairness of Markets

We mentioned earlier that the flow of new money capital shrinks when savers think that securities markets are unfair (i.e., fraudulent, deceptive, and manipulative). A lack of fairness in corporate securities markets brings with it an increase in risks associated with making investments. Such risks reduce returns that might otherwise be expected and therefore drive down the prices of securities. When prices of the securities they wish to sell are too low, businesses may not issue the securities as planned and thus may cease to grow or fail to replace worn-out equipment.

High-quality financial reporting contributes to fairness in financial markets. Such reporting shows the effects of business mergers and takeovers. It measures and reports the economic consequences of foreign exchange dealings, pension benefits available to employees, and future lease payments a company has agreed to make. Financial accounting reports establish how market prices of securities relate to financial positions and earnings of individual companies. The strength of accounting reports (together with other similar items of financial intelligence) has led many researchers in corporate finance to conclude that U.S. securities markets are efficient in the sense that securities prices quickly adjust to new information that becomes available.

Public Interest in Financial Reporting

If business managers do not report fairly the activities and financial affairs of their enterprises, investors make wrong investment decisions. As a consequence, securities markets will not allocate capital to its best use. When capital misallocations occur, some market participants gain at the expense of others. Securities markets are then unfair. Market manipulation creates excessive investment risks, which lead to capital withdrawal and sometimes even capital flight. The latter occurs in many developing countries where local savers do not trust local securities markets and therefore invest their savings outside their own countries.

For all of these reasons, the public has a substantial interest in the effective functioning of securities markets. Since financial accounting information plays a central role in market effectiveness and efficiency, there is also a high public interest in financial accounting.

STANDARD SETTING FOR FINANCIAL ACCOUNTING

Corporate securities markets have not always operated effectively. Many attribute the stock market crash of 1929 to abusive securities markets practices and deceptive financial reporting. These abuses were commented upon as early as 1927 by William Z. Ripley, a Harvard University professor of political economy and critic of American corporate reporting practices. In his book *Main Street and Wall Street*, Ripley describes his review of corporate annual reports of the time:

> Confronted with a great pile of recent corporate pamphlets on my table, the first impression is of their extraordinary diversity, in appearance, size, content, and intent. One premier concern, the Royal Baking Powder Company, fails to register any fiscal information at all, in as much as it has never issued a balance sheet or financial statement of any kind whatsoever for more than a quarter of a century. . . . Akin to it is the Singer Manufacturing Company, which handles 80 percent of the world's output of sewing machines. Neither hide nor hair of financial data for this firm is discoverable in the usual sources of information. The dance-card, bald balance-sheet, or picture-book variety of corporation report follows hard upon these examples of complete reticence. . . . Yet colored pictures of factories, brightly lighted at night,—as some of these must well have been in view of their extraordinary success,— tell no tales.[1]

A specific case in point is the house of cards built at the time by the so-called Swedish match king, Ivar Kreuger.

> The most widely held securities in America (and also the world) during the 1920s were the stocks and bonds of Kreuger & Toll, Inc., a Swedish match conglomerate. The reason Kreuger's securities were so popular was that they were sold in small denominations and paid high dividends. Dividends of over 20 percent annually were paid on both stocks and bonds. Unfortunately, these dividends were paid mostly out of capital, not profits. Kreuger was essentially operating a giant pyramid scheme, which was hidden from the investing public by Kreuger's insistence that financial statements not be audited. The bankruptcy of the company in 1932 was the largest on record and resulted in numerous changes in financial reporting. Articles in magazines and newspapers kept Americans aware of the extent of the fraud scheme at the same time Congress was considering the passage of a federal securities law. Thus the timing of the bankruptcy and the corresponding media coverage made it politically expedient to pass laws that would make it difficult for similar schemes to be successful in the future. Such laws were indeed passed, and the Congressional committee reports specifically refer to Kreuger. . . . The Ivar Kreuger fraud contributed significantly to the passage of the securities acts.[2]

These securities acts are the Securities Act of 1933 and the Securities Exchange Act of 1934. This legislation is central to financial accounting standard setting in the United States.

[1] William Z. Ripley, *Main Street and Wall Street* (Houston, TX: Scholars Book Co., reprinted 1972), pp. 162–64.
[2] Dale L. Flesher and Tonya K. Flesher, "Ivar Kreuger's Contribution to U.S. Financial Reporting," *Accounting Review*, July 1986, p. 421.

The Securities Act of 1933. The Securities Act of 1933 has two major objectives. First, it requires adequate and accurate disclosure of material data, financial or otherwise, concerning securities to be sold in interstate commerce or through the mail. Second, it specifically outlaws fraud in the sale of securities whether or not newly issued, and provides criminal penalties for offending parties and remedies for injured parties. The law clearly stops short of directly regulating the flow of funds in the corporate securities markets; that is, determining which enterprises are worthy of funds and/or the prices at which their securities may be fairly and equitably issued. Instead, the 1933 act is premised on full disclosure of all material facts about the issuer, leaving to a "free" market the determination of worth. The 1933 act is mainly directed at the primary corporate securities market.

The Securities Exchange Act of 1934. The Securities Exchange Act of 1934 established the Securities and Exchange Commission (SEC) and gave it authority to regulate trading in securities, securities exchanges, and the conduct and financial affairs of intermediaries. To accomplish its major objective of regulating trading in securities, the 1934 act exends the power of the SEC over the accounting practices of business enterprises. The 1934 act is mainly directed at the secondary corporate securities market.

The securities acts limit trading on national securities exchanges to securities registered with the SEC. Among other things, the acts require that the issuers of traded securities file with the SEC such annual reports and such quarterly reports as the commission may prescribe.

Thus, as a matter of law, any business enterprise that wishes to have its securities traded on a national exchange is subject to the prescriptions of the SEC in accounting for its financial condition, both at the time of first listing on the exchange and thereafter. Any issuer of securities listed on a national exchange that violates the requirements of the 1934 act may have trading in its securities suspended for up to ten days by the commission or up to ninety days with the approval of the President. Or, after appropriate notice and hearing, the commission may suspend for up to twelve months, or withdraw altogether, the registration of the enterprise's securities.

Setting Financial Accounting Standards

Although the 1933 and 1934 securities acts clearly gave the SEC the power to prescribe acceptable financial accounting standards, the SEC has never directly done so. By choosing which standards it will enforce on SEC registrant companies, the SEC retains absolute veto power over any and all accounting standards, both new and in existence. But the development and pronouncement of financial accounting standards is left to private-sector efforts. This arrangement has worked well ever since 1933.

The agency currently responsible for establishing financial accounting standards is the Financial Accounting Standards Board (FASB). A large private foundation, the Financial Accounting Foundation (FAF), was established to support the FASB. Annual contributions to FAF are limited to $50,000 per individual, company, or CPA firm.

The FASB currently has seven full-time members: three from professional accounting (CPA) practice; two from industry; and one each from academia and a government agency. Board members must sever all economic and organizational ties to prior places of employment or ownership in order to serve.

The FASB's function is best described in its own mission statement:

The mission of the Financial Accounting Standards Board is to establish and improve standards of financial accounting and reporting for the guidance and education of the public, including issuers, auditors, and users of financial information.

Accounting standards are essential to the efficient functioning of the economy because decisions about the allocation of resources rely heavily on credible, concise, and understandable financial information. Financial information about the operations and financial position of individual entities also is used by the public in making various other kinds of decisions.

To accomplish its mission, the FASB acts to:

1. Improve the usefulness of financial reporting by focusing on the primary characteristics of relevance and reliability and on the qualities of comparability and consistency;
2. Keep standards current to reflect changes in methods of doing business and changes in the economic environment;
3. Consider promptly any significant areas of deficiency in financial reporting that might be improved through the standard-setting process; and
4. Improve the common understanding of the nature and purposes of information contained in financial reports.

The FASB develops broad accounting concepts as well as standards for financial reporting. It also provides guidance on implementation of standards.[3]

The FASB is open to suggestions about which problems should be addressed from interested parties such as individuals, business enterprises, professional firms, courts of law, universities, and government agencies. The FASB also has an emerging-issues task force and an advisory council to help in identifying accounting and reporting problems in need of attention. Through these efforts the FASB develops its current work agenda.

After a new topic is placed on the agenda, a task force is appointed to prepare a comprehensive discussion memorandum on the problems identified, background issues, and pros and cons of possible solutions. Sometimes the task force contracts out research on specific aspects of an issue. Eventually position papers are prepared and public hearings held. After that, an exposure draft of a proposed new financial accounting standard is circulated, and again public hearings conducted. Once more feedback is considered and a final standard prepared. If this final standard receives a confirming vote from the FASB members and is accepted by the SEC, it becomes binding on all financial statements and reports prepared in accordance with "generally accepted accounting principles." Since considerable due process is involved in the procedure just described, it normally takes two years or more to develop and finalize a new financial accounting standard.

Generally accepted accounting principles (GAAP) are the sum total of all financial accounting standards, rules, and regulations which must be observed in the preparation of financial reports acceptable to the SEC. The FASB's State-

[3] Financial Accounting Standards Board, *Facts about FASB* (Norwalk, CT: FASB, 1990), p. 1.

ments of Financial Accounting Standards (SFASs) are the major component of GAAP.

GOVERNMENTAL ACCOUNTING AND REPORTING

Economic activities in the private sector typically involve a recognizable product or service that is sold in the marketplace at an agreed-upon price. Once a transaction has occurred, the transaction revenue can be measured, appropriate expenses matched against it, and net income determined. As pointed out in earlier chapters, the net income measurement becomes the performance indicator for the enterprise and its management.

Governmental agencies have some difficulty in defining their products. Often the product is a service which is seen as important in its general availability to the public—with little direct concern over who a particular user might be. There is no marketplace recognition of a service event and considerable difficulty in measuring the economic worth of such an event. Expenses or outlays are typically matched to a governmental program rather than to a defined product or service.

In accounting terms, the absence of profit measurability in governmental accounting creates three critical problems: (1) managerial performance in the public sector is difficult to determine; (2) there is no measure of comparable value across the wide range of governmental programs; and (3) economic costs of transactions and/or events have little motivating power in terms of the public or national interest.

Operationalizing the System. How can one operationalize a governmental accounting system in the absence of measurable product or service revenue and net income determination? The answer is—not very well. But governmental accounting is older than private enterprise accounting and thus has found ways of procedural development.

In process terms, direct legislation usually creates a program; that is, gives it legal validity. Subsequently, all or portions of an approved program may be funded through legislative money appropriations, which in turn creates expenditure authority. Control over a program or an agency is often exercised by comparing actual expenditures with money appropriations. In this respect, big cost overruns of some national defense programs have become legendary.

The astute reader recognizes quickly, of course, that spending money exactly as appropriated may be neither efficient nor effective in terms of program goals or governmental operations.

Focus on Accountability. The Magna Carta launched the idea that government is accountable to the governed. Ever since then, different concepts of accountability have guided governmental accounting, just as wealth and net income measurements have guided private enterprise accounting.

Elmer B. Staats, former Comptroller General of the United States, defined the idea of public accountability in a 1979 annual conference address to the National Council on Governmental Accounting.

Accountability requires a number of basic elements. First, information regarding the actions and decisions of the person or organization being held accountable must be transmitted. Second, the information must be received by someone who will examine it and take necessary actions. Third, a means must be found by which the information can be used to improve performance, correct deficiencies, or reward superior service. We have a responsibility to communicate information to the public, to open lines of communication between the government and its citizens, and keep them open. . . .

The accountability chain between the electorate and elected officials is a vital, indispensable element of democratic government. We must continue to develop ways of increasing citizen involvement in the process. Whatever can be achieved in this direction is clearly worth the effort.[4]

At the risk of some oversimplification, this accountability breaks down into three different categories.

1. Fiscal accountability: appropriate spending of public funds in a lawful way and with proper accounting. For example, the General Accounting Office (GAO) of the U.S. Congress has conducted audits and other examinations for decades to ensure that a high level of fiscal accountability exists at the federal level.

2. Process accountability: which requires that agencies or other governmental organizations carry out policies and programs in intended ways. For instance, bank examiners from federal home loan district banks conduct management audits at savings and loan banks to make sure that these savings institutions do not slip into commercial bank roles or perform unauthorized financial services.

3. Program accountability: which requires that governmental programs or policies produce results or changes intended. In this connection we might note that an in-depth review of the space shuttle program was initiated after Challenger was lost. Program accountability is triggering some major changes of the entire U.S. space program as a result of this loss.

Standard Setting for Governmental Accounting. Earlier in this chapter we noted that the Financial Accounting Foundation (FAF) is the parent unit of the FASB.

In 1985, after much political maneuvering, the FAF created a Governmental Accounting Standards Board (GASB) very similar to the FASB. The operations of the two boards are, for all intents and purposes, the same.

There are, however, two key differences. One is that governmental accounting is even more diverse than business enterprise accounting. Prior to the creation of the GASB, the National Council on Governmental Accounting (NCGA) issued various governmental accounting and financial reporting standards. Competing standards were issued by the Municipal Finance Officers Association (MFOA) as well as the GAO. Moreover, the Office of Management and Budget (OMB) of the Executive Office of the President of the United States imposed various administrative requirements through its accounting-related circulars. Then, professional organizations like the American Institute of CPAs issued various applicable audit and accounting guides, not to mention the standards and regulations promulgated by all the state and local governments. Therefore, the GASB inherited a much more voluminous, contradictory, and generally unclear set of prior standards and rules than did the FASB.

The second difference is that the GASB lacks an effective enforcement

---

[4] Elmer B. Staats, "Who Is Accountable? To Whom? For What? How?," *GAO Review,* Spring 1980, p. 33.

mechanism (the role served by the SEC for the FASB). Particularly, state and local governments do not always support the standards issued by the GASB.

In time, the GASB is likely to provide the benchmark accounting standards for all governmental accounting. There still is some dispute over the standard-setting jurisdiction regarding not-for-profit organizations. In 1989, accounting standards for public utilities, health care institutions, as well as colleges and universities, were assigned to the FASB; while all remaining not-for-profit sectors are the responsibility of the GASB. This division of responsibilities is likely to change in the future.

ACCOUNTING AS A SOCIAL FACTOR

We have established in earlier chapters that accounting does not follow any natural or biological laws and is therefore relatively indeterminate. All of its concepts, standards, and procedures are created by people and therefore, just like the discipline of law, are ever changing. Furthermore, we have determined that accounting standard setting is eclectic. Each of the several accounting measurement approaches we have studied in this text has its own distinct advantages and disadvantages.

Different economic entities are affected by the financial reporting process in different ways and to different degrees (in terms of costs and benefits). This means that different choices among financial accounting alternatives can lead to different distributions of wealth among various parties in the economy. Furthermore, since different entities may be better or worse off under one model than under another, there is no unanimity as to the best alternative on which to base present-day financial reporting practice.

The lack of unanimity as to the most appropriate financial accounting alternative and the implication that different alternatives may lead to different distributions of wealth in the economy prompt the question of what is the optimum *financial accounting policy*. This is a socioeconomic question rather than a question of accounting theory. All such questions are ultimately decided by some type of political mechanism.

The mechanism involved, as we have seen, is the shared power system between the FASB and SEC. In our current political and economic system, the FASB seeks to be responsive primarily to direct participants in the market system: securities markets participants, enterprise managements, professional accountants, and courts of law. The SEC, on the other hand, must accommodate large political constituencies. It is regularly subjected to congressional hearings and attempts to accommodate the general public interest. Hence the financial accounting policies that guide financial reporting in the U.S. system are best thought of as a social contract between all interested parties. Therefore financial accounting is a social phenomenon.

Historical Cost Measures

The social choice factor in financial accounting is readily apparent in the selection of historical costs as the conventional financial accounting measurement basis in the United States. Prior to 1935, the accounting practices and procedures followed by business enterprises in presenting their financial statements varied greatly from company to company. This great diversity was uncovered early in 1935 when some 2,500 enterprises listed on 20 national securities exchanges registered their securities for the first time under the 1933 and 1934 securities acts. Carman G. Blough was Chief Accountant for the SEC during those critical years. At an accounting symposium at the University of California at Berkeley in 1967, he recalled how historical cost measurements became the hallmark of SEC policy from its inception to the present day.

> One of the first members of the newly formed SEC to be appointed was a former General Counsel for the Federal Trade Commission who had been in charge of that Commission's very comprehensive investigation of the public utility holding companies. During that study the flagrant write-up policies of the holding companies and their subsidiaries and the havoc they caused when the crash came in 1929 and 1930 kept impressing themselves on the chief investigator to the point that their end became almost an obsession with him. It was only logical to expect that when he had an opportunity to outlaw write-ups he would do so. So strong were his convictions and so convincing were his arguments against write-ups that all of the other members of the Commission were persuaded to take a positive stand against them from the very first case in which the question arose.[5]

Thus historical cost measurements emerged as a U.S. social factor. Our entire federal income taxation system is based on it, as are tens of millions of business contracts. Many legal cases refer to historical costs, and gain or loss from a historical cost baseline is considered the best available measure of performance by many.

Somehow, historical cost measurements have captured the social imagination of U.S. people (as they have in Germany, Japan, and Switzerland; but less so elsewhere). Historical cost numbers are easily understood even by individuals not trained in bookkeeping or accounting. The system is easily taught in business colleges, high schools, and colleges and universities. It makes for easy programming into electronic computing systems. Also, it is a very objective system—any two people looking at the same transaction come up with the same answer. This system seems to fit the U.S. social spirit.

On the other hand, the current cost system is regarded with suspicion. Some of its measurements are based on statistical indexes, which are often regarded as unreal. Full applications of C-C systems tend to be costly, and enterprise managers appear to shy away from them when it comes to "hard" decisions. While a C-C reporting system has merit, especially during periods of changing prices, its strengths are widely questioned in the United States—particularly by corporate managers. This has nothing to do with intellectual merit between historical cost and current cost measurements. It is purely a social choice.

Financial Reporting Format

One element of a social choice approach to financial accounting is to allow business managements and others preparing financial reports a certain freedom of choice regarding acceptable accounting standards and procedures. As we have discussed and illustrated in earlier chapters, ranges of generally accepted accounting principles are available with regard to inventory and depreciation methods. Interest

---

[5] Carman G. Blough, "Development of Accounting Principles in the United States," *Berkeley Symposium on the Foundations of Financial Accounting*, (Berkeley, CA: University of California, 1967), p. 10.

accumulation and discount rates on company pension plans are permitted some choice, as are lease capitalization methods. But the entire system is one of *flexibility within defined boundary lines.* The only way to make such a choice-based system work is to require reporting units to describe in elaborate notes to their financial statements which choices among generally accepted accounting principles have been made. The information content of a U.S. financial report would indeed be minimal were it not for the elaborate disclosures in notes accompanying published financial statements.

Once again, no fundamental theory explains this practice and no one can prove that the U.S. financial reporting system is optimal. A social choice mechanism selected the system and reinforces it repeatedly. It has refined this system over time to a remarkable degree of effectiveness. Whether rational or not, the U.S. financial reporting system appears to work well in our economy in comparison to other national systems.

INTERNATIONAL ACCOUNTING

Almost no social or economic activities are strictly domestic. Americans drive cars built in Europe, Mexico, or Japan. They buy Italian shoes, cotton from Egypt, and sportswear produced in Hong Kong. They put kiwi fruit from New Zealand into their salads, eat bananas from Central America, and drink European wines. In turn, of course, other nations buy U.S. aircraft, heavy road-building equipment, and computer hardware and software technology. Every industrialized nation today is subject to the same global interdependence.

What does this have to do with accounting? Accounting must also be concerned with the global economy. If accounting were unwilling or unable to serve the international needs of business enterprises and the international securities markets, it would quickly lose most of its contribution as a key source of business information. Hence accounting has become international. As a brief introduction to international accounting, five of its critical issues are discussed in the remainder of this chapter.

Different National Accounting Practices. Earlier in this chapter we established that accounting policy is a matter of social choice. We also know that nations differ from each other with respect to their economic, legal, political, and social systems. Therefore, it stands to reason that accounting systems likewise differ.

By way of a general illustration we have already pointed out that several European countries, Japan, and the United States prefer historical cost measurements. On the other hand, most South American countries prefer or require P-L-A accounting. The Netherlands, New Zealand, and England, among others, tend toward current cost measurements. Financial statement consolidation is practiced in most English-speaking countries; was adopted in Japan only about ten years ago; was required only for domestic subsidiaries in West Germany; and is not practiced in most of the remaining countries. One would expect Soviet accounting to be quite different from British and American accounting, yet the differences between accounting in industrialized nations and accounting in developing countries are every bit as large. While there are many accounting similarities around the globe (e.g., double-entry bookkeeping), existing differences are substantial.

Multinational Corporation (MNC) Accounting. Examples of MNCs include Procter & Gamble and International Telephone & Telegraph; in Japan, Sony and Nissan; in Germany, Bayer and BMW; in Switzerland, Nestlé and Hoffmann LaRoche; in Holland, Philips Electric and Unilever; and in England, British Petroleum and Imperial Chemicals. Mammoth companies like these operate in up to one hundred different countries simultaneously. Thousands of companies worldwide operate in ten or more different countries.

From an accounting point of view the MNCs must somehow integrate all of their national accounting systems and come up with single language–single currency financial statements. This alone is a major task of translation and adjustment, since individual transactions occur in many different national currencies, and local accounting practices often contradict each other across national borders. For instance, large Japanese companies regularly prepare two sets of financial statements—one set for domestic use in Japan following Japanese company law, and another set for international use following internationally accepted accounting standards.

International Corporate Securities Markets. Almost five hundred companies have their securities listed not only on stock exchanges at home but also on stock exchanges in other countries. Major new international security issues, like that of British Telecom in 1985, are simultaneously sold in as many as six to ten different countries. The Eurobond market generates an annual volume in the $100 billion range. Many investment funds now specialize in corporate securities from other countries. In other words, the international market in corporate securities is so huge that it is almost beyond everyday comprehension.

This means that any foreign company wishing to sell securities in the United States must comply with SEC requirements. It also means that Swiss, Italian, or French financial statements must be translated into English and restated to U.S. accounting standards so that investors in the U.S. can understand these statements. Many believe that the international corporate securities markets would be significantly smaller and less efficient were it not for the international "adaptations" which financial accounting has made.

Technical International Accounting Problems. There are many technical accounting problems which exist internationally without domestic counterparts. One example is foreign currency translation. If one does business in several different currencies, one must *translate* foreign exchange to one's home currency. Should this be done transaction-by-transaction or in summarized form once a quarter or once a year? What exchange rate should be used, especially if a foreign country places restrictions on currency convertibility? What happens if exchange rates change but there has been no specific transaction? Should gain or loss be recognized for accounting purposes?

Regarding the latter, assume that a U.S. company borrowed 300 million West German marks during 1985 when the exchange rate was $1 = DM3. The loan involved is to be paid back in 1995. At December 31, 1985, assuming the exchange rate is still the same, this debt appears at $100 million in the company's U.S. consolidated financial statements.

By 1990, the U.S. dollar had depreciated against most major world currencies and by December 31, 1990, had reached $1 = DM1.50. Now if we again use the current foreign exchange rate, the debt would appear as $200 million in the year-end consolidated financial statements. Has there been a loss? Remember, there was no change in the actual German mark amount of debt. Rather complicated technical accounting rules apply to the solution of this dilemma.

International Financial Accounting Standards. Since there is so much financial accounting diversity around the world, and since increasing global interdependence demands that this diversity be reduced, many efforts are under way to coordinate accounting policy making between nations and develop special international standards of accounting. The United Nations is involved in this effort as is the Organization for Economic Cooperation and Development (OECD) headquartered in Paris. There are regional accounting associations in Central Europe, Scandinavia, Asia, Southeast Asia, South America, Africa, and the Middle East. Many of these organizations are making proposals for international standards regarding financial accounting and reporting.

Most effective to date has been the International Federation of Accountants (IFAC), whose membership consists of the important national accounting organizations from country to country. Professional accounting groups from more than 70 different countries now belong to IFAC. This group represents over one million of the world's practicing professional accountants.

IFAC has two major standard-setting committees: one for accounting and one for auditing. The International Accounting Standards Committee (IASC) has been at work since 1973, and published 29 international accounting standards through the end of 1989. Many MNCs use these standards when they report outside their home countries according to "internationally accepted accounting principles." Also, quite a few developing countries are adopting these standards since this saves them from developing their own.

But progress with international standardization in financial accounting is very slow. One of the worst offenders in this respect is the United States, since only domestic requirements are recognized for purposes of financial reporting by U.S. corporations. General Electric is one of the few United States corporations which states in its annual report that the report is in conformity with international accounting standards.

SUMMARY

This chapter is devoted to the broad policy context of financial accounting. We start with an explanation of how a market economy works. Securities markets are described as facilitators of exchanges of funds between savers and businesses making new or additional investments. In secondary markets, investors trade corporate securities previously owned. Accounting and financial reporting support a significant proportion of the decisions made in corporate securities markets.

There is a public interest in the nature of financial reporting. This public interest is safeguarded by federal securities acts. A private-sector board (FASB) sets financial accounting standards, which a regulatory commission (SEC) enforces for all companies whose securities are traded on a national exchange.

Governmental accounting and reporting are oriented to fiscal and program accountability. A private-sector board (GASB) recommends governmental accounting standards. The social choice factor in financial accounting explains the dominance of historical cost measurements in the U.S. It also explains why business managers have limited freedom of choice between different generally accepted accounting principles and financial reporting formats.

As global interdependence affects most business, accounting must also be concerned with the global economy. Since different accounting systems exist in different countries, special issues arise in accounting for multinational corporations and transactions in international corporate securities markets. International financial accounting standards are recommended by the International Accounting Standards Committee (IASC).

Questions for Review and Discussion

12–1. Define
  a. Free market economy
  b. Capital market
  c. Capital market intermediaries
  d. Primary corporate securities market
  e. Operational efficiency of securities markets
  f. Unfair securities markets
  g. Mission of Financial Accounting Standards Board
  h. Shared power system of financial accounting standard setting
  i. Government fiscal accountability
  j. Foreign currency translation

12–2. Why do controlled or manipulated markets result in relatively higher costs to consumers? State and briefly explain two relevant examples.

12–3. What functions are performed by financial intermediaries in capital markets? Is a savings and loan association a capital market intermediary?

12–4. Explain and briefly illustrate how a secondary market for corporate securities might become inefficient.

12–5. What is the role of financial accounting in corporate securities markets?

12–6. What is the relationship between the Swedish financial swindler Ivar Kreuger and the United States Securities Acts of 1933 and 1934?

12–7. State the two principal objectives of the Securities Act of 1933.

12–8. Describe briefly the procedure used by the FASB to set a financial accounting standard.

12–9. In the U.S., informed investors are considered to be the most important group as far as a direct interest in published financial reports is concerned. Do you agree with this focus for U.S. financial reporting? Who might be another important interest group for published financial reports?

12–10. How is governmental accounting different from business accounting?

12–11. Governmental accountability can be divided into three different categories. What are these categories and what does each mean?

12–12. Who sets governmental accounting standards and how? Be concise in your response.

12–13. In the text, historical cost measurements are identified as a "U.S. social factor." Explain whether you agree or disagree with this assertion.

12–14. Fundamental theory cannot explain existing U.S. accounting practices because U.S. financial accounting policy responds primarily to social choice factors. Given that this is the case, what are some important advantages and some important disadvantages of the financial accounting policy system in the U.S.?

12–15. What is meant by "global economic interdependence"? Is this interdependence a passing fad?

12–16. What are the two major standard-setting committees of the IFAC and what does each do?

Mini Cases

12–1. National Economic System Differences. Karen Evans and Martha Hanson, both CPAs, had worked for a large public accounting firm for several years. Recently they joined the financial executive staff of Micromax, a fast-growing and highly visible software concern. They each now have the job title of Senior Accounting Analyst.

"Guess what?" Karen came bursting into Martha's office one morning. "Our board of directors has just given approval to build and operate a subsidiary company in southern France and to enter into a joint venture with the People's Republic of China (PRC)." Martha responded a little quizzically. "What does this have to do with me?" Karen replied that one of them should take the France project and the other the PRC project to analyze the necessary procedures and costs for getting appropriate business accounting systems under way. Martha shrugged her shoulders. "So what's the big deal? We simply extend the financial accounting system we have in place here at Micromax headquarters, produce accounting data as we always have, and then make up whatever reports are required by local authorities. After all, what is good enough in the U.S. is surely good enough in France and in the PRC."

Karen, who had spent some time as a university exchange student in France, thought Martha's reaction to be fairly naive. Different economic systems seem to trigger different financial accounting systems and surely different types of financial reporting. But before talking to Martha further on this topic, Karen thought she better make herself some notes so that she and Martha wouldn't waste time on impressions and generalities.

Required:

1. How would you expect business financial statements to differ between the U.S., France, and the PRC?
2. In France the government sets one single standard for each accounting topic or issue and then requires every enterprise in the economy to follow this single standard. Is it likely that U.S. accounting standards are acceptable in France? Speculate on how financial accounting standards might be set in the PRC.
3. If French and PRC financial accounting rules turn out to be quite different from those in the U.S., should local business accounting systems be used locally and the board of directors of Micromax "educated" as to what these local numbers mean? What might be an alternative way for Karen and Martha to approach the accounting information needs of local managers and regulators, and concurrently, those at headquarters?

12–2. The Market Giveth (Not Always). Jeff and Craig just finished their junior year at State University. When they saw some advertising for the upcoming fall football ticket sales, they decided that the copy was really outstanding in appearance. It was multicolor, toned to the "old purple and gold" and covered with cleverly scrambled reproductions of the university's seal, triangular banners, the stylized name of the university, and the state's flag. They had never seen anything like this before.

"Why not use this design and sell it in some other form?" mused Craig late one evening. "We could have a bolt of cotton printed like this, hire out some sewing and make simple men's boxer shorts." "I bet they would sell like hotcakes—especially during the fall football season," was Jeff's quick response. And that is exactly what happened. The two pooled their modest savings to start a small business. With some help and advice from their respective families, the two obtained permission from the university's athletic department to use the design. They got a small mill in a nearby metropolitan area to print three bolts of appropriate cotton material and then had a local contract sewing company cut the material and produce the shorts in five different sizes. Craig and Jeff boxed the merchandise and were able to convince several local department and specialty stores to stock the item. Three weeks after school started in the fall the entire merchandise had been sold and there was considerable demand for more.

Now the two entrepreneurs developed bigger ideas. Why not produce Bermuda shorts and swim trunks using the same design? Also, why not order a larger quantity of the cotton material so that the unit price would be less? Also, why not rent a small warehouse space, purchase an industrial sewing machine, and hire a sewing operator for their own account? All of this would reduce costs and really get them going in business. Of course they had some pretty strong evidence from the unfilled orders for their shorts that solid market demand existed—at least for the shorts.

However, these plans needed substantial financial capital—somewhat like $250,000. On their first round of production and sales they had doubled the $4,000 they had to start with and thus had $8,000 to invest themselves. Armed with their facts and figures they went to see the branch manager of the bank who was a good friend of Jeff's family. While the banker (i.e., financial market intermediary) was very sympathetic and met with Jeff and Craig for about three hours, the conclusion was reached that the bank could not loan them any money at all unless one or both of their families would unconditionally guarantee the loan by possibly putting second mortgages on their respective family residences.

Required:

1. With regard to the bank loan application from Craig and Jeff, did the financial market react "efficiently"?
2. If you had $100,000 available (let's say as an inheritance from your grandparents), would you invest it in the proposed business venture? Why or why not?
3. What would you advise Craig and Jeff to do now?

12–3. The World According to GAAP. Great Circle Savings Bank was organized in 1906 as a mutual association. This meant that all along depositors and borrowers "owned" the bank. While the bank's performance was generally satisfactory over the decades and its reserves were fairly strong, it found difficulty with operating in the deregulated financial markets of the 1980s and 1990s. "Let's become a stock company; sell stock to depositors, borrowers, and the public at large; and thus bring in a substantial amount of new capital," urged President Eddy at a board of directors meeting. "We can loan out this new money at competitive interest rates without necessarily having to pay dividends to shareholders," he continued. The board agreed that this would improve the bank's income statements and thus voted to proceed with "going public."

For all of its internal and legal financial reporting purposes the bank had used regulatory accounting principles (RAP). RAP, in the bank's case, are financial accounting and reporting standards set specifically for banks by federal bank regulatory authorities. Federal supervision and control of banks are made easier and more uniform if all banks use strictly the same accounting standards.

In preparation for the sale of common stock, Great Circle Savings Bank financial statements had to be prepared in terms of generally accepted accounting principles (GAAP). For the most recent five years, GAAP accounting showed bank net income significantly lower than RAP accounting had. "If we could only use RAP accounting with our stock underwriters," lamented President Eddy. "Those guys will want an arm and a leg in underwriting fees when they see our GAAP financial statements."

Required:

1. Why is RAP accounting different from GAAP accounting? Speculate on what might be two items of differences.
2. RAP and GAAP financial reports are simply different expressions of the same underlying economic events and transactions. Would the initial issue price of Great Circle common stock likely be higher if the bank could use RAP accounting throughout?
3. Does it seem reasonable that the bank, after going public, must always prepare two sets of financial statements—RAP reports for bank regulatory authorities and GAAP reports for the SEC and the shareholders?

12–4. Mirror Mirror on the Wall. Joe and Leslie have been friends since university days. Joe is now the assistant administrator of a large hospital and Leslie practices tax law. "Did I ever drop a bundle in the stock market last week," reported Leslie. "With all this tax work I do, I think I understand financial statements, and then these big turnarounds appear out of nowhere!" Joe was most sympathetic. "Yeah, our pension plan administrative committee met two weeks ago and we sure wished we had never bought any common stocks. Our pension fund gained big over a couple of years but now we're literally back where we started." Joe continued, "I can't understand why the SEC gets an annual budget in excess of $120 million, and will not advise investors which companies are good investments. The least they could do is rank the Fortune 500 companies in terms of investment quality from 1 to 500!" Leslie had a different point of view. Even though she had experienced significant stock market losses, she thought it would be totally undesirable for the SEC to recommend individual common stocks for investment purposes. "This would destroy the entire capital market mechanism in the country," she observed. "In fact, such recommendations would put the government in the business of allocating investment funds to individual companies."

Required:

1. Do you agree with Leslie's final observation? Why or why not?
2. Should the SEC regularly publish dividend payouts, stock market price changes of individual securities, management fees charged by mutual investment funds, and similar other information now available from a wide variety of private news media and services?
3. What is the role of the SEC in the U.S. corporate securities markets? As far as you know or can judge, how effective has the SEC been in accomplishing its purpose since it was created in 1934?

12–5. Making the Rules. "We sure had a peculiar discussion in class today," reported Valerie Ambrose to her roommate. "Our accounting prof insisted that financial accounting standard setting in the United States is nothing but a big game among politicians, business managers, professional accountants, Washington, D.C. regulators, the courts, and Wall Street financiers. Do you think he was serious or was he just needling us?" "How should I know?" asked Nancy Runyan, a political science major. "We talked about regulatory processes in our public affairs class. My prof said you can't regulate unless you have a clear-cut mandate like a constitution. "Well, I am confused," Valerie came back. "In our economics course, we are always talking about theories and that without an appropriate theory you can't get to first base. It sure looks like there isn't any theory in accounting to help the FASB when they set financial accounting standards." "From what you have told me, it seems that your accounting prof is serious," Nancy answered. "If you don't have a theory, don't have a constitution or specific legislation that gives direction, accounting standard setting must be sort of a roulette game between everybody who stands to win some or lose some from the game."

Required:

1. Is the lengthy due process which the FASB uses in setting financial accounting standards a substitute for direct legal authority to set standards?
2. What are some pros and cons of the SEC's ability to exercise absolute veto power over any and all accounting standards, but at the same time refraining from setting financial accounting standards itself (i.e., letting the FASB do it)?

12–6. The Biggest of Them All. Exhibit 12–3 contains a recent financial report of the United States government as prepared by the U.S. Treasury Department.[6]

Required:

1. Who might use U.S. government financial statements and for what purpose?
2. What are six striking differences between the financial statements in Exhibit 12–3 and typical U.S. corporate financial statements?
3. The media make much of the fact that the U.S. is now the largest debtor country of the world. Does the balance sheet in Exhibit 12–3 reveal the size of the U.S. international debt?

12–7. Invisible Ink. The following extract is from an article by Richard Morais entitled "Invisible Ink."[7]

Consider West Germany, a natural magnet for international investors with its zero inflation, a GNP growing at 2.5% so far this year and a recent liberalizing of its stock market. The average German corporate annual report is a fairy tale. Management there strives to understate reported earnings, rather than overstate them, as its U.S. counterpart does. Why? Because German firms use the same set of books for tax purposes, and they don't like revealing to unions or to competitors how much they really earn. So, extraordinary items affecting earnings—the creation of special reserve funds, for instance—are not always fully disclosed. And German firms frequently cut their current pretax earnings sharply by deducting larger-than-necessary pension reserves.

Even to approximate an American-style earnings-per-share picture, investors have to make 70 adjustments to the typical annual report. An example: According to Germany's Financial Analysts Association, Volkswagen's 1985 adjusted net income was $547 million, vs. the $203 million reported. Bayer, the chemical giant, understated earnings by $374 million. At BASF, another chemical giant, net income should have been 60% higher.

German firms use a lot of invisible ink. Consolidated worldwide accounts are often so abbreviated they are useless to investors. The latest annual report of Kloeckner-Humboldt-Deutz, a $1.25 billion engineering firm, comes in two parts. The home market report includes 12 pages of detailed footnotes, while the worldwide figures are accompanied by $1\frac{1}{2}$ pages of airy type.

More: German cash flow usually looks a lot better when compared with international competitors', because German companies take advantage of generously accelerated regional depreciation allowances. In West Berlin, for example, up to 75% of the cost of buildings can be deducted immediately. In the U.K. buildings are generally depreciated over 50 years and in the U.S. over 30 years.

Then there is that nice little hiding place known as "uncertain liabilities." This

---

[6] United States Government, *Annual 1989 Report.* Compiled by the Financial Management Service, U.S. Department of the Treasury.
[7] Richard Morais, "Invisible Ink," *Forbes,* December 15, 1986, p. 44. Excerpted by permission of *Forbes* magazine; © Forbes, Inc., 1986.

EXHIBIT 12–3

Balance Sheet of the United States Government,* 1988–1989

	September 30, 1989	September 30, 1988
	(in millions)	

Assets

Cash and Monetary Assets:		
U.S. Treasury Operating Cash:		
Federal Reserve Account	$ 13,452	$ 13,024
Tax and Loan Note Accounts	27,521	31,375
Special Drawing Rights	9,487	9,074
Less: Special Drawing Rights Certificates		
Issued to Federal Reserve Banks	8,518	5,018
Monetary Assets with International Monetary	8,785	9,635
Other Cash and Monetary Assets:		
U.S. Treasury Monetary Assets	1,495	1,494
Cash and Other Assets Held outside the Treasury		
Account	8,101	8,818
Time Deposits Supported by 2% Depository Bonds	2	2
Total Cash and Monetary Assets	60,325	68,403
Miscellaneous Asset Accounts	8,426	4,635
Total Assets	**68,752**	**73,038**

Excess of Liabilities over Assets

Excess of Liabilities over Assets at Beginning of Fiscal Year	2,036,266	1,882,263
Add: Total Deficit for Fiscal Year	151,988	155,151[r]
Subtotal	2,188,254	2,037,414[r]
Deduct: Other Transactions Not Applied to Surplus or Deficit	667	1,148[r]
Excess of Liabilities over Assets at Close of Fiscal Year	2,187,587	2,036,266[r]
Total Assets and Excess of Liabilities **over Assets**	**2,256,339**	**2,109,304[r]**

Liabilities

Borrowing from the Public:		
Public Debt Securities Outstanding	2,857,431	2,602,183
Agency Securities Outstanding	23,680	12,398
Total Federal Securities Outstanding	2,881,112	2,614,581
Deduct: Federal Securities Held by Government Accounts	676,842	550,681[r]
Total Borrowing from the Public	2,204,270	2,063,900[r]
Premium and Discount on Public Debt Securities	15,448	13,902
Total Borrowing Less Premium and Discount	2,188,822	2,049,998[r]
Accrued Interest Payable to the Public	40,747	34,067
Special Drawing Rights Allocated by International		
Monetary Fund	6,270	6,322
Deposit Fund Liabilities	9,279	8,549[r]

EXHIBIT 12–3 (cont.)

Balance Sheet of the United States Government,* 1988–1989

	September 30, 1989	September 30, 1988
	(in millions)	
Liabilities (cont.)		
Miscellaneous Liability Accounts (Checks Outstanding, Etc.)	11,222	10,368
Total Liabilities	**$2,256,339**	**$2,109,304ʳ**

Details may not add to totals due to rounding.
ʳ-revised

**Statement of Operations
(in Millions)**

	Fiscal Year 1989	Fiscal Year 1988
Receipts		
Individual Income Taxes	$445,690	$401,181
Corporation Income Taxes	103,291	94,195
Social Insurance Taxes and Contributions:		
Employment taxes and contributions (off-budget)	263,666	241,491
Employment taxes and contributions (on-budget)	69,193	63,602
Unemployment Insurance	22,011	24,584
Contributions for Other Insurance and Retirement	4,546	4,658
Excise Taxes	34,386	35,540
Estate and Gift Taxes	8,745	7,594
Customs Duties	16,334	15,411ʳ
Miscellaneous Receipts	22,927	19,909
Total Receipts	**990,789**	**908,166ʳ**
Outlays		
Legislative Branch	2,094	1,852
The Judiciary	1,493	1,337
Executive Office of the President	124	121
Funds Appropriated to the President	4,302	7,252
Agriculture	48,414	44,003
Commerce	2,571	2,279
Defense—Military	294,876	281,935ʳ
Defense—Civil	23,427	22,047
Education	21,608	18,246
Energy	11,387	11,166ʳ
Health and Human Services, except Social Security	172,301	158,991
Health and Human Services, Social Security	227,473	214,178
Housing and Urban Development	19,680	18,956
Interior	5,308	5,147ʳ
Justice	6,232	5,426

EXHIBIT 12–3 (cont.)

Statement of Operations*
(in Millions)

	Fiscal Year 1989	Fiscal Year 1988
Receipts		
Labor	22,657	21,870
State	3,722	3,421
Transportation	26,689	26,404
Treasury	230,573	201,644[r]
Veteran Affairs	30,041	29,249[r]
Environmental Protection Agency	4,906	4,872
General Services Administration	−462	−281[r]
National Aeronautics and Space Administration	11,036	9,092
Office of Personnel Management	29,073	29,191
Small Business Administration	83	−54
Independent Agencies	32,323	23,446[r]
Undistributed offsetting receipts	−89,155	−78,474
Total Outlays	**1,142,777**	**1,063,318[r]**
Total Deficit	**−151,988**	**−155,151[r]**
Other Transactions Not Applied to Current Year's Surplus or Deficit		
Seigniorage (Gain on coin Production)	−594	−470
Profit on Sale of Gold	−15	−37
Proceeds from sale of loan assets	−24	−577[r]
Net gain (−)/loss for IMF loan valuation adjustment	−34	−63
Total Other Transactions not Applied to Current Year's Surplus or Deficit	$ −667	$ −1,148[r]

Details may not add to totals due to rounding
[r]-revised

* *This financial statement is confined to showing only those assets and liabilities of the United States government which are directly related to the cash operations of the Department of the Treasury and the rest of the Federal government.*

is an undisclosed reserve that is taken from pretax earnings to meet so-called potential liabilities—a fire at a plant, say, or a toxic cleanup. During boom periods companies stash large amounts in hidden reserves and then feed them back into earnings when times are hard.

Moral: American investors who are taking their first taste of international equities risk a nasty bout of indigestion if they forget the vagaries of foreign accounting.

Required:

1. Why does Richard Morais consider an average published West German corporate financial report a "fairy tale"?
2. If a U.S. investor were interested in buying some stocks or bonds of large West Germany companies, how would she or he go about finding or preparing reliable financial information for purposes of the desired investment decision?

EXHIBIT 12–3 (cont.)

SECRETARY'S LETTER

THE SECRETARY OF THE TREASURY
WASHINGTON 20220

January 10, 1990

To: The President of the Senate
Speaker of the House of Representatives
Citizens of the United States of America

In accordance with the provisions of Section 15 of the Act of July 31, 1894 (31 U.S.C. 331(c) and Section 114 of the Act of September 12, 1950 (31 U.S.C. 3513), I am transmitting herewith the Annual Report of the United States Government for the Fiscal Year Ended September 30, 1989.

The United States Department of the Treasury is proud of its 200 years of promoting the financial integrity of the Government through improved accounting and financial reporting. The furtherance of this tradition is reflected in the financial statements contained herein, showing budget results and the cash-related assets and liabilities of the Federal Government. Details supporting the summary in this Report are contained in the Annual Report Appendix.

Financial results for the year include total receipts of $990.8 billion, an increase of $82.6 billion over 1988 receipts; total outlays of $1,142.8 billion, an increase of $79.5 billion over 1988 outlays; and a $152 billion deficit, a decrease of 3.2 billion lower than the 1988 deficit.

Sincerely

Nicholas F. Brady

3. One answer to the dilemma posed in this mini case would be the universal adoption, at least by large companies, of international financial accounting standards as prepared by the London-based International Accounting Standards Committee. How likely is it that the FASB and the SEC in the U.S. would ever adopt an international accounting standard completely different from existing GAAP?

Financial Reporting and Analysis

CHAPTER THIRTEEN

The product of accounting is financial information. If the information produced is to have any social benefit, it must be communicated to interested users. This chapter discusses important communications avenues for financial accounting information. Throughout this discussion we maintain the focus on (investment) decision making introduced in Chapter One. Since different information users have different information needs, it is critical that these needs receive full attention in related reporting processes. Significant information characteristics for this purpose include timeliness, understandability, and reliability.

In the second half of this chapter we illustrate how investment decision factors are estimated from financial report information and how several widely used financial ratio statistics are calculated.

FINANCIAL REPORTING

Financial statements are the direct product of a large number of integrated accounting processes. These processes are discussed and analyzed in Chapters Three through Eleven. They yield periodic income, financial position, and cash flow statements. Financial statements are formal representations of an entity's financial activities and events during a specified period of time. The wide use of financial statements throughout the economy suggests that they have important information content.

Financial reporting is broader than financial statement preparation. Most financial reports contain full-fledged or abbreviated financial statements. But financial reports also contain other descriptions, explanations, and analyses. Examples of comprehensive financial reporting include corporate annual reports, various statutory annual financial information filings with regulatory commissions, and registration statements for new corporate securities to be sold publicly.

While we have referred to the usefulness of financial accounting information throughout this text, we now summarize this theme with a quote from Oscar S. Gellein. Gellein believes that the value of financial reporting can be gauged "by the extent to which it is helpful in making economic decisions."[1] He identified four user groups who rely heavily on financial reports.

1. Economic policy makers. They must determine the economic and other consequences which their policies have on individuals, companies, organizations and governments. Financial report information is typically a component in the assessment of economic consequences.
2. Government regulators (whose functions relate to financial affairs of entities). Examples include tax officials; banking authorities; utilities rate setters; and insurance, foreign trade, and financial markets regulators. Many of their regulatory activities are based on the contents of both general and regulatorily required financial reports.
3. Parties making economic decisions affecting their own relationships with an entity. Examples include investors, creditors, employees, customers and suppliers. These groups may have existing relationships with a reporting entity or may be contemplating one in the future. In the United States the investor group receives primary financial reporting attention.
4. Entities seeking funds from others. Included are individuals, business firms, social and civic organizations, and all levels of government. These entities want to obtain needed new funds at the lowest possible price (i.e., low interest rates when borrowing and high prices per share when selling stock). Effective financial reporting is of key importance in accomplishing this objective.[2]

If we accept Gellein's list of parties who find financial reports useful, the case for financial reporting is made. Professors Schall and Haley point out that "A company's financial statements are an extremely important source of information about the business. . . . Without the kind of information provided by financial statements, it is almost impossible to evaluate a company."[3]

Types of Financial Reports

The Gellein quote makes clear that a great many different types of financial reports are regularly prepared by different entities for various purposes. The following discussion is limited to a few typical corporate financial report types.

Annual Corporate Reports. A corporation receives a charter to do business from a state, and one of the responsibilities often imposed by law on that corporation is to report at least annually to the shareholders. This accountability

[1] Oscar S. Gellein, "Good Financial Reporting," *The CPA Journal*, November 1983, p. 40. Reprinted with permission from *The CPA Journal*, copyright 1983.
[2] Ibid., pp. 40–42.
[3] L. D. Schall and C. W. Haley, *Introduction to Financial Management*, 5th ed. (New York: McGraw-Hill, 1988), p. 441.

obligation often includes the distribution of copies of the corporation's annual financial report to each of the shareholders. Aside from this general statutory responsibility, additional requirements may be imposed on a corporation whose shares are listed and traded on an organized stock exchange, such as the New York Stock Exchange (NYSE). For example, a corporation listed on the New York Stock Exchange must submit its annual financial report to shareholders not later than 120 days following the end of its fiscal year, or 30 days prior to the annual stockholders' meeting, whichever comes first.

Generally the components of an annual report of a large corporation include

1. Report of management.
2. Report of independent accountants (see Chapter Fourteen).
3. Primary financial statements.
4. Management discussion and analysis of results of operations and financial condition.
5. Secondary financial statements (e.g., statement of stockholders' equity).
6. Notes to financial statements.
7. Ten-year comparison of selected financial data.
8. Selected quarterly data.
9. Supplemental financial information.

Of particular interest is the report of management. Here company management states its responsibility for the integrity and objectivity of the financial information presented in the report. There are also statements about the company's internal accounting control system and adherence to business policies and conduct guidelines. Also, the work of the independent auditors is referenced, as is the audit committee of the board of directors (see Chapter Fourteen). Thus the reader of the report is given strong assurances by management that the company's accounting information system is reliable. By implication, the quality of the information contained in the annual report is likewise reliable.

The primary financial statements are the consolidated statements of income, financial position, and cash flows. Nature and contents of these statements have been discussed earlier in the text.

The management discussion portion of corporate annual reports evolved as a part of the SEC's integrated financial disclosure system whereby information filed with the SEC is fully compatible with information provided in annual reports to stockholders. Regarding results of operations, important unusual events and uncertainties must be discussed. Financial trends must be pointed out and the effects of new products or new services elaborated. In connection with the discussion of financial position, significant past or anticipated changes in liquidity must be described and the overall status of capital resources discussed. The management-provided "discussion and analysis" is an important source of information about the financial situation of the reporting company.

The notes to the financial statements form an integral part of the statements themselves. They explain significant accounting policies utilized by the company, the extent of the company's involvement in multinational business operations, and the effects of specific financial accounting measurement policies selected by management. Readers of annual reports are often specifically interested in notes about taxation and segments of business products or services (i.e., lines of business).

The last three annual report components—ten-year comparison, selected quarterly data, and supplemental information—are statistical in nature. The ten-year statistical comparisons are provided so that the reader has a time-based perspective on the current numbers. The selected quarterly data relate to the discussion that follows regarding interim reports. Supplemental financial information covers such items as stock prices, costs and benefits of environmental protection efforts made, or numbers of employees working at different plant and office locations.

It should be noted that the contents of corporate annual financial reports vary somewhat among enterprises due to type of industry, size of company, manner of financing, and other such critical variables. For companies whose securities are publicly traded, items included in their annual reports originate from a mixture of laws and regulations, stock exchange listing requirements, and financial accounting policies.

Summary Annual Reports. In 1987, the SEC ruled that companies whose securities are publicly traded may henceforth issue annual reports in whatever form they wish so long as they continue to file all required financial information with the SEC and ensure that this information is available to their stockholders. Thus a number of companies have chosen to condense their traditional (and often quite lengthy) annual reports and publish them as *Summary Annual Reports* (SARs).[4] As condensed versions of comprehensive annual reports, SARs are less complex and therefore more readable. They are also more focused and less costly to produce. Caterpillar Inc., was among the first U.S. companies to unveil a SAR. Their 1989 SAR is reprinted as an appendix to this chapter. It is also the database for the section on financial ratio statistics at the end of the chapter.

Quarterly Financial Reports. While annual reports rank among the most useful financial communications, it is often desirable to have more frequent information about the financial progress of a corporation. Such information is provided by *interim financial statements*. Typically, interim financial statements are submitted to shareholders as quarterly financial reports (a requirement for most corporations listed on major stock exchanges).

Quarterly financial reports do not include the more elaborate discussion of the corporation's activities included in the annual report. Because the time period involved is shorter, additional measurement problems exist (for example, the impact of seasonal activity), and as a result the reports are generally considered somewhat less reliable than annual reports. Still, readers get an idea whether the interim financial statements "add up" to final annual totals. This is important in predicting the future cash-generating ability of a business, since some managements are more optimistic than others in reporting on the first quarter or two of the current period's operations.

SEC Reporting. Besides the annual financial reports sent to external parties, the SEC requires that all corporations subject to its jurisdiction file audited annual reports with the Commission. These annual reports are filed in SEC Form 10-K (and are usually referred to in the financial community as 10-Ks). The SEC 10-K report includes financial information similar to that included in the annual report to shareholders, as well as additional information that expands upon the amount of detail included in a typical annual report. An investor wishing to probe

---

[4] Charles H. Gibson and Nicholas Schroeder, "How 21 Companies Handled Their Summary Annual Reports," *Financial Executive*, November/December 1989, pp. 45–48.

more deeply into the diverse activities of a corporation may find it useful to obtain a copy of the 10-K annual report. Most companies furnish copies of their 10-Ks upon request and free of charge. Since the 10-K report is a document of public record, it may also be obtained at SEC offices (as well as at selected quasi-public repositories, such as the NYSE library). Many commercial financial services make available, on a subscription basis, copies of 10-Ks and other filings with the SEC.

In addition to the 10-K report, there are several other types of filings of financial information that are triggered by specified corporation activities. For example, if a corporation plans to make a public offering of a new stock issue, it must file an extensive description of its financial and economic affairs (including the prospectus it plans to issue offering the shares to the public). The SEC explicitly disclaims any endorsement of the value of a stock issue. It leaves this assessment of the company's future prospects to the prospective investor. But the Commission does attempt to monitor the accuracy of the factual representations included in the prospectus and other promotional material. Another SEC filing is the unaudited quarterly financial report (Form 10-Q). Thus, for the investor who is prepared and able to seek out and obtain the reports on file with the Commission, a considerable amount of information is publicly available.

News Announcements. Corporations also release selected financial information at various times throughout the year through the financial press. The large publicly held corporations whose securities are listed on national exchanges are actually required by the SEC to release certain financial information to the press and newswire services as soon as it is accurately measured. Typically, this information consists of data on sales and earnings for the quarter or the year. An example of this type of information is presented in Exhibit 13–1. While these news announcements contain highly aggregated data and primarily focus on revenue and earnings for the year, they are generally available at least 30 days prior to the release of the annual or interim reports. Thus they represent a timely source of information for the investor.

EXHIBIT 13–1

News Announcement Excerpt

Wall Street Journal Report of Fourth Quarter, 1989, and 1989 Annual Earnings for Caterpillar Inc.

Year Dec 31:	1989	1988
Sales	$10,882,000,000	$10,255,000,000
Net income	497,000,000	616,000,000
Shr earns:		
Net income	4.90	6.07
Quarter:		
Sales	2,694,000,000	2,610,000,000
Net income	107,000,000	163,000,000
Shr earns:		
Net income	1.05	1.61

Source: *"Digest of Earnings Reports,"* The Wall Street Journal, *January 19, 1990, p. B6. Reprinted with the permission of The Wall Street Journal, © 1990 Dow Jones & Company, Inc. All Rights Reserved Worldwide.*

EXHIBIT 13–2

Commercial Financial Service Report

UNITED STATES
CONSTRUCTION

CATERPILLAR, INC. (CAT)

Fiscal Year End: December 31	1989	1988	1987	1986	1985	1984
Financial Statement Data			(Millions of U.S. dollars)			
Income Statement						
Net Sales	10,882	10,255	8180.0	7321.0	6725.0	6576.0
Depreciation, Deple. & Amort.	471	434	403.0	436.0	476.0	492.0
Operating Income	582	820	482.0	249.0	302.0	-113.0
Interest Expense	372	340	209.0	197.0	234.0	265.0
Pretax Income	621	842	446.0	99.0	216.0	-541.0
Net Income	497	616	350.0	76.0	189.0	-654.0
Balance Sheet - Assets						
Cash & Short Term Investments	148	74	103.0	124.0	282.0	62.0
Receivables - Net	2,900	2,783	2163.0	1728.0	1337.0	1345.0
Inventories	2,120	1,986	1323.0	1211.0	1139.0	1246.0
Total Current Assets	5,708	5,317	3813.0	3363.0	2982.0	2915.0
Net Property, Plant & Equipment	3,505	2,802	2464.0	2433.0	2652.0	2945.0
Total Assets	10,926	9,686	6866.0	6292.0	6016.0	6223.0
Balance Sheet - Liabilities						
Total Current Liabilities	3,904	3,435	2392.0	2180.0	1742.0	1939.0
Long Term Debt	2,288	1,953	900.0	963.0	1177.0	1384.0
Preferred Stock	0	0	0.0	0.0	0.0	0.0
Common Equity	4,474	4,113	3565.0	3149.0	3068.0	2852.0
Liabilities & Equity	10,926	9,686	6866.0	6292.0	6016.0	6223.0
Sources & Uses of Funds						
From Operations	945	976	802.0	570.0	618.0	150.0
L.T. External Financing - Net	399	-9	197.0	-266.0	-191.0	-81.0
Dividends	121	77	50.0	49.0	49.0	120.0
Capital Expenditures	1,089	793	467.0	294.0	229.0	204.0
Change in Working Capital	-78	461	238.0	-57.0	264.0	-831.0
International Business						
Foreign Assets	2,116	1,821	1555.0	1374.0	1273.0	1109.0
Foreign Sales	2,993	2,977	2237.0	1866.0	1445.0	1283.0
Foreign Income	97	64	-16.0	-43.0	-16.0	-22.0
Supplementary Data						
Employees	60,784	60,558	54,463	53,731	53,616	61,624
R & D Expense	235	182	159.0	178.0	218.0	231.0
Common Shares (millions)	101	101	101.4	98.8	98.4	96.8
Financial Ratios and Growth Rates						
Profitability						
Operating Margin	5.3%	8.0%	5.9%	3.4%	4.5%	-1.7%
Effective Tax Rate	26.1%	31.1%	26.0%	23.2%	12.5%	n.a.
Net Margin	4.6%	6.0%	4.3%	1.0%	2.8%	-9.9%
Return on Assets	5.1%	9.0%	5.6%	1.3%	3.0%	-9.4%
Return on Equity	12.1%	17.3%	11.1%	2.5%	6.6%	-19.6%
Cash Flow/Sales	8.7%	9.5%	9.8%	7.8%	9.2%	2.3%
Sales Per Employee (000)	179.0	169.3	150.2	136.3	125.4	106.7
Asset Utilization						
Total Assets Turnover	1.0x	1.1x	1.2x	1.2x	1.1x	1.1x
Assets per Employee (000)	179.8	159.9	126.1	117.1	112.2	101.0
Capital Exp./Fixed Assets	n.c.	12.4%	7.5%	4.7%	3.7%	3.3%
Accum. Dep./Fixed Assets	n.c.	56.1%	60.6%	61.3%	57.5%	52.8%
Liquidity						
Current Ratio	1.5x	1.5x	1.6x	1.5x	1.7x	1.5x
Quick Ratio	0.8x	0.8x	0.9x	0.8x	0.9x	0.7x
Leverage						
Common Equity/Assets	40.9%	42.5%	51.9%	50.0%	51.0%	45.8%
L.T. Debt/Total Capital	33.8%	32.2%	20.2%	23.4%	27.7%	32.7%
EBIT/Fixed Charges	2.7x	3.5x	3.1x	1.5x	1.9x	-1.0x
Oper. Cash/Fixed Charges	2.5x	2.9x	3.8x	2.9x	2.6x	0.6x
Growth						
Net Sales	6.1%	25.4%	11.7%	8.9%	2.3%	21.2%
Operating Income	-29.0%	70.1%	93.6%	-17.5%	n.c.	n.c.
Total Assets	12.8%	41.1%	9.1%	4.6%	-3.3%	-10.7%
Earnings per Shr (cal year basis)	-19.3%	89.7%	315.6%	-61.9%	n.c.	n.c.
Div per Shr (cal year basis)	39.1%	53.3%	-10.0%	25.0%	-60.0%	-16.7%
Book Val per Shr (cal year basis)	8.8%	15.4%	10.3%	2.2%	5.8%	-16.0%
Per Share Data and Investment Ratios			(Calendar year basis)			
Earnings per Share	EF4.90	EF6.07	BEF3.20	DEF0.77	BEF2.02	BCE-4.47
Dividends per Share	1.20	0.86	0.56	A0.63	0.50	1.25
Book Value per Share	44.11	40.56	35.15	31.86	31.19	29.46
Market Price per Share	57.88	63.63	62.00	40.13	42.00	31.00
Total Return	-7.2%	4.0%	55.9%	-2.7%	37.1%	-31.7%
Price/Earnings Ratio	11.8x	10.5x	19.4x	52.1x	20.8x	def
Price/Book Value Ratio	1.3x	1.6x	1.8x	1.3x	1.3x	1.1x
Dividend Yield	2.1%	1.4%	0.9%	1.6%	1.2%	4.0%
Dividend Payout	24.5%	14.2%	17.6%	81.2%	24.8%	G

Notes: (A): DECLARED 5 DIVIDENDS IN 86; (B): INCLUDES OR EXCLUDES EXTRAORDINARY CHARGE OR CREDIT EXCLS $.31 CR IN 87, INCLS $.67 CHG & $.58 CR IN 85, INCLS $8.86 PRETAX CHG IN 84; (C): INCLS $1.65 PRETAX CHG IN 84 FOR EMPLOYEE BENEFITS; (D): PERIOD INCLUDES STRIKE; (E): BASED ON AVERAGE SHARES OUTSTANDING; (F): INCLS FOREIGN CURRENCY TRANSLATION GAIN/(LOSS) EQUAL TO $.16 IN 89, $.48 IN 88, $.86 IN 87, $1.01 IN 86, $.91 IN 85; (G): DIVIDENDS IN EXCESS OF EARNINGS.

General Information

Chairman & CEO
 G.A. SCHAEFER
President & COO
 D.V. FITES
Chief Financial Officer
 F.N. GRIMSLEY
Treasurer
 L.A. KUCHAN
Secretary
 R.R. THORNTON

Address:
 100 NORTH EAST ADAMS STREET
 PEORIA, IL 61629
 UNITED STATES
Telephone: (309) 675-1000

Exchange: NYSE BSE CIN MSE
Business:
 EARTHMOVING, CONSTRUCTION & MATERIAL HANDLING MACHINERY ACCOUNTED FOR 83%/76% OF 1989 SALES/OPERATING INCOME; ENGINES 17%/24%

Selected Data in U.S. Dollars ($Mil) At 1989 Fiscal Year End

Market Capitalization	5,869.6
Common Equity	4,474.0
Total Assets	10,926.0
Sales	10,882.0
Net Income	497.0

5 Year Annual Growth Rates

Net Sales	+10.6%
Net Income	n.c.
Total Assets	+11.9%
Employees	-0.3%
Earnings per Share	n.c.
Dividends per Share	-0.8%
Book Value per Share	+8.4%

Financial Ratios 5 Year Average

Operating Margin	5.4%
Net Margin	3.7%
Return on Assets	4.8%
Return on Equity	9.9%
Reinvestment Rate	7.6%
Price/Earnings Ratio	15.7x
Price/Book Value Ratio	1.5x
Dividend Yield	1.4%
Dividend Payout	22.1%

Accounting Practices

Acct. Standards: US STANDARDS (GAAP)

Acct. for Goodwill: AMORTIZED

Consol. Practices: ALL SUBSIDIARIES ARE CONSOLIDATED

Contingent Liab.: NONE REPORTED

Deferred Taxes: YES

Deprec. Method: ACCELERATED DEPRECIATION

Discretionary Reserves: NOT USED

EPS Numerator: NET INCOME AFTER PREFERRED DIVIDENDS

Fin. Stat. Cost Basis: HISTORICAL COST ENTIRELY

Foreign Curr. Gain/Los: TAKEN TO INCOME STMT AND/OR SHAREHOLDERS' EQUITY

Funds Definition: MODIFIED CASH

Inventory Cost Method: LIFO

Marketable Securities: LOWER OF COST OR MARKET

Minority Interest: BEFORE BOTTOM LINE ON INCOME STATEMENT; EXCLUDED FROM SHAREHOLDERS' EQUITY

Treas. Stock Gain/Loss: TAKEN TO SHAREHOLDERS' EQUITY

Financial Services. In addition to the information made publicly available by a company, investors also may have recourse to commercial financial services that tabulate information for a large number of corporations and compile it in an easily usable form. Such digests normally include more detail than is contained in news announcements, but less than is found in quarterly and annual reports. An example of commercial financial service information is presented in Exhibit 13–2. Companies like Moody's, Standard & Poor's, and Value Line provide this type of information.

Comparative Summary of Financial Report Characteristics

Exhibit 13–3 provides a summary of our discussion of different types of financial reports. Sometimes nonfinancial information such as the discovery of additional oil reserves or final approval of a breakthrough pharmaceutical product is covered in news announcements and SEC filings, but not in formal financial statements. The bottom row of Exhibit 13–3 covers Chapter Fourteen materials and should be referred to after study of that chapter.

FINANCIAL ANALYSIS

Investment Decision Perspective

The nature of the decision to invest in a business is simple in principle. In practice, however, it is a formidable challenge. The investment decision is an important, pervasive, and yet relatively definable kind of decision problem whose solution entails financial analysis of a variety of items from corporate annual reports. We will use the investment decision problem to illustrate the decision relevance of information from financial reports.

Business investment decisions begin with the task of specifying future cash flows (see Chapter Two). For the prospective owner, this task is quite open-ended. For the prospective creditor, the task is simplified somewhat by the typical cash flow specifications in contracts. On the other hand, both the creditor and the owner need to assess the risk associated with expected cash flows, because the greater the risk associated with a given future cash flow, the less it will be valued by either creditor or owner, other things equal. The need for risk assessment means that in addition to forecasting future cash flows, thought must also be given to the likelihood that the forecast flows will or will not materialize. Thus investors face the task of looking into the future and making fairly complex predictions about the amounts and probabilities of the cash payments the enterprise will be able to make to them in fulfillment of their rights as owners or creditors.

The ultimate objective of this forecasting-analysis process for the investor is the selection of a portfolio of investments with the optimum ratio of return to risk. Therefore, a representative decision model for the investor includes two major elements: (1) *expected return* (future cash flows); and (2) *expected risk*.

EXHIBIT 13–3

Comparative Summary of Financial Report Characteristics

Characteristics \ Reports	Corporate Annual Reports	Interim Financial Reports	SEC Reports	News Announcements	Commercial Financial Services
Timing of release	Annually	Quarterly for larger corporations	10-K annually, 10-Q quarterly; other reports when specified economic activities occur	At intervals throughout year (usually at least quarterly)	Usually monthly or quarterly, plus special reports
Scope of distribution	Shareholders (generally available to public on request)	Shareholders	SEC offices (available to public on request)	Newswire services; financial press	Available by subscription (and in many libraries)
Comprehensiveness of information	Extensive	Somewhat summarized	Most comprehensive source of information	Highly abbreviated	Somewhat summarized
Formality of report requirements	Relatively formal (compliance with generally accepted accounting principles)	Less formal than annual report	Highly formal (requirements imposed by SEC)	Few formal requirements	Based on source data formality
Level of assurance expressed by independent auditors	High (opinion audit)	Limited (review only)	High (opinion audit)	None	None

338

Estimating Investment Decision Factors from Financial Report Information

The use of information from corporate financial reports to estimate the expected return and the risk of an investment decision depends upon the assumption that historical data are relevant to future expectations. We have addressed this issue previously in developing the rationale for the conventional accounting model (see Chapters Three, Four, and Twelve). While many aspects of an enterprise's activities (like its product lines, production processes, etc.) change over time, many other aspects remain constant or change slowly. The immediate past thus provides a context in which to consider future possibilities.

In Chapter Six we introduced statistical procedures in connection with the calculation of price level indexes. Similar procedures apply to the development of financial statistics from financial reports.

Before considering the specific financial statistics that may be helpful in assessing investment alternatives, we first need to consider some general properties of these financial statistics. In one sense, the dollar values in corporate financial reports represent merely "numbers" with limited meaning and significance in themselves. Meaning and significance come from and depend upon an understanding of (1) the business environment which the numbers represent; (2) the relationship of the numbers to the underlying economic transactions and events that are the real items of interest; (3) the relationship of any particular number or set of numbers to other numbers included in the report; and (4) the relationships of the figures to previous years' performance and to performance of similar companies.

Example 13–1 | The High Profit Corporation reported net income for 1991 of $100,000. This measure in itself does provide some information to the investor in that it suggests a potential level of cash-generating ability that is relevant to the investment decision. However, the investor is interested in a broader, more comprehensive, measure of the corporation's performance as a basis for predicting future performance. In particular, given the amount of investment that the High Profit Corporation had in its productive facilities for the period, does the $100,000 represent good or bad performance? Additionally, how does the $100,000 reported profit stand compared with previous profits that the firm has generated or with profits or productivity by other firms in the same industry?

The questions raised in Example 13–1 suggest two important requirements for interpretation: (1) *scaling* of the reported, unadjusted "numbers," and (2) base figures, or *standards*, indicating performance over time (time standards) and by similar companies (industry standards).

Scaling. Scaling is the process of relating one number to another number based upon a presumably important relationship between the numbers. In Example 13–1, the matter addressed in the first question is the relationship, or ratio, between the net income for the year and the investment required to generate this return. By combining these two measures into a ratio, the investor generates a new measure of an important relationship—return on investment.

Time and Industry Standards. In addition to developing ratios, the investor is interested in the relationship between numbers (or ratios) and some standard.

Two standards of general interest to investors are *time standards* and *industry standards*. Time standards use numbers (or ratios) from preceding time periods so that the investor can assess the progress of the firm in relationship to prior performance.

Example 13–2 | Assuming capital investment is constant, if the High Profit Corporation had reported profits of $60,000 and $80,000 in 1989 and 1990, respectively, the $100,000 profit reported in 1991 suggests a continued improvement in the performance of the corporation *relative to its past performance*. A different picture would emerge if the reported profits for the preceding years had been $140,000 and $120,000.

Because time standards are important in evaluating the reported numbers for any particular time period, present accounting policy calls for the inclusion of data from the preceding period in corporate financial reports. In many instances a corporation also reports selected numbers from past financial reports for periods of five to ten years.

Industry standards use the performance of other business enterprises for comparison. In some cases, the standards are developed from the financial representations of all other corporations. More frequently, the standards represent norms developed from other corporations within the same industry.

Example 13–3 | If scaling produced a measure of return on investment of 10 percent ($100,000 net income divided by $1 million investment in production facilities), the investor still needs additional information regarding the level of performance implicit in this measure. If the average performance in this industry was an 8 percent return on investment, the investor might conclude that the management of High Profit Corporation was performing better than the industry norm. On the other hand, if the average return on investment in the industry was 12 percent, the particular investment alternative might not seem as desirable.

Because of the importance of industry norms, commercial financial services make them available to interested investors.

Statistical Measures

In analyzing the information provided in corporate financial reports, analysts have developed a number of statistical measures, or indicators, that they commonly use as a basis for reaching general estimates of expected risk and return factors. We briefly consider a few of the more important indicators to illustrate the analysis procedure. These indicators are grouped under the two decision factors, risk and return. However, the reader should be aware that the indicators often have implications for both decision factors.

The statistical measures (or indicators) introduced and illustrated in the remainder of this chapter use numbers from the *1989 Annual Report* of Caterpillar Inc. as reprinted in the Appendix to the chapter. Notice that the consolidated statement of cash flows was prepared on the indirect method and that Note 12 to the financial statements reports unaudited data. In 1989, 53 percent of Caterpillar's consolidated sales were outside the U.S. They received an unqualified opinion (refer to Chapter Fourteen) from their independent auditors.

Indicators of Return

The investor's principal interest in analyzing the returns of various investment alternatives is to compare rates of return. Hence investors are interested in several indicators of return. The general statistical measures of return reviewed here are (1) earnings per share and earnings yield; (2) net income to equity and/or assets; and (3) net income to sales (revenues).

Earnings per Share (EPS) and Earnings Yield. One indication of potential return is the earnings that will accrue to the investor's benefit. Thus the number of shares he or she possesses relative to the total number of shares outstanding can be scaled in terms of net income (or profit) as follows:

$$\text{Earnings per share} = \frac{\text{Net income accruing to common stock}}{\text{Total shares of common stock outstanding}}$$

$$= \frac{\$497,000,000}{101,418,773}$$

$$= \$4.90 \text{ per share}$$

EPS is the earnings attributable to each share of common stock, with the dividend requirements on any preferred stock (which does not share to any greater extent than the amount to which it has preference) deducted from net income in arriving at the income available to common-stock holders. Since Caterpillar does not have any outstanding preferred stock, no adjustment for dividend requirements on preferred stock is necessary in the calculation of earnings per share.

The calculation of earnings per share is complicated further when the firm has a capital structure that includes stock options, or bonds and/or preferred stock that are convertible into common stock. In this circumstance, the number of shares of common stock outstanding can increase, often substantially, should the holders of these convertible securities exercise their conversion options. The issue this poses for the EPS calculation is whether or not the number of common shares "outstanding" in the denominator of the ratio should be adjusted to reflect the conversion possibility. Current accounting policy provides for such an adjustment, but in a two-stage process. If, at date of issuance, the convertible security is determined to derive a "significant" portion of its market value from its conversion feature, it is considered "common-stock equivalent." Then the common shares that would be issued upon conversion are added to the common shares actually outstanding and EPS is labeled "primary earnings per share." If a convertible security at date of issuance does not meet the test of a common-stock equivalent, then the potentially issuable common shares are not included in the calculation of primary earnings per share. Hence the primary earnings-per-share statistic represents an upper bound on earnings per share generated for the period, as it is presumed to be unlikely that fewer shares of common stock will be outstanding in the future.

However, the convertible securities that are not classified as common-stock equivalents still may be converted at some future date. Therefore, a second earnings-per-share statistic, labeled "fully diluted earnings per share," also is calculated. In this calculation all the outstanding convertible securities are assumed to be converted into common stock, and the number of common shares that would be issued is added to the common shares actually outstanding in the denominator of the EPS ratio. The fully diluted earnings per share represents a lower bound on earnings per common share outstanding, as it is presumed unlikely that any more shares could be outstanding.

Application of these general principles involves many detailed operational rules, including specific tests for determining common-stock equivalents, procedures for modifying the numerator of the ratio consistent with the assumptions made in the denominator, and so forth. Examination of these rules is left to a more advanced course in accounting. It is sufficient for our purposes to note that for firms with a complex capital structure, the income statement will include the calculated values for both primary earnings per share and fully diluted earnings per share.

To relate EPS more directly to expected return, EPS may be divided by the price of a share of stock. The resulting statistical measure represents the current "earnings yield" on the required monetary investment. Customarily, cash dividends are subtracted from EPS to arrive at this yield. For Caterpillar 1989, we have EPS of $4.90 and cash dividends per common share of $1.20. Common stock price ranges were reported as follows on page 28 of the *1989 Annual Report*:

	1989			*1988*	
Quarter	*High*	*Low*		*High*	*Low*
First	69	$56\frac{1}{8}$		$67\frac{5}{8}$	$55\frac{7}{8}$
Second	$64\frac{5}{8}$	57		$68\frac{1}{2}$	$58\frac{3}{8}$
Third	66	$56\frac{7}{8}$		$67\frac{3}{4}$	$53\frac{7}{8}$
Fourth	62	$52\frac{7}{8}$		$64\frac{3}{4}$	57

On a 1989 low of $53 per share and a corresponding high of $69, the average is 61. Hence

$$\text{Earnings yield} = \frac{\text{Adjusted EPS}}{\text{Average annual share price}}$$

$$= \frac{(\$4.90 - \$1.20)}{\$61}$$

$$= 6.1\%$$

Net Income to Owners' Equity and/or Assets. As suggested in Example 13–1, the performance of a corporation is often judged in terms of the investment required to generate a particular return. Performance in this sense is an indicator of the efficiency of capital employed by the firm.

This type of return indicator is calculated by dividing net income for the period by the firm's capital investment. Two investment bases are customarily used: total assets and owners' equity (net assets). (Note: Since the purpose of return indicators is to show the efficiency of capital utilized *during* the period, the average levels of total assets or owners' equity are used).

When the total value of a firm's assets is used as the investment base, the return measure reflects the percentage return that the corporation generates on its total asset commitment, *regardless of the source of the investment* (i.e., whether from creditors or owners). This general measure of earning power is important in assessing the performance of two or more companies having different mixes of debt and owners' equity. The ratio of return to total assets is calculated as follows (amounts in millions of dollars):

$$\text{Return on assets} = \frac{\text{Net income} + \text{Interest expense}}{\text{Average total assets}}$$

$$= \frac{\$497 + \$251}{.5(\$10,926 + \$9,686)}$$

$$= 7.3\%$$

Since return on assets should be independent of the source of funds, the measure should not include the cost of the various types of financing. The interest expense of $251 million is therefore added back to net income. (Note that the $121 million of interest expense of financial subsidiaries is *not* added back since it is an operating as opposed to a financing cost of these subsidiary companies.) We have not attempted here to adjust for the income tax effect of interest expense, although a more precise calculation would do so.

Investors are also interested in the return to them as holders of common stock. In this case the denominator of the return-on-investment ratio is owners' equity (net assets), and the numerator is the net income accruing to owners. Note that in contrast to the return-on-assets ratio, we essentially exclude the value of assets supplied by creditors from the denominator and the interest paid to the creditors from the numerator.

The ratio of return to owners' equity is calculated for Caterpillar 1989 as follows:

$$\text{Return on owners' equity} = \frac{\text{Net income}}{\text{Average owners' equity}}$$

$$= \frac{\$497}{.5(\$4,474 + \$4,113)}$$

$$= 11.6\%$$

This measure of return reflects the scaled return accruing to shareholders on their contributed capital. It is larger than the return on assets because the return on total assets is larger than the cost of all the liabilities. This phenomenon is known as the *leverage effect*.

Net Income to Sales (Revenues). Another indicator of a firm's return efficiency is the ratio of net income for the year to total sales. It indicates the amount of profit that is generated from each dollar of sales. For our example, this is calculated as follows:

$$\text{Net income to sales} = \frac{\text{Net income}}{\text{Sales (revenues)}}$$

$$= \frac{\$497}{\$11,126}$$

$$= 4.5\%$$

For every dollar of sales (revenues), the expenses of producing this inflow amount to approximately 95.5 cents. The residual return accruing to the owners of the business is 4.5 cents.

Whether a particular return for a dollar of revenue is good or bad depends, of course, upon the total volume of revenue that a firm generates, as well as the investment required to generate this level of revenue. The net-income-to-revenue statistic is related to the return on investment (i.e., investment by owners) through the following relationship:

$$\text{Return on owners' equity} = \frac{\text{Net income}}{\text{Sales (revenues)}} \times \frac{\text{Sales (revenues)}}{\text{Average owners' equity}}$$

$$= \frac{\$497}{\$11,126} \times \frac{\$11,126}{.5(\$4,474 + \$4,113)}$$

$$= 4.5\% \quad\quad \times 2.6$$

$$= 11.7\%$$

The reasoning behind this equation is that the revenue-to-owners'-equity ratio indicates the number of times that the total owners' investment "turns over" during the year. Thus, if the firm earns 4.5 percent on each dollar of revenue, and the total investment of the owners is turned over 2.6 times per year, the total return on owners' equity is 2.6 times the return on revenue. Obviously, for firms that turn over total investment frequently (such as the grocery-chain industry), a lower profit per dollar of sales can be sustained while generating a reasonably good return on total investment. On the other hand, a firm that has a slow turnover of investment (such as a jewelry retailer) may require a higher return on each dollar of revenue in order to maintain a similar return on investment.

Indicators of Risk

Measures frequently used to estimate expected risk include: (1) current and acid-test ratios; (2) debt-equity ratio; and (3) times interest earned.

Current and Acid-Test Ratios. An important indicator of the potential riskiness of an investment is the company's short-term solvency, which is the ability to pay bills when due. Two different ratios are used as indicators of short-term solvency: the current ratio and the acid-test (or quick assets) ratio.

The current ratio is determined in the following manner:

$$\text{Current ratio} = \frac{\text{Current assets}}{\text{Current liabilities}}$$

$$= \frac{\$5,708}{\$3,904}$$

$$= 1.46:1$$

This ratio indicates that for each $1.00 of current liabilities, there are $1.46 in current assets to "back it up." The larger this ratio is, the less the risk of default and bankruptcy or takeover by the creditors (other things being equal).

The current assets in the numerator of the current ratio include, of course, the total value of inventories. In many cases, inventories are not readily available for settlement of liabilities. Therefore, a more stringent indicator of short-term solvency is determined by including only cash, marketable securities, and accounts receivable in the assets available to satisfy the current liabilities. This group of assets is referred to as quick assets, that is, those susceptible to fairly quick conversion into cash without any substantial loss in value. The acid-test ratio is determined as follows:

$$\text{Acid-test ratio} = \frac{\text{Quick assets}}{\text{Current liabilities}}$$

$$= \frac{\$2,961}{\$3,904}$$

$$= 0.76:1$$

This ratio means that for each $1.00 of current liabilities, there are $0.76 in quick assets available to satisfy it.

Debt to Assets Ratio. Another indication of the relative riskiness of a corporation is provided by the relationship between funds provided by creditors and funds provided by owners. The higher the percentage of funds provided by creditors, the potentially more risky the investment is in terms of its solvency. For our example, the debt to assets ratio for Caterpillar 1989 is:

$$\text{Debt to assets ratio} = \frac{\text{Total liabilities}}{\text{Total assets}}$$

$$= \frac{\$\ 6,452}{\$10,926}$$

$$= 59.1\%$$

Creditors of all types supplied 59.1 percent of the assets for Caterpillar, and the owners supplied 40.9 percent.

Since current liabilities may fluctuate in amount and may not represent permanent investment or capitalization, they may be excluded from creditor-supplied funds. In this case we obtain a measure of the firm's *long-term capitalization*:

Long-term liabilities	$2,548	36.3%
Owners' equity	$4,474	63.7%
	$7,022	100.0%

The debt to assets ratio, or alternatively the long-term capitalization of the firm, is important in an overall assessment of the riskiness of the particular investment to shareholders (or additional creditors whose claims would be subordinated to present creditors). It is also an indicator of potential return on investment. The larger the amount of funds supplied by creditors, the *potentially* larger the return that might accrue to the owners (in good times) from the leverage effect (noted earlier in this chapter when return on owners' equity was discussed). Thus, in assessing a firm's debt to assets ratio, the investor is confronted with a trade-off between the risk of having additional debt and the potentially high return on a smaller investment by the owners.

Times Interest Earned. The final indicator of risk examined here is the extent to which interest requirements are covered by net income. The larger the net income in relationship to contractual interest requirements, the smaller the possibility that the firm will be unable to make interest payments as they come due. On the other hand, if net income is not much larger than interest obligations, there is a good chance of insolvency, and thus a higher degree of general risk.

This measure utilizes income before interest and income tax expenses since that is the amount available to pay interest obligations. (Refer also to the discussion earlier in this chapter of return on assets.)

$$\text{Times interest earned} = \frac{\text{Before-tax income} + \text{Interest expense}}{\text{Interest expense}}$$

$$= \frac{\$621 + \$251}{\$251}$$

$$= 3.47$$

Here the required interest payments are covered by earnings amounting to 3.47 times the dollar amount of the interest requirement.

Some Limitations of Financial Ratios. We could continue to develop other relationships between various measures included in the financial statements. But the ratios covered illustrate the way in which the total package of financial information can be used to estimate decision factors.

One important point that should be kept firmly in mind is that each of the ratios is essentially evaluated in a *ceteris paribus* mode. That is, the interpretation of any single statistic in terms of evaluating its desirability or lack of desirability is based upon the assumption that all other measures remain constant. In point of fact, whether a higher or a lower value is desirable for any single statistic is a function of the values for all related financial statistics and all other sources of information about the enterprise as well.

Another important point is the effect of conventional accounting measurement policy on the extent to which financial ratios reflect underlying economic relationships. Present-day financial reports contain mixtures of unexpired original transaction amounts of assets and liabilities. Such values impose limitations on the usefulness of ratios in at least two respects: (1) Current market values may relate better to the intended information of a particular ratio—for example, the average efficiency of capital employed in a business might best be measured by the ratio of current-cost-based net income to total assets; and (2) the dollars of various original transaction amounts (established at various times in the past) do not represent the same economic sacrifice as time passes and the general level of prices changes.

These and other limitations (brought out in the next section) on the use of statistics based on present-day financial reports serve to emphasize again the complex information-processing problem faced by investors trying to assess the expected returns and risk associated with investments in business enterprises.

THE COMPARABILITY QUESTION

A key issue in the analysis of the financial reports (and financial statistics or ratios) of several investment alternatives is the comparability of the data over time and between firms. Generally, comparisons both with the past and with other firms are used in analyzing a particular company's data. Indeed, between-firm comparisons are at the heart of assessing the relative values of alternative investment opportunities. Whether or not actual comparisons are useful, however, is another matter—depending on the comparability of the accounting methods used by each firm and the particular situations.

Comparability Over Time

Comparability *over time* (i.e., stability in whatever relationship exists between accounting data and economic circumstances) is enhanced through the application of the same accounting policies each year. Accordingly, present accounting policy includes the *consistency principle*. It urges the use of the same accounting policies by a given firm from one time period to the next (assuming circumstances have not changed). In those instances when an accounting policy is changed, the consistency principle calls for prominent disclosure of the change and the dollar impact on affected items. Thus, although a corporation may choose among alternative accounting policies to value its resources and obligations, one can assume that the choices have been consistently applied over time unless there is a specific indication of a change. And when such a change is made, some information is provided to facilitate the modifications necessary for the investor to reconstruct comparable financial statements.

Comparability Between Firms

The question of comparability between firms, unfortunately, is not as well settled as that of comparability over time. Different firms in different industries, and in many cases within the same industry, use different accounting methods. This diversity creates a serious problem for the investor in comparing different companies. One obvious solution would be for appropriate policy makers (FASB or SEC) to require the uniform application of one approved set of accounting methods—either by all companies or within particular industries.

Notwithstanding its intuitive appeal, this solution also has its drawbacks. Although many measurement problems and situations appear to be similar, in most cases they are not identical. Hence there may be merit in allowing management some flexibility in choosing accounting policies that best represent the financial affairs of the firm. At present, the trade-off between the advantages and disadvantages of uniformity and flexibility has been resolved in favor of substantial flexibility for management. Accordingly, the external decision maker must adapt to this situation when making comparisons between companies.

Enhancing Comparability Between Firms

In seeking comparability across companies, the investment decision maker or financial analyst may wish to make some adjustments to the data included in the various financial reports. To facilitate this adjustment process, certain actions have been taken by accounting policy-making bodies. First, "full disclosure" of all important facts has long been a financial reporting rule and a legal requirement embodied in the securities acts of 1933 and 1934. Additionally, the interpretation of what constitutes important relevant information has been increasingly broadened by the FASB and the SEC. The investor now receives a large amount of supplementary information which may be helpful in reconciling differences in accounting methods between firms (see also Chapter Twelve).

A second adaptation to the need for comparability between firms is the elimination of some alternative accounting policies. While the accounting profession, and the business community, do not seem prepared at this time to accept *uniform* accounting methods, there is considerable consensus that the number of acceptable alternatives should be reduced. To the extent that a reduction of alternatives is achieved, the investor's adjustment process is simplified.

As long as management continues to have some flexibility in choosing the accounting policies to be used in preparing financial reports, however, it seems reasonable that investors will want some type of independent review (audit) of management's choices. Audits are provided by independent certified public accountants. The manner in which audits are undertaken, and some of the standards employed by the auditor, are the subject of the next chapter. Suffice it to say at this point that the auditing process is an important and integral part of the corporate financial reporting process.

SUMMARY

Periodic financial statements are a direct product of many financial accounting methods and accounting policy applications. They are also key components of financial reports, which expand and analyze financial statement information. Financial reports are important tools for investors when they evaluate companies for investment decision purposes.

Various types of financial reports are available. Corporate annual reports and their typical components are discussed in the chapter, as are summary annual reports, interim reports, SEC regulatory reporting requirements, press announcements, and information available from commercial financial services. The characteristics of the various types of financial reports are assessed and summarized.

From an investment decision perspective, expected return and expected risk are the major factors that must be analyzed. Information from financial reports assists in such analysis. Various financial statistics can be prepared, but the general properties of such statistics must be understood to ensure proper use. Financial ratios are customary statistical measures of investment decision factors.

The general measures of expected return which are presented include earnings per share and earnings yield, net income to owners' equity and total assets, and net income to sales (revenues). As indicators of expected risk, current and acid-test ratios, the debt-equity ratio, and times interest earned are presented. The chapter concludes with a discussion of comparability of financial report information over time and between firms.

Questions for Review and Discussion

13–1. Define or explain

    a. Corporate annual report
    b. Summary annual report
    c. Notes to financial statements
    d. Interim financial report
    e. 10-K and 10-Q
    f. News announcements
    g. Commercial financial services
    h. Expected return
    i. Expected risk
    j. Scaling
    k. Industry standards
    l. Consistency principle

13–2. There are four groups who use corporate financial reports regularly and heavily. Identify each group and describe briefly why each relies on corporate financial reports.

13–3. Interim financial reports are typically considered less reliable and more abbreviated than annual financial reports. Why then might the investor find interim reports useful in evaluating investment alternatives?

13–4. Rank the financial information reports provided by a company (annual report, etc.) according to the following criteria:

    a. Level of detail (comprehensiveness)
    b. Scope of distribution
    c. Formality or rigidity of reporting requirements
    d. Frequency of release

13–5. What are the major elements in a representative decision model for an investor?

13–6. "*Expected* return is a crucial factor of the investment decision. Accounting reports are historical in nature. Therefore, accounting reports are useless in the investment decision." Comment.

13–7. "Since it is impossible for the average investor to earn an above-average return on investments, brokerage houses can provide no useful financial information to the potential investor." Comment.

13–8. The meaning and significance of "numbers" reflected in corporate annual reports depend upon an understanding of several different variables and relationships. What are these critical factors.

13–9. Why is it important to scale the numbers reported in corporate annual reports?

13–10. What are the two main classes of standards used in interpreting financial statements, and how are they useful?

13–11. What are accountants or financial analysts attempting to measure or describe when they calculate various financial statistics? Are the financial statistics sufficient for this task, or is additional information necessary?

13–12. What usually is the *minimum* number of years for which financial data are included in a company's annual report? Why is this a minimum (i.e., why not include data only for the current year)?

13–13. What are the major classifications of financial statistics? Are these classifications mutually exclusive? Why or why not?

13–14. The naive interpretation of many financial statistics implies that "higher is better, lower is worse." However, such a sweeping generalization is incorrect. For example, a high current ratio may imply an unwarranted buildup in inventory, and the buildup in inventory may be a sign of an unfavorable situation in the future.

For each of the following statistics, given an example, if possible, of a high value that might *not* be interpreted favorably (or might have *unfavorable* connotations as well as a favorable interpretation):

a. EPS
b. Return on assets
c. Return on owners' equity
d. Net income to sales
e. Current ratio
f. Acid-test ratio
g. Debt-equity ratio
h. Times interest earned

13–15. "The problem of comparability between firms would be settled if a national uniform set of accounts were required for all industrial corporations (similar to the set of accounts prescribed by the Federal Power Commission for utilities under its jurisdiction)." Comment.

Problems

13–1. Analyzing Financial Statements. Using the financial statements contained in Caterpillar's 1989 annual report (found in the Appendix to this chapter):

1. Calculate the eight financial ratios listed in question 13–14 for 1988. (Use *year-end* amounts of total assets and owners' equity, since *average* amounts for 1988 are not available).

2. From resources in your business administration library, find the average annual share price of Caterpillar common stock for last year. Also find the EPS and cash dividends for the same year. On the basis of this information, what was the company's earnings yield for that year?

3. Calculate Caterpillar's owners' equity turnover for 1988 and 1989. Explain briefly how these turnover statistics relate to the indicator "return on owners' equity."

13–2. Interpreting Financial Ratios. Refer to the eight financial ratios calculated for 1988 in the previous problem.

1. Compare the return on assets ratios with the return on owners' equity ratios. Is any leverage effect present? Should Caterpillar leverage itself further? Be sure to explain your opinion adequately.

2. Find operating profit and sales statistics for Caterpillar's U.S. and outside-the-U.S. business. Which of these two business segments was more profitable in 1989?

3. From the viewpoint of an individual investor's decision making, is the expected risk of investing in Caterpillar common stock high, medium, or low? Please defend your answer by writing a paragraph in support of it.

13–3. Computing Financial Statistics. Condensed financial statements for Standard Corporation follow.

	(000s omitted)	
	1990	*1991*
Cash	$ 20	$ 15
Marketable securities	10	5
Accounts receivable	30	40
Inventory	50	70
Plant and equipment (net of depreciation)	290	370
	$400	$500
Current liabilities	$ 60	$ 80
Long-term debt	100	170
Owners' equity (10,000 shares outstanding)	240	250
	$400	$500
Sales		$480
Expenses:		
Cost of sales		320
Selling and administrative		70
Depreciation		20
Interest		10
Federal income taxes		30
		450
Net income for 1991		$ 30

Compute the financial statistics that may be used to evaluate the expected return and risk factors for Standard Corporation. Where the measures refer only to balance sheet relationships, calculate the statistics for both 1990 and 1991 (use year-end numbers only).

13–4. Calculating Financial Ratios. Here are certain data summarized from The Sting Stores' 1990 and 1991 financial statements. Calculate the following ratios for 1991:

1. EPS
2. Return on assets
3. Return on owners' equity
4. Current ratio
5. Times interest earned

	December 31	
	1990	*1991*
Current assets	$596	$628
Noncurrent assets	328	310
Total assets	$924	$938
Current liabilities	$298	$300
Noncurrent liabilities	168	158
Total liabilities	$466	$458
Common stock	$270	$290
Retained earnings	188	190
Total stockholders' equity	$458	$480
	$924	$938
Shares of stock outstanding	135	145

Sales	$4,366
Other revenues	32
Total revenues	$4,398
Cost of merchandise sold	$3,361
Interest expense	30
Taxes expense	51
Depreciation expense	307
Other expenses	616
Total expenses	$4,365
Net income	$ 33
Dividends	31
Increase in retained earnings	$ 2

13–5. Calculating Financial Ratios. The following data are summarized from Back Door's 1991 annual financial report. Calculate for 1991 the eight financial ratios listed in question 13–14 on page 350.

	December 31	
	1990	*1991*
Cash	$ 40	$ 50
Receivables	60	70
Merchandise inventory	200	220
Noncurrent assets	300	360
Total assets	$ 600	$ 700
Current liabilities	$ 50	$ 90
Noncurrent liabilities	150	130
Common stock	250	300
Retained earnings	150	180
	$ 600	$ 700
Shares of stock outstanding	250	300

Cash sales	$1,100	
Sales on account	500	
Other revenues	24	$1,624
Cost of merchandise sold	$ 830	
Salaries expense	500	
Depreciation expense	48	
Interest expense	9	
Other expenses	187	1,574
Net income		$ 50
Dividends		20
Increase in retained earnings		$ 30

13–6. Effect of Financial Leverage. Conservative Appliances, Inc., and Highly Leveraged Appliances Company both manufacture and distribute home appliances. Each company has total assets of $1 million, but Highly Leveraged Appliances Company has outstanding debt (current and long term) of $700,000; while Conservative Appliances, Inc., has no outstanding debt. The annual interest cost incurred by Highly Leveraged Appliances Company amounts to $50,000. For two consecutive years, the two companies earned the following rates of return on total assets (before considering interest expense):

Year	Return on Assets
1990	10%
1991	6%

Required:
1. Determine the net income for each company for each of the two years.
2. Determine the return on owners' equity for each company for each of the two years.
3. Explain the reason for the variation in performance (as measured by return on owners' equity) over the two years for the two companies, given that both earned the same return on assets deployed.
4. What factor(s) would be critical in choosing between the two companies as investment alternatives (assuming the price was the same)?

13–7. Relationship between Return on Owners' Equity and Net Income to Sales. For each independent case that follows, calculate the amount or percentage for each question mark.

Case	Sales	Net Income	Owners' Equity	Net Income to Sales (Percent)	"Investment" Turnover	Percent Return on Owners' Equity
1	$20,000	$ 2,000	$10,000	?	?	?
2	40,000	?	30,000	25	?	?
3	50,000	?	?	1	10	?
4	?	15,000	?	?	0.8	15
5	?	8,000	?	5	?	40
6	30,000	6,000	?	?	0.5	?
7	?	?	50,000	?	2	10
8	?	?	25,000	4	?	20
9	60,000	?	20,000	?	?	10
10	?	5,000	?	5	4	?

13–8. Effect of Transactions on Current and Acid-Test Ratios. The current asset and liability sections from a corporate balance sheet follow.

Current assests:
Cash	$ 150,000
Marketable securities	125,000
Accounts receivable	175,000
Inventory	500,000
Prepaid expenses	50,000
	$1,000,000

Current liabilities:
Accounts payable	300,000
Estimated federal income taxes payable	60,000
Accrued liabilities	40,000
	$ 400,000

For each of the following *independent* transactions, indicate whether the current ratio and the acid-test ratio would be *increased*, *decreased*, or *unaffected* after the transaction.

1. Collected $75,000 on account from customers.
2. Paid $80,000 on account to suppliers.
3. Borrowed $100,000 on a 90-day note.
4. Paid the federal income tax liability.
5. Sold the marketable securities for $125,000.
6. Purchased new equipment for the plant costing $200,000, and signed a 180-day installment contract with the seller.
7. Purchased inventory of $100,000 on account.
8. Purchased inventory of $100,000 for cash.
9. Purchased $50,000 marketable securities for cash.
10. Recognized expense of $20,000 from the prepaid expense account.

13–9. **Ratio Changes When Equipment Is Leased Rather than Purchased.** On December 31, 1990, Romex Ltd. bought $3,000 of equipment with an expected 10-year service life and no scrap value on retirement. The firm financed this purchase by issuing three $1,000, 12% notes payable, principal and interest of which are due on January 3, 1992, January 2, 1993, and January 2, 1994, respectively. From the following summaries of the firm's 1991 financial statements, calculate its December 31, 1991, debt-equity ratio. For the year 1991, calculate EPS, return on assets, return on owners' equity, net income to sales, and times interest earned.

| | *December 31* | |
	1990	*1991*
Total assets	$22,000	$24,000
Total liabilities	$14,000	$15,000
Stockholders' equity	8,000	9,000
	$22,000	$24,000
Shares of common stock outstanding	1,000	1,000
Sales		$41,310
Cost of goods sold	$23,050	
Salaries expense	11,700	
Depreciation expense	1,260	
Interest expense	470	
Other expenses	3,830	40,310
Net income		$ 1,000

Suppose instead that Romex Ltd. rented this equipment at a rate of $55 per month, paying on the last day of each month (with no prepayment).

1. Recalculate the summaries of the firm's 1991 financial statements.
2. Recalculate the firm's 1991 ratios as specified in the first part of this problem.
3. What general effect does leasing have upon a firm's ratios?

13–10. **Evaluating Long-Term Capitalization Structures.** C. Madelyn Panozzo, chief executive officer of the Ytel Corporation, is studying alternative means of financing a new 100-percent-owned subsidiary that is being set up to market a new soft drink. The total investment required is $2 million, and the return on assets (before interest costs) is expected to range between 5 percent and 15 percent.

Three alternative financing plans are under consideration:

	Long-Term Debt	*Common Stock*
Plan I	80%	20%
Plan II	50	50
Plan III	20	80

The interest rate on long-term debt issued by the subsidiary will be 10 percent. Whichever plan is selected, Ytel Corporation will furnish the total funds for the common stock and will therefore be a 100 percent owner of the equity interest in the subsidiary.

Required:

1. To evaluate these financing alternatives, Ms. Panozzo asks you to prepare a schedule that depicts net income, return on owners' equity, and times interest earned for each plan, assuming a return on assets (before interest) of

   a. 5 percent
   b. 10 percent
   c. 15 percent

Ignore the effect of income taxes in your solution.

2. Comment on the risk-return trade-off in the alternative financing plans.

13–11. Using Risk and Return Indicators. Based on (1) the partial information appearing in the following balance sheet; (2) the "additional information" given; and (3) the definitions of the various return and risk indicators described in the chapter, determine the amounts of the missing numbers. Ignore income taxes.

Partial Information, Incorporated

Balance Sheet
As of December 31, 1991

Assets

Cash	$ 2,000,000
Accounts receivable	2,000,000
Marketable securities	?
Prepaid expenses	1,000,000
Inventory	?
Total current assets	$?
Plant and equipment (net)	?
Total assets	$?

Liabilities and Stockholders' Equity

Accounts payable	$?
Wages payable	1,500,000
Taxes payable	1,000,000
Total current liabilities	$?
6% Bonds payable	10,000,000
Total liabilities	$?
Stockholders' equity:	
Common stock, $1 stated value, 10,000,000 shares authorized;	
____?____ outstanding	$?
Paid in excess over stated value	8,000,000
Retained earnings	?
Total stockholders' equity	$?
Total liabilities and stockholders' equity	$?

Additional Information:

Expenses	$16,000,000
Times interest earned	$7\frac{2}{3}$
Current ratio	2:1
Debt-to-equity ratio	2:3
Acid-test ratio	1.2:1
Earnings per share	.50
Permanent capital: ¼ long-term debt;	
¾ stockholders' equity	

13–12. Accounting Policy Effects on Financial Ratios. Xcan Corporation and Canco, Inc., are in the same industry. Both had disappointing 1990 profits but did better in 1991. Their financial statements would have been identical had Canco not done two things on December 31, 1990, both of which are reflected in its "Other expenses."

1. Wrote down partly obsolete merchandise to a current market value $200 lower than cost. (It sold this merchandise in 1991).
2. Wrote off a $400 book value for standby equipment retired from active service since 1988 but retained for possible future use. Canco had been depreciating this equipment at a rate of $100 per year.

Assume that neither action had any tax consequences. Here are summaries of the two firms' financial statements. Both have had 500 shares of common stock outstanding since 1982.

	Xcan		Canco	
	December 31		December 31	
	1991	1990	1990	
Total assets	$ 9,500	$ 9,000	$ 8,400	(9,000 − 200
Total liabilities	$ 4,100	$ 4,000	$ 4,000	−400)
Stockholders' equity	5,400	5,000	4,400	(5,000 − 200
	$ 9,500	$ 9,000	$ 8,400	−400)

	Xcan		Canco	
	December 31		December 31	
	1991	1990	1990	
Revenues	$13,000	$11,000	$11,000	
Cost of goods sold	$ 4,700	$ 4,000	$ 4,000	
Salaries expense	4,000	3,900	3,900	
Depreciation expense	500	500	500	
Other expenses	3,200	3,000	3,600	(3,000 + 200
Total expenses	$12,400	$11,400	$12,000	+400)
Net income	$ 600	$ (400)	$ (1,000)	
Dividends	200	0	0	
Change in retained earnings	$ 400	$ (400)	$(1,000)	

1. Calculate summaries of Canco's 1991 financial statements. Explain.
2. Calculate both firms' 1991 EPS, return on owners' equity, and net income to sales ratios. Which firm shows superior ratios?
3. Which firm was the more profitable? After publication of their 1991 financial statements, which would you expect to appear the more attractive to investors? Explain.

Financial Report
(Excerpt from 1989 Annual Report, Caterpillar Inc.)
(A Summary Annual Report)

Consolidated Results of Operations

CATERPILLAR®

Years Ended December 31 *(Millions of dollars except per share data)*	*1989*	*1988*
Sales	$10,882	$10,255
Revenues of financial subsidiaries	244	180
Sales and revenues	11,126	10,435
Operating costs:		
Cost of goods sold	8,727	8,011
Selling, general, and administrative expenses:		
Excluding financial subsidiaries	1,242	1,153
Financial subsidiaries	96	89
Research and development expenses (note 2)	235	182
Interest expense of financial subsidiaries	121	76
	10,421	9,511
Operating profit	705	924
Interest expense — excluding financial subsidiaries	251	264
	454	660
Other income (note 4)	167	182
	621	842
Provision for income taxes (note 5)	162	262
Profit of consolidated companies	459	580
Equity in profit of affiliated companies (notes 1A and 6)	38	36
Profit	$ 497	$ 616
Profit per share of common stock	$ 4.90	$ 6.07
Dividends paid per share of common stock	$ 1.20	$ .75

See accompanying Condensed Notes to Consolidated Financial Statements.

*The accompanying financial statements and notes have been prepared by the
management of Caterpillar Inc. The notes have been condensed to make them more
readable. For more comprehensive financial information, refer to the financial
statements and notes in the appendix to the proxy statement.*

Consolidated Financial Position

December 31
(Dollars in millions)

	1989	1988
Assets		
Current assets:		
Cash and short-term investments	$ 148	$ 74
Receivables:		
Excluding financial subsidiaries	2,228	2,221
Financial subsidiaries	585	448
Refundable income taxes	87	114
Deferred income taxes and prepaid expenses	540	474
Inventories (note 1B)	2,120	1,986
Total current assets	5,708	5,317
Land, buildings, machinery, and equipment — net (note 1C)	3,505	2,909
Long-term receivables:		
Excluding financial subsidiaries	100	104
Financial subsidiaries	938	798
Investments in affiliated companies (notes 1A and 6)	302	288
Intangible assets	147	71
Other assets	226	199
Total assets	**$10,926**	**$ 9,686**
Liabilities		
Current liabilities:		
Short-term borrowings (note 7B):		
Excluding financial subsidiaries	$ 734	$ 656
Financial subsidiaries	624	416
Accounts payable and accrued expenses	1,550	1,495
Wages, salaries, and employee benefits	454	485
Dividends payable	30	30
Income taxes	164	118
Long-term debt due within one year (note 7C):		
Excluding financial subsidiaries	30	32
Financial subsidiaries	318	203
Total current liabilities	3,904	3,435
Long-term debt due after one year (note 7C):		
Excluding financial subsidiaries	1,797	1,428
Financial subsidiaries	491	525
Deferred income taxes and other liabilities	260	185
Total liabilities	**6,452**	**5,573**
Ownership		
Common stock of $1.00 par value (note 8):		
Authorized shares: 200,000,000		
Outstanding shares (1989 — 101,418,773 and		
1988 — 101,414,138) at paid-in amount	822	824
Profit employed in the business	3,560	3,184
Foreign currency translation adjustment	92	105
Total ownership	**4,474**	**4,113**
Total liabilities and ownership	**$10,926**	**$ 9,686**

See accompanying Condensed Notes to Consolidated Financial Statements.

Consolidated Statement of Cash Flows

CATERPILLAR®

Years Ended December 31 *(Millions of dollars)*	*1989*	*1988*
Cash flows from operating activities:		
Profit	$ 497	$ 616
Adjustments for noncash items:		
Depreciation and amortization	471	434
Other	(23)	(74)
Change in assets and liabilities:		
Receivables — excluding financial subsidiaries	(36)	(365)
Inventories	(137)	(598)
Accounts payable and accrued expenses	162	311
Other — net	(27)	51
Net cash provided by operating activities	907	375
Cash flows from investing activities:		
Expenditures for land, buildings, machinery, and equipment	(984)	(732)
Expenditures for equipment leased to others	(105)	(61)
Proceeds from disposals of land, buildings, machinery, and equipment	37	30
Investments in affiliated companies	(10)	(24)
Additions to financial subsidiaries' receivables	(947)	(833)
Collections of financial subsidiaries' receivables	660	411
Other — net	1	(78)
Net cash used for investing activities	(1,348)	(1,287)
Cash flows from financing activities:		
Dividends paid	(121)	(77)
Common shares issued, including treasury shares reissued	1	4
Treasury shares purchased	(9)	(86)
Proceeds from long-term debt issued:		
Excluding financial subsidiaries	363	30
Financial subsidiaries	289	341
Payments on long-term debt:		
Excluding financial subsidiaries	(38)	(264)
Financial subsidiaries	(207)	(34)
Short-term borrowings — net:		
Excluding financial subsidiaries	86	848
Financial subsidiaries	207	117
Net cash provided by financing activities	571	879
Effect of exchange rate changes on cash	(56)	(48)
Increase (decrease) in cash and short-term investments	$ 74	$ (81)

See accompanying Condensed Notes to Consolidated Financial Statements.

1. Summary of significant accounting policies

A. Basis of consolidation

The financial statements include the accounts of Caterpillar Inc. and all its subsidiaries.

Affiliated companies (50% interest or less) are accounted for by the equity method (note 6). Accordingly, the company's share of the affiliates' profit is included in Consolidated Results of Operations as "Equity in profit of affiliated companies" and the cost of the company's investments in these affiliates plus its share of their retained profits are included in the Consolidated Financial Position as "Investments in affiliated companies."

B. Inventories

With minor exceptions, inventories are stated on the basis of the LIFO (last-in, first-out) method of inventory valuation. LIFO was first adopted for the major portion of inventories in 1950.

If the FIFO (first-in, first-out) method had been in use, inventories would have been $1,828 million and $1,611 million higher than reported at December 31, 1989 and 1988, respectively.

C. Depreciation

Depreciation is computed principally using accelerated methods. If the straight-line method had always been used, "Land, buildings, machinery, and equipment—net" would have been $633 million and $596 million higher than reported at December 31, 1989 and 1988, respectively.

2. Research and engineering expenses

Research and engineering expenses include both "Research and development expenses" for new product development and charges to "Cost of goods sold" for ongoing efforts to improve existing products.

3. Pension and other retirement benefit plans

Caterpillar has pension plans covering almost all employees. These plans provide a benefit based on years of service and/or the employee's average earnings near retirement. Pension expense for 1989 was $56 million, compared with $6 million in 1988. At the most recent plan year-ends, the market value of plan assets exceeded the projected benefit obligation by $434 million.

Caterpillar also provides health care and life insurance benefits for nearly all retired employees. The cost of providing these benefits is charged against operations as claims are incurred. For 1989 and 1988, these costs totaled $75 million and $63 million, respectively.

4. Other income

The components of other income were as follows:

Years ended December 31
(Millions of dollars)

	1989	1988
Foreign exchange gains	$ 16	$ 49
Interest income	71	53
License fees	43	44
Miscellaneous income	37	36
	$167	$182

5. Income taxes

In 1989 and 1988, Caterpillar's effective income tax rate was 26% and 31%, respectively. The lower 1989 rate resulted from higher tax credits related to U.S. federal and state income taxes and a change in the geographic mix of where 1989 profit was earned.

6. Affiliated companies

Caterpillar's investments in affiliated companies consist principally of a 50% interest in Shin Caterpillar Mitsubishi Ltd., Japan ($283 million). The other 50% owner of this company is Mitsubishi Heavy Industries, Ltd., Japan.

Profit of affiliated companies for the years ended September 30 totaled $76 million on sales of $2,561 million in 1989 and $74 million on sales of $2,110 million in 1988. Net assets of affiliated companies at September 30, 1989 and 1988, were $604 million and $554 million, respectively.

7. Credit commitments and debt

A. Credit commitments

At December 31, 1989, Caterpillar had confirmed short-term credit lines totaling $2,077 million, of which $2,006 million was unused. In addition to these short-term credit lines, a three year revolving credit agreement totaling $500 million was entered into with a group of commercial banks during 1988. This agreement was extended in 1989 and now expires in 1992. It may be extended on an annual basis subject to mutual agreement. It is currently being used to provide support for the issuance of commercial paper. Based on this agreement, $500 million of commercial paper outstanding at December 31, 1989 and 1988, was classified as long-term debt due after one year.

B. Short-term borrowings

Short-term borrowings at December 31, 1989, consisted of $1,279 million commercial paper and $79 million notes payable to banks.

C. Long-term debt

Long-term debt, including that due within one year and classified as current, totaled $2,636 million at December 31, 1989. This includes $500 million of commercial paper outstanding at December 31, 1989, which was classified as long-term debt due after one year in conjunction with the revolving credit agreement. The aggregate amounts of maturities and sinking fund requirements of long-term debt during each of the years 1990 through 1994 are $348, $365, $449, $173, and $189 million, respectively.

8. Capital stock

In 1977 and 1987, stockholders approved stock option plans for officers and other key employees. Options granted under both plans carry prices equal to the market price on the date of the grant. Under these plans, 140,635 shares were issued in 1989, most of which were purchased on the open market. At December 31, 1989, 3,459,889 options were outstanding.

Caterpillar has a stock purchase rights plan designed to protect stockholders from certain takeover attempts.

9. Profit-sharing plans

For 1989 and 1988, Caterpillar charged operations $45 million and $76 million, respectively, for profit-sharing payments due eligible employees.

10. Financial subsidiaries

Caterpillar's investments in financial subsidiaries consist principally of an investment in Caterpillar Financial Services Corporation, which assists customers in acquiring Caterpillar and noncompetitive related equipment by offering a wide range of financing services.

Combined financial information of the financial subsidiaries, before consolidating entries, was as follows:

Years ended December 31
(Millions of dollars)

	1989	1988
Results of Operations		
Revenues	$ 244	$ 188
Operating costs:		
Selling, general, and administrative expenses	97	94
Interest expense	122	81
	219	175
Operating profit	25	13
Other income	7	6
	32	19
Provision for income taxes	11	5
Profit	$ 21	$ 14

December 31
(Millions of dollars)

	1989	1988
Financial Position		
Assets		
Current assets:		
Cash and short-term investments	$ 14	$ 8
Receivables	587	450
Total current assets	601	458
Equipment on operating leases — net	199	142
Long-term receivables	938	798
Other assets	130	64
Total assets	$1,868	$1,462
Liabilities		
Current liabilities:		
Short-term borrowings	$ 624	$ 416
Accounts payable and accrued expenses	138	73
Income taxes	7	1
Long-term debt due within one year	318	203
Total current liabilities	1,087	693
Long-term debt due after one year	491	525
Deferred income taxes	21	15
Total liabilities	1,599	1,233
Ownership	269	229
Total liabilities and ownership	$1,868	$1,462

11. Segment information
A. Business segments

Caterpillar designs, manufactures, and markets products in two principal business segments: *Machinery* (Earthmoving, Construction, and Materials Handling) and *Engines*. The financial subsidiaries (note 10) are included in the general corporate lines unless otherwise indicated.

Years ended December 31
(Millions of dollars)

	1989	1988
Sales:		
Machinery	$ 8,478	$ 8,206
Engines	3,067	2,666
Elimination of intersegment engine sales	(663)	(617)
Consolidated sales	10,882	10,255
Revenues of financial subsidiaries	244	180
Sales and revenues	$11,126	$10,435
Operating profit:		
Machinery	$ 733	$ 932
Engines	235	243
	968	1,175
General corporate expenses	(263)	(251)
Operating profit	$ 705	$ 924
Capital expenditures:		
Machinery	$ 694	$ 509
Engines	229	199
General corporate (includes equipment leased to others)	166	85
	$ 1,089	$ 793

December 31
(Millions of dollars)

	1989	1988
Identifiable assets:		
Machinery	$ 5,574	$ 5,020
Engines	2,188	1,972
	7,762	6,992
General corporate assets	2,862	2,406
Investments in affiliated companies	302	288
Total assets	$10,926	$ 9,686

B. Geographic segments

Information on Caterpillar's geographic segments is based on the location of the company's manufacturing operations. The financial subsidiaries (note 10) are included in the general corporate lines unless otherwise indicated.

Years ended December 31
(Millions of dollars)

	1989	1988
Sales from:		
United States	$ 8,109	$ 7,546
Europe	1,936	1,992
All other	1,183	1,112
Elimination of intersegment sales from:		
United States	(220)	(268)
Europe	(44)	(49)
All other	(82)	(78)
Consolidated sales	10,882	10,255
Revenues of financial subsidiaries	244	180
Sales and revenues	$11,126	$10,435
Operating profit:		
United States	$ 871	$ 1,111
Europe	17	(11)
All other	80	75
	968	1,175
General corporate expenses	(263)	(251)
Operating profit	$ 705	$ 924

December 31
(Millions of dollars)

	1989	1988
Identifiable assets:		
United States	$ 5,646	$ 5,171
Europe	1,248	1,059
All other	868	762
	7,762	6,992
General corporate assets	2,862	2,406
Investments in affiliated companies	302	288
Total assets	$10,926	$ 9,686

C. Non-U.S. sales

Sales outside the United States were 53% of consolidated sales for 1989 and 50% for 1988. This chart shows data on Caterpillar sales outside the United States based on dealer location.

Years ended December 31
(Millions of dollars)

	1989	1988
Sales of U.S. manufactured product:		
Europe	$ 693	$ 684
Asia/Pacific	1,002	781
Latin America	447	420
Canada	661	606
Africa/Middle East	488	439
	3,291	2,930
Sales of non-U.S. manufactured product:		
Europe	1,246	1,191
Asia/Pacific	470	332
Latin America	382	309
Canada	117	135
Africa/Middle East	244	281
	2,459	2,248
Total sales outside the United States:		
Europe	1,939	1,875
Asia/Pacific	1,472	1,113
Latin America	829	729
Canada	778	741
Africa/Middle East	732	720
	$5,750	$5,178

12. Selected quarterly financial results
(unaudited)

Financial data for interim periods were as follows:

(Millions of dollars except per share data)   **1989**

Quarters	1st	2nd	3rd	4th
Sales	$2,626	$2,984	$2,578	$2,694
Revenues of financial subsidiaries	54	57	65	68
Sales and revenues	2,680	3,041	2,643	2,762
Cost of goods sold	2,071	2,390	2,074	2,192
Gross margin*	555	594	504	502
Profit	141	141	108	107
Profit per share of common stock	$ 1.39	$ 1.39	$ 1.07	$ 1.05

(Millions of dollars except per share data)   **1988**

Quarters	1st	2nd	3rd	4th
Sales	$2,346	$2,556	$2,743	$2,610
Revenues of financial subsidiaries	36	46	46	52
Sales and revenues	2,382	2,602	2,789	2,662
Cost of goods sold	1,858	2,006	2,129	2,018
Gross margin*	488	550	614	592
Profit	118	145	190	163
Profit per share of common stock	$ 1.16	$ 1.44	$ 1.87	$ 1.61

*Gross margin excludes revenues and costs of financial subsidiaries.

In 1989, the company began reporting financial results based on calendar quarters rather than internally developed cutoff schedules. As a result, 1989 and 1988 quarters are not necessarily comparable.

Profit for the fourth quarter was $107 million or $1.05 per share. This compares with $163 million or $1.61 per share in the same quarter of 1988. Profit declined, despite higher sales and revenues, because of higher costs and a reduction in the profit of the company's affiliated companies.

Sales and revenues of $2.76 billion were up $100 million from the same period a year ago. The increase resulted from improved price realization and a $16 million rise in financial subsidiaries' revenues. Physical sales volume declined slightly.

Fourth-quarter costs were higher than 1988 because of higher material prices, wage and benefit increases, higher start-up costs for the factory modernization program, increased research and development costs for new and updated product programs, and higher depreciation expense.

Report of Independent Accountants

Price Waterhouse

To the stockholders of Caterpillar Inc.:

We have audited, in accordance with generally accepted auditing standards, the consolidated financial statements of Caterpillar Inc. and its subsidiaries as of December 31, 1989, 1988, and 1987, and for the years then ended. These statements appear in the appendix to the proxy statement for the 1990 annual meeting of the stockholders of Caterpillar Inc. and have not been presented herein. In our report dated January 18, 1990, which also appears in the appendix to the proxy statement, we expressed an unqualified opinion on those consolidated financial statements. In our opinion, the information in the accompanying condensed consolidated financial statements appearing on pages 18 through 24, is fairly stated in all material respects in relation to the consolidated financial statements from which it was derived.

Price Waterhouse

Peoria, Illinois

January 18, 1990

Auditing

The earlier chapters of this book demonstrate how decision-relevant accounting information is produced by financial accounting. Now we address the question of the general reliability of this information. In so doing, our focus shifts from aspects of quantity and types of information to the quality of information. Quality of information generally is improved when completely independent and competent outside experts examine it and attest to its reliability, fairness, and other important characteristics. Investors have a large stake in such attestation, because it enables them to make decisions with better expected outcomes.

Certified Public Accountants (CPAs) perform most of the independent examinations (audits) of financial statements in the United States. According to occupational data from the U.S. Census, a total of 993,327 accountants and auditors were employed in the economy in 1980. This total excludes bookkeepers and other semiprofessionals. The 1980 total compares with 637,761 in 1970; 471,302 in 1960; and 378,055 in 1950. Thus the U.S. accounting profession has been growing at a much faster rate than the population of the United States. *Accounting Today*, a semimonthly accounting newspaper, reported in its October 23, 1989 edition that the demand for accountants will increase 40 percent during the 1990s. This estimated increase exceeds comparable estimates for all other professions. The U.S. Bureau of Labor Statistics conducted the study which produced these estimates.

The CPA Profession

CPA certificates, along with state licenses to practice as independent auditors, are issued by the individual states and territories. The issuing agency is normally the State Board of Accountancy. Typical prerequisites for a CPA certificate include

(1) a baccalaureate degree from an accredited college or university; (2) passing of the Uniform CPA Examination, which is a rigorous two-day examination covering accounting practice, accounting theory, auditing, and commercial law; (3) practical experience under the supervision of a CPA; (4) demonstrated knowledge of local professional ethics statutes; and (5) satisfactory personal references. Most jurisdictions now require specified periodic amounts of continuing education as a condition for renewal of the license to practice as a CPA.

Professional CPA organizations include the American Institute of Certified Public Accountants (AICPA) and the State Societies of CPAs. However, membership in these two types of organizations is not compulsory for practicing CPAs. The AICPA acts as the advocate of the profession vis-à-vis government, industry, and the financial community. In connection with the attest function, it establishes guidelines and standards for "generally accepted" auditing. It also conducts research and professional development activities on a wide scale. Furthermore, it prepares and administers the Uniform CPA Examination twice each year.

State Societies of CPAs are predominantly concerned with local or regional matters. They seek to safeguard professional interests in state legislatures, support state boards of accountancy in their various activities, and conduct scores of professional seminars and continuing education programs. Quite often they also operate speakers' bureaus, assist local social programs and charitable organizations, and encourage public professional involvement.

The Role of Auditing

In its 1989 brochure *Understanding Audits and the Auditor's Report*, the AICPA describes an independent audit as follows:

> An audit allows creditors, bankers, investors, and others to use financial statements with confidence. While the audit does not *guarantee* financial statement accuracy, it provides users with reasonable assurance that an entity's financial statements present fairly, in all material respects, its financial position, results of operations, and cash flows in conformity with GAAP. An audit enhances users' confidence that financial statements do not contain material misstatements because the auditor is an independent, objective expert who is knowledgeable of the entity's business and financial reporting requirements.[1]

The relationships between auditing and financial reporting are depicted in Exhibit 14–1.

In the process of providing the assurances contained in the typical independent auditor's report (described next), the auditor will assess whether

- All transactions and accounts that should have been recorded are reported in the financial statements.
- The assets and liabilities reported in the financial statements existed at the balance sheet date, and the transactions reported in the financial statements occurred during the period covered by the statements.
- All reported assets are owned by the entity, and the liabilities are owned by the entity at the balance sheet date.
- The financial statement elements (assets, liabilities, revenues, expenses, cash flows, and so on) are appropriately valued in accordance with GAAP.

[1] AICPA, *Understanding Audits and the Auditor's Report* (New York: AICPA, 1989), p. 3.

EXHIBIT 14–1

Relationships Between Auditing and Financial Reporting

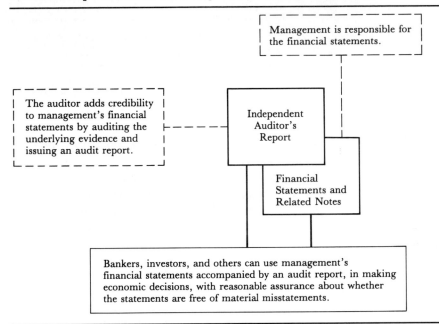

American Institute of Certified Public Accountants, Understanding Audits and the Auditor's Report (*New York: AICPA, 1989*), *p. 3.*

  • Financial statement elements are properly classified, described, and disclosed in conformity with GAAP.

AUDIT REPORTS

The CPA profession, with concurrence from the SEC, has adopted the following standard independent auditor's report which is used when an examination reveals no reservations about the adequacy of the financial statements under audit. The report is addressed to the board of directors and the shareholders of the company whose financial statements have been examined. Also, the report is dated and signed. It is presented in three paragraphs. Exhibit 14–2 illustrates the AICPA recommended format.

The report in Exhibit 14–2 is usually referred to as an unqualified or clean opinion. When the scope of an examination has been limited, when there is disagreement with one or more aspects of the financial statements, or when an inherent uncertainty exists, the auditor will issue a *qualified* opinion. Words like "except for" typify report qualifications. For example, suppose that a company has an affiliate company in a foreign country, and that this foreign investment and the earnings from it are included in the home company's financial statements. Also suppose that audited financial statements of the foreign affiliate company are not available. Under these circumstances, the auditor would describe the situation in a fourth special paragraph in the audit report and state in the opinion paragraph

EXHIBIT 14–2

Standard Independent Auditor's Report

A SAMPLE STANDARD AUDITOR'S REPORT

Independent Auditor's Report

To Sample Company, The Board of Directors, and Shareholders:

(Introductory Paragraph)

We have audited the accompanying balance sheets of Sample Company as of December 31, 19X2 and 19X1, and the related statements of income, retained earnings, and cash flows for the years then ended. These financial statements are the responsibility of the Company's management. Our responsibility is to express an opinion on these financial statements based on our audits.

(Scope Paragraph)

We conducted our audits in accordance with generally accepted auditing standards. Those standards require that we plan and perform the audit to obtain reasonable assurance about whether the financial statements are free of material misstatement. An audit includes examining, on a test basis, evidence supporting the amounts and disclosures in the financial statements. An audit also includes assessing the accounting principles used and significant estimates made by management, as well as evaluating the overall financial statement presentation. We believe that our audits provide a reasonable basis for our opinion.

(Opinion Paragraph)

In our opinion, the financial statements referred to above present fairly, in all material respects, the financial position of Sample Company as of December 31, 19X2 and 19X1, and the results of its operations and its cash flows for the years then ended in conformity with generally accepted accounting principles.

R. Johnson & Co.
Certified Public Accountants

February 14, 19X3

In our opinion, except for the effects of any adjustments which might have been necessary had we been able to examine evidence regarding the foreign affiliate investment and earnings, the financial statements referred to above present fairly, in all material respects, the financial position of Sample Company as of December 31, 19X2 and 19X1, and the results of its operations and its cash flows for the years then ended, in conformity with generally accepted accounting principles.[2]

The foregoing opinion paragraph signals a qualified auditor's opinion.

If a qualification is so extreme that the financial statements no longer "present fairly" an enterprise's financial position, the results of its operations, and so forth, an *adverse* opinion will be issued. This occurs, for instance, when there are material departures from GAAP so that the financial statements do not present fairly the financial position, results of operations, and cash flows of the company. Now the opinion paragraphs starts out

In our opinion, because of the effects of the matters discussed in the preceding paragraphs, the financial statements referred to above do not present fairly . . .[3]

A *disclaimer* of an opinion is given when the auditor has not been able to obtain sufficient audit evidence or the financial statements are fundamentally impacted by uncertainty—like a high probability of bankruptcy or other going concern risk.

Responsibility for Financial Statements

While the professional literature establishes the independent auditor as solely responsible for the audit report on financial statements, it is equally emphatic in pointing out that the enterprise management has the responsibility for the production and preparation of proper financial statements. Thus it is management's responsibility to adopt sound accounting policies, to maintain adequate and effective systems of accounts, to safeguard enterprise assets, and to devise control systems that will accomplish these objectives (see Exhibit 14–1).

The financial statements are an implicit and integral part of management's responsibility because no one knows a company better than its management. Consequently, management is usually in the best position to choose procedures and policies and ultimately financial statement formats that will most fairly report to others a company's financial position and results of operations.

The auditor's responsibility with respect to financial statements is therefore secondary. An unqualified audit report on a set of financial statements cannot be issued unless these statements represent actual business transactions and events and conform to established accounting principles. The London *Economist* once called the auditor's responsibility a "watchdog function." Later on in the chapter we describe how this function is performed.

Effects of Independent Audits

Much has been written on behavioral effects produced when auditors perform audit activities in a client's office. Company accounting personnel often feel uneasy when the independent auditors are around. That is, auditing produces what

---

[2] AICPA, *Understanding Audits and the Auditor's Report*, p. 29 (slightly altered for expositional clarity).
[3] *Ibid.*, p. 33.

might be called a report card effect. Jobs get done with fewer errors, and system improvements are constantly sought because of the periodic report card prepared by the independent auditors. Some observers feel that this effect may even prevent some contemplated frauds or lesser irregularities by employees. However, the typical financial audit review is not intended to *guarantee* fraud detection. This is discussed later.

Auditing usually results in producing valid and reliable financial information efficiently. Management clearly knows the most about the business enterprise and understands its strengths and weaknesses best. Therefore management usually is and should be most efficient in preparing financial representations about the firm.

Unfortunately, however, management also has a direct interest in the representations made. If things are not going well, then management, in its own interest, might make biased representations. Such biases might even shade into misrepresentations or dishonesty. Knowing that independent audit procedures will eventually test their financial representations, managements are probably less prone to make deliberately or intentionally biased judgments and estimates than would otherwise be the case.

Efficiency Provided by Independent Audits

Despite report card effects within enterprises, we mentioned earlier in this chapter that outside users of financial information want additional assurances about its validity and reliability. If users of financial information had to obtain and verify this information item by item and user by user, an immensely costly process would unnecessarily be repeated over and over.

Professor W. A. Wallace explored the substantial and persistent market demand over time for the audit function. Her basic conclusion is that "economic incentives exist for parties to have and to supply an audit."[4] According to Professor Wallace, the audit fulfills three explicit market demands: (1) demand for a monitoring mechanism; (2) demand for information production to improve investors' decisions; and (3) demand for insurance to protect against losses from distorted information.

Importance of Internal Control

Until the late 1940s, auditing was viewed as a process of examining the documentation supporting recorded transactions and of verifying their classification in financial statements. This approach to auditing has been characterized as "auditing the books."

In 1949, a committee of the AICPA issued a special report containing a comprehensive statement on the significance of internal control to the auditing process. In this statement *internal control* is defined as follows:

> Internal control comprises the plan of organization and all of the coordinated methods and measures adopted within a business to safeguard its assets, check the accuracy and reliability of its accounting data, promote operational efficiency, and encourage adherence to prescribed managerial policies. This definition possibly is broader than the meaning sometimes attributed to the term. It recognizes that a system of internal

[4] W. A. Wallace, *The Economic Role of the Audit in Free and Regulated Markets* (New York: Touche Ross & Co., Aid to Education Program, 1980), p. 49.

control extends beyond those matters which relate directly to the functions of the accounting and financial departments.[5]

Soon after the special report, independent auditors began to place greater reliance on internal control considerations. At the beginning of an audit process, they now carefully evaluate a company's internal control system. If internal controls operate well, the system is likely to produce reasonably complete and accurate financial data. In turn, such data are a good starting point for reliable financial statements. On the other hand, the financial data base of an enterprise is not very dependable when internal controls are either weak or absent altogether.

Example 14–1 shows selected internal control system components as they apply to the operations of a shopping center.

Example 14–1 | Rents and fees are collected from different tenants of a shopping center according to a wide variety of individual contracts. The controller's department of the shopping center has established the following internal control procedures, among others, to correspond to recognized internal control principles.

Procedure	*Reason*	*Principle*
1. The receptionist prepares and mails all bank deposits as checks are received. The bookkeeper reconciles each monthly bank statement to the company's cash records.	To avoid misuse of funds received (as can occur when the same individual who receives funds also controls the records) and to ensure timely bank deposits.	A plan of organization that provides appropriate segregation of functional responsibilities among employees.
2. Each advertising allowance made to tenant stores is individually authorized by the controller.	To control total amount of allowances granted and prevent kickbacks.	A system of authorization and recording procedures adequate to provide reasonable accounting control over assets, liabilities, revenues, and expenses.
3. New construction activities are recorded in accounts clearly separated from repair and maintenance accounts.	To ensure appropriate accounting classifications and control repair and maintenance operations.	Sound practices to be followed in the performance of duties and functions of each of the organizational departments.
4. The job description for the controller's position requires that appointees hold a CPA certificate.	To seek best possible job performance within budgeted salary range.	A degree of quality of personnel commensurate with responsibilities.

[5] Quoted in Philip L. Defliese, Kenneth P. Johnson and Roderick K. Macleod, *Montgomery's Auditing* (Ninth Edition). New York: Ronald Pren, 1975, p. 56. (This definition has been repeated and quoted extensively, including paragraph 320.09 of the AICPA's *Statements on Auditing Standards No. 1.*)

If an internal control system is found to be highly effective, independent audit procedures can be curtailed. With a well-functioning internal control system, relatively less extensive tests or samples may be required to supply the auditor with needed evidential matter. On the other hand, a weak system of internal control generally necessitates more extensive auditing procedures to provide sufficient evidence for an adequate evaluation of data quality and opinion formulation on the financial statements under audit.

AUDITING FRAMEWORK

When the independent auditor begins an audit assignment, it is assumed that (1) the internal control system of the enterprise is appropriate and effective; (2) generally accepted accounting principles have been applied in all accounting processes underlying the financial statements; (3) the generally accepted accounting principles utilized have been applied consistently between the current and the prior periods; and (4) there is an adequate amount of informative financial disclosure in the financial statements and footnotes. Evidence gathering and its evaluation enable auditors to reject or confirm these a priori assumptions.

The major steps of the auditing process are (1) become acquainted with the firm—its environment and its accounting, personnel, production, marketing, and other systems; (2) review and evaluate the management and the accounting control system in operation; (3) gather evidential matter on the integrity of the system; (4) gather further evidence related to the representations made in the financial statements; and (5) formulate an opinion on the basis of the evidence available.

Getting Acquainted. Auditing is an analytical process applied to everyday business situations. Without firsthand knowledge of existing business practices, the auditor would have to rely exclusively on available financial data. This would jeopardize both audit efficiency and effectiveness. Therefore a getting-acquainted phase (which usually includes a visit to a client's facilities and certain analytical preliminary tests and inquiries) initiates the typical audit process. The likely activities of this phase are described in Example 14–2.

Control System Review. We already know that the auditor's evaluation of the control systems operating within the enterprise has a direct influence on the scope of the examination and the nature of the tests conducted. However, even though preliminary evaluation of control systems is an essential ingredient of planning the audit scope, we must remember that eventually both the system and the data it produces are covered by the audit process.

Example 14–2 | The Brothers Three Shopping Center has leased space to Mr. Hines, who operates a quality restaurant named The Duncan Inn. Lease payments are based on the minimum monthly amount sufficient to cover taxes and insurance on the building plus a graduated percentage of the restaurant's gross sales to patrons. No percentage payments are due on catering services.

Restaurant receipts of The Duncan Inn are collected in cash and from credit card billings. A select few patrons have the privilege of open credit with monthly billings. In planning the initial audit of The Duncan Inn's financial statements, a CPA finds that virtually no internal control exists over cash receipts. Hence tests covering cash receipts are scheduled more comprehensively than those related to credit sales.

Evidential Matter. Evidential matter supporting financial statements consists of the underlying accounting data and all corroborating information available to the auditor. The auditor tests underlying accounting data by analysis and review. Some of the procedural steps followed in the original accounting process are retraced and reconciled with the information reported.

The auditor's evidential material is the result of tests, selected observations, and statistical sampling where large compilations of data may be involved. The auditor must always balance the natural desire for more evidential matter against the costliness and social usefulness of completely reconstructing the data and processes that produced the financial statements. One key justification for independent audits, as we have seen, is the economy that results from producing expert opinion-based judgments from limited but reliable evidential matter.

Example 14–3 | Among tests covering cash receipts of The Duncan Inn, the CPA determined what the expected average ratios should be between food and beverage items purchased, number of meals served, and the average total price of luncheons and dinners purchased by patrons. Making appropriate allowances for credit card sales, the CPA was then able to make a reasonable estimate of cash receipts for the period under audit. The estimate of the cash receipts constitutes evidential matter for purposes of the audit. (Note that the foregoing test has physical and financial dimensions. A purely financial test would be to analyze total bank deposits to arrive at cash restaurant receipts. In an actual engagement, an auditor might have undertaken both types of tests.)

Professional Judgment. The object of an independent audit is to express a professional opinion on a set of financial statements. Rendering such an opinion is a matter of judgment. Professional evaluation of audit evidence gathered is therefore a key function of the independent auditor. The AICPA puts it into the following context:

> Most of the independent auditor's work in forming his opinion on financial statements consists of obtaining and evaluating evidential matter concerning the assertions in such financial statements. The measure of the validity of such evidence for audit purposes lies in the judgment of the auditor; in this respect audit evidence differs from legal evidence, which is circumscribed by rigid rules.[6]

The foregoing statement can be rephrased to say that judgment of what evidential matter should be obtained and how it is to be interpreted permits confirmation or rejection of the assumption that the financial statements examined are in conformity with established financial reporting standards.

Standards and Procedures

AICPA literature carefully distinguishes between auditing standards and auditing procedures:

> Auditing standards differ from auditing procedures in that the "procedures" relate to acts to be performed, whereas "standards" deal with measures of the quality of

---

[6] AICPA, *Codification of Statements on Auditing Standards Nos. 1 to 51* (New York: AICPA, 1987), p. 119.

EXHIBIT 14–3

Generally Accepted Auditing Standards

General Standards

1. The audit is to be performed by a person or persons having adequate technical training and proficiency as an auditor.
2. In all matters relating to the assignment, an independence in mental attitude is to be maintained by the auditor or auditors.
3. Due professional care is to be exercised in the performance of the audit and the preparation of the report.

Standards of Field Work

1. The work is to be adequately planned and assistants, if any, are to be properly supervised.
2. A sufficient understanding of the internal control structure is to be obtained to plan the audit and to determine the nature, timing, and extent of tests to be performed.
3. Sufficient competent evidential matter is to be obtained through inspection, observation, inquiries, and confirmation to afford a reasonable basis for an opinion regarding the financial statements under audit.

Standards of Reporting

1. The report shall state whether the financial statements are prepared in accordance with generally accepted accounting principles.
2. The report shall identify those circumstances in which such principles have not been consistently observed in the current period in relation to the preceding period.
3. Informative disclosure in the financial statements is to be regarded as reasonably adequate unless otherwise stated in the report.
4. The report shall either contain an expression of opinion regarding the financial statements, taken as a whole, or an assertion to the effect that an opinion cannot be expressed. When an overall opinion cannot be expressed, the reasons therefor should be stated. In all cases where an auditor's name is associated with financial statements, the report should contain a clear-cut indication of the character of the auditor's work and the degree of responsibility the auditor is taking.

the performance of those acts and the objectives to be attained by the use of the procedures undertaken.[7]

Exhibit 14–3 lists the ten generally accepted auditing *standards* which are binding upon CPAs performing an independent audit. The binding force of these standards is established by (1) AICPA membership and the corresponding requirement to observe its Code of Professional Conduct; (2) state CPA licensing requirements, which sometimes build these standards into a state accountancy statute; and (3) regulatory enforcement of these standards by administrative agencies like the SEC. It is noteworthy that the CPA profession itself sets the standards by which it conducts its independent audit activities.

Auditing procedures are less clearly established because the nature, substance, and importance of any single procedure varies with the circumstances. No two companies and no two transactions are completely alike. The AICPA makes clear that the choice among various possible auditing procedures is a matter of professional judgment.

[7] *Ibid.*, p. 7.

The nature, timing, and extent of the procedures to be applied on a particular engagement are a matter of professional judgment to be determined by the auditor, based on the specific circumstances. However, the procedures adopted should be adequate to achieve the audit objectives developed by the auditor, and the evidential matter obtained should be sufficient for the auditor to form conclusions concerning the validity of the individual assertions embodied in the components of financial statements. The combination of the auditor's reliance on internal accounting control and on selected substantive tests should provide a reasonable basis for his opinion.[8]

From time to time, the AICPA issues formal *Statements on Auditing Standards* (SAS). These statements serve as guidelines for the work of independent auditors. Known as generally accepted auditing standards (GAAS), they are to auditors what GAAP are to financial accountants. GAAS, in short, are intended to guide professional judgments of independent auditors.

As an example, SAS No. 59 (issued April 1988) is entitled *The Auditor's Consideration of an Entity's Ability to Continue as a Going Concern*. It requires the auditor to evaluate in *every audit* whether there is a substantial doubt about the client's ability to continue as a going concern for one year beyond the balance sheet date. If, after considering information about management's plans for the future, a substantial doubt about the ability to continue remains, the auditor would add an explanatory paragraph to the audit report *regardless* of whether the assets and liabilities are appropriately valued or classified.

In the international environment (see Chapter Twelve for details), the International Auditing Practices Committee (IAPC) sets and publishes *International Auditing Guidelines* (IAGs). The IAPC is a senior committee of a federation of the most important international professional accounting organizations—the *International Federation of Accountants* (IFAC). IAGs are similar to corresponding statements on auditing standards issued in English-speaking countries. They do not override local regulations, but are intended for global acceptance. Third World countries often initially adopt IAGs, because it is an efficient way to set professional standards and establish connections with the international community.

An Audit Engagement

The CPA profession consists of individual practitioners, small local firms, medium-sized regional firms, and large national and international firms. Most firms are organized as partnerships, including the largest firms. Some local and regional firms operate as professional services corporations.

In the organizational structure of the typical CPA firm, each partner works with several audit managers, each of whom in turn is responsible for a number of supervising accountants. Staff accountants work under the direction of supervising accountants. Hence a pyramid of responsibility exists. Usually a small team of auditors performs an engagement.

Start of an Engagement. Independent audit engagements begin as a consequence of (1) SEC requirements; (2) referrals by head offices of companies or home offices of large international CPA firms; or (3) suggestions from attorneys, bankers, or other business persons.

---

[8] *Ibid.*, p. 121.

Example 14–4 | When Mr. Hines, owner of The Duncan Inn, realized that his restaurant was highly profitable, he discussed with his banker the possibility of a large loan for the purpose of building The Second Duncan Inn. The banker suggested an independent audit of the Hines Company's financial statements as a condition for the loan. Furthermore, three to five years hence the Hines Company, which owns The Duncan Inn and would be the owner of The Second Duncan Inn, might offer some of its stock for sale to the public. This could require SEC registration and therefore audited financial statements. To explore the possibility of an independent audit for his company, Mr. Hines made an appointment with Jonathan Lee, a partner in the CPA firm of MacLean & Co.

Mr. Hines came to the meeting with two sets of financial statements prepared by his controller—one for the year just ended and one for the preceding year. After short introductory amenities, Mr. Hines came right to the point by asking how much it would cost to have the two sets of financial statements audited by MacLean & Co. Mr. Lee explained that his firm has an hourly billing rate for each staff classification and that Mr. Hines's company would be billed for the exact number of hours spent on the audit at an appropriate billing rate for each auditor. Mr. Lee then estimated a range for the probable cost of an annual audit for Mr. Hines's company.

The estimate satisfied Mr. Hines and he agreed to appoint MacLean & Co. as his company's auditors. (This is possible because Mr. Hines is at present the sole stockholder.) In further discussion it was agreed that because retroactive audits are difficult and costly to undertake, the engagement would begin with the year just ended. Based upon these various understandings, Mr. Lee drafted an appropriate engagement letter for Mr. Hines' signature. The appointment of MacLean & Co. as independent auditors of the Hines Company became official with the execution of the engagement letter. The engagement letter also spelled out the services to be performed and responsibilities to be undertaken by MacLean & Co., along with the necessary cooperation and access to records to be provided by Hines.

Planning Audit Activities. Once an engagement is agreed upon, many different procedures take place. Within the CPA firm, appropriate staff assignments are necessary. Dates for the auditors' visits must be agreed upon and needed documents and information made available. Personal introductions and tours of facilities are another type of essential preliminary activity.

As established earlier in this chapter, a comprehensive evaluation of a company's internal control system is a significant determinant of the types and amounts of evidential matter needed for a given audit. The effectiveness of other organizational and operational controls must also be considered.

Example 14–5 | Continuing the case of The Duncan Inn, an initial visit from two MacLean & Co. auditors was scheduled almost immediately. The purpose of the initial visit was to gather facts about the Hines Company in general and to collect data on its internal control system.

During the visit, the auditors acquainted themselves with all the company's management personnel and its physical facilities, and a long list of such relevant information as membership on the board of directors, name and address of the company's attorney, and copies of governmental and tax reports filed. Some desk space was arranged for the auditors, and they began their assignment. The task was finished in two days. Evidence gathered was recorded in audit working papers and standard review questionnaires which MacLean & Co. uses.

Setting of a Regular Audit Examination. Independent auditors always keep in mind that their primary purpose is the expression of an opinion on the fairness of representations in financial statements. Hence it is not surprising to find that each audit step and each audit test are a building block toward the final expression of a professional opinion.

A partial list of things an auditor would wish to know about sales revenues appearing in the financial statements of the Hines Company might include the following:

1. Have actual revenues been recorded *properly* and *completely*? Tests like the one described in Example 14–3 help to answer this question. The auditor begins with evidence of products or services provided to customers and compares the corresponding amount of revenue with the amount recorded.
2. Were reported revenues earned in the *period* for which they are reported? In this connection the auditor performs so-called cutoff tests, making sure that all December sales, for instance, are recorded in December and not carried forward to January. Improper cutoffs of revenues and/or expenses represent misallocations of reported net income between successive periods.
3. Do accounts receivable shown at year-end reflect *bona fide receivables* and are they *collectible*? Correctness is tested by direct correspondence with debtors to confirm outstanding balances. Analysis of subsequent actual payments received helps to establish whether any bad accounts were among the receivables listed. Overstatement of receivables may again overstate reported net income (because of insufficient provision for uncollectibles) as well as financial position amounts and ratios.

With an appreciation of what is needed to achieve fair presentation in financial statements, an auditor can evaluate an individual company situation and the state of its control systems for purposes of setting scope and depth of needed audit examinations. In determining which aspects of an accounting system should be tested and in what fashion, the auditor typically relies on guidelines available in the professional literature.

Audit Completion and Reporting. The tests and other necessary procedures that are included in an audit are documented in a set of audit working papers. The AICPA recommends that audit working papers include or show the following:

1. Data sufficient to demonstrate that the financial statements or other information upon which the auditor is reporting are in agreement with (or reconciled with) the client's records.
2. That the engagement had been planned, such as by use of work programs; and that the work of any assistants was supervised and reviewed—indicating observance of the first standard of field work. (See Exhibit 14–3).
3. That the client's system of internal control was reviewed and evaluated

in determining the extent of the tests to which auditing procedures were restricted—indicating observance of the second standard of field work.

4. The auditing procedures followed and tests performed in obtaining evidential matter—indicating observance of the third standard of field work. The record in these respects may take various forms, including memoranda, checklists, work programs, and schedules and would generally permit reasonable identification of the work done by the auditor.

5. How exceptions and unusual matters, if any, discovered by the independent auditor's procedures, were resolved or treated.

6. Appropriate commentaries prepared by the auditor indicating conclusions concerning significant aspects of the engagement.

Working papers are reviewed by managers and partners of the CPA firm conducting the audit. Eventually, a partner signs an appropriate auditor's report on behalf of the CPA firm.

Example 14–6

Let us assume now that all necessary field work was completed on the first annual audit of Hines Company. The supervising auditor on the engagement completed the working papers and sent them to his manager for review. Thereafter, a number of accounting adjustments were suggested to Mr. Hines and his controller so that the financial statements would be brought into conformity with generally accepted accounting principles. The representatives of the Hines Company agreed, and the financial statements were adjusted accordingly.

At this point, Mr. Lee reviewed all of the working papers that were prepared, as well as the drafted financial statements and footnotes. Mr. Lee asked quite a few questions of the audit manager and received satisfactory answers so that he felt justified in signing the auditor's opinion on the Hines Company financial statements. Copies of the statements and the opinion were then mailed to Mr. Hines as the sole shareholder. A statement (bill) for professional auditing services rendered by MacLean & Co. was sent to the company as well.

Special Auditing Tools and Techniques

The case just described is highly simplified to illustrate the essential steps in conducting an audit. Engagements for large clients are more complicated and often involve large-scale coordination between client locations and subsidiaries not only across North America but in many overseas countries as well. In addition, auditors rely on some rather sophisticated techniques in conducting large-scale engagements. Two of these techniques are described briefly in the following paragraphs.

Statistical Sampling. Where the sets of documents constituting evidential matter are relatively large and homogeneous, statistical sampling can be applied to good advantage. Statistical sampling uses formal statistical theories and methods to evaluate the characteristics of a population of data on the basis of one or more samples drawn from the total data population. This is most likely to apply to auditing procedures involving invoices payable to creditors, accounts receivable from customers, inventories, and payroll applications. By using statistical sampling in these areas, the auditor is often able to reduce the number of documents actually examined and at the same time control the precision and the confidence levels. As a result, statistical sampling may reduce audit costs to clients.

Computer-assisted Auditing Procedures. Another sophisticated auditing technique is the use of computers in the auditing process. Among the more simple tests in this connection is deliberate processing of nonsensical or impossible transactions to determine the client company's computer system's reaction. For instance, if a payroll program would process a monthly payroll check exceeding, let us say, $500,000, then the internal control of the system is weak. It should reject any wage payment exceeding reasonable maximum amounts.

Computer audit software packages are increasingly efficient in expediting audit tests and procedures. The larger CPA firms have developed such software packages to perform predetermined test and check functions on the client's computerized information systems and records. These packages have enabled auditors to audit "with the computer" rather than "around" the computer. The availability of portable personal computers has accelerated the use of computer-assisted auditing procedures.

Detection of Errors and Irregularities (Including Fraud)

In the course of an ordinary audit, the independent auditor is aware that the possibility of errors in the client's records or the possibility of irregularities such as fraud may exist. Financial statements may be misstated as a result of errors, defalcations, or deliberate misrepresentations by management. The auditor recognizes that errors or irregularities, if substantial enough, will affect the opinion on the financial statements. Therefore, an audit made in accordance with generally accepted auditing standards includes reasonable procedures designed to detect material errors or irregularities.

SAS No. 53 (issued April 1988) requires the auditor to design the audit to provide reasonable assurance of detecting errors and irregularities that are material to the financial statements under audit. It also requires the communication of all consequential errors and irregularities to the client's audit committee (discussed later in this chapter). If a client does not have an audit committee, the communication must be to persons of equivalent authority and responsibility. In small business cases, the owner-manager must be informed.

THE AUDITOR

Professional Independence

Independence is the cornerstone of the auditing profession. Ideally, CPAs should be completely independent when they perform audits related to financial statements. The second general auditing standard listed in Exhibit 14–3 requires that in all respects related to the audit of financial statements, an independence of mental attitude is to be maintained. Public confidence in independent auditors' reports would be impaired if there were evidence that this independence was lacking. Confidence might also be impaired by the existence of circumstances that reasonable people might interpret as an impairment to this independence. To be independent, the auditor must be intellectually honest. To be recognized as independent, he or she must be free from any obligation to or interest in the client, its management, or its owners. For example, independence rules require that outside auditors cannot own any stock in the companies they audit. Through the AICPA's *Code of Professional Conduct*, the profession guards itself against any public presumption of loss of independence. The code requires that CPAs acting as independent auditors must avoid situations that may lead outsiders to doubt their independence.

The requirement for complete independence creates several dilemmas for the CPA. One dilemma is *economic*. Since managements often directly pay auditors' fees, an economic relationship necessarily exists between the auditor and the auditee. The creation of audit committees among corporate boards of directors as the boards' conduits to their independent auditors has alleviated but not eliminated the dilemma. Board audit committees typically are comprised of outside (i.e., not corporate officers or employees) directors. They monitor management activities, periodically review all corporate internal control procedures, receive reports from internal auditors, and serve as primary liaison with independent auditors. When board audit committees exist, auditors have an opportunity to become more independent of a company's top operating management. The New York Stock Exchange requires that all companies whose securities are listed on the NYSE have audit committees consisting of outside board members. The SEC and the AICPA strongly recommend audit committees. SAS No. 61 (issued April 1988) is entitled *Communications with Audit Committees* and requires that certain specified matters related to the conduct of an audit be communicated.

Another dilemma is *behavioral*. Mental attitudes are difficult to change by means of laws and codes of conduct. Despite all outward appearances of independence, the behavioral makeup of some persons simply precludes a consistent and pervasive mental attitude of independence on their part. Some CPA licensing rules and continuing professional education requirements for license renewals mitigate this dilemma, but do not eliminate it.

SEC Influence. The SEC administers the Securities Acts which provide for the adequate and accurate disclosure of all material facts relating to financial information filed by companies with the Agency. The SEC believes that an auditor's independence is fundamental in implementing the purposes of the Securities Acts. Most filings of financial statements with the SEC must include an independent auditor's report on such statements.

SEC *Accounting Series Release No. 126* is entitled "Guidelines and Examples of Situations Involving the Independence of Accountants." The following examples are taken directly from the release.

1. An accountant has a sister-in-law whose husband is a 40 percent stockholder of a company. There is no other business connection between the company, the stockholder, the accountant, or his wife. Conclusion: *Independence is adversely affected because of the family relationship between the accountant and a major stockholder in a client company.*

2. A partner in an accounting firm is a member of an investment club. The club owns stock in a company which is a client of the accounting firm. Neither the number nor the value of the shares purchased is material to the club or the company. Conclusion: *The firm's independence would be adversely affected as a result of the partner's interest in the investment club. In this regard, an investment club does not stand on the same footing as a mutual*

fund, because the former is comprised of relatively few members, and each member plays an active part in the selection of investments.[9]

Rule 101 of the AICPA's *Code of Professional Conduct* covers independence requirements. Interpretation 101-9 defines effects of family relationships.[10] For instance, if a CPA's spouse is employed by an audit client company, does not exercise "significant influence" over the operating, financial or accounting policies of the company, and is not in an "audit sensitive" position (e.g., general accounting clerk, purchasing agent or internal auditor), the CPA's professional independence is *not* impaired with regard to the audit client.

Legal Liability of Auditors

Various court cases have extended the professional liability of independent auditors to third parties. Until the 1960s, professional liability of auditors was limited to clients and others with a *direct* economic interest in audited financial statements. Now third parties with only general interest in an auditor's work can also sue. Reasons for legal complaints include professional negligence, nonobservance of GAAS and/or GAAP, lack of due care in the conduct of an audit, association with misleading or fraudulent financial statements, and lack of independence. An early case was Bar Chris Construction Corporation (1968). In this action, the suing bondholders did not accuse the underwriters, auditors, or outside directors of trying to *deceive* them or anyone else *intentionally*. But were the auditors nevertheless liable for the demonstrably incorrect information that management had distributed? *Yes*, ruled U.S. District Court Judge Edward C. McLean, because they had *not* made a *reasonable* effort to check the facts.

The Continental Vending Machine Corporation case produced criminal convictions against some auditors. Illegal funds transfers and other irregularities involving Continental's president were not properly reported in the audited financial statements, which had shown $250,000 cash as an asset when in fact a cash deficit of more than $1 million should have been reported. Continental went into receivership in 1963.

Among more recent cases, E.S.M. Government Securities, Inc. (1985), stands out. This Florida government securities dealer owed customers some $320 million at the time it went bankrupt. Its audit firm, Grant Thornton, was held liable for negligence and breach of contract. The audit partner, Jose L. Gomez, pleaded guilty to fraud charges for receiving bribes from E.S.M. officers and issuing unqualified opinions on E.S.M.'s financial statements knowing they were misleading and false. A federal jury ordered the audit firm to pay $70.9 million in damages to the creditors of the defunct E.S.M. Mr. Gomez was sentenced to 12 years in prison.[11]

Most observers seem to agree that there is a trend toward greater third-party responsibility for auditors. Since the CPA title is legally established and protected, it grants auditors a preferential economic position when it comes to performing independent audits. In return, users of audit services are entitled to expect high-quality audits. Since user expectations do not always match realistic

[9] Securities and Exchange Commission, *Accounting Series Release No. 126*, "Guidelines and Examples of Situations Involving the Independence of Accountants." Published by the Bureau of National Affairs, Inc., Washington, D.C. 20037.
[10] "Guidance on Independence Issues," *Journal of Accountancy* (May 1986), pp. 56–60.
[11] *The Wall Street Journal*, January 27, 1987, p. 6.

audit performance possibilities, law suits will result. Of course, there are also occasional audit failures where the resulting damages are determined through court actions.

EXTENSIONS OF THE AUDIT FUNCTION

Auditing of financial statements is clearly an attest function. The expertise auditors have, though, is leading to extensions of their services throughout the economy. Strong competition among audit firms and trends toward an overall service economy have intensified such extensions.

In its 1986 *Statement on Standards for Attestation Engagements*, the AICPA defined the activities covered by the *Statement*.

> An attest engagement is one in which a practitioner is engaged to issue or does issue a written communication that expresses a conclusion about the reliability of a written assertion that is the responsibility of another party.

Attestation work is a natural activity for auditors who express professional opinions after analyzing large sets of data. Also, auditors are proficient in making professional judgments. These qualities are the ingredients for success in attestation engagements.

There are 11 attestation standards compared with 10 GAAS (see Exhibit 14–3). The attestation standards are *extensions* of the generally accepted auditing standards. They do not supersede them. Attestation engagements to which the newer standards apply might include

1. Occupancy, enrollment, and attendance data.
2. Labor data for union contract negotiations.
3. Technical accuracy of college textbooks.
4. Audience and media circulation data.
5. Investment performance statistics.
6. Integrity and security of a computer network.
7. Financial feasibility of a rapid transit system.

Another extension of the audit function is the so-called social audit. Social auditing concerns the social impact of business enterprises in such areas as work environment, noise and air pollution, inefficient use of natural resources, and minimum performance and safety standards for consumer products. Social audits are required in France and strongly recommended in several other European countries.

AUDITING IN THE PUBLIC SECTOR

The auditing profession also is extending its traditional boundaries in the public sector. The General Accounting Office, which is the auditing watchdog of the U.S. Congress, increasingly engages in "performance" audits—an audit function addressed more to the effectiveness of a particular agency or program management than to its financial affairs and conditions. The GAO has published a body of audit standards applicable to all forms of government organizations and activities.[12] These standards are intended to apply to government and private auditors alike when audit work is performed in the public sector.

Aside from the GAO, most large federal cabinet-level departments and state governments maintain growing audit agencies of their own. These auditors, while internal to the respective organizations, typically have the power to publish their findings without jeopardy and are able to deliver their reports and recommendations to the highest management levels of the organizations they serve. Large audit organizations of this type are found in the Department of Defense and the Department of Health and Welfare. State auditors and their staffs are similarly organized, even though in some states the state auditor is publicly elected and therefore subject to at least some influence from political pressures.

SUMMARY

Independent audits allow creditors, bankers, investors, and others to use financial statements with confidence. Mandated audits are performed by CPAs. Thus the CPA profession is explained, the role of auditing in the business community elaborated, and the responsibility for financial statements clarified. Then we turn to the auditing process. There are discussions of internal control, the nature of professional audit judgment, and the standards and procedures employed in the performance of an audit. There is a complete listing of the ten generally accepted auditing standards.

The essential steps in an audit engagement involve proper planning of audit activities and gathering of relevant evidential matter. Thereafter a professional opinion is formulated whether the financial statements under audit present fairly, in all material respects, the financial position, results of operations, and cash flows of the client company. The opinion is communicated in a written report.

The chapter concludes with brief discussions of several special topics. Statistical sampling and computer-assisted auditing procedures are explained. Detection of errors and irregularities is mentioned and professional independence is explained and illustrated. Also discussed are legal liability to third parties, extension of the audit function to attestation engagements, and auditing in the public sector.

Questions for Review and Discussion

14–1. Define the following:
- **a.** Audit reports
- **b.** Internal control
- **c.** Independent audit
- **d.** Auditing standards
- **e.** Evidential matter
- **f.** Auditor opinion formulation
- **g.** Qualified opinion
- **h.** Adverse opinion
- **i.** Disclaimer of an opinion
- **j.** Attest engagement

14–2. What is the objective of audits of financial statements of enterprises by independent professional accountants?

---

[12] U.S. General Accounting Office, *Standards for Audit of Governmental Organizations, Programs, Activities & Functions*, rev. ed. (Washington, D.C.: The Comptroller General of the United States, 1981).

14–3. Who has primary responsibility for the preparation of financial statements? Why?

14–4. Explain how independent audits generally provide economies in the production of reasonably reliable corporate financial reports.

14–5. What is the relationship between an internal control system of an enterprise and the scope of an audit of financial statements performed by independent auditors?

14–6. What are the typical prerequisites for obtaining a CPA certificate?

14–7. The standard audit report makes a number of representations about audit performance and financial statement characteristics. List and explain briefly three additional items to which a standard audit report might refer.

14–8. Explain the connection between incomplete or unreliable financial information and financial capital formation processes within an economy (refer to Chapter Twelve).

14–9. Independent audits are said to fulfill three explicit market demands. What are these demands?

14–10. Why do auditing procedures that the independent auditors actually use differ from year to year and from company to company?

14–11. What kinds of things do independent auditors typically want to accomplish on an initial visit to the offices of a new client?

14–12. List three things that independent auditors might want to know in forming an opinion about the liabilities listed in a company's statement of financial position.

14–13. Describe briefly the benefits, as you perceive them, that result from the use of statistical sampling procedures in auditing.

14–14. What is the relationship between detection of fraud and an audit of financial statements for the purpose of expressing an independent opinion thereon?

14–15. Why is the SEC concerned with professional auditor independence?

14–16. Find the description of a recent third-party liability suit involving independent auditors (from *The Wall Street Journal* or another financial newspaper) and explain concisely the charge against the auditors.

14–17. Is the professional audit function limited to private enterprises? If not, how and where else does it operate?

14–18. Why do Third World (i.e., developing) countries often adopt *International Auditing Guidelines* as soon as they are published?

Problems

14–1. Management Interest in Financial Statements.   The management of a business enterprise has legal, contractual, and fiduciary ("stewardship") responsibilities for the production and preparation of proper financial statements. Thus management exercises judgments and makes a variety of estimates regarding the periodic preparation of enterprise financial statements.

Required:

1. Explain why management might bias its financial statement judgments and estimates in its own favor (i.e., making things look better than they really are).
2. Give five reasons why management might decide to report the financial status of an enterprise less favorably than it really is.
3. How do regular independent audits affect management's financial representations?

14–2. Internal Control System Design.   Jerry Mander is chairman of the Committee to Reelect Stan the Man as State Governor. The committee has its own offices and a large number of workers. All campaign workers are regarded as having high dedication and integrity. Nevertheless, Jerry is concerned about the control over the handling of donations.

Potential donors are listed in a directory kept at the committee's offices. Each day Phil E. Buster (Jerry's second-in-command) allocates several names from the list to each of his campaign workers. They then visit the prospective donors and, if possible, collect a check or cash from them. No donations are ever received by mail. At the end of the day the campaign workers return to the offices and hand Phil their collections, which he places in a safe. Periodically, the contents of the safe are deposited in the committee's checking account. Devise an effective but simple internal control system for the solicitation and receipt of donations.

14–3. Professional Independence Case Analysis. For each of the following cases, state whether the independence of the auditor concerned is adversely affected, and give brief reasons for your answer.

1. A partner in an accounting firm is the trustee of the estate of a deceased friend and administers the estate on behalf of the friend's children. A material portion of the value of the estate consists of stocks of a company that is an audit client of his accounting firm.
2. A partner in a public accounting firm is a member of a tennis club of which his brother is president. The club has raised a relatively large amount of funds to finance the eventual construction of additional courts and social facilities. Most of these funds have been invested temporarily in common stocks. Half the total investment has been made in a company that is an audit client of the accounting firm.
3. A manufacturing company employs a small firm to handle most of its advertising activities. Without the revenue generated by this association, the advertising firm could not remain in business. The owner of the advertising firm has a son who is a partner in an accounting firm. The manufacturing company is an audit client of the accounting firm.
4. A partner in an accounting firm has not completed repayment of a large loan made by a bank. The money had been borrowed to enable payment of damages resulting from a car accident involving a member of the partner's family. The bank has now appointed his firm as its auditors. The partner will not be involved in the audit of the bank, and he now resides in a state in which the bank has no branches.

14–4. Conflict of Interest Resolution. Some have claimed that a reasonable degree of independence is rarely maintained by CPAs, chiefly because remuneration of the CPA comes from clients. However, there is little evidence of agreement on possible alternatives to the present practices. Three possible alternatives may be

1. Appointment of independent auditors and negotiation of scope of services and fees by an "audit committee" composed of nonmanagement members of the board of directors, or
2. A requirement that companies change their auditors fairly frequently, for example, every three years, or
3. Performance of the attest function by a governmental body.

Required:
Critically evaluate each of the three alternatives.

14–5. Physical Inventory Program. You are an audit manager in a large accounting firm. One of the clients for whose audit you are responsible is the Diaper Distributors Company. The company purchases fully completed and packaged diapers from major suppliers and arranges the distribution throughout the state. You are now developing an audit program for the verification of inventories. The company's inventories will be counted on December 31, 1991, and you intend that your staff auditors will be present on that day at all locations where inventory counting is to be undertaken. From past experience you know that a substantial quantity of inventories will be in transit between locations on that day. For example, inventory from the head office warehouse will leave by truck on December 30 and will not reach the company's regional warehouse until January 2, 1991.

Required:

Draw up an audit program that will ensure that no inventories on hand or in transit are counted twice or omitted altogether from the inventory records compiled in the count.

14–6. Marketable Securities Audit. A large company holds a substantial number of bonds and stocks in other companies. The stocks and bonds are kept in a safe at the company's offices, with the exception of some that are kept at the bank. Ignoring the problems of valuation of the stocks and bonds, how would you verify their existence? That they are actually owned by the company? How would you ensure that dividends and interest have been recorded properly?

14–7. Leased Equipment Audit. Hubert's Hirings specializes in the leasing of construction equipment—compressors, welders, pneumatic drills, and bulldozers. On any given day, approximately 75 percent of its lease equipment will not be in the company's yards, but out on lease to customers of Hubert's Hirings. Design an audit program to verify the existence of the equipment shown on the company's records at any given time.

14–8. Accounts Receivable Analysis. Debts due from customers, that is, accounts receivable, normally constitute a significant portion of an enterprise's total assets. How would you audit accounts receivable? What steps would you take to ensure that they have not been overstated due to inadequacies in the recognition of potentially uncollectible accounts?

14–9. Contingent Liability Procedure. When an individual is being sued, or guarantees repaying of loans made to others by his local bank, he has a contingent liability; that is, he may have to pay out money if a certain future event occurs. Likewise companies may have contingent liabilities which should be disclosed to stockholders. How would you approach the problem of satisfying yourself that the company you are auditing has no undisclosed contingent liabilities?

14–10. Auditors' Professional Judgment. Exhibit 1–1 in this text is a graphic representation of Stages in the Decision-making Process. Prepare a similar representation of the Independent Auditors' Professional Judgment Process.

14–11. Reasons for Internal Control Weaknesses. After their interim audit of a small company, the auditors sent their client a letter, listing weaknesses in the client's system of internal control. Among the weaknesses were the following:

1. Checks and cash are accumulated for three or four days before being deposited.
2. The cashier (who handles all cash receipts) has access to the accounts receivable ledger from which monthly statements are prepared.
3. The person responsible for preparing the bank deposit and depositing funds at the bank also prepares the bank reconciliation.
4. Persons who are authorized to sign checks for payment of accounts payable do not cancel the supporting documentary evidence (e.g., invoices).
5. There is no rotation of employees' duties, nor are annual vacations compulsory.

Required:

Give a brief explanation of why each of these facts involves an internal control weakness.

14–12. Fraud Discovery Yecch Breakfast Foods Company is a small family business which specializes in breakfast cereals. Its financial statements have never been audited by a CPA. To the owner's chagrin, he eventually finds that

1. Bags of spices which ostensibly filled a large portion of his warehouse were arranged in hollow stacks. In some cases, bags were found to be filled with sand. In addition, the quality (and hence the cost) of many of the spices actually in stock was inferior to the quality specified in the company records.
2. The company accountant occasionally pocketed receipts from customers which had arrived by mail. He would then sign a credit note for the amount, so that the balance of the statement eventually mailed to the customer would be in accordance with the customer's records. To Yecch Breakfast Foods Company, the credit note indicated that the client had received a reduction in the amount due because goods delivered to him were spoiled on arrival.
3. The company accountant had also sold some of the company's marketable securities for $10,000. When the stock market price of these securities subsequently dropped, he replaced them at a cost of $4,000. No records of the transactions were made in the company's books, and the accountant retained the $6,000 net proceeds for himself.

Although examinations by independent auditors are not specifically designed to discover fraud, it is possible that their presence and their procedures might have prevented or more quickly disclosed these defalcations. For each of the above examples of fraud, indicate how the independent auditor might have detected it during the course of a normal audit examination.

14–13. Analysis of a Fraud Situation. Lisa Young is a third-year staff auditor in a large public accounting firm. As a member of an audit team, she was performing examinations of the financial records of a large pulp mill. Her specific assignment was to check truck-weighing tickets so that the recorded amounts of trucked-in raw material (logs) could be established as a reliable basis for the cost of the pulp manufactured. No log inventory was kept at the pulp mill; all logs were fed directly into the shredding machinery as delivered.

Checking weighing tickets was not a particularly exciting task for Lisa. They all seemed to be in order, with serial numbers properly accounted for and authorization initials appearing on each. After she had established the totals for the month she was checking, she wondered what the daily usage rate was. After she had computed that amount, she was struck by the fact that the plant superintendent had quoted a total capacity for the shredding machinery which was below the actual volume she had calculated.

Lisa then checked her findings with the auditor in charge of the team. They both went over the calculations and found that, indeed, the reported amount of logs delivered could not have been used by the available shredding capacity. Since the most important cost item of the pulp mill was affected, the partner in charge of the audit was contacted and brought into the picture immediately.

Since there existed the possibility of fraud at the plant superintendent's level, top production management at corporate headquarters was informed of the suspected irregularity. The corporate vice-president in charge of production then confronted the plant superintendent, who was both surprised and embarrassed. An unobtrusive surveillance system was then put into effect over the scale master. Telescopic scale readings were compared with imprinted weighing tickets. Over the course of several days, it was discovered that the scale master was in collusion with three driver-operators. He advanced his scales from actual readings by as much as 10 to 20 percent on individual loads being delivered. The copies of weighing tickets which remained with the truck operators even had the fictitious weight differential noted!

Over a three-year period, the company had paid for approximately 20 percent more than it should have on the logs it had purchased from those operators.

Required:

1. Identify three internal control procedures that might have prevented these defalcations.
2. Did a specific procedure lead to the discovery of the fraud? Explain.
3. What is likely to have happened if there had been intentional collusion of the fraudulent activities between the plant superintendent and the scale master?

14–14. International Auditing Guidelines.   In your business administration library, use an index to professional accounting literature, official pronouncements, or the *IFAC Handbook* to find a list (or lists) of the titles of all *International Auditing Guidlines* issued through December 31, 1989. Copy this list and bring it to class. Which of all these *Guidelines* appears to be most relevant to independent auditing in the United States? Why?

14–15. Audit Committee Duties.   The chapter text briefly mentions audit committees of corporate boards of directors as communication channels for the potential concerns of independent auditors. Using your own imagination and library resources available to you, develop a list of ten likely duties that could be assigned to an audit committee of a corporate board of directors.

14–16. Audit Committee Decision Making.   After a highly successful career, Arthur Stanwood retires as senior financial executive of Y Corporation. An intensive executive search procedure reveals that the best candidate for the resulting job opening is the CPA firm partner who has been in charge of the Y Corporation independent audit for the past eight years. Should Y Corporation hire the partner "away" from his firm? Since the partner necessarily has had a close relationship with his firm's audit staff, would this create any difficulties if he were employed? In case of his employment, should Y Corporation change CPA firms?

Required:
Write a short essay in response to the questions posed.

14–17. International Audit Activities.   Assume that you are a partner in a medium-sized CPA firm that does not have offices outside North America. One of your clients has acquired several subsidiary companies in Europe and the Far East, whose business volume is important in relation to total consolidated sales, net income, and assets. The client proposes that local audit firms be employed to perform independent audits of the subsidiary companies in question.

Required:
Draft a short memorandum to the client outlining the conditions precedent to your acceptance of the work and opinions of foreign auditors.

14–18. Qualified Reports of Independent Auditors.   Sometimes CPA auditors have reservations about the results of their audit activities and thus issue so-called qualified reports. Utilizing the resources of your closest library, make a copy of a qualified report of an independent auditor and state why the qualification occurred.

14–19. Other Attestation Reports.   Consider the following report on nonfinancial (fictional) CPA attestation engagement.

Sigma & Omega

One Metropolitan Place
Key City, Main State 01001
Telephone (999) 090-9090
Fax (999) 909-0909
Telex 001001

Master Publishing Company
College Division
Ten Corner Street
Key City, MX 01100

We have examined the text of PRINCIPLES OF ACCOUNTING, New Edition, by Alpha, Beta and Delta, together with its accompanying Instructor's Solutions Manual. Our examination, which was directed at this work's technical and mathematical accuracy, internal consistency, and the appropriateness and accuracy of references to professional and other pronouncements, was made in accordance with standards established by the American Institute of Certified Public Accountants and, accordingly, included such procedures as we considered necessary in the circumstances. Our examination was carried out during the composition process and before final page proof. In our opinion, the material in this book is technically and mathematically accurate, internally consistent, and references to professional and other pronouncements are accurate and appropriate.

SIGMA & OMEGA

November 1991

Required:

1. Is it appropriate for independent professional auditors to issue such reports? Why or why not?
2. Under what conditions should a CPA refuse to become associated with a proposed "extended" attestation engagement?

14–20. Requirements to Become a CPA. For your state or U.S. territory, determine all legal requirements to become a CPA, receive a license to practice as a CPA, and renew such a license periodically. Consult references in your business administration library, the Department of Accounting at your university, or your State Board of Accountancy directly.

Appendix A

TABLE A-1

Present Value of One Dollar

n/r =	.01	.02	.03	.04	.05	.06	.07	.08	.09	.10	.12	.14	.15	.16	.18	.20
1	.990	.980	.971	.962	.952	.943	.935	.926	.917	.909	.893	.877	.870	.862	.847	.833
2	.980	.961	.943	.925	.907	.890	.873	.857	.842	.826	.797	.769	.756	.743	.718	.694
3	.971	.942	.915	.889	.864	.840	.816	.794	.772	.751	.712	.675	.658	.641	.609	.579
4	.961	.924	.888	.855	.823	.792	.763	.735	.708	.683	.636	.592	.572	.552	.516	.482
5	.951	.906	.863	.822	.784	.747	.713	.681	.650	.621	.567	.519	.497	.476	.437	.402
6	.942	.888	.837	.790	.746	.705	.666	.630	.596	.564	.507	.456	.432	.410	.370	.335
7	.933	.871	.813	.760	.711	.665	.623	.583	.547	.513	.452	.400	.376	.354	.314	.279
8	.923	.853	.789	.731	.677	.627	.582	.540	.502	.467	.404	.351	.327	.305	.266	.233
9	.914	.837	.766	.703	.645	.592	.544	.500	.460	.424	.361	.308	.284	.263	.225	.194
10	.905	.820	.744	.676	.614	.558	.508	.463	.422	.386	.322	.270	.247	.227	.191	.162
11	.896	.804	.722	.650	.585	.527	.475	.429	.388	.350	.287	.237	.215	.195	.162	.135
12	.887	.788	.701	.625	.557	.497	.444	.397	.356	.319	.257	.208	.187	.168	.137	.112
13	.879	.773	.681	.601	.530	.469	.415	.368	.326	.290	.229	.182	.163	.145	.116	.093
14	.870	.758	.661	.577	.505	.442	.388	.340	.299	.263	.205	.160	.141	.125	.099	.078
15	.861	.743	.642	.555	.481	.417	.362	.315	.275	.239	.183	.140	.123	.108	.084	.065
16	.853	.728	.623	.534	.458	.394	.339	.292	.252	.218	.163	.123	.107	.093	.071	.054
17	.844	.714	.605	.513	.436	.371	.317	.270	.231	.198	.146	.108	.093	.080	.060	.045
18	.836	.700	.587	.494	.416	.350	.296	.250	.212	.180	.130	.095	.081	.069	.051	.038
19	.828	.686	.570	.475	.396	.331	.277	.232	.194	.164	.116	.083	.070	.060	.043	.031
20	.820	.673	.554	.456	.377	.312	.258	.215	.178	.149	.104	.073	.061	.051	.037	.026
21	.811	.660	.538	.439	.359	.294	.242	.199	.164	.135	.093	.064	.053	.044	.031	.022
22	.803	.647	.522	.422	.342	.278	.226	.184	.150	.123	.083	.056	.046	.038	.026	.018
23	.795	.634	.507	.406	.326	.262	.211	.170	.138	.112	.074	.049	.040	.033	.022	.015
24	.788	.622	.492	.390	.310	.247	.197	.158	.126	.102	.066	.043	.035	.028	.019	.013
25	.780	.610	.478	.375	.295	.233	.184	.146	.116	.092	.059	.038	.030	.024	.016	.010
26	.772	.598	.464	.361	.281	.220	.172	.135	.106	.084	.053	.033	.026	.021	.014	.009
27	.764	.586	.450	.347	.268	.207	.161	.125	.098	.076	.047	.029	.023	.018	.011	.007
28	.757	.574	.437	.333	.255	.196	.150	.116	.090	.069	.042	.026	.020	.016	.010	.006
29	.749	.563	.424	.321	.243	.185	.141	.107	.082	.063	.037	.022	.017	.014	.008	.005
30	.742	.552	.412	.308	.231	.174	.131	.099	.075	.057	.033	.020	.015	.012	.007	.004

TABLE A-2

Future Value of One Dollar

n/r =	.01	.02	.03	.04	.05	.06	.07	.08	.09	.10	.12	.14	.15	.16	.18	.20
1	1.01	1.02	1.03	1.04	1.05	1.06	1.07	1.08	1.09	1.10	1.12	1.14	1.15	1.16	1.18	1.20
2	1.02	1.04	1.06	1.08	1.10	1.12	1.14	1.17	1.19	1.21	1.25	1.30	1.32	1.35	1.39	1.44
3	1.03	1.06	1.09	1.12	1.16	1.19	1.23	1.26	1.30	1.33	1.40	1.48	1.52	1.56	1.64	1.73
4	1.04	1.08	1.13	1.17	1.22	1.26	1.31	1.36	1.41	1.46	1.57	1.69	1.75	1.81	1.94	2.07
5	1.05	1.10	1.16	1.22	1.28	1.34	1.40	1.47	1.54	1.61	1.76	1.93	2.01	2.10	2.29	2.49
6	1.06	1.13	1.19	1.27	1.34	1.42	1.50	1.59	1.68	1.77	1.97	2.19	2.31	2.44	2.70	2.99
7	1.07	1.15	1.23	1.32	1.41	1.50	1.61	1.71	1.83	1.95	2.21	2.50	2.66	2.83	3.19	3.58
8	1.08	1.17	1.27	1.37	1.48	1.59	1.72	1.85	1.99	2.14	2.48	2.85	3.06	3.28	3.76	4.30
9	1.09	1.20	1.30	1.42	1.55	1.69	1.84	2.00	2.17	2.36	2.77	3.25	3.52	3.80	4.44	5.16
10	1.10	1.22	1.34	1.48	1.63	1.79	1.97	2.16	2.37	2.59	3.11	3.71	4.05	4.41	5.23	6.19
11	1.12	1.24	1.38	1.54	1.71	1.90	2.10	2.33	2.58	2.85	3.48	4.23	4.65	5.12	6.18	7.43
12	1.13	1.27	1.43	1.60	1.80	2.01	2.25	2.52	2.81	3.14	3.90	4.82	5.35	5.94	7.29	8.92
13	1.14	1.29	1.47	1.67	1.89	2.13	2.41	2.73	3.07	3.45	4.36	5.49	6.15	6.89	8.60	10.70
14	1.15	1.32	1.51	1.73	1.98	2.26	2.58	2.94	3.34	3.80	4.89	6.26	7.08	7.99	10.15	12.84
15	1.16	1.35	1.56	1.80	2.08	2.40	2.76	3.17	3.64	4.18	5.47	7.14	8.14	9.27	11.97	15.41
16	1.17	1.37	1.60	1.87	2.18	2.54	2.95	3.43	3.97	4.59	6.13	8.14	9.36	10.75	14.13	18.49
17	1.18	1.40	1.75	1.95	2.29	2.69	3.16	3.70	4.33	5.05	6.87	9.28	10.76	12.47	16.67	22.19
18	1.20	1.43	1.70	2.03	2.41	2.85	3.38	4.00	4.72	5.56	7.69	10.58	12.38	14.46	19.67	26.62
19	1.21	1.46	1.75	2.11	2.53	3.03	3.62	4.32	5.14	6.12	8.61	12.06	14.23	16.78	23.21	31.95
20	1.22	1.49	1.81	2.19	2.65	3.21	3.87	4.66	5.60	6.73	9.65	13.74	16.37	19.46	27.39	38.34
21	1.23	1.52	1.86	2.28	2.79	3.40	4.14	5.03	6.11	7.40	10.80	15.67	18.82	22.57	32.32	46.01
22	1.24	1.55	1.92	2.37	2.93	3.60	4.43	5.44	6.66	8.14	12.10	17.86	21.64	26.19	38.14	55.21
23	1.25	1.58	1.97	2.46	3.07	3.82	4.74	5.87	7.26	8.95	13.55	20.36	24.89	30.38	45.01	66.25
24	1.27	1.61	2.03	2.56	3.23	4.05	5.07	6.34	7.91	9.65	15.18	23.21	28.63	35.24	53.11	79.50
25	1.28	1.64	2.09	2.67	3.39	4.29	5.43	6.85	8.62	10.83	17.00	26.46	32.92	40.87	62.67	95.40
26	1.30	1.67	2.16	2.77	3.56	4.55	5.81	7.40	9.40	11.92	19.04	30.17	37.86	47.41	73.95	114.48
27	1.31	1.71	2.22	2.88	3.73	4.82	6.21	7.99	10.25	13.11	21.32	34.39	43.54	55.00	87.26	137.37
28	1.32	1.74	2.29	3.00	3.92	5.11	6.65	8.63	11.17	14.42	23.88	39.20	50.07	63.80	102.97	164.84
29	1.33	1.78	2.36	3.12	4.12	5.42	7.11	9.32	12.17	15.86	26.75	44.69	57.58	74.01	121.50	197.81
30	1.35	1.81	2.43	3.24	4.32	5.74	7.61	10.06	13.27	17.45	29.96	50.95	66.21	85.85	143.37	237.38

TABLE A–3

Present Value of an Annuity of One Dollar

n/r =	.01	.02	.03	.04	.05	.06	.07	.08	.09	.10	.12	.14	.15	.16	.18	.20
1	.99	.98	.97	.96	.95	.94	.93	.93	.92	.91	.89	.88	.87	.86	.85	.83
2	1.97	1.94	1.91	1.89	1.86	1.83	1.81	1.78	1.76	1.74	1.69	1.65	1.63	1.61	1.57	1.53
3	2.94	2.88	2.83	2.78	2.72	2.67	2.62	2.58	2.53	2.49	2.40	2.32	2.28	2.25	2.17	2.11
4	3.90	3.81	3.72	3.63	3.55	3.47	3.39	3.31	3.24	3.17	3.04	2.91	2.85	2.80	2.69	2.59
5	4.85	4.71	4.58	4.45	4.33	4.21	4.10	3.99	3.89	3.79	3.60	3.43	3.35	3.27	3.13	2.99
6	5.80	5.60	5.42	5.24	5.08	4.92	4.77	4.62	4.49	4.36	4.11	3.89	3.78	3.68	3.50	3.33
7	6.73	6.47	6.23	6.00	5.79	5.58	5.39	5.21	5.03	4.87	4.56	4.29	4.16	4.04	3.81	3.60
8	7.65	7.33	7.02	6.73	6.46	6.21	5.97	5.75	5.53	5.33	4.97	4.64	4.49	4.34	4.08	3.84
9	8.57	8.16	7.79	7.44	7.11	6.80	6.52	6.25	6.00	5.76	5.33	4.95	4.77	4.61	4.30	4.03
10	9.47	8.98	8.43	8.11	7.72	7.36	7.02	6.71	6.42	6.14	5.65	5.22	5.02	4.83	4.49	4.19
11	10.37	9.79	9.25	8.76	8.31	7.89	7.50	7.14	6.81	6.50	5.94	5.45	5.23	5.03	4.66	4.33
12	11.26	10.58	9.95	9.39	8.86	8.38	7.94	7.54	7.16	6.81	6.19	5.66	5.42	5.20	4.79	4.44
13	12.13	11.35	10.63	9.99	9.39	8.85	8.36	7.90	7.49	7.10	6.42	5.84	5.58	5.34	4.91	4.53
14	13.00	12.11	11.30	10.56	9.90	9.29	8.75	8.24	7.79	7.37	6.63	6.00	5.72	5.47	5.01	4.61
15	13.87	12.85	11.94	11.12	10.38	9.71	9.11	8.56	8.06	7.61	6.81	6.14	5.85	5.58	5.09	4.68
16	14.72	13.58	12.56	11.65	10.84	10.11	9.45	8.85	8.31	7.82	6.97	6.27	5.95	5.67	5.16	4.73
17	15.56	14.29	13.17	12.17	11.27	10.48	9.76	9.12	8.54	8.02	7.12	6.37	6.05	5.75	5.22	4.77
18	16.40	14.99	13.75	12.66	11.69	10.83	10.06	9.37	8.76	8.20	7.25	6.47	6.13	5.82	5.27	4.81
19	17.23	15.68	14.32	13.13	12.09	11.16	10.34	9.60	8.95	8.36	7.37	6.55	6.20	5.88	5.32	4.84
20	18.05	16.35	14.88	13.59	12.45	11.47	10.59	9.82	9.13	8.51	7.47	6.62	6.26	5.93	5.35	4.87
21	18.86	17.01	15.42	14.03	12.82	11.76	10.84	10.02	9.29	8.65	7.56	6.69	6.31	5.97	5.38	4.89
22	19.66	17.66	15.94	14.45	13.16	12.04	11.06	10.20	9.44	8.77	7.64	6.74	6.36	6.01	5.41	4.91
23	20.46	18.29	16.44	14.86	13.49	12.30	11.27	10.37	9.58	8.88	7.72	6.79	6.40	6.04	5.43	4.92
24	21.24	18.91	16.94	15.25	13.80	12.55	11.47	10.53	9.71	8.98	7.78	6.84	6.43	6.07	5.45	4.94
25	22.02	19.52	17.41	15.62	14.09	12.78	11.65	10.67	9.82	9.08	7.84	6.87	6.46	6.10	5.47	4.95
26	22.80	20.12	17.88	15.98	14.38	13.00	11.83	10.81	9.93	9.16	7.90	6.91	6.49	6.12	5.48	4.96
27	23.56	20.71	18.33	16.33	14.64	13.21	11.99	10.94	10.03	9.24	7.94	6.94	6.51	6.14	5.49	4.96
28	24.32	21.28	18.76	16.66	14.90	13.41	12.14	11.05	10.12	9.31	7.98	6.96	6.53	6.15	5.50	4.97
29	25.07	21.84	19.19	16.98	15.14	13.59	12.28	11.16	10.20	9.37	8.02	6.98	6.55	6.17	5.51	4.97
30	25.81	22.40	19.60	17.29	15.37	13.76	12.41	11.26	10.27	9.43	8.06	7.00	6.57	6.18	5.52	4.98

Index